Wilfrid Philip Ward, William George Ward

Essays on the Philosophy of Theism

Vol. II.

Wilfrid Philip Ward, William George Ward

Essays on the Philosophy of Theism
Vol. II.

ISBN/EAN: 9783337076405

Printed in Europe, USA, Canada, Australia, Japan

Cover: Foto ©Thomas Meinert / pixelio.de

More available books at **www.hansebooks.com**

ESSAYS

ON THE

PHILOSOPHY OF THEISM

BY THE LATE

WILLIAM GEORGE WARD, Ph.D.

SOMETIME FELLOW OF BALLIOL COLLEGE, OXFORD
AND PROFESSOR OF MORAL PHILOSOPHY AND DOGMATIC THEOLOGY
AT OLD HALL COLLEGE, WARE

REPRINTED FROM THE "DUBLIN REVIEW"
**PRESENTED TO ST. MARY'S COLLEGE LIBRARY
BY REV. T. CALLAGHAN**

EDITED, WITH AN INTRODUCTION, BY

WILFRID WARD

IN TWO VOLUMES
VOL. II.

LONDON
KEGAN PAUL, TRENCH & CO., 1, PATERNOSTER SQUARE
1884

CONTENTS OF VOL. II.

ESSAY X.—SUPPLEMENTARY REMARKS ON FREEWILL.
(*October*, 1879.)

	PAGE
Purpose of the essay to re-state, so as to meet criticisms received, the argument for freewill	1
Familiar examples	3
Nature of "anti-impulsive effort"	11
Argument therefrom for freewill	14
Power of habit in determining the will's impulse	21
Technical terms explained	22
Objections replied to	24

ESSAY XI.—MR. SHADWORTH HODGSON ON FREEWILL.
(*October*, 1880.)

New opponent to our teaching on freewill	36
Determinism defined	37
What is "stronger" and "weaker" desire?	39
Illustrative case	40
Critical issue between Mr. Hodgson and the writer	42
Ultimate appeal to experience	44
Illustrations of anti-impulsive effort	44
Objection: such effort equally determined by circumstances	50
Reply	52
Mr. Hodgson's replies to writer's arguments	54
Virtue and self-interest may often be pleasurable motives	58
Latent thoughts or qualities admitted	59

Contents.

	PAGE
What are motives of anti-impulsive effort?	60
Mr. Hodgson's objection illustrated and refuted	62
Determinists confuse different kinds of moral action	65
Anti-impulsive effort made by personal exertion	65
Comments on Mr. Hodgson's affirmative position	76
Determinism and guilt	79

ESSAY XII.—ETHICS IN ITS BEARING ON THEISM.
(*January*, 1880.)

The human mind forms various moral judgments	83
The ideas "virtuous," and "wrong" implied in those judgments are simple ideas	84
They are also metempirical	87
Certain moral truths self-evidently necessary	88
These are intued in the *individual case*, and not as general propositions	89
From the ideas of freedom and morality we come to recognize a supreme rule of life from which it is wicked to deviate	94
This rule is no mere catalogue of truths, but is of the nature of a law imposed by personal authority	95
Our perception of this truth not always explicit	102

ESSAY XIII.—PHILOSOPHY OF THE THEISTIC CONTROVERSY.
(*January*, 1882.)

Our present purpose is against phenomenistic atheism	107
Summary of former statements against it	109
Phenomenism shown to be self-contradictory	110
Consistent phenomenists cannot make use of memory	116
Reason of the contempt of Phenomenists for intuitionist reasoning	119
Reason why so many Phenomenists are also Antitheists	121
Service rendered by M. Ollé-Laprune's "Certitude Morale"	129
Implicit proofs of religious doctrine more solid and penetrating than argument	132
Proofs of God's existence for the uncultured	137
Certitude whether metaphysical or physical has the same meaning	143
Influence of "will" on religious certitude, and need for exertion of it in antitheistic dealing with religious truth	145

Contents.

Essay XIV.—SCIENCE, PRAYER, FREEWILL, AND MIRACLES.
(*April,* 1867.)

	PAGE
Objections against religion founded on the fact of phenomenal uniformity	158
Intimate connection of physical science with theology	165
Phenomenal uniformity in no way disproves God's unintermittent premovement of phenomena	172
Physical phenomena taken by themselves rather tell in favour of such premovement	175
The same argument holds in regard to that particular premovement, Divine Grace	193
The doctrine of freewill explained	194
Objections to it answered	197
Extent to which this doctrine interferes with the strictly scientific character of psychology	201
Miracles, however frequent, in no way affect the foundation of physical science	205

Essay XV.—EXPLICIT AND IMPLICIT THOUGHT.
(*October,* 1869.)

F. Kleutgen on the non-philosophical knowledge of God, readily attainable by all mankind	216
Implicit reasoning	223
Implicit thought	226
Distinction between reasoning and argument	228
Vital importance of philosophy	229
Correctness of implicit reasoning is best secured by simplicity of intention	232
Catholic instincts	234
A Catholic atmosphere	235
It is only the few whose business it is to argue	239
Mixed education	239

Essay XVI.—CERTITUDE IN RELIGIOUS ASSENT.
(*April,* 1871.)

F. Newman's "Grammar of Assent"	244
Statement of the chief contemporary anti-Catholic philosophical principle	245
Reply to that principle as stated	249
Suggested amendment to it	251

Contents.

	PAGE
Reply to its amended exposition	251
Evidences of Theism accessible to all men	256
Evidences of Catholicity possessed by the most uneducated Catholics	257

Essay XVII.—THE EXTENT OF FREEWILL.
(*July*, 1881.)

Purpose of present essay	274
Thesis to be defended on the extent of freewill	275
A preliminary map of man's moral nature and action	276
"End" of moral action	277
What "virtual" intention is	282
Measure of the *degree* of virtuousness or sinfulness	292
Liberty of moral acts	296
What "perfectly voluntary" acts are	304
Theory of some Libertarians on the extent of freewill assailed	312
Reasons against it: universal testimony of mankind	318
Secondly, frequency of anti-impulsive effort	323
Man's self-intimate and continuous sense of freewill	326
The relation between freewill and morality	332
Consideration of the thesis that in order for an act to be mortally sinful there must be explicit advertence to its sinfulness	336
The doctrine of "inordination"	345
This doctrine applied to Catholic obdurate sinners	347
Concluding remarks	349

ESSAYS ON

THE PHILOSOPHY OF THEISM.

X.

SUPPLEMENTARY REMARKS ON FREEWILL.

AMONG all the philosophical verities which reasonably count as premisses of Theism, there are two in particular, closely correlated, on which we are disposed to lay quite exceptional stress. These are (1) the doctrine that man's will is free; and (2) the doctrine that there is a certain moral code, a certain authoritative rule of life, cognizable by reason as of intrinsic obligation. These two, we say, are, to our mind, much the most important of Theistic premisses. For we heartily follow Cardinal Newman, in regarding men's natural sense of right and wrong as by far the strongest of those foundations on which belief in God is reasonably built.[*] We have just now, therefore, arrived at the very heart and crisis of our argument, and every step as we proceed must be carefully made good.

For this reason, before proceeding to any further subject, we wish to establish on an entirely satisfactory basis the position assumed in our previous essays on Freewill. To prove the existence of Freewill, we set forth an argument, in regard to which we are not certain that it has

[*] F. Kleutgen also gives to this particular argument the first and most prominent place.

ever been exhibited in the precise shape we gave; though we are bound to add, that the more we consider it the more confident we are of its validity and decisiveness. Under those circumstances, we cannot be surprised that some critics have importantly misunderstood our meaning; while others, who rightly understand it, have advanced grave objections against our reasoning. We do not here refer to any published replies, but to comments which have been made in private, sometimes by way of response to our request of criticism. On our side, these criticisms have shown us that we have been by no means uniformly so full and clear as might be desired, in setting forth what we intended. It will not be necessary to pass all these objections explicitly under review, because most of them will be sufficiently answered by a clearer exposition of what we intended to say. But there are one or two which it will be better to cite and answer in due course.

There was one particular class, then, of mental phenomena on which we rested our whole argument for Freewill: the phenomena of what we called "anti-impulsive effort." That which, above all things, we now desire to effect in our reader's mind is (1) that he shall understand precisely what those phenomena are, which we call "anti-impulsive efforts;" and (2) that he shall see how entirely certain is the fact that such phenomena exist. When these two results are obtained, he will, we expect, recognize it as a very obvious and immediate inference that the human will is free. What, therefore, we especially wish is, that he may observe accurately in his own mind a certain class of facts which frequently therein occur. Accordingly, we shall not hesitate to indulge, during the few following pages, in what some philosophical readers may consider a very unnecessary prolixity of detail. When any persons may have fully mastered what it is which we intend, they can easily skip over remaining illustrations. But, on the other hand, there are assuredly others who *require* varied illustrations, in order to apprehend our meaning. In these illustrations, however, we shall purposely avoid technical terminology as much as possible. We shall not explain our technical terms by using other technical terms. On the contrary, in explaining such terms we shall here use such language as, we think, will be most readily understood by an ordinary educated Englishman, who has received no special philosophical training.

We would beg such a person first to consider what is the general attitude of his will throughout the day. There may be short periods, probably enough, of what we have in former essays called "vacillation and vibration." A devoted son falls in love. At various moments, then, he may go through much vacillation and vibration of will; as he is solicited by his desire of seeing the young lady on one hand, and, on the other hand, of solacing his widowed mother's old age by his company. We will not fail to take into due account these moments of vacillation and vibration. But we would begin by pointing out that, in the enormous majority of instances, such moments are comparatively rare in a man's mental history. We would point out that, during far the larger portion of most men's life, the spontaneous impulse of their will is altogether stable.

Take a most ordinary case to begin with. I am a merchant possessing regular habits of business. I rise on any given morning at my usual time; breakfast; after breakfast, at my usual time I take a cab down to my office; when there I read the letters which I find waiting for me; at my usual time I go on 'Change and duly transact business; I meet some friends and converse with them on such topics as occur; I return to my office and attend to routine work; at my usual time I go back home again, where I have asked some friends to dinner; while waiting for the dinner-hour, I amuse myself with my children; when my friends arrive, I chat with them on current topics; when they depart I go to bed. During the whole day I seem to have been doing at each moment exactly the one thing which was natural and spontaneous for me to do. We will not here inquire what scope there has been throughout for what we shall presently commemorate under the name of "anti-impulsive effort." But at all events there has been no vacillation or vibration of will, unless in very small matters and at very rare intervals.

Let us suppose, however, a very slight complication of circumstances. My cab is in the morning at my door, when a friend of mine pays me a visit. I have an appointment of great importance to keep, at a little distance beyond my office, and if I do not start at once I shall be too late for it. I beg my friend to get into my cab with me, but he cannot. Under these circumstances, it is possible that my will shall enter into a state of vacillation and vibration; that I shall be distracted by the two conflicting motives, of pleasure in his conversation on one side, and momentous business on the other. Let us hope, however, that my character is not so weak. And if it is *not*, the motive which leads me to go off at once entirely preponderates over the motive which prompts me to stay with my friend at home. The latter may be a strong motive, but the former is indefinitely stronger. Perhaps I beg my friend to give me a call next Sunday. At all events, my will's spontaneous impulse remains so stable that I have no more doubt or hesitation about starting off at once, than I had before my friend arrived.

Before I get to my office, however, another event occurs of far greater importance. Let it be supposed—in order more vividly to colour the picture—that the engagement to which I am bound is of most critical moment in my commercial life. Let it be supposed that for the last week I have been so anxious about it, that I have hardly been able to think about anything else, and that now I am intensely bent on bringing the matter to a crisis. The result is, that some symptoms befall me connected with a *heart complaint* under which I occasionally suffer. The symptom is not a painful one, nor does it interfere with my full power of transacting business. But a physician, in whom I have entire confidence, has told me that it is simply as much as my life is worth to transact agitating business while I am afflicted with such symptoms. And in every way the circumstances are such, that if I choose to ask myself the question, I know perfectly well that returning home at once is my one right and reasonable course. Let us now consider the different ways in which my will and conduct may imaginably be affected, under the state of things we have mentioned.

Perhaps (1) the thought of this danger produces on me at once so strong an *emotional* effect of recoil, that my will's spontaneous impulse is now as stably moved towards *avoiding* the interview, as it was, a moment before, towards *encountering* it. Nay, I remember that when I get to my office, it is abundantly possible I may find *there* some agitating letters. So I at once order the cabman to drive me home again. Perhaps (2) my conduct may be the same, but the preliminaries somewhat different. The *emotional* effect, produced on me by the advent of these heart symptoms, is little or nothing. Nevertheless, I have so firmly established a *habit* of prudence, that, just as in the former case, the motive which prompts me to avoid the engagement preponderates absolutely, unquestionably, triumphantly, over the motives which prompt me to keep it. Here, therefore, as in the first case, my will's spontaneous impulse is just as stably directed towards *avoiding* the interview, as it was, a moment before, towards *encountering* it. Perhaps, however (3), my will's spontaneous impulse ceases for the moment to be stable. I see plainly enough that my one reasonable course is to decline the interview. But, then, so intense is my anxiety to bring the business matter to a point, that my *emotions* are as keenly enlisted on one side as on the other. My emotional impulse is for one instant in one direction, for the next instant in another. Then, as I have no *habit* of prudence worth mentioning, my will remains for some time in a state of vacillation and vibration. Shall I order the cabman to return, or shall I not? Shall I, at all events, go on to my office and see whether anything I find *there* may make the thing plainer? or what else shall I do? Perhaps, again (4), my will's spontaneous impulse remains unchanged. I am still unswervingly and unquestioningly bent on effecting my business transaction; though of course I am a good deal less *intensely* bent on it than I was before. On the one hand, the force of my emotions urges me most strongly to get through the matter at once, at whatever peril of death. On the other hand, my emotions, so it happens, are not keenly aroused by my knowledge of the danger which I shall incur; nor yet have I a habit of prudence sufficiently firm to counterbalance the effect produced on my will by my current of emotion.

All these four alternatives are contemplated by the Determinist, and square most easily with his theory. But there is a fifth alternative, which he does not—and consistently with his theory cannot—admit to be a possible one. It is imaginable that I may put forth "anti-impulsive effort" on the occasion. In explaining what the phenomenon is which we designate by this term, we must begin with the beginning. We will assume, then, as first existing, such a stable spontaneous impulse of the will as that exhibited under the *fourth* of the preceding alternatives. The spontaneous impulse of my will is still stably directed towards keeping my business appointment. On the other hand, I see clearly enough that the course, to which the impulse of my will stably solicits me, is violently unreasonable. And what we confidently maintain is this. Under such circumstances, I have a real power of *resisting* my will's stable spontaneous impulse. I am not its *slave;* though neither am I in such sense its *master* that I can at once compel it to desist from its urgent solicitations. I can exercise "self-government" and "self-restraint." While my will's spontaneous impulse remains both stable and powerful, I can, nevertheless, refuse to do what it prompts. I see plainly the very serious evils which will befall me, if I blindly follow its solicitation. And I feel that I can act in a way, which is on the one hand accordant with *reason,* while on the other hand it is opposed to *desire* and *impulse.* However vehemently impulse may press me to the unreasonable course, at that very moment, in the teeth of that very impulse, I can exercise what we call "anti-impulsive effort." I can put my head out of window, and tell the cabman to drive me back home again.

For a certain period after I have done this, the two conflicting movements proceed simultaneously in my mind. I *desire* to keep my appointment, but I *resolve* that I will *not* keep it. My strongest present *desire* is on one side, my *action* is on the other. Meanwhile, however, I probably proceed to ponder on the grievous evil which would ensue, if I blindly obeyed impulse. Then, as this course of salutary meditation proceeds, my emotions become more and more enlisted on the side of reason; and perhaps, by the time I get back home, the struggle has ceased. By that time my will's spontaneous impulse has, perhaps, come to be on the side of reason. Reviewing, however, the proximately antecedent period, what I come to see as having been its mental history is the following :—It has not at all depended on me during that period, whether my will's spontaneous impulse have been stable or vibratory; nor yet, supposing it stable, in what direction it have stably solicited me.

But it has absolutely depended on me whether I should follow the promptings of such stable impulse, or refuse to follow them; whether I should or should not put forth "anti-impulsive effort." If my will chose to remain passive in regard to forming its own decision,* its movement would, no doubt, be infallibly determined by the circumstances, internal and external, of the moment. But, then, my will *need* not have remained passive in regard to forming its own decision; it might have exerted itself actively in decreeing what that action should be. On myself—that is, on my soul—has depended the alternative, whether it have so exerted itself or no.

Now, were it not for the philosophical and religious issue involved, we do not believe there is any man of ordinary culture and self-observation who would doubt that such cases occasionally occur. How *frequent* they are, is a question which, in our last essay, we reserved for future consideration. What we here have to point out is merely that they are psychologically possible, and exist from time to time. I may, all will admit, be very certain of the fact that I feel cold, or that I experience the sensation which is called a pain in my finger. But, it is just *as* simply a matter to me of unmistakable certainty, on such an occasion as we have described, that two definite mental phenomena are now simultaneously proceeding in my mind. It is a matter, we say, of unmistakable certainty that at this moment the spontaneous *impulse* of my will is in one direction, and my *act* of will is in the opposite direction. My spontaneous *impulse* prompts me at every moment to

---

* "Passive in regard to *forming* its own decision." Of course it is not passive as regards *executing* its decision. Suppose I yield to my spontaneous impulse, and go to the business interview. My will is active in several ways—I tell the cabman to wait for me at my office, while I am reading my letters; I tell him to drive me to the place appointed for the interview, etc. Nevertheless, my will has been passive *in regard to forming its own decision*. It has passively acquiesced in the promptings of its own spontaneous impulse.

order my cabman back to the office; while my *act* of will at every movement energetically *resists* that impulse.

In the early part of our preceding illustration, we were pointing out how frequent a fact it is that my will's spontaneous impulse remains stable—*i.e.* free from all vacillation and vibration—throughout the day. We confined ourselves, however, to the mere facts of my external life: getting up; breakfasting; going to my office, etc. But it is worth while, for more reasons than one, to initiate a similar inquiry as to the workings of my mind and thought. As regards *these* facts also, we suppose that with the mass of men a similar conclusion holds. My mind is probably never altogether quiescent, during any part of my waking life. But, nevertheless, with most men, one thought usually succeeds another throughout most part of the day, without any active intervention of will, according to the laws of human nature taken in connection with external circumstances. As I drive down to my office, I begin thinking what letters will probably await me there; what business engagements I have for the day; what is the present state of my finances; what the state of the money market, and what hope of improvement. I remember, with bitterness and disgust, how greatly this or that firm has lately stood in my way. I look at the extraordinary success of some particular scheme, which an acquaintance of mine has started. I draw attractive pictures of the amount which I, in my turn, shall realize by some ingenious speculation I have just thought of. And my fool's paradise is only brought to an end by the cab stopping at my office. Here, however, as we observed in a former essay, one difference is to be noted, of extreme importance between the interior and the worldly man respectively.* The difference,

* "A similar remark may be made," we pointed out, "on numberless other instances, where men agree with each other, as a matter of course, in doing the external act, but differ indefinitely as to the spirit in which they do it. It is really difficult to determine how often the good man's probation

however, relates not to vacillation and vibration of the will, but to anti-impulsive effort. If I am happy enough to be a person steadily pursuing a course of spiritual advance, I by no means permit my mind to move unchecked along its own spontaneous course. I am keenly alive to the fact, whenever thoughts of discontent, or envy, or hatred, or undue worldly solicitude, or undue worldly hopefulness, threaten, like thorns, to choke my spiritual growth. On all such occasions—unless I am to lay up for myself matter of subsequent self-accusation—I interfere in the course of mental events with vigorous anti-impulsive effort, and fight God's battle in my soul. Then, even when nothing sinful is in my mind, I frequently interrupt the natural and spontaneous course of my thoughts by holy aspirations, intercessory prayers, theological acts. Not unfrequently, of course—in virtue of my pious habits—such acts present themselves spontaneously, in accordance with the natural workings of my mind. But at other times I introduce them by anti-impulsive effort, when my mind is naturally moving in a different direction, and when its spontaneous impulse is stably opposed to these holy occupations.

We hope by this time we have made clear to our readers what that compound phenomenon is to which we beg their careful attention. Two mutually related acts are simultaneously proceeding in my mind. The first of these acts is my will's stable spontaneous preponderating impulse in one given direction. The second of these acts is my firm and successful resolution to resist that impulse, and proceed in a different—perhaps the opposite—direction.

In the illustrations which we have hitherto given, what

consists, not in the external act which he has to do, but in the motives for which he does it. During the greater portion of his life, his growth in virtue mainly depends either (1) on his choice of good motives for everyday acts; or (2) on acts altogether interior, such as patience, self-examination, humility, forgivingness, equitableness of judgment, purity, under circumstances of trial."

is the characteristic which will have impressed our reader,
as specially distinguishing "anti-impulsive efforts" from
those other mental acts with which we have contrasted
them? Perhaps this, that they involve constant *struggle*
and *effort*. But it is of vital importance for our argument
to make it clearly understood, that there are very many
acts, involving great struggle and effort, but which,
nevertheless, are not acts of *anti-impulsive* effort. Acts of
anti-impulsive effort are one thing; acts of what we call
"congenial" effort are quite another thing. Acts of *congenial* effort are those done in *accordance* with my strongest
present desire, in accordance with the stable and preponderating spontaneous impulse of my will. Acts of *anti-impulsive* effort, on the contrary, are acts done in *resistance*
to such desire and impulse. As an instance of "congenial"
effort, we have before now referred to a gallant soldier in
action. He will very often put forth intense effort; brave
appalling perils; confront the risk of an agonizing death.
But to what end is this effort directed? He puts it forth,
in order that he may act in full accordance with his
preponderating spontaneous impulse; in order that he may
gratify what is his strongest present desire; in order that he
may defend his country, overcome his country's foe, obtain
fame and distinction, gratify his military ardour. In cases
of *anti-impulsive* effort, the agent practises "self-restraint
and self-control." But most certainly no one would commemorate the "self-restraint" of one who should be so
carried away, breathlessly, as it were, by military ardour,
by desire of victory, by zeal for his country's cause, by a
certain savage aggressiveness—who should be so carried
away, we repeat, by these and similar impulses, that,
under such influences, he performs prodigies of valour.
In seeking to gratify these overwhelming and sovereign
desires, he tramples underfoot an indefinite number of
those weaker wishes which have just now no such hold on

his will. He faces appalling dangers without one pause for deliberation or reflection, because his overmastering crave of the moment intensely impels him so to act. If our readers would carry with them a clear notion of the contrast which we intend, between "anti-impulsive effort" on one side, and "congenial effort" on the other, they cannot, we think, have a better guide, than to keep in mind two distinct courses of action, pursued by the same brave and gallant soldier. Let them first consider him, on the one hand, as he puts forth intense struggle for victory in the heat of action. Then let them consider him, on the other hand, as putting forth struggle no less intense —the struggle of self-restraint and self-control—in order to exercise full Christian patience and meekness under insult and humiliation.

On a former occasion, we have entirely admitted that there may be sometimes difficulty in deciding whether this or that given effort be "congenial" or "anti-impulsive." But these, we added, will always be instances belonging to what may be called the border-land; cases in which the influences acting on me are so nearly equivalent, that it requires very careful self-inspection on my part to see on which side the balance preponderates. But if there are extreme cases—where it is not easy to be certain in which direction lies the preponderating impulse—the great majority of cases are quite different in character. By far the greater number of "anti-impulsive efforts" are of such character, that no one possessing the most ordinary power of self-inspection can possibly doubt their being what they are. And as, hitherto, we have given fewer instances of what we call "congenial effort" than of any other phenomenal class with which our argument is concerned, we will conclude this particular part of our subject by giving two more instances of what we mean by this last term. By doing this we shall make still clearer how radical is the distinction between "congenial" and "anti-impulsive" efforts respectively.

First, let us go back to our merchant seized with heart symptoms. One probable alternative with him is, that his preponderating spontaneous impulse, whether in consequence of predominant emotion or of confirmed prudential habits, prompts him vigorously to going back home. Nevertheless, there is a strong emotional current setting in the *opposite* direction. He puts forth much effort and struggle to *resist* this emotional current. True, but such effort is "congenial," and proves nothing against Determinism. The effort is *prompted*, not *opposed*, by his preponderating spontaneous impulse.

Second illustration. I am at sea in a pleasure-boat, when to my dismay I discover plain signs of a rapidly approaching storm. I at once set to work at rowing towards shore for the sake of dear life. The effort which I put forth is intense. I vigorously, continuously, energetically, unflaggingly resist every antagonistic desire. But in which direction, all this time, is my *desire*—my *strongest* present desire? my stable spontaneous *impulse*? my natural *tendency*? Of course, in the very same direction with my *act*. Contrast this with my state of mind when, for Christ's sake, I strenuously resisted my desire of retaliating injury. In that earlier case, my effort was put forth in order that I might *oppose* the predominant desire, impulse, and tendency of my will. But in the present case, they are put forth in order that I may *gratify* that desire; that I may obey more *thoroughly* that impulse; that I may give fuller and freer *scope* to that tendency. In the earlier case, my efforts were directed to an end from which the spontaneous impulse of my will recoiled; whereas they are now directed to an end which my will, according to its spontaneous impulse, intensely desires. In the earlier case, my will put forth vehement effort in order to resist its own urgent tendency; *now* it puts forth such effort in order to give that tendency its freest and most unfettered play. In the earlier case I exercised unremitting, energetic, vigilant "self-government" and "self-control." But it would be droll enough to hear any one say that a man exhibited "self-government" and "self-control" by the mere fact of straining every nerve to escape a watery grave.

Here, then, we close the first portion of our essay. By means of these multiplied and diversified illustrations, we trust we have made clear to our reader what we wished to make clear. We hope he will now (1) understand what we *mean* by "anti-impulsive effort;" and (2) see that acts of such effort do really from time to time take place in the human mind. Our next task, then, will be to exhibit the argument deducible from these acts in favour of Freewill. It may be remembered that, during the larger portion of our preceding essays on this subject, we were merely arguing for "Indeterminism"—*i.e.* for the negative doctrine, that the doctrine of Determinism is false. It was not until we reached the later portion of our last essay, that we argued for the full doctrine of Freewill. Here we will, therefore, refer respectively to these two stages of our reasoning.

The mental facts, on which we directly based that reasoning, are, as we have so often said, those of "anti-impulsive effort." In every case of this kind there exists what we have called a "compound phenomenon;" or, in other words, there co-exist in my mind two mutually distinct phenomena. First phenomenon. My will's preponderating spontaneous impulse is stably set in one given direction. Second phenomenon. My will *resists* that preponderating spontaneous impulse, and I act in a different—often an entirely opposite—direction. To fix the fact in our mind more definitely, let us recur to the merchant who, on being seized with recognized symptoms of heart complaint, acts reasonably, but very much against the grain, by telling the cabman to drive him home again. He is acting, by supposition, very much *against the grain*. One distinctly pronounced and strongly marked mental phenomenon is his restless, impatient, and predominant desire to bring this very troublesome business matter to a conclusion. So strong is the predominance of this desire, that, unless he exercised unintermitting self-resistance, self-government, self-control, he would infallibly countermand his recent order, and direct the cabman back to his office. Here is one unmistakable phenomenon. A second, no less distinctly pronounced and strongly marked phenomenon, is this very self-resistance, self-government, self-control, of which we have been just speaking. One one side is that phenomenon which we call his will's predominant spontaneous *impulse ;* on the other is that phenomenon which we call its firm and sustained *resolve*.

Now, firstly, let us set forth the *negative* argument which we deduce from such mental facts—the argument directed merely to show that the doctrine of Determinism is false. We drew this out at length in our essay on Mr. Mill's denial of Freewill, and will here very briefly sum up what we there said. The doctrine of Determinists is precisely this : that my will's action at any given moment is infallibly determined by the preponderant influences and attractions of that moment. Now, during the greater part of my waking life, my consciousness directly testifies what *is* that course of conduct to which the preponderant influences and attractions of the moment dispose me. For my will's *spontaneous impulse* directly supplies me with such testification. My will's spontaneous impulse, we say, whenever it is stable, precisely testifies what is that course of conduct to which my preponderant desires and attractions of the moment dispose me. But, as we have been urging at such length, it is an undeniable fact of experience that at certain periods I pursue a course of conduct *divergent* from that prompted by my will's spontaneous impulse. It is most clear, then, that at those particular periods, be they more or fewer, my will is *not* infallibly determined by the preponderant influences and attractions of the moment. In other words, the phenomena of those periods make it irrefragably certain that the doctrine of Determinism is false.

But we now proceed, from the negative argument disproving Determinism, to the positive argument establishing Freewill. And this, we maintain, is even more direct and immediate than the former. We solicit for it our readers' careful attention, because we feel that we did not state it in our last essay with sufficient prominence and emphasis. Consider respectively those two distinct phenomena—preponderating spontaneous impulse on one side, anti-impulsive effort on the other side, to which we have so earnestly drawn attention. If we examine them successively with due care, we shall see that they differ from each other in character not less than fundamentally. In experiencing one of them, my will is entirely passive; in experiencing the other, it is intensely active.* Consider my will's spontaneous impulse; the impulse, *e.g.*, which prompts me to bid the cabman drive me back to my office. In experiencing this impulse, my will, we say, has been entirely passive; the impulse has *befallen* me, *come upon* me, *taken hold* of me: such are the phrases which I should naturally use. On the other hand, my *resistance* to this impulse has been

---

* So Mr. H. W. Lucas (*The Month* of February, 1878, p. 251) distinguishes emphatically between "what has *been given to* me" and "what *proceeds from* me;" between "what I *have*" and "what I *do*." And, again (p. 254), "I deny entirely that, in resisting a temptation, I am *the mere passive spectator* of a battle between *conflicting impulses*. . . . I know what it is to witness the succession of my thoughts, to feel their solicitations; and I know, on the other hand, what it is to exert myself to *govern* that succession of thoughts and *resist* the solicitations. *In the one case I am a spectator, in the other an actor.*"

not merely *experienced* by my soul, but has rather been put forth by my soul's *intrinsic strength*. I am not only conscious that I *elicit* the act of resistance; I am no one whit less directly conscious that I elicit it *by the active exertion of my soul*. The consciousness of one single moment suffices to show me unmistakably that I have the power at that moment of resisting preponderant impulse by my soul's intrinsic strength. I know unmistakably that I have the power to do this, because I know unmistakably that I am actually doing it.

So important is the doctrine, which may reasonably be based on the consciousness of one moment. But we need hardly add that still more important inferences may be drawn, if we contemplate the experience, not of one moment only, but of a continuous period. This we urged in our last essay. The experience which I obtain, even in one single period of protracted and vehement struggle against impulse, is amply sufficient to give me an intimate and infallible knowledge of one all-important fact. We refer to the fact that, at every moment of the struggle, it has depended simply on my own choice, with what degree of efficacy I have struggled against the temptation.

It will be admitted by every philosopher, be he Libertarian or Determinist, that such a power as we have just described is the very power which every one designates by the name "Freewill." It is this very power of which Libertarians maintain, and Determinists deny, the existence. In the essay referred to we proceeded to show this in some detail; and we need not here repeat what we there said. There is, no doubt, a very important supplementary question, viz. during how many moments of the day, in what acts, under what conditions, do I *possess* the power of acting freely? But of this question, while earnestly expatiating on its importance, we postponed our treatment to a somewhat later portion of our course.

Still, there are two further matters of philosophical doctrine, which it will be necessary to consider even on the present occasion, previously to our leaving this part of our subject. The first of these has very little comparative importance, and what we have to say on it in no way affects our argument on one side or the other. Still, we must explain ourselves, in order to avoid the possibility of our being misunderstood on one subordinate point. In our whole discussion, then, we have put entirely into the background any consideration of those exceptional moments during which there exists what we have called vacillation and vibration of the will. We have founded our whole argument on those other indefinitely more frequent instances, in which the will's preponderating spontaneous impulse is entirely stable. We have done this because it is instances of *the latter* kind, which so unmistakably exhibit that phenomenon of anti-impulsive effort, on which our whole reasoning has depended. But, at the same time, we must not for a moment be supposed to admit that the will is not *free*, even during a period of vacillation and vibration. On the contrary, we are confident that by no means unfrequently, though, we admit, by no means universally, vacillation and vibration are simply *caused* by freedom. The will first languidly and falteringly resists its own spontaneous impulse, and then, for want of due energy, sinks back into acquiescence. Then another languid effort probably succeeds, to be again followed by relapse. And this kind of movement may go on for a considerable period of time. We are not here, of course, *arguing* for this conclusion : such an argument is not yet in place. But it has been necessary to make this explanation, as our reasoning might otherwise be importantly misapprehended.

The other matter of philosophical doctrine to which we just now referred is one which we have discussed, indeed, on earlier occasions, but to which we must once more recur. We wish our readers expressly to observe that, in dealing with "spontaneous impulse," there are two questions entirely distinct from each other, which are sometimes inadvertently confused to the great detriment of philosophical lucidity. It will be admitted by every one that, during far the longer portion of my waking life, my will is affected at every successive moment by some stable preponderating spontaneous impulse. Again, it will also be admitted, we suppose, universally, that this stable preponderating spontaneous impulse is infallibly determined at each moment by my *circumstances* of that moment, internal and external. These two statements being accepted and taken as our foundation, there are two entirely distinct questions, we say, which are introduced by them.

The first of these questions is that on which we have been mainly labouring in the present and previous essays. Is this spontaneous impulse infallibly and necessarily followed by accordant action? Or, on the contrary, have I the power of resisting it, and acting in a different direction? We have argued earnestly, we need hardly say, for the *latter* of these alternatives. And we shall here, of course, assume that we have argued successfully.

But there is a second question, entirely irrelevant, indeed, to the Deterministic controversy, yet undoubtedly of great philosophical importance. Nor, indeed, can we ourselves escape the necessity of saying a word or two concerning it, because its consideration is involved in the answer we must give to one particular objection which has been urged against our reasoning. The question may be thus stated. My will's preponderant spontaneous impulse at any given moment is infallibly determined, we have said, by the circumstances, internal and external, of that moment. We proceed to ask by *what* circumstances? Among all the co-existing circumstances of the moment, which are those that influence the will's impulse? And this being known, further, in what mutual *proportion* do they influence it? Or let us put the same question in other terms. Of co-existing circumstances, (1) which are those that are factors of my will's impulse? and (2) with what *proportionate* degree of *efficacity* do these respective factors act on it? This question, our readers see at once, is a very comprehensive one; but there is only one particular part of it on which our purpose requires us to lay prominent stress. We ask, then, more particularly—what are the mutual relations of *habit* on one side, and *emotion* on the other, in determining the will's spontaneous impulse? Determinists sometimes express themselves incautiously, as though they thought that the mere balance of *emotional craving* determines the impulse. But we suppose they cannot really mean this; most certainly Dr. Bain does not mean it. In our essay on Mr. Mill's denial of Freewill, we set forth his theory on the subject, as far as we were able to understand it, and proceeded to express our own substantial agreement therewith. We dissent, of course, intensely from his opinion that the will's spontaneous impulse infallibly issues in accordant *action*; but we are disposed substantially to agree with what he says concerning the *genesis* of that impulse. We do not mean that he has even come near to fathoming and exhausting the subject; for it is one which, we think, has been most unduly neglected by psychologians. But Dr. Bain has gone much further into it than any other philosopher with whom we happen to be acquainted, and we substantially agree with all which he has said thereupon.

Our own concern, however, as we have already said, is only with a small part of a very large theory. On earlier occasions we have protested against any such notion, as that the will's spontaneous impulse is always determined by the mere balance of emotional craving. And as we find, from certain criticisms which we have received, that we have been misunderstood on this point, we will here repeat what we have said in former essays. Certainly it is a most shallow view to suppose that the will's spontaneous impulse at any given moment is determined by the mere balance of emotional craving and excitement at that moment. *Habits* of the will are also most important factors of the result. Suppose, *e.g.* I have acquired a firm habit of rising at some particular time in the morning. When that hour arrives, nothing is more probable than that the balance of my emotional craving is towards remaining in bed. But it results from my acquired habit of early rising that the confused thought of all those various benefits which result from the practice of early rising—that this confused thought spontaneously resists the stream of emotion. This confused thought, we say, of future advantage so effectively influences my will that my spontaneous impulse is towards rising. In this case, the desire engendered by habit is a more influential desire than that engendered by emotional craving; and I rise from bed, as a matter of course, without the need of any anti-impulsive effort. What effort there is—and perhaps a good deal may be exercised—is, nevertheless, entirely "congenial" effort.* A few pages back we made a similar supposition, when considering our old friend the merchant seized with heart symptoms. One among the alternatives which we supposed—and one by no means uncommon in such a case—was this. We suppose that, in virtue of his firmly acquired habit of prudence, habit prevailed against emotion. His desire of avoiding the peril which his business interview would cause was indefinitely more influential than his antagonistic desire of terminating his long anxiety at once by *proceeding* to the

---

* We have fully admitted, our readers will remember, that there are not a few instances in which it may be reasonably doubted whether some given act be one of "congenial" or "anti-impulsive" effort. But we have made it, we trust, abundantly clear that there is a much larger number of instances in which there cannot reasonably be any such doubt.

interview. The latter desire might be accompanied with much stronger emotional excitement; but habit on this occasion was stronger than emotion, and his will's spontaneous impulse prompted his return home. Often enough, then, habit spontaneously prevails against emotion; often, on the other hand, emotion spontaneously prevails against habit. We will not here attempt any psychological analysis of either phenomenon. We will only repeat the remark which we have already made, viz. that psychologians have, in our humble opinion, been very unduly remiss in exploring the matter scientifically.

Here, then, our remarks incidentally offer a very convenient point of transition to the next portion of our task. This next portion is the giving a brief explanation of certain technical terms which we have used in preceding essays, and which some of our critics have failed rightly to apprehend.

Firstly, then, when we speak of desire A being "stronger" than desire B, we are far from meaning necessarily to say that A is accompanied by a stronger *emotional craving* than B. We mean that A has more influence than B on the will's spontaneous impulse. It follows, therefore, that, according to our use of words, "my strongest present desire at this moment" means neither more nor less than "my will's spontaneous impulse at this moment."

Further. By the term "effort" we mean "resistance to desire." "Congenial effort" is "resistance spontaneously offered to some (at the moment) weaker desire, in order to the gratification of some (at the moment) stronger desire." "Anti-impulsive effort" is "resistance offered by my will's intrinsic energy to my strongest present desire, for the purpose of advancing towards some end, which my intellect proposes to me (at the moment) as worth my so aiming at."

Once more. Inducements influencing the will are

evidently of two fundamentally different kinds, accordingly as they respectively influence (1) its spontaneous impulse, or (2) its active exertion in *resisting* impulse. Since, therefore, they are of two essentially different kinds, we have thought it important to give them distinct names. So far as my will's spontaneous impulse is concerned, our readers have seen that my will has had no active part whatever, has put forth no intrinsic energy whatever of its own, towards the origination of that impulse. The various circumstances, therefore, which have combined to originate it, may well be paralleled to those physical attractions which at any given moment solicit some inanimate particle. Accordingly, we have called such influential circumstances by the name of "attractions." Moreover, we have divided them into "emotional" and "non-emotional" attractions. The latter term we apply to those cases—just now considered by us—in which the desire is not mainly *emotional*. Take, *e.g.* the thought of those confusedly remembered advantages which result from the practice of early rising. This thought will be very powerfully influential, if a strong habit have been acquired in the appropriate direction; but its attractive efficacy is not exercised mainly through the medium of *emotion*.

So much as regards those influences which act more or less powerfully on the will's spontaneous impulse. We have called these "attractions," and we have reserved the term "motives" for a different kind of influence altogether, and we will here add a few words on the broad contrast which exists between "attractions" and "motives." Firstly, the word "attraction" may perhaps be suitably so extended as to include other influences besides *thoughts*. If I pass a gentleman's park which is open to the public, so delightful a scent of flowers may reach me as to produce a certain influence, whether predominant or no, on my will's spontaneous impulse, prompting me to turn aside and enter the park. This scent may, perhaps, suitably be called an "attraction." But, putting this consideration aside, and supposing it were agreed that the term "attraction" should be confined to attracting *thoughts*—even so the distinction is signal between "attractions" and "motives." Those thoughts which we call "attractions" occur to my mind without any active intervention of the will, according to the spontaneous working of psychical and physical laws. And these laws, moreover, infallibly determine what is the amount of influence which such attractions shall exercise on my will's spontaneous impulse. But a "motive" is the thought of such or such an end which the will, by its own active resolve, chooses to pursue. Moreover, these thoughts remain in my mind, not mainly through the spontaneous working of psychical and physical laws, but, far more, by the will's own anti-impulsive effort. My will fixes my attention on those thoughts—in opposition to the preponderating impulse which may prompt me to think about something else—in order that I may more vigorously pursue the end which they indicate. At the same time, we are, of course, as far as possible from forgetting that those very thoughts which my will's anti-impulsive effort selects as "motives," far more commonly than not, while present in my mind are also "attractions," and affect, in greater or less degree, my will's spontaneous impulse.

We are now, at last, in a position to examine those few among the friendly criticisms received by us which seem to need distinct consideration.

I. One critic (unknown to us, but evidently a Catholic) thus comments on our fundamental argument:

A Determinist might say [in reply to that argument], "If the soul has been furnished by education with moral habits of some considerable strength, they would be the proximate cause of a resistance to the strongest present desire. That is to say, the strongest present desire would fail in its effect, because of a motive-power existing in the soul."

Now, if our critic means by a "motive-power of the soul," a power residing in my soul of putting forth anti-impulsive effort at my free choice, he and we are here entirely at one. But it is plain, we think, that he means something quite different. He has apparently understood us to use the term "my strongest present desire" as synonymous with "my strongest present emotional craving." But we think that the reference we have made in past articles to "non-emotional attractions," ought sufficiently to have averted such misapprehension. At all events, we have made our meaning abundantly clear on the present occasion. We are the very last to forget that "moral habits of considerable strength" preponderate again and again over emotion, in the influence exercised by them on my will's spontaneous impulse. But the question on which our fundamental argument turns is not how that impulse is *engendered* or *influenced*. Our sole essential question is whether that impulse, however engendered, be ever resisted.

We do not at all deny—on the contrary, we expressly maintained—that moral habits are of great service not only in elevating the will's spontaneous impulse, but also in facilitating anti-impulsive effort. But we have given our reasons for holding that any act of true anti-impulsive effort, however much it my be facilitated by habit, is, nevertheless, a conclusive proof of Freewill.

II. In this first objection, then, so we submit, the writer has failed to apprehend our precise argument. His second objection, however, is indubitably relevant, and we must simply fight the matter out with him. He would, himself, he says, be prepared to "acknowledge that the will is a *cæca potestas;* that it cannot act without a motive, and that, therefore, it cannot resist its strongest present desire while that desire is held before it." But, then, he would maintain against Determinists, that the will "has full power to *turn to other motives;*" and he says that this latter power, at all events, can be easily proved to exist. In this last statement, of course, we entirely agree; the question is, whether a much stronger power of resistance to "motives" cannot also be established.

Putting the statement into our own language, what we understand our able and intelligent critic to maintain is this:—"So long as my will's spontaneous impulse is in one direction, I have not the power of acting in an opposite direction. I have no further immediate power of resistance beyond that of turning my attention to opposite inducements; and of otherwise suspending my action, until the thought of those inducements—acting by way of attraction —shall have diverted my spontaneous impulse into the direction which I desire." We are well aware that many thoughtful Catholic philosophers take this view; but, with sincere respect for their authority, we cannot ourselves see reason to accept it. Let us go back to our old illustration of the merchant seized with heart symptoms, who at once by anti-impulsive effort resolves to return home, though very much against the grain. Under such circumstances, as soon as I have had a moment for reflection after experiencing those symptoms, I order my cabman to take me back home. My preponderating spontaneous impulse, my strongest present desire, is directed vigorously and intensely towards going on to my office; but by strong anti-impulsive effort I resolve to order my cabman back again. It is not merely that I begin to ponder on other "motives," but that, without waiting for any change of my spontaneous impulse, I perform the critical bodily act of putting my head out of window and turning the cabman back. Our critic, on the contrary, must say that such an act on my part is impossible, according to the laws of human nature. Here, then, precisely is the question which inquirers have to consider. According to the constitution of the human mind—have I, or have I not, the power of ordering my cab home again, at a moment when my will's spontaneous impulse still prompts me in an opposite direction? Those who consider that such conduct as we have described is psychologically impossible, will be on our friendly opponent's side; those who think it entirely possible will be on our side. We cannot fancy that, when this alternative is fairly placed before minds unwarped by theory, there will be much doubt on the response.

Perhaps here we shall make our precise point still clearer, and show also how much we can concede to our opponent, if we have recourse to another illustration of anti-impulsive effort. I have asked to be called at a somewhat early hour, in order that I may visit a sick dependent, whom I could not otherwise have time to see. At the moment of being called, so far am I from springing up with promptitude, that, on the contrary, my will's spontaneous impulse—not merely its emotional craving, but its spontaneous impulse on the whole—is intensely averse from rising. As soon, however, as I have time to collect my energies, I freely exercise with some vigour the power I possess of resisting my strongest present desire. The effort which I have made indeed is not sufficient to *counterbalance* my spontaneous impulse, and I still, therefore, remain in bed. What, then, will be my state of will immediately after this first moment of effort? The spontaneous impulse of my will, in the direction of staying in bed, has immediately become importantly weaker than it was just before; weaker by the whole extent of force corresponding with the effort I have made. Or, to put the matter algebraically, "My new spontaneous impulse towards staying in bed" equals "my old spontaneous impulse towards staying in bed," minus "the force freely exercised by my will in the opposite direction."

But this first free act of my will produces by degrees a *further* effect also on my spontaneous impulse, entirely distinct from that which we have just mentioned. The motive of my anti-impulsive effort was the thought of a certain benevolent action, for which I should lose my opportunity if I went to sleep again. Consequently, during my effort, I have fixed my thoughts on this. But the thought of this visit is to me a very attractive thought; whether by way of emotion, or by way of habit, or of both; and much more the thought of *missing* the visit is exquisitely repulsive. By this means a second favourable modification —and a very considerable one—takes place, of my original spontaneous impulse towards staying in bed. Very soon some moment will arrive in which my predominant impulse is, indeed, still towards staying in bed, though very far less intensely than at first; but in which, on the other hand, my motive for getting up is presented far more vividly to my mind than it was originally. Our opponent must say that, even at this much more favourable moment, I have still no psychical power of rising from bed. He must say that I have no power of rising, until my preponderating impulse itself comes to be in that direction. We venture strongly to maintain the opposite position. No other ultimate appeal is, of course, possible, except to the observed facts of human nature. But we cannot think that such appeal will favour our opponent's doctrine.

III. A Catholic friend, of much ability, who takes great interest in things philosophical, has, at our request, put on paper the following criticism, which he had at first more briefly expressed in conversation :—

The position assumed by the Determinist is this. The same ("similar" is more correct) antecedents *in all respects* being given, the same ("similar") act of will will infallibly follow.

This statement you deny, and maintain, in opposition, that all the antecedent circumstances being precisely similar, the *consequent*, viz. the act of will, will at one time be in accordance with these antecedents constituting the "*preponderating attraction*," and at another time in opposition to them, viz. an act of resistance to this "*preponderating attraction.*" Your proof consists in an appeal to every man's experience. Now, on this I remark that if this act of will, viz. resistance to "preponderating attraction," were *without a motive* to serve as a fresh antecedent, then (on the supposition that consciousness testifies to this *motiveless* resistance) the Determinist is completely answered by the experience of all mankind. But neither he nor you admit that the act of resistance is motiveless. He in his own language would say that it has a fixed antecedent, which does not form one of those included in what you call the "preponderating attraction;" and you, if I understand you rightly, would say that we are induced to resist by "motives," using the term in your sense of the word. If, then, it is admitted on both sides that the act of resistance has an *antecedent*, or is consequent upon a *motive*, such as a resolution always to pursue what is virtuous, I can well conceive the Determinist replying to you in this way. You maintain, in relation to the will, he will say that, all the antecedents being the same, the *consequent* act of will will not always be the same. On the contrary, it will sometimes be just the contrary of what it was before. The man, you say, will *resist* instead of *complying* with the "preponderating attraction"—but then, you add, he will resist "*for some worthy motive*," "induced to do so by one or other of these two classes of motives." Now, this *motive*, for the sake of which he resists, or which induced him to resist, must necessarily have been in the man's thoughts *before* he willed or determined to resist, and thus formed a fresh antecedent. Nor does it affect the question at issue of what kind this motive may be,—it is immaterial whether it be a dictate of reason, or a previous act of will resulting in a present fixed resolution; for my present fixed resolution—to pursue, for example, what is virtuous—is quite a distinct act from that by which I determine that I will not in the present instance follow the impulse urging me to commit this particular sin. The case therefore stands thus. A man is violently tempted to *resolve* upon an act of vengeance; for the moment the antecedents are such as always have been and always will be followed by the resolve "I will take revenge"—the "preponderating attraction" is to yield to the temptation. The next moment, and before the man has time to make his resolve, the thought springs up in his mind that it is wrong to take revenge; that it is contrary to his fixed resolution always to pursue what is virtuous. And now the case is completely changed: a fresh antecedent has been added to those previously existing—and in consequence of this fresh antecedent, that which before was the "preponderating attraction" has ceased to be so. No wonder, therefore, that the *consequent* act is also different, and that the man, instead of resolving that he will be revenged, resolves that he will not. In making his resolve he follows what *was* not but *is* the "preponderating attraction." Such is the answer that I fancy a Determinist would give to your essays, and which I meant to imply when I last saw you. I think upon that occasion that I put it briefly thus, you show that a man resists his *sensitive appetite* ("preponderating attraction"), but not that he will resist "motives" and sensitive appetite combined.

Our critic quite rightly understands us, as resting our case on observed and unmistakable mental phenomena. But he does not rightly apprehend, we should say, what those phenomena *are* on which we rest our case. He thinks, if we rightly understand him, that we appeal to experience, as *immediately* disproving Determinism. He thinks we appeal to the experience of two different moments, as immediately evincing that two precisely similar groups of mental antecedents may exist at two different moments, and may nevertheless be followed respectively by a dissimilar mental consequent. But we never alleged anything of the kind; nor do we for a moment think that any such *immediate* experience of Indeterminism is possible. Certainly we appeal with great confidence to, and found our whole argument on, what we consider to be an unmistakable fact of immediate experience. That fact is, that very frequently my will's spontaneous impulse is in one direction, at the very moment when my conduct is in a different— often the very contrary—direction. If this statement of ours were disproved, no doubt our whole argument would be overthrown; but we think that the period of such disproval will not be earlier than the Greek Kalends. On the other hand, our present critic seems to understand us as resting on *inference* or *conjecture* our response to the inquiry, what is at this moment my will's spontaneous impulse? But, on the contrary, *this* is the very fact which we base on *immediate* experience. We say, not that in all cases, but that in very many cases, experience pronounces on this matter immediately and unmistakably. I know immediately and most unmistakably, by the self-inspection of this moment, that my *conduct* of the moment is proceeding in a direction different from my *spontaneous impulse* of the moment. We are not comparing one moment and its thoughts with another moment and *its* thoughts. We are dwelling on one compound phenomenon, as we have called it, which exists at one and the same moment. This is our fundamental premiss, our phenomenal fulcrum. From this premiss we *infer* (1) the doctrine of Indeterminism, and (2) the full doctrine of Freewill. In the preceding pages we have duly set forth, according to our earlier essays, what is the process of reasoning by which we purport to establish those two doctrines. We cannot see that our able friend has written anything which invalidates our position. Firstly, we cannot see that he has said anything to throw doubt on the correctness of that report, given by self-inspection, to which we have referred. Nor, secondly, can we see that he has said anything to throw doubt on the validity of that argumentative process which we have *based* on the report given by self-inspection. But if that report be correct, and if that argumentation be also valid, Determinism is disproved and Freewill established.

It will be seen, then, that the criticisms which have reached us have not led us to change our opinion in any particular; though we feel how such a confession may leave us open to the charge of obstinacy and undue self-confidence.

But, at all events, we feel deeply that our critics have conferred on us service of great moment, by making us aware of several particulars in which our language had been obscure, and by thus enabling us to amend and strengthen our exposition.

We will conclude, for the present, our treatment of Freewill with a remark which has already been made by Dr. Mivart in one of his admirable papers. We have more than once asked Determinists to explain, on what argumentative ground they base their Determinism. They do not venture to allege that direct self-inspection furnishes them with phenomena which, taken by themselves, even invest their case with strong *probability*. The answer they commonly give to the inquiry is the same with that which we quoted from Dr. Bain in our last essay. They consider the fact sufficiently established, that the general *rule* of Nature is phenomenal uniformity; and they argue that this rule is to be accepted as holding in all doubtful cases, until an exception is made good. We maintained, in reply, that such an argument "does not carry with it so much as the slightest appearance of probability," unless Dr. Bain begins by *assuming*, on his own side, what is the one vital and fundamental point of difference between him and his opponents. But, even were there far more force than we can possibly admit in Dr. Bain's analogies and conjectures, they would avail him nothing against our direct appeal to experience. We have argued, that our own Libertarian conclusions do not rest in any way on any kind of analogy or conjecture; but that they are inferred demonstratively, from what is the unmistakable and immediate report of direct self-inspection. We retort, therefore, Dr. Bain's premiss directly against his own position. We accept his premiss, that Freewill is a complete anomaly and eccentricity in Nature. To this we subjoin our own premiss, that Freewill indubitably exists. The inference which may legitimately be drawn by combination of these two premisses is, we think, of much importance and significance.

We entirely concur, then, with Dr. Bain in holding that, among other phenomena whatever, among all phenomena, except those of the human will, the law of uniformity ordinarily prevails.* This particular class of phenomena stands out in isolated and startling opposition to the otherwise universal law of phenomenal existence. Surely the most ordinarily inquiring philosopher, to whom such a circumstance shall be made clear, cannot do otherwise than muse on the *meaning* of this, as it were, miraculous and bewildering fact. There is no tenet held by *Antitheists*, which throws on it any light or significance whatever. On the other hand, what is well known to be among the most characteristic and fundamental doctrines of *Theism*, is precisely and emphatically correlative to that abnormal and prodigious anomaly which is called Freewill. According to the Theist's doctrine, the one reason for which men are placed in this world is their moral probation. Even their physical well-being is, in the Theist's eye, a matter of indefinitely minor moment, except so far as it is connected with their moral advancement. And as to the rise and fall of empires, the intellectual triumphs of philosophies, the marvels of mechanical invention, the one primary importance of these things—predominating indefinitely over all others put together—is their ministration to the moral interests of mankind. We hope, in our future course, to establish this doctrine firmly on the foundations of reason. What we are now pointing out is its deep harmony with those experienced facts on which we have dwelt in this and earlier articles. There can be no such thing as morality in the Theistic sense, without Freewill. *Admit* Theistic

---

* We say "ordinarily," because, of course, we hold that *miraculous* intervention is a sufficiently frequent fact.

morality, Freewill becomes, one may say, a matter of course. Deny Theistic morality, Freewill is an uncouth, unmeaning, portentous exception to the whole course of Nature.

After we had written the immediately preceding paragraphs, we called to mind a passage of Mr. Hutton's, so singularly bearing on their purport, that we are sure our readers will be pleased by our inserting extracts from it. We italicize a word or two here and there.

The consciousness of moral obligation, and that of moral freedom which accompanies it, are due to no abstracting process. . . . They are the essential characteristics of a very positive experience, which . . . forces on us the sense of a power which besets our moral life, while absolutely penetrating all the physical conditions of our existence. . . . Accustomed as man is to feel his personal feebleness, his entire subordination to the physical forces of the universe—unable as he is to affect in the smallest degree either the laws of his body or the fundamental constitution of his mind—it is not without a necessary sense of supernatural awe that, *in the case of moral duty*, he finds this almost constant pressure *remarkably withdrawn* at the very crisis in which the import of his action is brought home to him with the most vivid conviction. . . . The absolute control that sways so much of our life is *waived* just where we are impressed with the most profound conviction that there is *but one path* in which we can walk with a free heart. . . . The sense that a supernatural eye is upon us in duty is so strong, because the *relaxation of restraint* comes simultaneously with a *deep sense of obligation*—just as the child is instinctively aware, when the sustaining hand is taken away, that *the parent's eye is all the more intent on his unassisted movement.*—" Essays " (Second Edition), vol. i. pp. 33, 34.

XI.

*MR. SHADWORTH HODGSON ON FREEWILL.

It has resulted, from various circumstances, that our proposed argument for God's Existence has been gradually developed in successive papers published from time to time, instead of being exhibited once for all in one or two volumes, as the case might be. This course involves, no doubt, certain serious drawbacks; but it is also attended with certain conspicuous advantages. Among the latter is to be reckoned, that we are able to profit by incidental criticisms, and correct our view on this or that minor particular. Another advantage is that, if we may so express ourselves, we can feel our readers' pulse as we proceed; that we can discover what parts of our philosophical structure we may assume as sufficiently established, and what are those other parts on which further discussion is needed. A prominent instance of the latter sort has already occurred. We set forth in an early paper what seemed (and seems) to us conclusive proof that certain propositions are cognizable as "necessary." Our reasoning, however, on this head was assailed in various different quarters, and it was requisite to write several successive essays in its defence. Something similar is now happening on the doctrine of Freewill—a doctrine which, in our humble judgment, is hardly less important as a philosophical

* *Dr. Ward on Freewill.* By SHADWORTH HODGSON. *Mind*, April, 1880. Williams and Norgate.

foundation of Theism, than is the very doctrine of Necessary Truth. In our essays on Mr. Mill's Denial of Freewill, we exhibited what we consider an absolute disproof of Determinism. However, we have had to supplement those essays in reply to successive objectors; and the imperative task of rejoinder has not even yet terminated. In addition to our original opponent, Dr. Bain, a new champion has taken the field, Mr. Shadworth Hodgson.

We are tempted, indeed, to say, "*Italiam sequimur fugientem:*" it seems as though we should never be permitted to arrive at the final stage of our reasoning—the direct argument for God's Existence. But, for the reasons we have given, we hope the course we propose will be generally admitted by our friends to be less unsatisfactory than the other alternative.

Two preliminary remarks. (1) Mr. Hodgson has a philosophical system of his own, to which, very naturally, he refers throughout. We shall not attempt any appreciation of this system as a whole, but only so far as it impinges on the doctrine of Freewill, or on our reasoning in behalf of that doctrine. (2) Then we shall have no scruple in inserting frequent and sometimes lengthy repetitions of what we have already said—often, indeed, in the very same words as before. We cannot expect our reader to refer to all that we have previously written on this subject; and we must, therefore, place directly before him whatever we desire him to bear in mind.

Mr. Hodgson is a consistent and very decided advocate of Determinism; though, in our view, most strangely, he considers himself also to maintain Freedom of the Will. On this latter head we shall say a few words before we conclude; but the former is, of course, our chief theme. Now, what is the doctrine of Determinism? Briefly this, that every man at every moment infallibly and inevitably, by the very constitution of his nature, elicits that precise

act of will to which his entire circumstances, external and
internal, of the moment dispose him. Mr. Hodgson, then,
we say, is a Determinist. That "Freedom" which he
admits is merely "the action and reaction of motives with
each other within the mind, not fettered by external
restraint, but free to exert each its own kind and degree of
energy" (p. 229). All Determinists, we need hardly say,
admit that, *so* understood, Freewill exists. In a later
passage (p. 248) he states with great candour the Libertarian's well-known objection: "Since we did not make
our own nature," argues the Libertarian, "then, if our
acts of choice are determined by our nature, as they are
in the last resort on the Determinist's theory, we should
not be morally responsible for our acts of choice, unless we
suppose that we have a power of choosing *independent* of
our nature." Mr. Hodgson expresses himself "not insensible to the great apparent cogency" of this argument, and
accordingly attempts a reply; but in his reply he entirely
identifies himself with the Determinist's position. Nor is
it only with Determinism in general that he identifies
himself, but also in particular with what may be called
"Hedonistic" Determinism; we mean with the doctrine
that man's will is always infallibly and inevitably determined by *the balance of pleasure*. Thus he says by most
manifest implication, in p. 238, that at any given moment
the stronger pleasure will, with infallible certainty, carry
the day against the weaker; though, in *judging* the comparative strength of "disparate pleasures," "often the
only way open to us is to see which of the two is actually
obeyed at the moment of choice." But we need not proceed
with further citations; as no one who reads Mr. Hodgson's
paper can doubt—nor would he himself dream of denying
—that he is a Determinist pure and simple.

For our own part, in treating this most vital theme,
before entering on the direct question of Freewill, we have

always begun with maintaining a purely negative doctrine, which we have called Indeterminism. This, we say, is a purely negative doctrine, being neither more nor less than the doctrine that Determinism is untrue. And so much having first been securely established, we have afterwards proceeded by help of further considerations to demonstrate the full doctrine of Freewill. Mr. Hodgson (p. 280) considers that "nothing can be clearer or more convenient" than this arrangement. At the same time, as he most truly proceeds to say, in one sense our doctrine of Indeterminism is positive and "aggressive" enough. We have brought, he says, "a long array of cases"—he is kind enough to add "well-chosen cases"—"to prove no negative point, but a positive fact, viz. that the course of the will's action is often in opposition to the man's strongest present impulse." We cannot wish the purpose of our argument to be more clearly stated.

Now, in arguing against Determinism, we have commonly—as we think most controversialists on either side have done—bestowed our chief attention on that particular class of cases in which two, and two only, alternatives are at the moment open; so that the agent has no resource but to choose between these two alternatives. Whatever doctrine is established in regard to these cases may most easily be extended to those other occasions, on which the agent has *several* different courses of action at his disposal. Let us suppose, then, that at this moment I am obliged to make a choice between two mutually inconsistent alternatives, both of which I more or less desire. Mr. Hodgson alleges that, under such circumstances, the "stronger" of the two antagonistic desires infallibly and inevitably carries the day. This statement, unless it be simply tautological, and therefore unmeaning, is one which, in virtue of our theory, we entirely repudiate. But before we come into conflict thereon with Mr. Hodgson, we must begin by attaching to it some precise signification. What, then is meant by a "stronger" or "weaker" desire? If by the "stronger" desire be merely meant "that desire which in action prevails over its rival," then the statement is, as we just now implied, purely tautological: it is purely tautological to say, that that desire which prevails over its one rival infallibly carries the day. On the other hand, if we use Mr. Hodgson's terminology—if we say that the "stronger desire" means precisely "the desire of that alternative which at the moment is apprehended as the more pleasurable"—then we fall into a serious difficulty. There are many Determinists who are very far from holding, in any obvious or intelligible sense, that the desire of that pleasure which is apprehended as greater, invariably prevails over the desire of that pleasure which is apprehended as less. As regards Dr. Bain himself, e.g.—no obscure or subordinate champion of Determinism—we pointed out this fact in our essay on Mill's denial of Freewill; see also the note there appended.* With the hope, then, of avoiding such equivocations, many Libertarians repudiate altogether the phrase "stronger," "weaker," desire. For ourselves, however, we have always thought that the phrase may be used in a very serviceable sense; and that, if used in that sense, it throws great light on the psychological questions connected with Freewill. In order to explain this sense, we will first set forth what is a very critical and fundamental fact in relation to our whole argument.

When two different desires come into collision, it happens very far more commonly than not, that there results at once a certain spontaneous, direct, unforced impulse of the will in one direction or the other. For example: A, an

* Our point in the essay referred to, was that, by help of certain very forced and recondite explanations, Dr. Bain's theory might be brought into accordance with that of "Hedonistic" Determinism. We are now drawing attention to the correlative fact, that Dr. Bain's theory *cannot* be brought into accordance with the doctrine of Hedonistic Determinism, *except* by means of certain very forced and recondite explanations.

extremely keen sportsman, is called very early on the first of September. Two different desires come into antagonism: on the one hand, a desire to sleep off again; on the other hand, a desire to be among the partridges. Under the circumstances, his spontaneous, direct, unforced impulse is, we may expect, unmistakably, and indeed most strongly, towards the latter alternative. On the other hand B, who is no sportsman, has also ordered himself to be called on the same morning, for a very different reason. He will be busy in the middle of the day, and he would rise betimes to visit a sick dependant. His spontaneous, direct, unforced impulse, on being called, may very probably be towards sleeping off again. We do not of course, deny that he has full power to resist such impulse; on the contrary, that is the very conclusion which in due course we shall maintain: but we say that his spontaneous, direct, unforced impulse, at the moment he is called, may very probably be towards renewed slumber. In defining, then, the terms "stronger" and "weaker" desire, we take as our foundation the fact of this spontaneous direct, unforced impulse. We say that A's desire of being early among the partridges was "stronger" than his desire of renewed sleep; whereas B's desire of renewed sleep was at the moment "stronger" than his desire to visit his sick dependant. Or, to put the thing generally, my "stronger" desire or motive * is

* For convenience' sake, we will use the word "motive" as expressing inclusively any *assemblage* of motives which at the moment may be influencing the mind in one or other direction.

In our earlier essays we distinguished between two different ideas, which are commonly expressed by this word "motive." We still regard this distinction as of much importance in the *exposition* of what we account sound doctrine. But when we wrote our last paper we had come to think that, in arguing with an opponent, we may conveniently waive this distinction. Here, therefore, we use the word "motive" to express any thought, which in any way prompts the will to act in any given direction. In pp. 233, 234 Mr. Hodgson criticizes our original use of the word "motive." We shall argue, before we conclude, that his criticism is entirely baseless; but, in this earlier portion of our essay, we no longer employ the terminology to which he objects.

that which at the moment prevails over the other in generating my spontaneous, direct, unforced impulse. That which at any given moment I "most desire," is that to which at the moment my spontaneous impulse prompts me.

One further explanation is of great importance towards a clear comprehension of several facts. My "strongest desire" at any moment is very far from being synonymous with my "strongest *emotional craving*" at that moment. We should hold a most shallow view, if we supposed that the will's spontaneous impulse is determined as a matter of course by the mere balance of emotional craving and excitement. Habits of the will, *e.g.* are also important factors in the result. Suppose I have acquired a firm habit of temperance, and an unwholesome dish is placed before me. My *sensitive appetency* may prompt me to indulgence: but my spontaneous, direct, unforced impulse, under the influence of habit, prompts me to forbearance; and I should be doing violence to the predominant impulse of my nature, if I succumbed to the solicitation. Or consider the case of paternal affection. A father who severely pinches himself for his son's temporal benefit, may in many instants of the day feel more vivid emotional pain from his own privations than he feels of emotional delight at the thought of his son's well-being. Yet the spontaneous unforced impulse of his *will* is no less unrelentingly directed at that moment, than at others, to the continuance of his benefaction. Here again possibly, as in the former instance, is seen merely the result of *habit;* but we should ourselves be disposed to explain the phenomenon much more prominently by this or that man's natural temperament and mental constitution. Certainly habit is not the *only* reason why the spontaneous impulse of a man's will diverges at times from his preponderance of emotion. Consider what Dr. Bain calls the influence of "fixed ideas," "infatuation," "irresistible impulse." "There are sights that give us almost unmitigated pain, while yet we are unable to keep away from them." * In such cases the abnormal impulse of the will conquers the emotional repugnance. Enough, however, of such matters for the present occasion. We certainly think that this general question—an investigation, namely, of those pyschological laws which determine the will's spontaneous impulse—is of extreme scientific importance, and that it has been very unduly neglected by psychologians. But at last it has of course no direct relevance to the Free-will controversy.

We have now said enough on the first stage of our argument. We have made clear, we think, what we mean by "the will's spontaneous, direct, unforced impulse." We next proceed to point out another fact, which is as heartily admitted by Mr. Hodgson as by ourselves. Every man's spontaneous impulse of the moment is the infallible and inevitable outcome of his entire circumstances, external and internal, as they exist at the moment. This spontaneous impulse, according to Mr. Hodgson, results from the "inner necessity of his nature" (p. 228); from "the action and reaction of motives on each other within the mind" (p. 229); from "internal circumstances reacting on external" (p. 232). Mr. Hodgson, in fact, will say just what we say—viz. that my spontaneous impulse of this moment faithfully and infallibly indicates what it is to which my entire circumstances (internal and external) of this moment are disposing me. And we are thus at last brought to what is the critical issue between our able opponent and ourselves. Mr. Hodgson, as a Determinist, holds that all men at every instant elicit that precise act of will to which their entire circumstances, external and internal, of that instant dispose them; or, in other words,

* "Emotions and the Will," third edition, p. 390. We are disposed to agree with Dr. Bain on every point, as to the genesis of the will's spontaneous impulse. Our difference from him is the fundamental one, that we maintain confidently men's power of *successfully resisting* that impulse.

that they must elicit that precise act of will to which their spontaneous impulse prompts them. "What a man is," he says, epigrammatically (p. 238), "*manifests itself* in what he does." If, therefore, we are able to show that on various occasions men are found successfully to *resist* their will's spontaneous impulse, we thereby show that on various occasions men do *not* elicit that act of will to which their entire circumstances of the moment dispose them. And if we establish that conclusion, *ipso facto* we overthrow Determinism. Here, then, is the main battle to be fought out between Mr. Hodgson and ourselves: Do men, or do they not, ever successfully resist their spontaneous unforced impulse? Our opponent answers this question in the negative, while we confidently answer it in the affirmative.

Or let us express the same issue in a somewhat different shape. By the term "effort" we understand "resistance to desire." Mr. Hodgson, of course, agrees with us, that "effort" is a sufficiently common phenomenon in human life. The difference between him and ourselves is this. On his view no kind of effort is possible, except that which crushes a "weaker" desire under influence of a "stronger:" as, *e.g.* the sportsman, when called on the first of September, crushes his desire of lying in bed by his stronger desire of being early among the partridges. This kind of effort we have ourselves always called "congenial." By "congenial effort" we mean, then, "resistance to some, at the moment, weaker desire or weaker motive, in order to the gratification of some, at the moment, stronger desire or stronger motive." But we earnestly maintain against Determinists that a kind of effort is possible, and, indeed, frequent enough, which is fundamentally different from what we have just described; a kind of effort whereby I successfully resist what at the moment is my *strongest* desire and my *strongest* motive. This kind of effort we have always called "anti-impulsive effort;" and Mr.

Hodgson holds, as heartily as we do, that if the human will be really capable of anti-impulsive effort, his doctrine of Determinism is fundamentally false. It bodes favourably for the fruitful result of our discussion, that our opponent is so entirely agreed with us as to what is the point at issue.

Further, the appeal between Mr. Hodgson and ourselves is to experienced psychical facts; and, from the very nature of the case, can be nothing else. We have never denied, indeed, that there are various instances in which it is not easy, perhaps not possible, to distinguish with certainty between "congenial" and "anti-impulsive" effort. But we have further maintained that there are also instances— and those, indeed, very numerous—in which the contrast between the two classes of effort is vividly and clamorously exhibited; so vividly and clamorously, that no competent judge can shut his eyes to it, unless he be blinded by some adverse philosophical theory. What we have next, therefore, to do, is to reproduce some of the instances we have alleged in earlier essays for our conclusion; and then to examine Mr. Hodgson's adverse method of explaining those instances.

I. A military officer, possessing real piety, and steadfastly proposing to grow therein, receives at the hand of a brother officer some stinging and, as the world would say, intolerable insult. His nature flames forth, and urgently solicits him to inflict some retaliation, which shall at least deliver him from the charge of cowardice. Nevertheless, it is his firm resolve to conduct himself Christianly; and his *resolve* contends vigorously and successfully against his predominating *desire*. Mr. Hodgson, who quotes our passage verbatim (p. 239), does not attempt to deny that such a case as we have supposed may well exist in real life. Yet surely no one can look such a fact fairly in the face and doubt that the agent of whom we speak is *disposed*, by his aggregrate of circumstances, external and internal, to *retaliate;* that his spontaneous unforced impulse, his strongest desire, is in that direction. But if so, it is a plain matter of fact that the act of will which he does elicit is something entirely different from, or rather directly contradictory to, his spontaneous impulse. His will moves in a direction *opposed* to that towards which his entire circumstances of the moment predominantly and vehemently dispose him.

Now, take a fundamentally different class of case. Consider some gallant soldier in the heat of action. He puts forth intense effort, braves appalling perils, confronts the risk of an agonizing death. He is so carried away by military ardour, by desire of victory, by zeal for his country's cause, by a certain indwelling savage aggressiveness, that under the influence of these and similar motives he performs prodigies of valour. In seeking to gratify these overwhelming and sovereign desires, he tramples underfoot an indefinite number of those weaker wishes which have just now no such hold on his will. He faces the most fearful dangers without one pause for deliberation and reflection, because his overmastering crave of the moment intensely impels him so to act. The effort in this case may be no less intense than in the other; but, as is manifest, it is of an essentially different kind. And the difference of kind consists precisely in this, that the last-named soldier is putting forth effort *in accordance* with his strongest desire, whereas the other was putting it forth *in opposition* to such desire. We allege this fundamental difference of character between the two classes of effort as a fact obvious to any one who shall choose to examine carefully the two cases.

We have already pointed out that, in a controversy of this kind, no appeal is possible except to observed facts; and if therefore an individual inquirer choose to ignore those facts, against him personally it is difficult to see what further step can be taken. For instance: Psychologians point out the elementary truth, that such a mental act as the desire of wealth differs fundamentally in kind from such a mental act as the recognition of a mathematical axiom; and they then proceed to investigate the laws which regulate these two different classes of psychical action. But suppose me to exclaim, "I see no difference of kind whatever between the two acts:" what resource does a philosophical teacher possess? I have pretty well taken the wind out of his sails. He will do all he can, of course, to fix my attention on the very salient characteristics which so clamorously distinguish the two acts from each other; but if I still tell him that I really don't catch his point, what is he to do? He must leave me alone; though, of course, he will call on my fellow-students to join him in protesting against the abnormal puzzle-headedness of which they have been witnesses. Now, we must really maintain that the difference in kind between "congenial" and "anti-impulsive" effort respectively—in such cases as we have been setting forth—is every whit as salient and unmistakable a phenomenon, as is the difference in kind between two such mental acts as desiring wealth and recognizing a mathematical axiom. If an individual inquirer fails to see this, what can be done, except to appeal—not, perhaps, from Philip drunk to Philip sober—but from Philip's strange idiosyncrasy to the common sense of mankind? And, indeed, we might make much controversial capital out of such idiosyncrasy; because we could point out to the world at large that he who denies our thesis is obliged to close his eyes against one of the most obvious and undeniable phenomena in the whole mental world.

But before proceeding to this "ultima ratio," perhaps we can induce the individual dissentient to accept the arbitration of an umpire. We will not, of course, ask him

to take a philosophical Libertarian as umpire, any more
than we should be content with a philosophical Determinist
in that capacity. We will not, then, resort on either side
to the arbitration of philosophers. At the same time, as is
clear, neither can we satisfactorily appeal to the verdict of
rough and uneducated minds, which may be wholly incapable of correct introspection. It may be plain, indeed,
to an impartial observer that the intimate conviction of
such minds is on this side or on that; but we cannot expect
that they will *depose* accurately to its existence. The fair
arbitrator, then, will be some person, on the one hand, of
sufficiently cultivated faculties; but, on the other hand,
who has not given special attention to philosophical
inquiries. In order that we may obtain from such a one
his genuine avouchment, we would deal with him in some
such way as the following:—

"How do you account," we first ask him, "for those
intense deeds of valour performed by the military hero
during the heat of action?" "I have no difficulty whatever in accounting for them," he replies. "In his original
nature bravery was a most conspicuous quality; he has led
a life eminently calculated to strengthen that quality; the
surrounding circumstances of battle afford the very motives
best calculated to stimulate it, and to dwarf in his mind for
the moment every antagonistic desire." "But, then," we
reply, "look at that soldier who has received so stinging an
insult, and is now so strenuously resisting the impulse
which prompts him to retaliation. Is *that* act also explained, by considering on one side his natural or acquired
character, and considering on the other side those circumstances in which he is placed?" "Just the contrary,"
replies our arbitrator. "One sees at once what his nature
under his present circumstances would prompt him to do;
for it would prompt him to vigorous retaliation. This is
just what, as a Christian, I so admire in him; for, under

his existent circumstances, he is resisting the urgent impulse of his nature by vigorous personal action." Such would be the verdict of our impartial arbitrator, for such, we are confident, would be the verdict of all persons possessing common sense and common powers of observation, who are not entrammelled by a philosophical theory. Now, be it observed, we are not appealing to our imaginary arbitrators for the purpose of showing that in this latter case the soldier was exerting self-originated *personal action*. We hold this proposition, indeed, to be most certainly true; but its enforcement belongs to a later stage of our argument. What we are here insisting on is that, at all events, the act of will exerted by this Christianly principled soldier was essentially different from—nay, point-blank contradictory to—that which was prompted by his nature and circumstances. But if there be even one such case, the doctrine of Determinism is false.

II. To make our view still clearer, let us set forth another case of intense effort, which we entirely admit to be "congenial." I am at sea in a pleasure boat, when to my dismay I discover plain signs of a rapidly approaching storm. I at once set to work at rowing to reach the shore for the sake of dear life. The effort which I put forth is intense. Vigorously, continuously, energetically, unflaggingly, I resist every antagonistic desire. Nevertheless our arbitrator will certainly pronounce that all this effort is fully explained by my nature and circumstances. My strongest desire, or spontaneous impulse, or natural tendency—whichever you like to call it—are prompting me in the exact direction which actually I pursue. Contrast this with my state of mind many weeks back, when for Christ's sake I strenuously resisted my desire of revenging an insult. At the earlier period my effort was put forth in order that I might *oppose* the predominant desire, impulse, tendency of my will; and our arbitrator will ascribe my course to vigorous personal action, resisting the promptings of my nature and circumstances. But in the present case my efforts are put forth for an end, which my will, according to its spontaneous impulse, intensely desires; and, as we have said, they are most amply and easily explained, without supposing any other factor than that nature and those circumstances which we have just commemorated.

III. We will conclude this part of our subject by a longer and more consecutive illustration, which we set forth in our reply to Dr. Bain,* and which exhibits one or two further points in the argument.

I am a keen sportsman, and one cloudy morning am looking forward with lively hope to my day's hunting. My post, however, comes in early; and I receive a letter, just as I have donned my red coat and am sitting down to breakfast. This letter announces that I must set off on that very morning to London, if I am to be present at some occasion on which my presence will be vitally important for an end which I account of extreme public moment. Let us consider the different ways in which my conduct may imaginably be affected, and the light thus thrown on the relative strength of my motives.

Perhaps (1) the public end for which my presence is so earnestly needed happens to be one in which I am so personally interested, which so intimately affects my feelings, that my balance of *emotion* is intensely in favour of my going. This motive, then, is indefinitely stronger than its antagonist. I at once order my carriage, as the station is four miles off and time presses; and I am delighted to start as soon as my coachman comes round. Perhaps (2) the balance of my *emotion* is quite decidedly in favour of the day's hunting, because the public end, though intellectually I appreciate its extreme importance,

* This reply is not here republished.—ED.

is not one with which my character leads me *emotionally* to sympathize. Nevertheless, through a long course of public-spirited action, I have acquired the firm and rooted habit of postponing pleasure to the call of duty. Here, therefore, as in the former case, there is not a moment's vacillation or hesitation. My spontaneous impulse is quite urgently in favour of going. My balance of *emotion*, indeed, is in favour of staying to hunt; but good habit, by its intrinsic strength, spontaneously prevails over emotion; and the motive which prompts me to go is indefinitely stronger than that which prompts me to stay. Or (3) when I have read the letter, my will may possibly be brought into a state of vacillation and vibration. My emotional impulse is one moment in one direction and the next moment in another. Then, as I possess no firm *habit* of public spirit, I take a long time in making up my mind: the strength of my motives is very evenly balanced, whichever may finally prevail. Lastly (4), I have perhaps very little public spirit, and am comparatively fond of hunting; so that I do not even entertain the question whether I shall offer up my day's sport as a sacrifice to my country's welfare.

Now, all these four alternatives are contemplated by the Determinist, and square entirely with his theory. In each case my conduct is determined by my strongest present motive. There is, however, a fifth case which he does not—and consistently with his theory cannot—admit to be a possible one; but in regard to which we confidently maintain, by appeal to experience, that it is abundantly possible, and by no means unfrequent. It is most possible, we say, that I put forth on the occasion anti-impulsive effort; that I act resolutely and consistently in opposition to my spontaneous impulse, in opposition to that which at the moment is my strongest desire. Thus. On one side the spontaneous impulse of my will is quite decidedly in favour of staying to hunt; or, in other words, the motive which prompts me to stay is quite decidedly stronger at the moment than that which prompts me to go. On the other hand, my reason recognizes clearly how very important is the public interest at issue, and how plainly duty calls me in the direction of London. I resolutely, therefore, enter my carriage, and order it to the station. And now let us consider what takes place while I am on my four miles' transit. During the greater part, perhaps during the whole, of this transit, there proceeds what we have called in our essays " a compound phenomenon ; " or, in other words, there co-exist in my mind two mutually distinct phenomena. First phenomenon. My spontaneous impulse is strongly in the opposite direction. I remember that even now it is by no means too late to be present at the meet, and I am most urgently solicited by inclination to order my coachman home again. So urgent, indeed, is this solicitation, so much stronger is the motive which prompts me to return than that which prompts me to continue my course, that, unless I put forth unintermitting and energetic resistance to that motive, I should quite infallibly give the coachman such an order. Here is the first phenomenon to which we call attention—my will's spontaneous impulse towards returning. A second, no less distinctly pronounced and strongly marked phenomenon is that unintermitting energetic *resistance* to the former motive of which we have been speaking. On one side is that phenomenon which may be called my will's spontaneous, direct, unforced *impulse* and preponderating desire; on the other side, that which may be called my firm, sustained, active, antagonistic *resolve*. We allege, as a fact obvious and undeniable on the very surface, that the phenomenon which we have called "spontaneous impulse" is as different in kind from that other which we have called "anti-impulsive resolve," as the desire of wealth is different in kind from the recognition of a mathematical axiom. Our imaginary arbitrator will at once thus explain the distinction. On one side, he will say, is that impulse which results, according to the laws of my mental constitution, from my nature and external circumstances taken in mutual connection. On the other side, he will say, is that *resistance* to such impulse, which I elicit by vigorous personal action.

The scope of our argument, so far as we have gone, will perhaps be made clearer if at this point we expressly encounter an objection which has been sometimes urged against us in one or other shape. It may be thus exhibited.

"Doubtless a man's spontaneous impulse is infallibly and inevitably determined by his entire circumstances, external and internal, of the moment. But how can you prove that his *anti-impulsive effort* is not *equally* due to the combination of those circumstances? When the pious Christian receives an insult, what right have you to assume that his Christian forbearance is less inevitably determined by circumstances than is his spontaneous burst of indignation? And so on with every other illustration you have given."

We have again and again, as we consider, implicitly refuted this objection; but we may probably do service by setting forth such refutation explicitly. Our preceding argument, then, may be thus summed up. We are purporting to disprove the doctrine of Determinists—*i.e.* the doctrine that every man at every moment, by the very constitution of his nature, infallibly and inevitably elicits that precise act of will to which his entire circumstances of the moment, external and internal, dispose him. Now, we allege that this doctrine is disproved by taking into combined consideration these two facts :—(1) In a large number of cases, I know, by certain and unmistakable experience, *what* is that act of will to which my entire circumstances of the moment dispose me. (2) In many of such cases, I know, by certain and unmistakable experience, that, as a matter of fact, I elicit some *different* act of will from this. By the very force of terms, that act to which my entire circumstances of the moment dispose me is in accordance with my spontaneous, direct, unforced impulse. If, then, I act at any moment *otherwise* than according to such impulse, I act in some way *different* from that to which my entire circumstances of the moment dispose me. And if I ever so act, Determinism is thereby disproved. We do not pretend that Determinism is disproved, merely because I act at times in opposition to what would be my more *pleasurable* course; for we entirely admit that my spontaneous impulse may often enough tend to the less pleasurable course. We do not pretend that Determinism is disproved merely because I put forth intense effort in opposition to some desire which urgently solicits me; for we entirely admit that my spontaneous impulse often *prompts* such effort. But if it be shown that I can successfully contend against my *spontaneous impulse itself*, then it is most manifestly shown that Determinism is false, because it is shown that I can act in some way *different* from that to which my entire circumstances of the moment dispose me. Determinists, therefore, are obliged to maintain, and do maintain, that no such thing is possible to man as anti-impulsive effort; that I can put forth no effort, except that to which my spontaneous impulse prompts me, and which we have called "congenial." To this we have replied that, as regards the more strongly accentuated cases, the phenomenal difference of kind between "congenial" and "anti-impulsive" effort is no less manifest than is the phenomenal difference of kind between the act of desiring wealth and the act of recognizing a mathematical axiom. But this fact, if admitted, is of course conclusive against Determinism.

So much on our preceding course of argument. As for the objection we drew out, we thus reply to it in form :—It is a *contradiction in terms* to say that my entire circumstances of the moment can possibly dispose me to anti-impulsive effort. For consider. We are not here referring to those comparatively few cases of vacillation and vibration which we have treated at abundant length in earlier essays. In the great majority of instances, however—and it is these to which we here refer—that to which my entire circumstances of the moment, external and internal, by their combined influence, dispose me, is one stable, definite, given course of action : a course of action accordant with one stable, definite, and spontaneous impulse. If you affirm, then, that my circumstances of the moment, by their combined influence, dispose me to anti-impulsive effort, what can be the possible meaning of your statement? If you mean anything, it must be, (1) that my whole assemblage of existent circumstances, external and internal, by their combined influence, dispose me to one stable, definite course; and (2) that at the same moment they do *not*, by their combined influence, dispose me to that course, but to some other. A contradiction in terms.

Before proceeding to the next stage of our argument, we will examine Mr. Hodgson's replies to our reasoning as far as it has gone. And we must say at once, that nothing can be controversially fairer than his course throughout. He takes real pains to understand rightly our various points, and encounter them in their true significance. Of course, however, we are very far from thinking that he succeeds in his enterprise.

I. He alleges, in the first place (p. 230), that the words " self-restraint," " self-command," which we had used to express " anti-impulsive effort," in common parlance express quite as naturally " congenial " effort. We cannot think that this is a true interpretation of those phrases; but, as the question is a purely verbal one, we abstain from such terms in our present essay.

II. Mr. Hodgson next refers (p. 281) to one of our incidental and minor illustrations. A young man has been warned by his dentist to brush his teeth carefully every morning; but one day he is in a great hurry to get to his breakfast and go out hunting. He is on the point of disregarding his dentist's advice; but, on second thoughts, compels himself, by anti-impulsive effort, to perform the important dental operation. According to Mr. Hodgson, all which really passes in such a case is this. By the working of natural laws, some new motive—Mr. Hodgson suggests "the dignity of keeping a good resolution"—enters the youth's mind. By the further working of natural laws he is led to ponder with due earnestness on this motive, and thus he is induced to change his course of action. We reply that nothing is more possible or more frequent than a psychical fact of the kind Mr. Hodgson describes. As we should express the matter—under the influence of this new motive, which his existent circumstances dispose him thus earnestly to ponder, the youth's spontaneous impulse gradually changes, and by a "congenial" effort he sets to work brushing his teeth. Nothing, we say, is more intelligible than such a psychical phenomenon; and, as we heartily admit, it proves nothing whatever against Determinism. We only say that the mental phenomenon on which we relied was not the phenomenon described by Mr. Hodgson, but one fundamentally different. What we urged was that, on certain occasions, *while my spontaneous impulse is unchanged*, my will, nevertheless, may—whether in the matter of tooth-brushing or any other—successfully resist that impulse, and put forth "anti-impulsive" effort. In one word, we allege phenomenon A as disproving Determinism; and Mr. Hodgson replies that phenomenon B does *not* disprove Determinism. Of course we never thought it did. What we said was that phenomenon A disproves Determinism; and what Mr. Hodgson had to prove, if he could, was that phenomenon A is psychically impossible. But this task Mr. Hodgson has not even attempted to perform, though it is simply indispensable to his controversial position.

III. Later on (p. 239), Mr. Hodgson criticizes an illustration which we have set forth in the earlier pages of this essay. We refer to the illustration we derived from contrasting the military officer's efforts in the heat of battle with his effort in forgiving a gross insult. It is a manifest fact of observation, we have said, that the former class of efforts are "congenial," the latter "anti-impulsive." Mr. Hodgson replies that, on the contrary, in the latter case, just as in the former, the agent overcomes a "weaker desire" by a "stronger one." The agent, says Mr. Hodgson, "opposes a desire which is in process of becoming a resolve, by a desire which has already become one; opposes a new desire which derives its strength from its vividness, by an old desire which derives its strength from its fixity." We answer this objection precisely in the same way in which we answered the last. But before proceeding to do so, we will make one or two short comments on Mr. Hodgson's treatment of this particular instance.

Firstly, on what ground does he assume that the desire of forgiving an insult is "an old desire"? It may very easily happen that only on this very day have I adopted the firm resolution of living Christianly; and that, before the day is over, my good purposes are assailed by the endurance of a stinging insult.

Then, secondly, as a critic asks in the *Spectator*, "how in the world can a desire derive strength from its fixity? We can barely imagine a desire deriving fixity from its strength, but certainly not strength from its fixity. Let a desire be ever so permanent, yet if it be but faint it will be overcome by a stronger desire."

Thirdly, on our reading of human nature, it is extremely doubtful, to say the very least, whether such a case can ever occur as Mr. Hodgson supposes. If I possess those qualities of character which presumably distinguish a military officer, would my *spontaneous impulse*, on receiving a gross and bitter insult, *ever* be towards forgiving it? Would forgiveness ever be possible to me, except by anti-impulsive effort?

At last, however, we may waive these three points. Let us grant the supposition to be a possible one, that on some given exceptional occasion my spontaneous impulse, when I receive some stinging insult, is towards forgiveness. In that case, no doubt, the fact of forgiveness proves nothing against Determinism; nor did we ever say it did. It is here just as it was before. We allege phenomenon A as disproving Determinism; and Mr. Hodgson answers that phenomenon B—a fundamentally different one—does *not* disprove Determinism.

In truth, Mr. Hodgson throughout, with the fairest intentions, has nevertheless entirely failed to apprehend what it is which we allege. He understands us, no doubt, and so far rightly, as maintaining that acts of anti-impulsive effort differ in kind from acts of congenial effort; and he would, indeed, entirely agree with us on this head, if he admitted that acts of the former kind can possibly exist. But we make a further allegation. On many various occasions—such is our contention—it is matter of direct and unmistakable *observation*, that this or that act is an act of anti-impulsive and *not* of congenial effort. He argues as though we accounted this quality of the act to be a mere matter of *inference;* and he contends that our inference is not conclusively established. But, on the contrary, as we trust we have made sufficiently clear in the earlier part of our essay, our whole point is that the fact on which we rest is one of repeated and most unmistakable *experience*.

IV. The last objection of Mr. Hodgson's which we will here consider refers (p. 237) to a doctrine which we have not yet mentioned in our present essay. In our first paper on the subject we inquired, What are the *motives* in any given case which induce a man to resist his spontaneous impulse? "There are two, and two only, classes of motives," we said, "which occur to our mind as adequate to the purpose. First, there is my resolve of doing what is right; and, secondly, my desire of promoting my permanent happiness in the next world, or even in this." We are still disposed to account this sound doctrine, though the question has no essential bearing on the Free-will controversy. No other motive occurs to our mind now, any more than it did when we then wrote, adequate as a reason for anti-impulsive effort, except only the two we named. But Mr. Hodgson has here seriously misunderstood our meaning in more than one particular.

For instance, he asks (p. 237) whether "virtue and self-interest are such thoroughly unpleasant things, that the pursuit of them can in no degree be owing to their attractiveness:" as though we gave an affirmative answer to this question. Again, in p. 238, he says that we speak "as if virtue and self-interest had not a pleasure of their own, often very intense, and in most cases very abiding." But in the very passage which he quotes from us in p. 237, we implied our entire agreement with Mr. Hodgson on this matter. "We do not for a moment deny"—these were our words—"that Determinists include both the pleasurableness of virtue and the pleasurableness of promoting our permanent interest, among the attractions which influence a man's will." Moreover, we entirely agree with our opponent, that such pleasurableness may be on occasion very intense, and is in most cases very abiding; and exercises accordingly important influence on the will's spontaneous impulse. But we go still further than this in our concessions to the Determinist, if concessions, indeed, they are to be called. We have implied in our previous remarks that, in proportion as a habit of virtue may have been acquired, *virtuousness* itself is attractive, apart from its pleasurableness altogether. In truth, where an intense habit of virtue exists, virtuousness by its own strength is most powerfully influential over the will's spontaneous impulse. There is many a good man who on occasion conspicuously exemplifies this. Let him have a chance to escape the keenest present suffering by some act of gross ingratitude or treachery—there will be no need of his resisting such solicitation by anti-impulsive effort. His *spontaneous impulse* will be in the direction of virtue; his desire of avoiding basest ingratitude and treachery will be at the moment stronger than his desire of avoiding anguish. No thinkers who do not bear this fact carefully in mind can escape a very inadequate, or rather a very false, appreciation of human nature and of human character. Nevertheless, it is not a fact which bears directly one way or other on the Freewill controversy.

We mention this truth, then, merely as a preliminary, before we encounter the objection which Mr. Hodgson has built on that doctrine of ours, which we have just named; our doctrine, that virtue and self-interest are the main, or perhaps even the sole, motives of anti-impulsive effort. Another preliminary must also here be mentioned. There are such things, he says (p. 238), as "abiding latent thoughts, ready to spring forward into distinct consciousness in intervals of reflection." We should be very sorry if we were thought to deny this truth or undervalue its significance. Such "latent thoughts"—or, as we should ourselves rather express it, latent mental tendencies or qualities which on occasion spring into quite unexpected actuality—are, we think, very important parts of the mind's furniture; and deserve, at the hands of psychologians, much more notice than they commonly obtain. "I had not the least idea how warm was my affection towards A. B. till he fell into trouble, poor fellow, and I felt how vehement was my wish to assist him." "Little did I suspect how much envy there was in my composition, until circumstances befell me which gave large incitement to that passion," etc. A moment's thought, however, will evince that facts of *this* kind, again, however interesting and momentous in themselves, have absolutely no relevance on Mr. Hodgson's argument. They are often of great value in elucidating the *genesis* of my spontaneous impulse on this or that occasion; but they throw no particle of light on the question, whether I have or have not the power of successfully *resisting* such spontaneous impulse.

And now, as a third and final preliminary, what do we exactly *mean* by that doctrine of ours, concerning the motives of anti-impulsive effort, to which Mr. Hodgson objects? It is necessary to say a few words on this; because, though to our mind the thing is as plain as a pikestaff, Determinists seem to have much difficulty in apprehending it. Thus Dr. Bain, commenting on the frequent reference made by Libertarians to the "Ego," complains of them as introducing into psychology a certain arbitrary and unintelligible "meation." And Mr. Hodgson again has evidently altogether failed to catch our point. We would thus, therefore, explain ourselves.

If at this moment I pursue some given course of action, my reason for doing so must either be (1) that I *predominantly desire* such course, that I gratify my strongest desire of the moment by pursuing it; or else (2) that I regard such course as a more *reasonable* one than that which I do predominantly desire. On the former supposition, I am acting in accordance with my spontaneous impulse; * but on the latter supposition, I am putting forth anti-impulsive effort. Whenever, therefore, I put forth anti-impulsive effort, my reason or "motive" for doing so must be, that I regard such effort as being at the moment a more reasonable course than acquiescing in my spontaneous impulse. Now, there are only two classes of consideration which have occurred to us as possibly effecting, that anti-impulsive effort shall in any given case be regarded by me as more reasonable than acquiescence in spontaneous impulse. One of these is my thinking that the former course is more *virtuous* than the latter; the other is my thinking that it is more conducive than the latter to my *permanent happiness*. We hold, therefore, that virtue and self-interest are frequently motives of anti-impulsive effort; and we cannot think of any other motive for it except these.

What, then, at last is Mr. Hodgson's *objection* to this doctrine? We will state it in his own words:—

Are virtue and self-interest such thoroughly unpleasant things, that the pursuit of them can in no degree be owing to their attractiveness? Yet, if some tinge of attractiveness is theirs, then, on Dr. Ward's principles, they must be *pro tanto* contributories to the resultant spontaneous impulse of the will, which, nevertheless, as motives of its anti-impulsive action, they resist. Their position in the economy of volition is then a truly critical one: they are divided against themselves; they resist in one character what they contribute to form in another (p. 237).

We have seldom been more surprised than by the circumstance that our opponent attaches any weight whatever to such an objection as this. Let us exhibit a concrete illustration. I see clearly that A. B. is the best

* A further subdivision is possible, though we need not pursue it. Either (1) that course which I predominantly desire is regarded by me as my most reasonable course; or (2) it is not so regarded.

person I can appoint to some important place in my gift, and I therefore resolve to nominate him. Yet in forming this resolve I put forth a certain anti-impulsive effort. Some near relatives of his inflicted grievous suffering on some of my dearest friends, nor has he ever dissociated himself from solidarity with those relatives. My spontaneous aversion, therefore, to doing him a service is considerable. This, indeed, is so much more the case because I might without any discredit appoint to the post one who has undeviatingly been my kind personal friend. On the other hand, no doubt, there are various attractions which more or less strongly urge me towards nominating him, who is eminently the fittest candidate. The pleasure of doing what I feel to be right is in itself great; and, for obvious reasons, still greater under existing circumstances. Then, as I have acquired strong habits of virtue, the virtuousness itself of so acting has a great special attractiveness of its own, apart altogether from pleasurableness. There is a further attraction again acting on my will's spontaneous impulse, when I remember that by acting as I propose I am preparing for myself increased reward in heaven. At the same time, all these attractions combined do not suffice to effect that my *spontaneous impulse* is towards giving him the appointment. On the contrary, my aversion towards doing him, rather than my own kind friend, so signal a good turn constitutes my predominant impulse; and my desire of giving the place to my personal friend is decidedly my strongest desire. Under these circumstances, I *resist* my spontaneous impulse. I do so, partly that I may please God by acting in a more virtuous way, and partly also in order that I may increase my future blessedness. These two motives have already performed one function, in effecting that my spontaneous impulse towards giving my personal friend the preference is far less intense than otherwise it would be; and now they do a *second* good work, in affording me good reason for *resistance* to my spontaneous impulse. What can be more simple and intelligible? We cannot answer Mr. Hodgson's difficulty, because we cannot even remotely guess wherein it consists. He proceeds, indeed, to say, "The line which separates Dr. Ward from the Determinists is in this place narrow indeed, and to me, I confess, invisible." But such words, we must declare, convey no more meaning to our mind than if they were written in some unknown tongue.

There is a terse and pithy sentence of Mr. Hodgson's in page 240, which may be taken as summing up his view on this particular part of the subject; and which, we think, conspicuously exhibits the necessary narrowness of a Determinist's psychological insight. Whenever we resist predominant impulse in order to comply with the dictates of virtue, "what we *most desire* at the very moment of choice," says Mr. Hodgson, "is to do our painful duty." We maintain that, in so speaking, he mixes into one two fundamentally different classes of moral action; and that he thereby throws a cloud of confusion and misconception over the whole body of relevant psychical phenomena. On many occasions, we heartily admit, it is most certain that what men most desire under such circumstances is to do their painful duty; but on many other occasions, we maintain, the opposite is equally certain. Let us give an illustrative case under each head.

I have a son, for whom I entertain the tenderest affection, and in whose prospects, here and hereafter, I feel the keenest interest. He has exhibited some very serious fault, and one on which it gives me special pain to address him; while, on the other hand, I clearly see that his whole future may depend on my administering a severe rebuke. My spontaneous impulse, then, is quite intensely directed to so acting, though I distinctly bear in mind how exquisite will be my own suffering on the occasion. In Mr. Hodgson's words, what I *most desire* is to do my painful duty.

Now take an opposite case. I am a large landed proprietor, and I rejoice in my thereby assured income, as a means of securely prosecuting my physical, or literary, or philosophical studies. Otherwise I am profoundly uninterested in my estate : I cannot distinguish wheat from barley; I am quite indifferent to field sports ; I have no value whatever for my social position ; I have no tendency towards personal relation with my agricultural dependants. Information reaches me that my agent has been acting with gross injustice to various of my tenants, and is endeavouring to stifle their complaint. What is my spontaneous impulse? Probably to invent some salve for my conscience as regards the tenants, and plunge myself afresh in my favourite studies. I have no particular affection for my tenants, any more than I have for any *other* farmers who may happen to live in my neighbourhood and pursue their (to me utterly unintelligible) avocations. I can easily persuade myself, if I choose, that I may conscientiously ignore the information I have received, and continue, without further inquiry, to repose trust in my agent. On the other hand, if I am really conscientious, I am able by means of due thought to see clearly where my duty lies. Accordingly, I put forth anti-impulsive effort. With sighing and weariness of heart, I bid adieu to my studies for the necessary interval of painful and laborious inquiry. I resolve to exercise herculean labour ; to interview the complaining tenants ; to apprehend (1) the meaning and (2) the merits of the accusation they bring ; and, finally, to take such practical steps as I may judge necessary. What can be more unmeaning than to say, that during all this time what *I most desire* is to do my painful duty ? And what judgment shall be formed of a theory which mixes up under one head two such fundamentally different kinds of moral action as those we have specified?

On looking Mr. Hodgson's paper through and through, we can find no other replies than those we have now récited to the reasoning we have set forth in the earlier part of this essay. We must consider ourselves, therefore, to have established the doctrine of Indeterminism; or, in other words, to have established the negative doctrine, that Determinism is untrue. And here the controversy, as a controversy, is practically at an end. There never was, and we may be sure there never will be, a thinker—who admits, indeed, that the will is from time to time determined by some agency different from phenomenal antecedents, and who nevertheless considers that agency to be other than the will's free choice. For the sake, however, of philosophical completeness, it is important to exhibit the argumentative grounds for our *further* statement. In other words, we are now to reproduce, and vindicate against Mr. Hodgson's criticisms, the arguments which we have alleged in previous papers for our conclusion, that when I successfully resist my will's spontaneous impulse, I do so by my own intrinsic strength and personal exertion.* We will first, then, reproduce the chief of our earlier passages on this subject; and we will then consider Mr. Hodgson's comment on these passages. In the two passages we cite we make certain small verbal changes, indicated by brackets, to a mention of which we shall afterwards recur.

In our essay entitled "Freewill," we thus expressed ourselves; and Mr. Hodgson (p. 243) has quoted part of our words:—

* We need hardly say that, when we speak of the will's "intrinsic strength," we do not imply a word against in many cases the necessity of *divine grace*. But this, of course, is quite another and further question.

Consider those various periods of time during which I am occupied in vigorously resisting certain solicitations—*e.g.* to revengefulness—which intensely beset me. It is a matter of direct, unmistakable, clamorous consciousness that, during those periods, it is my own [self], and no external agency, which is putting forth active and sustained anti-impulsive effort. Nor, indeed, is this remark less applicable to *all* cases of anti-impulsive effort; though, of course, where the effort is less vigorous, the consciousness of which we speak is less obtrusive.

But more than this may be said. The experience which I obtain even in one such protracted and vehement struggle is amply sufficient to give me an intimate and infallible knowledge of one all-important fact. We refer to the fact that at every moment of the struggle it has depended on my own free choice, with what degree of efficacity I have contended against the temptation.

Later on we expressed this argument still more pointedly :—

We now proceed, from the negative argument disproving Determinism, to the positive argument establishing Freewill. And this, we maintain, is even more direct and immediate than the former. We solicit for it our readers' careful attention, because we feel that we did not state it [in our last essay] with sufficient prominence and emphasis. Consider, respectively, those two distinct phenomena—preponderating spontaneous impulse on one side, anti-impulsive effort on the other side—to which we have so earnestly drawn attention. If we examine them successively with due care, we shall see that they differ from each other in character not less than fundamentally. In experiencing one of them my will is entirely passive; in experiencing the other it is intensely active. Consider my will's spontaneous impulse—the impulse, *e.g.* [which prompts me to retaliate some stinging insult]. In experiencing this impulse, my will (we say) has been entirely passive: the impulse has *befallen* me, *come upon* me, *taken hold* of me; such are the phrases I should naturally use. On the other hand, my *resistance* to this impulse has been not merely experienced by [me], but has rather been put forth by my [own] *intrinsic strength*. I am not only conscious that I elicit the act of resistance; I am no one whit less directly conscious that I elicit it *by* [*my own*] *active exertion*. The consciousness of one single moment suffices to show me unmistakably that I have the power to do this, because I know unmistakably that I am actually doing it.

All this seems to us as entirely conclusive now, as it did when we originally wrote it; and we were not a little curious to see how Mr. Hodgson would meet our reasoning. He replies (p. 243), that such an argument cannot be legitimately adduced until we shall have excogitated a consistent scientific theory on "the existence and nature of the soul *per se*." We do not think that Mr. Hodgson could have accounted his own reply as possessing even superficial force had it not been for some awkward expressions used by us, to which we refer in a note.* Well, let us receive all due blame for our awkward expressions, and let Mr.

---

* The awkward expression to which we mainly refer is, that in two or three sentences of the preceding extracts we spoke of "my *soul*" where our meaning was "myself." We have now made the requisite change throughout, and our readers will have seen how entirely unaffected is our meaning.

Connected with this method of expression on our part is the following paragraph. Mr. Hodgson has not adverted to it; but we think, on reflection, that it is very obscurely expressed, and might naturally lead to serious misconception of our meaning. These were our words:—

"Many Libertarians, when explaining Freewill, are in the habit of introducing reference to the human personality; to the 'Ego.' We do not find this necessary; and if it be not necessary, we think it very undesirable. Those questions which concern the 'Ego' are so intricate, and so mixed up with theological dogma, that their treatment requires most anxious care. Nor can we see that the true doctrine of human personality, whatever it may be, has any special relevance to the exposition with which we are here engaged. Without further reference, therefore, to the 'Ego,' we now proceed with that exposition."

In so expressing ourselves, there was one opinion which we wished to disavow, and one question of which we wished to steer clear. Some Libertarians seem to think that the "Ego," which puts forth anti-impulsive effort, differs in some respect from the "Ego," which experiences spontaneous impulse. For this opinion, with very great deference to those writers, we can see no sufficient ground; and we disclaimed it in the above-cited paragraph. Then, further, we wished to steer clear of that intricate question, which inquires wherein precisely consists the *personality* of a rational being. But in real truth we imply no judgment whatever on this question, by availing ourselves of that most convenient term, the "Ego;" and we avail ourselves therefore thereof without scruple in our present essay. What we mean by the term will be made abundantly clear as we proceed in the text.

Hodgson so far be condoned; but this is a personal matter. What is required in the interests of truth is that the value of Mr. Hodgson's reply be duly considered in its bearing against those arguments of ours which we just now cited. And we venture to think that that reply is at once overthrown by appealing to the most elementary and universally admitted facts of psychology. We would give our exposition of these rudimentary facts in some such way as the following:—

When I am conscious of some mental phenomenon, one indivisible act of consciousness informs me, not only that the phenomenon is such or such, but also that it is I who experience it, and no one else. The "Ego" is as absolutely, immediately, clamorously testified by consciousness as is the mental phenomenon itself. If the existence of this phenomenon as a phenomenon must be accepted as a first and most certain premiss in psychological science—and Mr. Hodgson will, of course, admit that such is the case— so no less must the existence of the "Ego" be so accepted. The latter is no one whit less certainly an immediate deliverance of consciousness than is the former. But Mr. Hodgson's language implies that I do not really know my own existence, as of one who experiences this or that mental phenomenon, until I have been able to excogitate some "theory" in regard to my "soul, its nature, and its powers." He is surely putting the cart before the horse. First, in order of time, comes my knowledge of *myself*; and upon that most certain, immediate, unmistakable knowledge is to be founded any process of discussion, which shall issue in results—whether certain or in various degrees probable—concerning the nature and properties of my soul. Let us now apply this principle to the particular case before us.

1. Preliminary illustration. Some one has died, for whom I have the tenderest affection. Such an event has

never occurred to me before; and I experience for the first time, as a mental phenomenon, that particular kind of grief. Firstly, it is I, and not you, or any of my friends, who experience—who am the subject of—this phenomenon. Secondly, the phenomenon is what may be called " passive." It *befalls* me; it *comes upon* me from without, not through any exertion or agency of my own.

2. Spontaneous impulse. I have received some stinging insult, and spontaneously flame forth into passionate desire of retaliation. Here, again, just the same remark may be made as in the last case. Firstly, the "subject" of this mental phenomenon is the "Ego." It is I, not you, or any of my friends, who experience the impulse in question. Secondly, the phenomenon is entirely passive. It befalls me; it comes on me from without, not through any exertion or agency of my own.

3. Anti-impulsive effort. I vigorously and intensely *resist* my last-named impulse, my desire of retaliation. Here is a mental phenomenon, fundamentally different in kind from the preceding. The subject of the phenomenon, indeed, as before, is the "Ego;" it is I, and not any one else, who am conscious of the phenomenon as my own. But, then, that of which I am conscious is not that some experience *befalls* me, or comes on me without activity or energy on my part, but the very contrary. That of which I am conscious is that I exert *power;* that I put forth vigorous exertion *from within*. The fundamental difference in kind between these two classes of phenomena—spontaneous impulse, on one side, anti-impulsive effort, on the other—is, in the more strongly accentuated cases, a fact which cannot possibly be ignored; a fact which forces itself most distinctly and forcibly on my immediate observation. We may here repeat an illustration which we have already employed. It is a matter of most distinct and immediate observation—so much no one will deny—that the desire of

wealth is a mental phenomenon, fundamentally different in kind from the recognition of a mathematical axiom. But surely it is no *less* manifest, no less a matter of distinct and immediate observation, that such an act as we have described of *spontaneous impulse* differs fundamentally from such an act as we have described of *anti-impulsive effort*. In this latter act *the one most prominent feature* is that which is *entirely absent* from the former. I put forth vigorous and intrinsic exertion of *my own* by *self-originated effort*. I row against the stream of impulse, and force myself to resist successfully my strongest desire.

In our essay entitled "Freewill," we argued at length that the controversy, whether man do or do not possess such a power as this, is substantially identical with the precise controversy, whether he do or do not possess Freewill. Here Mr. Hodgson will be entirely at one with us. He will at once admit that if I possess the power of successfully resisting my strongest desire, I am thereby proved to possess Freewill in the very sense in which he denies its existence. What he so strenuously repudiates is the notion that I *do* possess the power of successfully resisting my strongest desire.

To the reasoning which we have now set forth, we can find but two replies in Mr. Hodgson's paper, over and above those which we have already encountered. Firstly, let us take the following :—

Dr. Ward, I think, is in this dilemma: either the free choice or resolve of the soul is caused by the soul, and then he is a Determinist; or else the free choice or resolve of the soul is caused by the bare power in the soul of freely choosing or resolving, and that is tautology and trifling. I argue, therefore, that unless Dr. Ward is a Determinist without knowing it, the only meaning attributable to his doctrine of Freewill is this, that a free act is an act without an agent (p. 247).

Here, firstly, we must protest against Mr. Hodgson's method of using the word "free." He uses the words "free choice," to include a choice which is infallibly and inevitably determined for the agent by his circumstances, external and internal. Such terminology is, we think, entirely at variance with that of all other Determinists; nor do we see that anything but confusion of thought can arise from its adoption. On this we may have a word or two more to say before we conclude our essay.

Otherwise, the complete irrelevance of the reply we have just quoted seems to us so obvious on the very surface that we feel real difficulty in formulating arguments which shall render such irrelevance more apparent. Let it be supposed that I elicit some act of will by anti-impulsive effort different from that to which my circumstances of the moment dispose me. Determinists maintain that the supposition is an impossible one; that I *cannot* elicit such an act; that the constitution of my nature renders it impossible. Libertarians say, on the contrary, that I *can* do this if I choose, and that I can choose to do it. But who in the world, before Mr. Hodgson, ever said that such an act of mine, if I could elicit it, would be "an act *without an agent*"? In what imaginable way can an "agent" more irresistibly establish his own existence as such than by "acting" in direct opposition to the promptings of his nature? And we need hardly say that, according to *our* way of stating facts, "the free choice or resolve of my soul" is not caused by "the bare *power* of my soul," but by my soul's own self-originated act. Mr. Hodgson, indeed, with amazing misconception considers (p. 247) that, on our theory, my "soul does not" even "*contribute*" to my "free choice." On the contrary, our theory is that my soul is the one proximate *cause* of my free choice.

But, in truth, Mr. Hodgson's whole description of our theory is quite incredibly strange. "We are required" by it, he says (p. 247), "to conceive a perfectly *colourless* power of choice." Why, the act of choice, in our humble view, is motived by one or other of the highest and worthiest motives which can well be conceived, viz. the motive (1) of virtue, and (2) of permanent self-interest. By what extraordinary application of language is such a "power of choice" to be called colourless?*

Mr. Hodgson's other reply is that "the exercise and even the existence of such a power as" we allege to exist "is not capable of being intelligibly construed in thought" (p. 246). Well, here our appeal must be to the common sense of mankind, who do *most* intelligibly "construe it in thought." Surely Determinists themselves construe our theory in thought, no less intelligibly than do Libertarians, as is shown by the zeal and intenseness with which they combat it. The last thing they would say is, that what they thus earnestly encounter is a mere shadow.

We have now replied to all those objections of Mr. Hodgson which we can observe in his article. But, further, he has fallen into one or two misconceptions of our meaning, which this will be the most convenient opportunity for setting right. For instance (pp. 241, 242), he quotes textually a certain passage from one of our articles, as exhibiting with special force our view on "the full doctrine of Freewill." But we did not direct this illustration to any such end at all. We avowedly employed it for the mere purpose of showing that the definition of Freewill, which we had "given in our own language and in

* Even as regards (what we, of course, account) the lowest form in which a man's permanent interest is pursued—viz. his interest merely on this side the grave—Mr. Stuart Mill makes a most just remark. "The power," he says, "of sacrificing a present desire to a distant object or a general purpose, which is indispensable for making the actions of the individual accord with his own notions of his individual good—even this is most unnatural to the undisciplined human being" ("Essay on Theism," p. 50). It is surely a most worthy resolve, on some given occasion, to do that which is "unnatural"—*i.e.* at variance with the promptings of Nature—and resist present desire for the sake of permanent well-being. How amazing to hear such a resolve described as "colourless"!

accordance with our earlier remarks," is in effect " precisely equivalent" to that given by certain representative Catholic theologians and philosophers.

A much more important misconception regards the whole import of our remarks on "Causation and Freewill." Mr. Hodgson apparently considers that the main purport of those remarks was to establish controversially the Freewill doctrine. On the contrary, this was a comparatively small portion of their purport. A few words will explain their general drift. Our course of essays, as a whole, is directed to the argumentative proof of Theism ; and we need hardly say that what we account the true doctrine of Causation is an indispensable link of such argumentative chain. In our essay on Causation, we had set forth this doctrine to the best of our power ; and what we aimed at in our essay on Freewill, was to adjust it with the particular doctrine of Freewill. As we explained at starting, our intention was, "by introducing the metaphysical principle of Causation, to develop the negative psychological doctrine of Indeterminism into the positive metaphysical doctrine of Freewill." We considered such questions as the following :—" In what sense can an intermediate cause be originative ? " " What is to be accounted the proximate cause of free acts ? " etc. Any one who reads that section of our essay to which we refer, will see that we are here rightly describing its contents. Indeed, it will have been seen from a quotation which we have already given, that in our supplementary essay, we were dissatisfied with our earlier paper, on the very ground that it had not given sufficient prominence to the controversial establishment of Freewill.

No doubt, on this general doctrine of Causation, Mr. Hodgson and we are fundamentally at variance. We hope, indeed, to take an early occasion of replying to his criticisms of us, both on that subject and on other parts of our humble philosophical structure. But all this is external to the proper question of Freewill.

One concluding remark on our terminology. Determinists, we venture to think, no less than their opponents, will be disposed to admit that, if our doctrine be true, our original distinction between "attractions" and "motives" will be found much conducive to its clear exposition. In our present essay we have used the word "motive" to express "every thought which prompts my will to action." But there are two senses, fundamentally different, in which some given thought may prompt me to action. On one side, it may prompt me to action by influencing my will's spontaneous impulse; while, on the other side, it may prompt me to action, by showing me that anti-impulsive effort is more reasonable at the moment than is *acquiescence* in spontaneous impulse. In the former case, we have called the thought an "attraction;" in the latter case, a "motive." Nor have we failed to point out that again and again the very same thought may serve in both capacities. Mr. Hodgson's objection to this terminology (p. 234) rests entirely on his objection to the doctrine which it expresses. Nor will any Determinists, we think, doubt, on reflection, that our distinction between "attractions" and "motives" is calculated to bring into much clearer and stronger light the essential proposition for which we contend.

In the preceding arguments, as we explained at starting, we have so spoken as to embrace those instances only in which the agent's choice is practically confined to two rival alternatives. But nothing can be easier than so to express our reasoning as to include those more frequent instances in which there are several various methods of procedure from which a selection may be made. In all the more strongly marked of such instances, I can know with absolute certainty to *which* one, among those various methods of procedure, my will spontaneously gravitates. I can know

with absolute certainty what is the resultant of those
various attractions which at the moment solicit me; what
is the exact course of action to which my entire circumstances of the moment, external and internal, dispose me.
I can know this with absolute certainty; because I can
recognize quite unmistakably what at the moment is my
will's spontaneous impulse and desire, its direct unforced
tendency. This spontaneous impulse or unforced tendency
measures, of course, with infallible accuracy the preponderating influence exercised over my mind, in its present
condition, by that complexus of attractions, which for the
moment is combinedly at work. But I know also, by
actual experience, that on various occasions I put forth a
vigorous self-originated effort, whereby I compel myself to
act in some way entirely *different* from that prompted by
my will's spontaneous impulse. On such occasions, then,
I know through experience that I compel myself, by a self-
originated and vigorous effort, to act in some way entirely
different from that to which my balance of attractions at
the moment disposes me. But Determinists will be the
first to admit that such self-originated resistance to the
balance of attractions, did it exist, would be a fact inconsistent with Determinism.

We have now, we think, vindicated against Mr. Hodgson
our whole argument for Freewill, as we submitted it on
earlier occasions. Nay, we venture to hope that, by encountering this new opponent, we have been able to exhibit
our reasoning in still clearer and fuller light. This, of
course, is all which is essential to our purpose, and we
might very fairly here leave the matter. Still, it will be
more satisfactory if we append a few comments on Mr.
Hodgson's affirmative position; though those comments
must necessarily be very brief, as we have but little more
space at our disposal.

1. As we have already said, Mr. Hodgson is not only a Determinist, but a Hedonistic Determinist. In other words, not only he holds that my act of will at any given moment is infallibly and inevitably determined by my circumstances, external and internal, as they *exist* at that moment, but he holds that the determining circumstances are simply the balance of *pleasure* as then apprehended. He admits, indeed (p. 238), as we have already quoted him, that "in *judging* the comparative strength of disparate pleasures, often the only way open to us is to see which of the two is actually obeyed at the moment of choice." But this very mode of expression implies that, as a matter of course, what "is obeyed at the moment of choice" is always the "strongest" proposed "pleasure." We have already drawn attention to the fact that Dr. Bain's doctrine is different from this.

2. Mr. Hodgson writes as a Theist (see pp. 248, 250). In this respect he differs, we fancy, from the great majority of contemporary Determinists; and, in our judgment, we need hardly add, differs for the better. We must frankly say, indeed, that those passages of his which bear on Theism impress us as less considered and less thoughtful than any others in his paper. But, so far as we may wish to criticize them, we must take a later opportunity for doing so. We may not ourselves here assume the truth of Theism; because we are advocating Freewill as a premiss, for the argumentative *establishment* of Theism.

3. According to Determinism, there are at every moment two factors which, taken in combination, infallibly and inevitably determine a man's conduct; one of these being his internal disposition of mind, the other his environment of external circumstances. Yet Determinists, we think, much differ from each other as regards the comparative *prominence* which they give to these two factors; and Mr. Hodgson lays far more relative strength on *the former*

than is, we think, common in his school. "The decision depends on" a man's "*state of mind*" (p. 232). "What the agent *is* manifests itself by what he does" (p. 246). We have ourselves far more sympathy with this form of Determinism than with the other. Such a mode of exhibiting Determinism as Mr. Hodgson's tends far more to encourage moral culture and the formation of moral habits, and does far more justice to the inexhaustible variety of human development; whereas the opposite method tends to represent men's acts as proceeding in a kind of wooden uniformity, under the pressure of external circumstances.

4. On this speciality of Mr. Hodgson's depends his strange use of the word "Freedom;" a terminology, which at first sight is startling in the extreme, and in which he differs, we think, from all other Determinists. He considers that, on his view, the human Will may be termed "Free;" because its movements are by no means enslaved to the domination of external circumstances, but are the unforced result of the mind's own constitution and temperament. To us such a terminology appears as inappropriate and inconsecutive as it is indubitably misleading. My Will, any one would say, is equally *enslaved*, whether its bondage be to my external circumstances or to my mental constitution. In no intelligible sense can it be called "Free," unless it be enfranchised from *both* tyrants.

5. Nevertheless, Mr. Hodgson considers (p. 229) that his sense of the term "Freewill" is that "in which it is understood by mankind at large." We emphatically deny this. When men declare that they possess an unmistakable and ineradicable "sense of freedom," they claim, we are confident, a very different freedom from that which Mr. Hodgson allows them. Take first an illustration. Through what we have called in earlier essays "self-intimacy," *i.e.* through my intimate acquaintance with my own series of mental and physical acts, I have a prevalent and pervasive

knowledge that I can move my arms in this or that direction; that I can rise up from my seat when I please, and then sit down again; that I can utter those words which present themselves to my mind, etc. In exactly the same manner, so we maintain, through self-intimacy, I have a prevalent and pervasive knowledge that, within certain limits, I can resist my will's spontaneous impulse whenever I please to do so. It is precisely this prevalent and pervasive knowledge, on our view, wherein consists my "sense of freedom." In our next essay on the subject we shall not fail to set forth this proposition, and exhibit the ground on which it rests. Here we would point out how signally Mr. Hodgson himself corroborates our doctrine; the more signally in proportion as the more unintentionally. He points out (p. 238), in a passage we have already quoted, how often it happens that "the only way open to us," in order to judge "the comparative strength of disparate pleasures," "is to see which of the two is actually obeyed at the moment of choice." He then adds these very remarkable words: "It is in this moment of *ignorance*, previous to choice, that a man has that sense of being able to choose which is called the sense of freedom." He admits, then, in direct contradiction to what he had said in p. 229, that when men account themselves "free," they account themselves "able to choose" between two "disparate" alternatives. Mr. Hodgson's statement, in fact, comes to this: "In real truth I *never* have the power of choosing for myself between two alternatives; but at certain periods of my daily life I am under a *delusion* that I *have* this power of choice; then, and then only, I have a sense of freedom." In other words, according to this dictum of Mr. Hodgson's, my sense of freedom is, on the Determinist theory, a mere delusion. This is the very conclusion for which we contend.

6. Nevertheless, Mr. Hodgson maintains (pp. 247, 248)

that the Deterministic theory is by no means inconsistent with "the existence of guilt and sin;" "the existence of morality in the Christian sense;" "a moral government of the world." In this, no doubt, he is at one with the Calvinistic necessitarians, such as Jonathan Edwards; but we think very few non-Calvinistic Determinists will be found on his side. We can take a curious corroboration of our statement from Dr. Bain. That philosopher puts the case of a schoolmaster, who is rebuking some pupil for having perpetrated a breach of discipline. We may suppose that, with the selfish recklessness of his age, some youth has broken out of bounds; insulted and outraged such persons of lower rank as may happen to have crossed his path; and, finally, indulged in a bout of drunkenness or worse sensuality. Dr. Bain ascribes no more *moral guilt* to our youth under these circumstances than to a dog who had broken loose, or to a sheep who had made his way through the hedge. These are Dr. Bain's words; and we italicize a few of them:—

The schoolboy, on being found guilty of a breach of discipline, will sometimes defend himself by saying that he was carried away, and could not restrain himself. He is frequently answered by the assertion that he *could* have restrained himself if he had chosen to do so. Such an answer is *a puzzle or a paradox*. The offender was in a state of mind such, that his conduct *followed according to the uniformity of his being;* and if the same antecedents were repeated, the same consequence would certainly be reproduced. In that view, therefore, the foregoing answer is *irrelevant, not to say nonsensical*. The proper form and the practical meaning to be conveyed is this:—" It is true that, *as your feelings then stood*, your conduct resulted as it did. . . . But I now punish you, or threaten you, or admonish you, in order that an *antecedent motive* may enter into your mind, as counteractive to your mind, spirit, or temper on another occasion; seeing that (acting as you did) you were plainly *in want of a motive*. I am determined that your conduct shall be reformed; and therefore, every time that you make such a lapse, I will supply more and stronger *motives in favour of what is your duty.*" Such is the plain unvarnished account of what the master intends in the address to his erring pupil. Finding a delinquency, *he assumes at once* that a repetition will occur if *the same feelings and ideas* occur under the same *outward circumstances ;* and accordingly there is nothing left for him but to *vary the antecedent,* and make sure that a new and potent spur shall be *mixed up with the previous combination,* so as to turn the conduct in the direction sought.—" Emotions and Will," third edition, pp. 477, 478.

According to Dr. Bain's theory, then, supposing me to be a schoolmaster, my position is this: If a pupil of mine breaks out into moral mischief, I should act as unreasonably and preposterously in *blaming* him, as I should in blaming him because some dose of medicine had not produced in him the expected result. In either case, circumstances show that a more copious supply—whether of quinine or of "motives"—urgently needs to be administered; and there is an end of the matter.

We warmly sympathize with Mr. Hodgson in his repudiation of this hideous theory; but we must strenuously maintain that it is Dr. Bain, and not Mr. Hodgson, whose view on the matter is accordant with Determinism. And perhaps we cannot more suitably conclude our controversy with our present opponent than by briefly defending this affirmation. Such defence, indeed, is the more appropriate as coming from ourselves, because it is some incidental statements of our own which have led him to speak on the subject.

That there can be no moral good or evil where there is no Freewill, is a doctrine, we consider, which legitimately results from every ethical theory, which recognizes ethical truth as such; from every theory which recognizes ethical truth, as distinct from truth psychological or otherwise experimental. For our own part, however, we are to assume that particular ethical theory which we ourselves accept as true. Human reason, we consider, intuitively recognizes as necessary a certain series of propositions—viz. that this, that, or the other act possesses that attribute which is termed "moral evil." *Universal* moral judgments, we further hold, which are more or less approximately true, are obtained by generalization from these intuitive *individual* judgments. We are now, then, to examine some one of these individual judgments; and we are to see whether its truth could possibly be admitted by those who accept Determinism.

My mother, who has been throughout life my most faithful and self-sacrificing friend, dies. Under the impulse of my grief, I am led to reflect on my past conduct to her, and I bitterly reproach myself for the many, many instances in which I have repaid her love by selfish neglect. A philosophical friend, however, assures me, for my comfort, that on every such occasion my self-indulgent conduct was infallibly and inevitably determined for me by my circumstances, external and internal; that I had no more power to pursue any less selfish course of action than a football has power to trace a path of its own, different from that impressed on it by physical agencies. If I could bring my mind to believe this kindly-intentioned Determinist—and if I brought home his theory to my feelings and imagination—I should be, no doubt, entirely relieved from my whole burden of compunction. At the same time, it is in the very highest degree improbable, we think, that I could possibly lay any such flattering unction to my soul: my intimate sense of my past freedom would be too strong to be overcome by sophistry however plausible. But whether I do or do not repose trust in my Determinist friend, on either alternative our conclusion equally holds. It is simply impossible for me to believe that my conduct on these various occasions was wrong and blameworthy, if I realize the doctrine that I had no power of acting otherwise. In other words, the notion of moral evil cannot be reconciled with Determinism. For the truth of this statement we appeal to all human beings who are able to understand it, be they virtuous or vicious, cultured or rude.

This was the argument on which we rested in those episodical sentences of ours which Mr. Hodgson (p. 247) cites. That with which he credits us (p. 248) is entirely different, though we should be quite prepared on occasion to defend it. The argument, however, which Mr. Hodgson ascribes to us, implies, if we rightly understand him, the Existence of God. But, as we have already more than once pointed out, we are advocating the Freewill doctrine as a premiss for the establishment of Theism; and we must not, therefore, *assume* Theistic doctrine in the course of our discussion.

The more we consider the doctrine of Freewill, the more strongly we feel (1) its absolute certainty on grounds of reason; and (2) its incalculable importance, as peremptorily disproving those philosophical tenets on which contemporary antitheists rest. We are very desirous, therefore, of exhibiting it with all obtainable completeness; and we hope in our next essay, accordantly with our previously expressed intention, to consider carefully its *extent*.* " Our own humble view," we have said, " is that a man's Will is Free during pretty nearly the whole of his waking life." It will be our business, then, to defend this proposition; a proposition which throws, we think, important and quite unexpected light on man's whole moral constitution.

* The essay here referred to is the last in the present volume.—ED.

XII.

ETHICS IN ITS BEARING ON THEISM.

SOME FIRST PRINCIPLES OF ETHICAL SCIENCE.

WE should be glad if our readers at this point would peruse our essay on "The Foundation of Morality." Even, however, supposing them to have done so, it will be important to exhibit once more those particular parts of it on which our purpose requires us especially to insist. And we begin with drawing attention to those psychical phenomena which stand at the foundation of our argument.

The human mind, as a matter of fact, forms a very large number of what we will call "moral judgments." "I am bound to do what I am paid for doing." "How conscientious a man is H!" "K behaved far better than L under those circumstances." "M is really an unmitigated scoundrel." "No praise can be too great for N's noble sacrifice." "O treats his children in a way which won't bear thinking of." "It was a matter of strict obligation on P to pay his debt at that particular time." "Of course, if God gives a command, it is man's duty to obey," etc. All these moral judgments, which so constantly occur, are reducible, directly or indirectly, to one or other of three types. (1) "Act A is virtuous in this or that degree;" (2) "Act B is wrong in this or that degree;"* (3) "Act C is more virtuous than Act D."† There is hardly

* We use the word "wrong" as the best single word we can think of to express the idea "anti-virtuous." But it is not quite a satisfactory word.

† When it is said in common parlance that this or that act is "of obliga-

any other question, we think, in all philosophy so momentous as that which concerns the true nature and the authoritativeness of such judgments. In order the better to fix our thoughts in its discussion, we will imagine, as we did in our essay above referred to, a concrete case. It is founded on, but much exaggerated beyond, Lord Macaulay's exposition of Lord Bacon's conduct.

A politician of high and unblemished character, with whose public principles I am heartily in accordance, has admitted me to his friendship, loaded me with benefits, and trusted me with his dearest secrets. I find, however, as time goes on, that my best chance of advancement lies in attaching myself to the opposite side. Filled with passionate desire for such advancement, I make political capital by disclosing my benefactor's confidences to the adverse party, and I embark heartily in a course of enterprise which has for its end his ruin. As I am about to reap the worldly fruit of my labours, I am seized with a violent illness. The crisis of the illness having passed away, in the tedious hours of slow recovery "I enter into myself," as ascetical writers would say. I judge that my successive acts have been signally wrong and wicked. Now, let us fix our attention on some one in particular of these judgments. For instance, let us take the following:—
"That past act, in which I divulged my benefactor's secrets to the opposite party for the sake of my own advancement, was an intensely wrong act." Let us take this moral judgment as the specimen instance whereby to test alternative ethical theories.

Firstly, we maintain that the idea "wrong"—or its correlative "virtuous"—is an entirely simple idea, entirely incapable of being analyzed into component parts. There

tion," no more is meant, we think, than that to omit the act would be wrong. Whether in *scientific* language this is a proper use of the term "obligation," we need not here inquire.

are many Intuitionists, we are well aware, who differ from us on this head; but we are very confident, nevertheless, that our thesis is true. And as, in our humble opinion, the importance of this thesis, in the Theistic controversy, is unspeakably great, we must not fail—even at the risk of tedium—to place arguments before our readers which shall suffice to exhibit it conclusively. This we shall best do by first passing under review some one antagonistic theory in particular. A certain number, then, of those Intuitionists who deny that the idea "virtuous" is simple, analyze it thus: "A 'virtuous' act," they say, "means a 'free act' directed by me to my true ultimate end;' and a 'wrong' act means 'a free act oppositely directed.'" We need hardly explain how entirely we agree to the proposition that "every free act directed by me to my true end is 'virtuous.'" * What we affirm, however, is that the term "virtuous" does not *mean* "freely directed to my true end;" but, on the contrary, expresses an idea distinct from, and superadded to, that other idea. Let us turn, then, to our specimen instance, and see whether the proposed analysis will hold water.

Surely not. When, under my new impressions, I first reflect on the baseness of that particular act in my past history, I clearly recognize that baseness before I so much as begin to think of the end for which I was created. At one and the same moment, there starts up in my mind a keen emotion of bitter shame, and, in company with that emotion, the clearest and most pungent perception how foully and atrociously I have acted. We repeat, I perceive *at once* with piercing clearness, that I have acted most wrongly, wickedly, basely. *Afterwards*, no doubt, I may begin to think about my ultimate end. I may reflect that I was created for something very different from this; and

---

* We assume, of course, that there is no flaw in what Catholics call its "object" and "circumstances."

that my having so gravely thwarted my high vocation has been a grievous calamity. But this is felt by me as a *new* reflection; a reflection entirely distinct from, though very directly founded on, my original reflection, that my conduct has been wrong, wicked, base.

In real truth, however, it is only necessary to exhibit in logical shape the tenet we are opposing, in order that every one may see its falsehood. According to this tenet, the term "a wrong act" means neither more nor less than "a free act put forth in opposition to my true ultimate end." Now consider the following proposition: "It is wrong for me to put forth freely an act in opposition to my true ultimate end." According to the tenet which we are opposing, this proposition means neither more nor less than the following :—"to put forth a free act in opposition to my true ultimate end, is to put forth a free act in opposition to my true ultimate end." The proposition, then—according to the tenet which we oppose—is as simple and bare a truism as the proposition that "a chair is a chair," or "a triangle is a triangle," or "an apple is an apple." When the matter is put in this shape, surely no reader of ordinary intelligence can be taken in by so preposterous a notion. When I say "it is wrong in me to put forth a free act in opposition to my true ultimate end," every person of ordinary intelligence will understand me to mean something very different from a bald and naked truism. Every one will see that I am uttering an ampliative proposition, and one of considerable importance. In other words, every one will see that the idea "wrong" is not *identical* with the idea "freely put forth in opposition to my ultimate end," but entirely *distinct* from the latter. And this is the precise thesis which we wished to establish.

An argument in every respect similar may be most easily drawn out, against any *other* suggested analysis of the idea "virtuous." We consider ourselves, then, to have sufficiently established our first thesis, viz. that "virtuous" is a simple idea. Secondly, we would point out, that the reality which that idea represents is absolutely "metempirical."* In the course of our series we have already maintained this, concerning the two ideas "necessary" and "cause:" here we are to exhibit the same truth, as regards the idea "virtuous." Of course the idea itself, as existing in the mind, is a psychical phenomenon; but what we say is, that the *objective attribute*, which that idea represents, is entirely metempirical. Suppose I form the judgment that such or such a course of conduct will probably preserve me in good health; or will conduce otherwise to my worldly advantage; or that it will obtain for me special help here and a special reward hereafter from some Invisible Being. In all such instances, the attribute which I predicate † is intelligible to me (so far as it is intelligible) by direct or indirect reference to phenomena of my experience. But when I form the judgment that such or such a course of conduct is "virtuous," and its contradictory "wrong," the attribute which I predicate cannot be even approximately represented in terms of phenomena at all. And yet—though such is undeniably the case—the meaning of this attribute "virtuous" is as clearly and readily intelligible to me as is the most simple phenomenon in the whole world. For the truth of this last statement, we refer to the only possible standard of appeal—the testimony of each man's consciousness. In every moral judgment, then, the subject is a certain phenomenal act, or certain phenomenal acts ; and the judgment itself ascribes a certain metempirical *attribute* to

* The word "metempirical" was invented by a Phenomenistic philosopher—the late Mr. G. H. Lewis—to express "external to the sphere of phenomena."

† For convenience' sake, we have always used the term "subject," "predicate," concerning *judgments* no less than concerning *propositions*.

that act or those acts. This is our second thesis on the present occasion.

Our third thesis is, that certain moral truths are self-evidently necessary.* Let us here revert to our pattern specimen, "That past act of mine, wherein for my own selfish purposes I betrayed my benefactor's confidence, was a wrong act." Now, in our treatment of necessary truth we mentioned one particular premiss, as having often been employed by us for the purpose of showing that this or that truth is a necessary one. The premiss, it may be remembered, runs thus: If in any case, by merely pondering on my conception of some *ens*, I know that a certain attribute, not included in that conception, is truly predicable of that *ens*, then such predication expresses a self-evidently necessary ampliative truth. Moreover, when we cited this premiss, we trust we sufficiently showed how incontestable is its soundness. Now, it can hardly be needful for us to say how obviously applicable is this premiss to the case in hand. I ponder on this past phenomenal act of mine, as I remember myself to have perpetrated it. And, by the mere process of thus pondering, I come to know that the attribute "wrong"—which is not included in my *conception* of the phenomenal act—is nevertheless truly applicable thereto. Consequently, the proposition, "that act was wrong," expresses a self-evidently necessary truth.

The Phenomenist, in replying to this argument, sometimes urges a consideration, which we are bound, no doubt, carefully to bear in mind. Inferences from experience, he urges, are often so obviously and spontaneously drawn that they may most easily be mistaken for intuitions. We have always entirely admitted the force of this consideration, which indeed has a very important bearing on questions concerning the existent divergence of moral standards.

* By "moral truths," we need hardly say, we mean "the objects of true moral judgments."

We have always fully admitted that we have no right to treat any given judgment as intuitive, until we have clearly shown that it is not inferential. But without at all denying that many moral judgments are inferential, it is evident on a moment's consideration, that, if our previous theses be admitted, *some* moral judgments are most certainly immediate. Take the case of some inferential moral judgment. Its predicate, as we have shown, is one or other exhibition of a certain simple and metempirical idea : " virtuous " or " wrong." Now, such an idea cannot possibly be found in the conclusion of a syllogism, unless it be found in one of the premisses.* Some one of its premisses, therefore, is a moral judgment. If this premiss be itself a conclusion, we are only thrown back on some earlier premiss. In due course, therefore, we must by absolute necessity arrive at some moral judgment which is immediate, not inferential. And there are no moral judgments which we *allege* to be intuitive, unless they belong to this class.

Our fourth thesis, in accordance with our view on axioms in general, is, that self-evidently necessary moral truths are first intued in the individual case. When reflecting on my past life, I intue, as a self-evidently necessary truth, that this particular past act of treachery to my benefactor was wrong, base, foul. No doubt I may carry my speculations further. I may come to intue, as a self-evidently necessary truth, that *any one else*, who under circumstances precisely similar should do precisely what I did, would also act wrongly, basely, foully. But we incline to think that in a vast majority of cases the agent does not carry his speculations so far. Moral axioms, like other axioms, are *potentially* universal ; but we much doubt

* If "virtuous" were a complex idea, it might imaginably be found in the conclusion of a syllogism, without appearing in the premisses except as regards its constituent elements. But here the idea *has* no constituent elements.

whether ordinary men commonly intue them as such. This particular question, however, is one of no great practical importance that we can see.

But there is a view, not uncommonly taken by Intuitionists, which is of far greater practical moment, and from which we must dissent with some confidence. In considering that judgment of mine whereby I recognize the intense baseness of my past act, they would deny that this judgment is immediate and self-evident. They would regard it, on the contrary, as an *inference* from more vague and general judgments, which they do regard as self-evidently necessary. " Benefactors ought not to be harmed ; " " secrets ought not to be disclosed ; " " men ought not to pursue their own advancement at another man's expense ; " etc. On our side, we need not here inquire to what extent a list of general moral propositions can be drawn out, which shall be reasonably accepted as self-evidently necessary, and as admitting therefore of no exception.* But we submit, with great confidence, that such an individual moral judgment as we have taken for our pattern specimen, is in no way an inference from any general moral judgment. Of no syllogism can the conclusion be more keenly manifest to me than are the premisses.† Yet it is with indefinitely more keenness manifest to me that my past act was base, than that those general propositions are true which we just now recited.

We have no space to pursue this particular question

* Mr. Sidgwick discusses this question with great care and signal ability in his "Methods of Ethics," Book iii. chaps. 4-11. We think that his remarks deserve most serious attention from all ethical students. For ourselves, we will here only say that we are very clear indeed on one point. Mr. Sidgwick's arguments against Intuitionism, we are confident, would be quite immeasurably less plausible than they are, if he more distinctly confronted Intuitionism under the shape exhibited in our text. He recognizes that phase of doctrine, indeed, as one existing in many minds ; but (for whatever reason) does not argumentatively confront it.

† We are supposing, of course, that the conclusion is not *otherwise* known to me than as resulting from those premisses.

further; but we venture to think it of quite critical importance, in the controversy against Utilitarians and other Phenomenists. For our own immediate purpose, however, the matter is comparatively irrelevant. Whatever be held concerning our fourth thesis, the three earlier theses remain; and we have established, therefore, that there are certain self-evident necessary moral axioms. Now, on this fact ethical science is founded. These axioms, as is evident, may be made premisses in many a different chain of reasoning; and thus a large number of moral judgments will result by way of inference, in regard to which it is certain or probable, accordingly as the reasoning may have been more or less cogent, that they are necessarily true. Then, again, my "moral sense," in proportion as it is "properly cultivated," to use F. O'Reilly's phrase, largely increases the number of moral judgments, which to me are self-evident as necessarily true. And it is by these various methods, as we look at the matter, that the great fabric of ethical science receives verification and enlargement.

A Catholic moralist, as distinct at all events from a non-Christian, has to make a further point. The Church claims to teach infallibly concerning moral truth; nor indeed do we see how it can be denied by any believer in Scripture, that the apostles claimed the same power. A Christian philosopher, then, has to show, as he very easily can, that this claim of infallible moral teaching involves no interference with the legitimate rights of reason. We merely mention this episodically, to show that we have not forgotten it; but the matter has no bearing on our argument, and we have no space to enter on it. For the same reason—want of space—we will not here attempt a reply to two different objections urged against our thesis, which we have sufficiently met on earlier occasions. The first of these objections is directed "ad homines" against Christians, on the ground of God's apparent interferences, as recorded in

Scripture, with those ethical verities which we maintain to be necessary and immutable. This objection we briefly answered, by help of Catholic theologians, in our essay on "The Foundation of Morality" (the third of this series); and we have treated the question in our "Philosophical Introduction," pp. 165-190. The second of the objections to which we refer, is the notable divergence of *moral standard*, which has existed in different times and countries. On this we must be content with referring our readers to our detailed reply in the essay referred to.

THE BEARING OF ETHICAL SCIENCE ON THEISM.

We are now, in conclusion, to exhibit the bearing on Theism of those fundamental ethical verities which we have laboured to establish. And we might commence this task by mentioning one ethical truth in particular, which all men will accept as self-evidently necessary who believe that there *is* such a thing as necessary truth. If a Holy Creator exist, it is wrong, base, wicked, to refuse Him unreserved obedience, love,* etc. Then we might further refer to the doctrine already mentioned, that all necessary truths, and moral truths therefore inclusively, are founded on the Nature of God; that they are what they are, because He is what He is. These are, doubtless, ethical truths closely bearing on Theism. Yet they are not exactly in the number of those which we are here considering. We are considering those ethical truths only which tend to the *argumentative establishment* of Theism.

Now, there is more than one class of ethical truths which directly or indirectly tend to the establishment of

---

* It is a very singular fact, that non-Catholic Theistic writers so often omit all reference to duties *towards God* in their ethical discussions. They speak of what are now called "egoism" and "altruism;" but apparently forget that there are other fundamental duties, besides those owing to myself and to my fellow-men.

Theism. It is only, however, the chief one of these on which we are able to insist in our present essay. What we would here, then, urge, is a consideration of all which is involved in that most unique and signally significant idea "virtuous," with its correlative "wrong." We ventured to say in the third essay of this series—and subsequent reflection has but confirmed us in our opinion—that there is probably no other psychical fact whatever so pregnant with momentous consequences, in the existing state of philosophy, as man's possession of this idea. In this statement, however, we include, of course, not merely his *possession* of the idea, but his cognizance of its correspondence with an objective reality.

Before setting forth at greater length what we here mean, we must make an introductory remark on a doctrine which has occupied us in several preceding philosophical papers—the doctrine of Freewill. Let us go back to our pattern instance of a moral judgment: the reflections of a repenting politician on his bed of sickness. In recognizing the fact that this or that past act of treachery was on his part wrong and base, he intues, as we have been urging, that the baseness of this act is a self-evidently necessary truth. It is not *only*, however, this moral truth which he recognizes. At the same moment he recognizes another verity, the verity that those past acts were *free*. As to the *former* verity, he intues it through that endowment of the human faculties whereby they are enabled to recognize certain self-evidently necessary truths. As to the *latter* verity, of that he is most intimately cognizant through his close and unintermittent familiarity with his own mental phenomena.

Whereas, then, self-intimacy acquaints me with the fact that I am true master of my own actions—that the conduct of my life depends on my own free choice—my various moral judgments instruct me, with varying degrees of certainty, in the all-important lesson what that conduct ought to be. These judgments, taken individually, direct me in individual acts. But it is not our present purpose to dwell on them in this point of view.* What we here wish to urge is concerned, not with individual moral judgments, but with my moral judgments, taken collectively. As time goes on, then, this, that, and the other act are successively known to me as not permissible—as wrong, base, wicked, whatever their attractiveness to my inclinations. Again, this act is known to me as more virtuous than that, whichever of the two, exercising my liberty, I may choose to perform. In proportion, therefore, as I give more attention to the ethical conduct of my life, in that proportion the number of such necessary moral truths brought within my cognizance increases unintermittently and inexhaustibly. I thus obtain an ever clearer perception of the fact that I am in contact with a certain necessarily existing and pervasive Supreme Rule of life; † from which, indeed, as regards its actual injunctions,‡ I cannot swerve without wrong-doing and wickedness. No other motive of action has any claim on me at all so paramount as the claim of this Rule. No other course of action is so reasonable as that of conforming myself more and more with its counsels; nor can any other thing be so intensely unreasonable as the doing that which it pronounces to be intrinsically evil.§ We have already, therefore, arrived at

---

* The question in itself is of course very momentous, how my various moral judgments may acquire increasing clearness and rectitude on matters of detail. On this see our essay already referred to; and for a fuller treatment, Dr. Ward's "Philosophical Introduction," pp. 119-161.

† We cannot, of course, refer to the Natural *Law* without assuming the Existence of God.

‡ When we mention the "actual injunctions" of this Rule, we refer to those particular moral judgments which are of the type "act B is wrong."

§ One or two collateral points here emerge, on which we would refer for our view to Dr. Ward's "Philosophical Introduction."

Thus (1) the case is imaginable, that, by doing what my moral judgment dictates, I shall impair my own permanent felicity. Dr. Ward submits

a very remarkable and noteworthy conclusion. There is a certain purely invisible and metempirical standard which claims to be the only true measure and arbiter of man's whole conduct in this visible scene. Man is proverbially monarch of the visible world; and it is precisely man who is *de jure* subject to the authoritative judgments of an invisible tribunal.*

Here we take a further and most momentous step forward. This Supreme Rule is no mere catalogue of metempirical moral truths, but a *Law* imposed on me by *rightful personal authority*. Or, to express the same proposition in somewhat different terms, whatever is known by my reason

(pp. 419-421) that such a case, though conceivable, is metaphysically impossible.

Then (2) some Intuitionists express themselves as though they held that men cannot pursue virtuousness for its own sake, but merely as a *means* to beatitude or felicity. We do not think that this is in general intended by such writers, though they certainly express themselves obscurely. Dr. Ward, at all events (pp. 409-417), exhibits strong theological authority in the opposite direction. He cites Scotus, Suarez, Vasquez, Viva, and others writers of name. See also pp. 404-409.

* Our argument will be interestingly illustrated if we quote a few of Bishop Butler's expressions, concerning what he calls "the principle of reflection or conscience," and its due authority.

"The very constitution of our nature requires, that we bring our whole conduct before this supreme faculty; wait its determination; enforce upon ourselves its authority; and make it the business of our lives to conform ourselves to it."

"This is the most intimate of obligations; which a man cannot transgress without being self-condemned, and—unless he has corrupted his nature—without real self-dislike."

This superior principle "without being consulted, without being advised with, magisterially exerts itself, and approves or condemns the doer of certain actions; and if not forcibly stopped, naturally, and as of course goes on to anticipate a higher and more effectual sentence, which shall hereafter second and affirm its own."

"Had it strength as it has right, had it power as it has manifest authority, it would absolutely govern the world."

There is one important difference between Bishop Butler's position and our own, viz. that he throughout assumes the Existence of God. But we think he lays very little stress on this in his argument.

Among the very many imperishable services which Cardinal Newman has rendered to the cause of Christianity and of Catholicity, none to our mind exceeds the example he has given, in always laying such prominent and emphatic stress on man's naturally implanted sense of right and wrong.

to be intrinsically and necessarily wrong, is also known by my reason to be necessarily forbidden by some Superior Being, who possesses over me rightful jurisdiction.

Before entering, however, on our grounds for this vitally important conclusion, it is of extreme moment that we guard against a possible misconception of what is involved therein. We must on no account be misunderstood as alleging that the idea "wrong" is *equivalent* to the idea "forbidden by some Superior Being," etc.; and, by parity, that the idea "virtuous" is equivalent to the idea "approved by some such Person." We have already argued—conclusively, we trust—that "virtuous" and "wrong," while mutually correlative, are at the same time absolutely simple ideas. Still there is one particular shape wherein a denial of this latter truth has been embodied, which to us seems so full of most serious evil consequences that we cannot be contented without considering it expressly and at some little length.

It has been held, then, by some Intuitionists, that the idea "wrong" is equivalent to the idea "forbidden by my Creator;" and that the former idea, therefore, is complex, being correctly analyzed into the latter. To this allegation we have already given, we trust, one amply sufficient answer. Take this very fundamental and momentous proposition: "It is wrong to disobey my Creator." According to the allegation which we are opposing, this proposition would not be momentous at all: it would be a bald and naked truism, with no more significance than the proposition that an apple is an apple, and a chair a chair. For, according to the allegation which we are opposing, the proposition we have just mentioned would mean neither more nor less than this: "To disobey my Creator is to disobey my Creator." Such a supposition, we need not say, is among the absurdest which can be conceived. It is most plain, then, that the term "wrong" introduces into the proposition some new idea which is *not* identical with the idea of "disobeying my Creator."*

Here, then, is our first argument against the allegation that the word "wrong" means "forbidden by my Creator," or "forbidden by my Holy Creator." A second is urged by F. Liberatore with great force, though perhaps it is hardly more than the preceding argument displayed in a somewhat different shape. Theists themselves must admit—such is F. Liberatore's argument—that, even after God has issued some command, the act commanded will still be destitute of obligation, unless an *antecedent* premiss be assumed: unless it be assumed that "to disobey God is wrong, sinful, wicked." If you can say nothing more than that "to disobey God is to disobey God," you will have given morality no foundation whatever ("Ethica," nn. 27, 29).†

There is a third argument, however, which has frequently been adduced for our conclusion, and on which for ourselves we would always lay greater stress than on either of the preceding. It is addressed, of course, to Theists, and we put it thus: Consider any one of God's Attributes, say, His Omnipotence. This is an attribute entirely analogous to the attribute "power," as possessed by a Creature; entirely analogous, but existing in an infinite degree. In

---

* An explanation should here be appended. Is it a self-evidently necessary and universal truth, that "it is wrong to disobey my Creator?" We submit that this is not the case, unless the attribute "Holy" be known as appertaining to the Creator. The supposition is conceivable—though of course intrinsically impossible—that some not perfectly virtuous being possesses creative power. Such a creator might impose some immoral command; and if so, assuredly could not be obeyed by me without my doing what is wrong.

The proposition then, as amended, stands thus: "It is wrong to disobey my perfectly Holy Creator." We have already explained that we account this a self-evidently necessary ampliative proposition.

† F. Liberatore's expressed thesis is merely, that morality does not depend on the *Free* Will of God. But those who read the sections to which we refer in our text, will see that he is also emphatically opposed to the doctrine that (as he expresses it in n. 27) "*God's Will*,"—not merely God's *Free* Will—"is the first root and source of morality."

like manner consider God's attribute "Infinite Holiness." This is entirely analogous to the attribute "virtuous," as possessed by a reasonable creature; entirely analogous, but existing in an infinite degree. Now, if "virtuous" merely meant "conformable with my Creator's Will," then the Uncreated could have no Attribute of "Holiness" at all, and would lose, as one may say, the brightest jewel of His crown.

We must maintain it, then, as most certain, and even most evident, that that attribute which is designated by the word "wrong" includes in its notion no reference whatever to God or to any Superior Being. Yet, as we just now alleged, there is another fact in the opposite direction, which is not less certain, and perhaps even hardly less evident. This is the fact to which we urgently solicit our readers' careful attention. We supposed throughout, it will be remembered, that the genuine avouchment of my faculties is entirely trustworthy and without appeal. Now, it is surely an undeniable matter of fact that when I contemplate a black catalogue of evil actions committed by me in time past, I contemplate them, not merely as intrinsically wrong and wicked, but as offences—as a rebellion—against some Superior Being, whose displeasure I have thereby incurred. Cardinal Newman expresses, with unsurpassable force and clearness, those experienced facts of human nature which bear in this direction. We italicize a few words and clauses.

No *fear* is felt by any one who recognizes that his conduct has not been *beautiful*, though he may be mortified at himself if perhaps he has thereby forfeited some advantage. But if he has been betrayed into any kind of *immorality*, he has a lively sense of responsibility and guilt, though the act be no offence against society; of distress and apprehension, even though it may be of present service to him; of compunction and regret, though in itself it be most pleasurable; *of confusion of face, though it may have no witness.* These various perturbations of mind, which are characteristic of a bad conscience, and may be very considerable—self-reproach, poignant shame, haunting remorse, chill dismay at the prospect of the future; and their contraries, when the conscience is good, as real though less forcible, self-approval, inward peace, lightness of heart, and the like;—these emotions constitute a generic difference between conscience and our other intellectual senses—common sense, good sense, sense of expedience, taste, sense of honour, and the like. . . .

Conscience . . . always involves the recognition of a living object, towards which it is directed. Inanimate things *cannot stir our affections;* these are correlative with persons. If, as is the case, we feel responsibility, are ashamed, are frightened, at transgressing the voice of conscience, *this implies that there is One to whom we are responsible,* before whom we are ashamed, whose claims upon us we fear. If, on doing wrong, we feel the same tearful, broken-hearted sorrow which overwhelms us on hurting a mother; if, on doing right, we enjoy the same sunny serenity of mind, the same soothing satisfactory delight, which follows on our receiving praise from a father—*we certainly have within us the image of some person,* to whom our love and veneration look, in whose smile we find our happiness, for whom we yearn, towards whom we direct our pleadings, in whose anger we are troubled and waste away. These feelings within us are such as *require for their exciting cause an intelligent being.* We are not affectionate towards a stone, nor do we feel shame before a horse or a dog; we have no remorse or compunction on breaking mere human law; yet, so it is, conscience excites all these painful emotions, confusion, foreboding, self-condemnation : and, on the other hand, it sheds upon us a deep peace, a sense of security, resignation, and a hope, which there is no sensible, no earthly object to elicit. "The wicked flees when no one pursueth:" then why does he flee? and whence his terror? *Who is it that he sees in solitude, in darkness, in the hidden chambers of his heart?* If the cause of these emotions does not belong to this visible world, the object to which his perception is directed must be Supernatural and Divine; and thus the phenomena of conscience, as a dictate, avail to impress the imagination with the picture of a Supreme Governor, Holy, Just, Powerful, All-seeing, Retributive; and *is the creative principle of religion.**

---

* " Grammar of Assent," fourth edition, pp. 108-110.

Similarly, F. Liberatore—whom we have seen so firmly opposing the notion that the word "wrong" means "prohibited by God"—nevertheless uses such language as this: "Natural reason itself," he says, "in discerning actions as suitable or repugnant to human nature, places before us a *Divine prohibition or command*" (n. 79). "This dictate of [moral] reason is so perceived by man with a certain internal auscultation (auditu quodam interno) that he feels himself truly bound *by a certain command*. . . . To which *voice interiorly commanding* if any man refuse obedience, he is so pierced by the stings" of conscience "as to expect some penalty from some Supreme Authority" (p. 80). In moral judgments "there is always involved the obscure at least and indistinct perception of *some hidden power*, which, objectively considered, is no other than God" (n. 78). So again F. Kleutgen: "God makes Himself felt within us by His Moral Law, as an August Power to which we are subject."

Here we must explain, as accurately as we can, the exact point on which we are at this moment insisting. We suppose ourselves of course preliminarily to have established our *earlier* doctrine—the doctrine that there exists most indubitably a certain Supreme Rule of life, the precepts of which, so far as known to me, cannot be disobeyed without wrongdoing and wickedness. If any men, then, choose to live in moral callousness and obduracy, they act on one hand with monstrous wickedness, and on the other hand with extremest unreasonableness. Nor do we here maintain that such men as these have any means of arriving explicitly at the further cognition on which we wish to insist, unless they begin to amend their ways, and to act more in accordance with sound reason. But we make *this* allegation. If I be not altogether morally callous and obdurate, if I practise a certain sedulousness in avoiding whatever I know to be wrong, or even if I keep alive in my mind the express remembrance that wrong *is* wrong, then I come to cognize with ever increasing clearness the ampliative truth, that all acts of wickedness are acts of rebellion against some Superior Being. So universal, intrinsic, irresistible, is this conviction among all men who are not morally callous and obdurate, that, if man's intellectual faculties are really trustworthy, the conviction *must* be well-founded. Either the judgment is intuitive, or it is an inference so universal and inevitable as to be tantamount in authority with an intuition. Those who believe in an intrinsic and necessarily existing distinction between right and wrong, and who keep alive in their mind the remembrance of that belief, are quite invariably found *also* to believe that acts intrinsically wrong are forbidden by some Superior Being. We must not fail indeed to set forth what seems to us the true account of that psychical process, which issues in this universal dictate of reason. Still, we entreat our readers to bear in mind that the *existence* of this dictate is a fact indefinitely more undeniable, than is the correctness of any given theory which may be suggested; and it is on the universal existence of this dictate that we base our conclusion. Our own theory on its genesis would be the following :—

Cognitions of every kind may be explicit or implicit. If they are explicit, I am explicitly conscious of them; if implicit, I am implicitly conscious, or, as it is now sometimes called, "sub-conscious," of them. Suppose I am interrupted in my literary work by the roar of a neighbouring cannon: if I were asked whether I *heard* it, I should laugh at my interrogator's joke. But if he asks me whether I have heard a certain low rumbling sound which has gone on near me for some time, my first impression perhaps will be that I have *not* heard it : yet, by carefully examining my recent consciousness, I may find that the sound did in fact reach me. My cognition of it then was real but implicit.

Now take the case of some moral judgment: "this my past act of treachery to my benefactor was wrong, wicked, base." This judgment is most explicit, we need not say. But we submit that such a judgment is always in fact accompanied by another, though this other is *not* always explicit. We should thus express the second judgment: "That past act of treachery was an act of rebellion against some Superior Being, who possesses over me rightful jurisdiction." This judgment, when I contemplate merely some one evil act, may possibly enough be altogether implicit: but when I contemplate a *series* of past evil acts, it assumes more and more an explicit shape. In defence of this conclusion, we argue as follows:—

Let us first repeat what we have already said. By means of my various moral judgments, this, that, and the other act is successively cognized by me, as not permissible —as wrong, base, wicked—whatever may be its tendency to worldly advantage. In proportion as I give more attention to the ethical conduct of my life, in that proportion the number of moral truths brought within my cognizance increases in a more rapid ratio. And I am thus brought into a constantly clearer perception of the truth, that I am in contact with a certain metempirical and pervasive Rule of Life, from which I cannot swerve without wrongness, wickedness, baseness; that the whole conduct of my life is *de jure* subject to the pronouncements of a certain invisible tribunal. Such was our earlier statement.* But as soon as I have arrived at the conviction expressed by that statement, a further step is strictly inevitable and irresistible. The notion of a Supreme Rule from which I cannot swerve

* We do not here refer to those other moral judgments included in the Supreme Rule, which are of the type "act A is virtuous," "act C is more virtuous than act D." We abstain from this, because our argument, though applicable to all these judgments, is exhibited with more irresistible clearness in the case of those particular judgments which are of the type "act B is wrong."

without wickedness, passes inevitably and irresistibly into the *further* notion of a Law imposed on me by some Superior Being. The notion of an invisible tribunal, by which my actions are authoritatively praised or blamed, passes into the further notion of some Personal Judge sitting on that tribunal. To dwell on the earlier of the two convictions without passing into the later—to remain content with the notion of a Supreme *Rule*, without carrying it forward to the notion of a Natural *Law*—is as impossible psychically as to pass my life standing on one leg is impossible physically. If ever there were a general intuition it is that on which we are insisting. That rule to which profound, continuous, unreserved allegiance is due from free and reasonable beings, cannot be a mere *abstraction;* it must be the Law of some personal Superior possessing rightful authority.

Of course our whole train of reasoning from first to last is entirely futile, unless inquirers admit what we have called " the principle of intrinsic certitude." But then, as we have so often argued, those who refuse to admit that principle descend to the level of brutes—nay, to a level below that of brutes—as regards the knowledge which they can consistently claim to possess. Their knowledge, were it possible for them to carry out their principle faithfully, would be strictly limited to the passing consciousness of each individual moment. On the other hand, if persons admit the genuineness and trustworthiness of those particular intuitions which are called acts of memory, they have no pretext for refusing to admit the genuineness and trustworthiness of those *other* intuitions, which are undeniably no *less* immediate declarations of the human mind than are acts of memory themselves. It is on such intuitions that we have constructed our argument. Those which we have alleged for our purpose are divisible, our reader will remember, into two classes. The first class consists of those intuitions which declare that certain moral judgments possess self-evidently necessary truth; while the second consists of those which declare, as a self-evidently necessary truth, that all wrong acts are prohibited by a certain Superior Being.

Now, further. Since it is a necessary truth that all wrong acts are prohibited by a certain Superior Being—and since it is very certain that wrong acts *are* committed—it manifestly results that the Existence itself of that Being is a necessary truth.

Moreover, as Viva argues, this Superior Being has on me such paramount claims that, though all other beings in the universe solicited me in the opposite direction, my indispensable duty would in no way be affected of submitting myself unreservedly to His command. His will, then, is more peremptorily authoritative than the united will of all existent or possible persons who are not He.

Once more. As F. Franzelin puts it, moral laws hold good for all persons existent or possible. All other persons, therefore, existent or possible, are no less unreservedly subject to the command of this Being than I am. Consequently, he is Supreme Legislator over the universe of reasonable and free individuals.

We are thus landed in the conclusion that there is a certain Necessary Being, faultlessly Holy, possessing authority rightful, absolutely supreme, exclusive, without appeal, over the whole existent or possible universe of rational and free individuals. We are well aware, of course, that objections more or less plausible may be raised against the reasoning which issues in this conclusion. But, then, we are also confident that a review of these objections will only make the force of our argument more obviously certain and irresistible. Any such review, however, must be deferred to a future occasion.

Here, then, for the moment we terminate our discussion,

having arrived at the threshold—and, indeed, at some little distance beyond the threshold—of that disquisition, to which all our preceding essays have been introductory. The next stage of our argument will be to engage in direct conflict with Agnosticism as such; to examine those arguments which have been adduced for the conclusion, that nothing of practical importance can be certainly known concerning the Great First Cause. On this head we shall take Mr. Herbert Spencer as representing the Agnostic party, and they will certainly admit that we could not choose a more powerful expositor of their doctrine. We expect, however, that our readers will be greatly amazed when they see the extraordinary weakness and futility of the Agnostic position; a position which not even Mr. Spencer's genius can invest with so much as superficial plausibility.

XIII.
PHILOSOPHY OF THE THEISTIC CONTROVERSY.

THROUGHOUT our present series of essays we have explained that, whereas our affirmative argument for Theism will be such, we hope, as to hold its own against all gainsayers, the opponents, nevertheless, whom we directly assail are those only of one particular school. We do not directly encounter Hegelians and Pantheists, but only Phenomenists and Agnostics. This statement must, of course, be understood with obvious qualifications: we cannot, *e.g.*, establish the existence of a Personal God, without replying to whatever objections are raised by the Pantheist. But we shall not directly criticize the spirit and teaching of any Antitheistic school, except only that which proceeds on the lines of Phenomenism and which opposes Theism in the name of Inductive Philosophy. No other Antitheistic School has large influence in England; nor again, as we shall point out in the sequel, is any other so fundamentally and obtrusively opposed to religion in regard to the very meaning and due conduct of life. When we began our series we dealt with Mr. Stuart Mill as representing this school, for he was its acknowledged leader and most typical specimen. Since his death, however, not only his philosophical reputation has declined in quite an extraordinary degree; but, which is partly, no doubt, the cause of that declension, his posthumous "Essays on Religion" have exhibited one or two most remarkable instances of hesitation in carrying out his principles to their full and legitimate issue. On the present occasion, therefore, and hereafter, we shall treat him as one only out of many, and refer to those only of his utterances which are common to him with all Phenomenists.

The purpose of our present essay, we may say briefly, is to exhibit in their mutual relation these two antagonistic doctrines of Theism and Phenomenistic Antitheism. We hope first to summarize and emphasize what we have said on former occasions concerning the intellectual inanity, or rather self-contradictoriness, of Antitheistic Phenomenism in the shape which it now assumes. We hope next to consider what are the reasons of that profound antipathy to Theism which is so conspicuous in the adherents of Phenomenism; for this is, of course, an absolutely necessary inquiry if we are to fight against its adherents with any hope of success. We hope, lastly, to exhibit a catalogue of those arguments for Theism which we shall successively enforce in future essays; to indicate their general character; and to exhibit their ground of conclusiveness. We begin, then, with the first of these three themes.

It was a remarkable characteristic of Mr. Stuart Mill that he invariably treated his opponents not with courtesy only, but with kindliness and generosity. Dr. Bain, also, we must say, is uniformly courteous and respectful in his language. But such habits are far from universal among living members of the school. Thus Professor Huxley—as quoted in the *Tablet* of Aug. 20, 1881—says of those who believe that God created the universe, that "they have not reached that state of emergence from ignorance in which the necessity of a discipline to enable them to be judges has, as yet, dawned on the mind." Here is bounce and swagger with a vengeance: no Christian, then, possesses even the rudiments of due mental discipline. Without calling into question the Professor's possession of due mental discipline, we shall, nevertheless, contend that the philosophical system which he maintains is so feeble and self-contradictory as to be destitute of all claim on the slightest intellectual respect.

We here speak of Phenomenists, be it observed, as Philosophers, not as scientists. We heartily admit that innumerable truths of great importance have been established by inductive science; and that no men have laboured more ably and more successfully in the vineyard of inductive science than these our opponents. So far we have, of course, no quarrel with them whatever, and would only point out that many others have wrought with equal success in the same field who have been firm believers in Religious Doctrine. But Professor Huxley and his sympathizers are not content with holding that the processes of inductive science are reasonable and legitimate; they take an all-important step farther. According to them, the fact that inductive processes are legitimate suffices to establish a certain philosophical tenet which we call Phenomenism. And they then set forth a further premiss, with which we entirely concur—viz. that, if this tenet be true, man has no means of knowing God's Existence. We entirely admit, then, that Phenomenism is Antitheistic; but we maintain that, as held by them, it is most manifestly false and self-contradictory.

What, then, is Phenomenism? Nothing can be more easily understood by any one who will use his mind, than the distinction between this tenet and its contradictory, Intuitionism. The Phenomenist, as such, professes to build his intellectual fabric exclusively on "experienced facts;" to accept nothing except some experienced fact as a first premiss in argument, as a truth immediately known. It is by so comporting himself that he thinks he sympathizes with the true spirit of inductive science; and guards against the evil habit so common among other philosophers, the erecting gratuitously into the rank of objective truths what are merely impressions of the speculator's own mind.* On the other hand, the Intuitionist alleges that there are various truths, immediately evident and admissible therefore as primary premisses, which are in no sense "experienced facts." These he calls "truths of intuition." Accordingly we have, on former occasions, defined an "intuition" to be "an intellectual avouchment, reliably declaring as immediately certain some truth other than the mere existence and characteristics of such avouchment." The Intuitionist considers accordingly that these "truths of intuition" are no less immediately certain, no less trustworthy as primary sources of knowledge, than are experienced facts themselves.

We said just now that Phenomenism, as held by the contemporary school of Antitheistic Phenomenists, is most manifestly false and self-contradictory. What we meant was, that if Phenomenists were true to their characteristic tenet—if they honestly and consistently held to their principle, that experienced facts are the exclusive basis of real knowledge—they would commit philosophical suicide; they would contradict those affirmations, to which they have committed themselves most confidently and unanimously. This is to be our first ground of attack.

* "The notion that truths external to the mind may be known by intuition independently of observation and experience, is, I am persuaded, for these times the great intellectual support of false doctrines and bad intentions. By the aid of this theory every inveterate belief and every intense feeling, of which the origin is not remembered, is enabled to dispense with the obligation of justifying itself by reason, and is erected into its own all-sufficient justification. There never was such an instrument devised for consecrating all deep-seated prejudices."—Stuart Mill's "Autobiography," pp. 225, 226.

"The difference between these two schools of Philosophy—that of Intuition and of Experience and Association—lies at the foundation of all the greatest differences of practical opinion in our age of progress."—*Ib.* p. 273.

Certain persons "addict themselves with intolerant zeal to those forms of philosophy in which intuition usurps the place of evidence, and internal feeling is made the test of objective truth."—"Essays on Religion," p. 72.

They consider that the strongest and most irresistible proof of the Phenomenistic tenet is to be found in the marvels wrought by inductive science. " Inductive science," they say, "has achieved its incredible successes precisely by its stern rejection of all first premisses except experienced facts." Now, Dr. Bain (" Deductive Logic," p. 273) points out what is very obvious, viz. that "the guarantee, the ultimate * major premiss of all induction," is "nature's uniformity." And we are now going to argue that this first premiss of all induction, the premiss, without which no experienced fact can have the slightest scientific value —that this premiss is itself quite incapable of being proved on the exclusive basis of experienced facts. But, if this our thesis be established, it follows that "the stern rejection of all first premisses except experienced facts" not only is not the characteristic of inductive science, but on the contrary would be the absolute destruction of that science. We proceed at once to develop this argument.

What do Dr. Bain and his sympathizers understand by the phrase " nature's uniformity " ? They mean (1) that no phenomenon ever takes place without a corresponding phenomenal antecedent; and (2) that any given phenomenal antecedent is invariably and unconditionally followed by the same phenomenal consequent. It is their own emphatic statement that the uniformity of nature, understood in this precise sense, is absolutely essential as a foundation for inductive science. Suppose it were possible, *e.g.*, that I should compose a substance to-day of certain materials, and find it by experience to be combustible; while I might compose another to-morrow of the very same materials, united in the very same way, in the very same proportions, and by experience find the composition *in*combustible. If such a case were possible, argues the Phenomenist, the whole foundation of inductive science would be taken from under

* Should not this word rather be "primary"?

my feet.* Belief, then, in the uniformity of nature is admitted by Phenomenists themselves to be an absolutely essential condition, for the prosecution of inductive science.

The first question, then, we ask them is, by what right they *assume* this fact of nature's uniformity? How can they prove, unless they admit intuitive premisses, that phenomena throughout the universe do proceed with that undeviating regularity which their science requires? Mr. Stuart Mill, in controversy with ourselves, professed to give such a proof as we challenged; but his argument was so flimsy, that we had difficulty in believing him really to have given his mind to the subject. Dr. Bain, on the contrary, frankly admits that no such argument is forthcoming; and that the fact of nature's uniformity must be taken for granted without any proof whatever. (See his "Deductive Logic," p. 273.) "We can give no reason or evidence," he says, " for this uniformity." For our own part, however, we are disposed to admit that the *present* uniformity of phenomenal sequence may be

* We do not ourselves admit that the uniformity of nature is by any means so complete as Phenomenists consider. Their statement, indeed, as it stands, is directly anti-religious; it denies the existence of Freewill and of miracles, and it virtually denies also the efficacy of prayer, whether offered for temporal blessings, or for strength against temptation, or for progress in virtue. We set forth at sufficient length what we here mean, in our essay on "Science, Prayer, Freewill, and Miracles." In that essay—while we protest vigorously against any such sweeping proposition concerning the extent of nature's uniformity as Phenomenists love to set forth—we entirely admit, nevertheless, and maintain, that there does exist a certain very extensive uniformity throughout the phenomenal world. We consider, indeed, that both Freewill and Miracles constitute a very large exception to that uniformity; and we consider also that God is ever premoving and stimulating the natural action of natural forces in the direction marked out by His Providence. But a very large area of uniformity still remains, and one, we maintain, which amply suffices as a basis of solid induction.

In our present essay, our argument does not require that we dwell at greater length on this particular divergence between Phenomenists and ourselves: and we shall accept, therefore, for argument's sake and without further protest, their understanding of the term "nature's uniformity."

inferred from experienced facts—not indeed with certainty, but with very considerable probability. Inductive science proceeds on this basis; and in these modern centuries its fecundity has been marvellous indeed. The supposition is certainly improbable in a very high degree, that investigations, proceeding on a thoroughly false basis, can have issued in so vast a multitude of entirely unexpected, yet experimentally verified, conclusions. The incredibly rapid progress, then, of inductive science has endued with a rapidly increasing degree of probability the fundamental principle on which that science rests—viz. the uniformity of phenomenal sequence. We should, indeed, confidently maintain that even such an argument as we have here given possesses no real validity, except by the help of this or that implicit intuition, which men unconsciously and irresistibly assume as genuine. This, however, is a question on which we shall not now insist, because we wish here to content ourselves with the broadest and most palpable considerations. We will willingly admit, therefore, for argument's sake, that the modern progress of inductive science has enabled the Phenomenist, consistently with his own principles, to regard the *present* uniformity of nature as sufficiently established.

But now it is manifest on the surface that these grounds of probability, whatever their value, apply exclusively to what may be called *the scientific epoch*. Go back three thousand years, not to speak of an indefinitely more recent period, there was no assemblage of facts, discovered by careful processes of induction; nor any persistent exploration of nature. Phenomenists declare that they will accept no conclusion unless it be rigidly deduced from experienced facts. What facts in the world are there to which they can point as premisses for the conclusion that uniform phenomenal sequence existed three thousand years ago? If *experienced facts* were all the premisses on which the argument could reasonably proceed, there is hardly so much as a preponderance of probability for the conclusion that nature's uniformity existed then as it exists now. Assuredly, the notion of there being any approximation to *certainty* on the matter is absolutely childish. Yet Phenomenists, in their whole argumentation concerning creation, evolution, and similar themes, invariably assume, as a matter of course, that the laws of nature proceeded during thousands, not to say millions, of years ago, with the same regularity and uniformity with which they proceed now. Was there ever poorer and more paltry child's play than this? Let it be carefully observed that we are not here attempting any inquiry whatever, direct or indirect, how far *intuitive* premisses may be producible, which shall suffice for establishing the past uniformity of nature: we are but criticizing these repudiators of intuition, these devotees of experienced facts. And it is really too absurd when one finds them ridiculing with lofty contempt the dogma, *e.g.*, of creation, and resting their criticism on no stronger basis than their extravagant assumption—extravagant, that is, on *their* principles—concerning the laws of nature in time past. In fact, their argument is exactly like what is uncomplimentarily called a lady's reason: "It is because it is." "We hold firmly that creation never took place." "Why?" "Because the laws of nature always existed." "On what ground do you hold that these laws always existed?" "Because otherwise it might be necessary to admit the dogma of creation."

And if, on Phenomenistic principles, there is such very slender probability for the statement that nature proceeded uniformly throughout time past, what shall we say of the statement that nature will proceed uniformly in time *future?* Yet, as Dr. Bain himself observes, "all our interest is concentrated on what is yet to be: the present and past are of no value, except only as a clue to the events that are to come" ("Deductive Logic," p. 273). The processes of induction lose their whole practical use, unless there be assurance that the laws of nature will be hereafter the same which they now are. But to say, as the Phenomenist must consistently say, that *experienced facts* can afford assurance for this, is simply a contradiction in terms. Experienced facts belong to the past or present. And it is self-contradictory to say that any inference can be drawn from them in regard to the *future*, except by help of some premiss alleged to be intuitive; as, *e.g.*, "the future will resemble the past;" or, as Dr. Bain more accurately words it, "What has uniformly been in the past will be in the future." "This assumption," Dr. Bain proceeds ("Deductive Logic," p. 274), "is an ample justification of the inductive operation: without it we can do nothing; with it we can do everything. Our only error is in proposing to give any reason or justification of it; to treat it otherwise than as *begged* at the very outset." Is Saul, then, also among the prophets? Is Dr. Bain at last an Intuitionist? For as to this "assumption" of which he speaks, what is it at last but precisely what we have called an alleged "truth of intuition"? Manifestly, if inductive science cannot reasonably be constructed except on the basis of this "assumption," it cannot reasonably be constructed at all on the exclusive basis of experienced facts.

Here, therefore, we will revert to what we just now said. The stern rejection, we said, of all first premisses except experienced facts, not only is not a characteristic of inductive science, but would be the destruction of that science. Take Dr. Bain's thesis that "the future will resemble the past." It would, of course, be an unspeakable absurdity to say that this is an experienced fact. But neither can any experienced facts be alleged which in any combination will suffice by themselves logically to *prove* this thesis, or even to make it ever so faintly probable. A science, then, which should be based exclusively on experienced facts would not throw one glimmering of light on the future. It might show that, *at this moment*, such or such a medicine is a remedy for such a disease; such or such a chemical combination issues in such or such a result; such or such an arch bears such or such a weight, etc. But it would throw absolutely no light whatever on the question whether such statements will be even proximately correct, a day or an hour beyond this moment. Dr. Bain points out very truly that such a science would be absolutely valueless. What we are ourselves saying is that, at all events, it would be fundamentally different from what is now called "inductive science." That which is now called "inductive science" would be utterly overthrown and subverted, if its votaries rejected all first premisses except experienced facts.

We have argued that, if no first premisses were admissible except experienced facts, two grave consequences would inevitably ensue. Firstly, man could have neither certain nor even probable information concerning nature's uniformity in times long past; nor, secondly, could he form so much as any reasonable conjecture of the kind concerning even the most immediate future. Here, however, a further question will most reasonably be asked. Let intuitive premisses be admitted no less than phenomenal—in other words, let true, and not false, philosophical principles be assumed—what will *then* be ascertained as sound doctrine in regard to man's extent of knowledge concerning past and future phenomenal uniformity? We merely indicate this question to show that we have not forgotten its reasonableness. Plainly it is quite irrelevant to our own argument; and we really do not happen to be acquainted with any writer who, to our mind, fairly confronts it. Its consideration is one of the various philosophical lacunæ—much more numerous, we think, than might have been expected—which arrest the course of a straightforward student, and dissatisfy him with existent philosophical treatises.

So much, then, on that one foundation of inductive science—of the science which Phenomenists specially claim as their own—the doctrine of phenomenal uniformity. But all this is really as nothing compared with the further objection to Phenomenism, which we have pressed on many former occasions, and to which we have never received a reply even superficially plausible. Every man, throughout every minute of his waking life, is eliciting one or other of those intuitive acts which are called acts of *memory*. If he accept these acts as testifying objective truth, he is *ipso facto* an Intuitionist and no Phenomenist. If he do not so accept them, his knowledge is below that of the very brutes, being strictly confined to his consciousness of the present moment.* Let us explain our meaning in this statement.

The Phenomenist purports to build his whole philosophical structure on "experienced facts;" and he must mean, of course, facts which he *knows* to have been experienced. We ask him how he can possibly know that there is any given fact in the whole world which has been experienced by any one whomsoever. Most certainly he does not know more as to what *others* have experienced than of what he has experienced *himself*. We ask him, then, straightforwardly, how can you possibly know, concerning any given mental phenomenon in the whole world, that you have once experienced it? You reply that you have the clearest and most articulate memory thereof. Well, we do not doubt at all that you have that present *impression* which you call a most clear and articulate memory. But how do you know—how can you legitimately

---

* We have here often made an explanation, which it may be better to make again. Those avouchments of memory, to which we refer in the text, are those only which concern a man's *quite recent* experience—the memory of a minute or a few minutes back. A man's memory of what took place a long time ago is often far from infallible.

even guess—that your present impression corresponds with a past fact? See what a tremendous proposition this is which you, who call yourself a cautious man of science, unscrupulously take for granted. You have been so wonderfully endowed—such is your prodigious assertion—that in every successive case your clear and articulate present *impression* and *belief* of something as past corresponds with a past mental *fact*. That this should happen even once is surely, on Phenomenistic principles, a very remarkable coincidence; but you assume, as a matter of course—without so much as any attempt at proof—that this marvellous fact occurs some thousand times in every hour of your waking life. What is the true *rationale* of your proceeding? There is but one answer which can possibly be given. You are acting like a reasonable man, *i.e.* like an Intuitionist. You accept your intuitive act of memory as an infallible voucher for your firm conviction, that certain experiences have befallen you in time past which are entirely external to your present consciousness.

Had space permitted, we might with advantage have recapitulated a much larger portion of our earlier controversies against Phenomenism; but we must proceed, without further delay, to point our moral. Mr. Stuart Mill complains that the opposite school alleges certain tenets as self-evident; "erects them into their own absolutely sufficient vouchers and justifications; and uses them for the purpose of consecrating all deep-seated prejudices." Now, a truth which is "its own absolutely sufficient voucher and justification," is precisely what we call a truth of intuition; and we have admitted throughout that, without the assumption of intuitive premisses, Theism cannot be argumentatively established. But, as we have now been arguing, Theism is not the *only* important doctrine so circumstanced. On the contrary, there is absolutely no doctrine, existent or conceivable, which *can* be established without the help of intuitive premisses; nay, if men do not avail themselves of such premisses, their knowledge will be below that of the very brutes. Whatever else, therefore, may or may not be true, the Phenomenist's position, at all events, is a suicidal absurdity.

Of course, an Antitheist, having become an Intuitionist, may most reasonably raise a further question. He may maintain that, whereas the intuitions alleged by him are genuine, those alleged by his opponents are spurious. In our future essays we shall have to join issue on this indictment, as regards each successive tenet, which we shall allege as intuitive. We may as well, however, point out at once that our opponent will here have an uncommonly difficult part to play. "It is an undoubtedly valid intuition," he will have to say, "which declares that the uniformity of nature dates back, say, six thousand years. It is an undoubtedly valid intuition which declares that the said uniformity will continue in the future for quite an indefinite period. It is an undoubtedly valid intuition which declares in each successive case that my feelings of five minutes ago were what my memory now declares them to have been. But it is no valid intuition which declares that $2 + 5$ necessarily equals $3 + 4$; or that to slander my neighbour is necessarily wrong." Here is surely a startling and paradoxical position, if ever such there were. Still, all this is external to our immediate theme. What we are now urging is this. The proposition maintained by Mr. Mill and his school that there are *no* genuine intuitions, no truths external to present experience, "which are their own sufficient vouchers and justifications"—this proposition, at all events, is out of court. It is a proposition clamorously repudiated by the common sense and clear insight of mankind: it expresses a theory which may now fairly be relegated to the limbo of exploded philosophical absurdities.

It will be asked, If the characteristic tenet of Phenomenism is so entirely destitute of philosophical foundation, how can it have happened that so many men of such undoubted, and in many cases most conspicuous, ability have prevailed on themselves to accept it? Still more, how is it that they have conceived so great an antipathy to Theism? This question leads us to what we proposed at starting as the second theme to be discussed in our present essay. There are, no doubt, very many successful labourers in the field of physical science, who exhibit a violent antipathy to the kind of reasoning adopted for the establishment of Theistic doctrine, and a still more intense antipathy to that doctrine itself. It is our business, then, here to account for this antipathy. We will begin with the former, the antipathy exhibited by Phenomenists to Theistic *reasoning*. And we will preface our remarks by drawing attention to the truly marvellous results which physical science has achieved in these late centuries. Lord Macaulay has vigorously depicted this fact in a well-known passage, which we may as well quote:—

The new Philosophy has lengthened life; it has mitigated pain; it has extinguished diseases; it has increased the fertility of the soil; it has given new securities to the mariner; it has furnished new arms to the warrior; it has spanned great rivers and estuaries with bridges of form unknown to our fathers; it has guided the thunderbolt innocuously from heaven to earth; it has lighted up the night with the splendour of the day; it has extended the range of the human vision; it has multiplied the power of the human muscles; it has accelerated motion; it has annihilated distance; it has facilitated intercourse, correspondence, all friendly offices, all despatch of business; it has enabled men to descend to the depths of the sea, to soar into the air, to penetrate securely into the noxious recesses of the earth, to traverse the land in cars which whirl along without horses, and the ocean in ships which run ten knots an hour against the wind. These are but a part of its fruits, and of its firstfruits. For it is a philosophy which never rests, which has never attained, which is never perfect. Its law is progress. A point which yesterday was invisible is its goal to-day, and will be its starting-point to-morrow. (" Essay on Lord Bacon.")

We cannot be surprised that any one who fixes his keen interest and attention on studies which have issued in results like these, still less one who is himself occupied in relevant physical investigations, should become, as it were, intoxicated under such an influence. We cannot be surprised at his assuming, as a matter of course, that it is experimental methods, and no others, which can afford solid foundation of argument for important truth. No doubt, as we have been pointing out above, the whole cogency of a physicist's argument in each successive case rests in last analysis on intuitive premisses; and without the assumption of such premisses, his experiments would be entirely valueless. Still, what his mind incessantly dwells on are not such premisses as these; on the contrary, he entirely forgets them, or would even, on occasion, deny their existence. When, therefore, he hears of propositions the most extensive, being predominantly proved by intuitive assumptions—unless he is an unusually large-minded and dispassionate man—he is tempted to regard such a method of reasoning with angry contempt. His life is mainly occupied with such arguments as those, *e.g.*, which establish that diamonds are combustible, or that oil and alkali taken in combination produce a soap. Let us suppose, then, that such an argument is placed before him as that on which we have insisted, and which occupies so prominent a place in Theistic advocacy. "Whatever is known to me," we said, "as intrinsically and necessarily wrong, is also known to me intuitively as necessarily forbidden by some Superior Being, who possesses over me rightful jurisdiction." This proposition, if true, is manifestly one of insurpassable importance; and our scientist asks us for its ground. We have, of course, nothing to reply, except that mental phenomena, if studied carefully and with prolonged attention, show the genuineness of this alleged intuition. Such a method of argument is one with which his own studies bring him into no sort of contact; and, again, it is one the validity of which is incapable of being tested in this world by any subsequent verification—such verification, *e.g.*, as attends his researches concerning the combustibleness of a diamond or the composition of oil and alkali. For his own part, then, he could as readily believe, with the astrologers, that by studying the course of the stars one may obtain knowledge of future human events, as he could believe that by merely studying the human mind one can acquire knowledge of a Superhuman Being. His reasoning is, of course, poor and shallow enough, but it is surely very natural in any scientist who has not been carefully trained in different principles, unless, as we have said, he is unusually large-minded and dispassionate. Consequently (which is our immediate point), the fact that certain most brilliant and successful explorers of external nature deride the intuitional method as unsubstantial and even childish, constitutes no kind of presumption that this method may not, nevertheless, be, as we have shown that it is, the only possible foundation of human knowledge.

Lord Macaulay, in the article from which we have just quoted, unintentionally, but effectively, confirms our reasoning. His own sympathies with physical science have quite incapacitated him for appreciating any less superficially tangible course of speculation. In most manifest sympathy with Bacon, he points out that the English philosopher "did not consider Socrates' philosophy a happy event." He adds on his own account that Socrates, Plato, Aristotle, and the rest cultivated an "unfruitful wisdom;" "systematically misdirected their powers;" "added nothing to the stock of knowledge;" gathered in no other "garners" than of "smut and stubble." As to the great Christian thinkers—S. Augustine, S. Thomas, and the rest—he does not even condescend in this connection to hint at their existence. We suppose Lord Macaulay's warmest admirers cannot read, without a blush of shame, various parts of the paper which we are criticizing. Still, our point remains untouched. If so accomplished a writer, and one so versed in human affairs, could—even in some chance moment of excitement or aberration—have expressed such sentiments as these, how much more easily credible it is that the exclusive votaries of physical science may be guilty of the like perverse and shallow injustice, towards a line of thought essentially differing from their own.

Here an ingenious objection may perhaps be started, which shall take the shape of an argument *ad hominem*. We cannot ourselves deny, so some opponent of ours may suggest, that God desires the cultivation of physical science. How, then, can we maintain, he may proceed to ask, that such cultivation tends to the overthrow of religious belief, and to the establishment of secularism on its ruins ? In reply, we heartily concede that God desires the cultivation of physical science, but we do not for a moment admit that the sedulous cultivation of such science has of itself an irreligious tendency. The evil effect which we deplore arises from the fact that physical science is cultivated by a large number of persons who have not been previously trained in the general elements of religious philosophy. Cardinal Newman's noble work on "The Idea of a University" is fruitful in dissertation on this theme. He descants on the grievous calamity which befalls mankind so far as at any given time or place the various branches of knowledge are exclusively pursued, each on its own special ground, and are thus deprived of the safeguard afforded to each one by combination with other portions of the scientific cyclopædia. In a wisely conducted Christian university the danger on which we are commenting would be entirely removed, while there would be at the same time abundant scope for the most diligent investigations in the sphere of physical science. Indeed, true as it is that the pursuit of physical science urgently needs the corrective afforded by science metaphysical and religious, it is no less true, we strongly think, that metaphysical and religious science derive greater advantage from the contemporaneous presence of physical. But this is a theme on which we have no space here to enlarge.

So much on the antipathy exhibited by Phenomenists towards the reasoning which a Theist draws out for his doctrine. Still more intense, as we have said, is their antipathy to that doctrine itself. This antipathy is founded on their own amazing notions concerning human life and human conduct; and we will therefore introduce our treatment of it by a short comment on those notions. I know intimately two persons, A and B. I have found A a man of spotless integrity; remarkable for steady self-command; strictly just to all with whom he has dealings; carefully considerate to his dependants; discriminatingly and most abundantly generous to the necessitous; full of public spirit; exemplary in all his domestic relations.* I have found B, on the contrary, cowardly and self-indulgent; selfish in his family and indifferent to the public good; steering very near the wind on matters of common honesty and straightforwardness; evincing no sense of his own defects, nor making any effort to correct them. If I am a Phenomenist, I am compelled by my principles to recognize no other distinction between A and B than one entirely similar to the distinction which exists between an efficient

---

* We do not speak in the text of A's love and obedience towards Almighty God—which, of course, we account the highest crown of a virtuous life—because we are arguing with Antitheists.

and a rickety locomotive. The course of conduct pursued by A cannot, in any intelligible sense, be called by me "higher," "nobler," "more excellent," than that pursued by B. All which I can say is, that A's life is more *beneficial to mankind* than B's; just as an efficient locomotive is more beneficial to mankind than a rickety one. Then, secondly, even if A's conduct could be called higher and nobler than B's, still I could not award him any *praise* for it, because I hold that he has no Freewill, and that he is as simply, therefore, at the mercy of surrounding circumstances as is the locomotive with which we are comparing him. Now, it will throw light on the utter unnaturalness of Phenomenism if we proceed to point out that no Phenomenist on earth can possibly confront A and B as concrete persons —can come across them in the actual affairs of life—and so think of them as his principles require. He has, literally, no more physical power of withholding his respect from A, or his disrespect from B, than he has of jumping over a fence twenty feet high. Does he feel *respect*, then, for a serviceable locomotive ? Or does he feel *disrespect* for one which, by permitting itself to be blown up, inflicts fearful injury on human life ?

One might have fancied, on first thoughts, that such a crucial fact as this would disabuse him of his unnatural and revolting tenet. But every one knows how marvellous is the power possessed by a theorist of withholding attention from individual cases which militate against his theory. Let us fix our attention, then, on the theory of Phenomenists, and we shall cease to wonder at their detestation of Theism. They consider (1) that man knows not the existence of any life beyond the grave; (2) that no such quality exists as that which Intuitionists call "virtuousness," and which we have treated in two preceding essays; (3) that every man is as simply at the mercy of his circumstances, internal and external, as is a football of given composition when kicked about by players in a field. As regards, therefore, the standard of moral value in any given act, no other standard is to them even possible, except only the tendency of that act to promote earthly enjoyment. As regards the reasonable motive of human actions, no other motive, on their view, is consistent with common sense, except that each man try to grasp for himself all the earthly enjoyment he can. As regards education, they must account any attempt to train some given youth by means of *praise* or *blame* a dishonest " pious fraud ; " nor have they any other resource, except to do their utmost that he be taught to find his own pleasure in what most promotes the earthly enjoyment of his fellow-men. The furtherance of earthly enjoyment in each and in all—this is that ethical end which alone is consistent with their theory; and their whole mind is saturated with the thought of it. Moreover, men's earthly enjoyment is the one purpose to which their favourite processes of inductive science are directed.

In this state of mind they turn their thoughts to Theism. Now, as M. Ollé-Laprune points out in the treatise to which we shall presently draw attention, genuine Theism is vitally connected with certain other doctrines also. Full Theistic belief includes, not only belief in God's Existence, but also in Freewill; in the necessary character of Ethical Truth; and in the Soul's Immortality. The genuine Theist, then, regards this world mainly and predominantly as a place of probation. With him the real and true interests of life are almost entirely concentrated on that which follows after death; the present brief period of existence having in his eyes little other value except as regards its bearing on the life to come. On the other hand, he accounts that bearing so close that no words can exaggerate the intimacy of its connection ; and Freewill, as he views the matter, is granted by God to men in order that, by patient continuance of well-doing, they may avoid future woe and reap future reward. Now, we do not, of course, mean that the great mass of Theists act with steady consistency on this doctrine: of enormous numbers, one does not see how it can be said that they act on it at all. Still, the four Theistic doctrines which we mentioned above, when taken together, *mean* what we have just said, or they mean nothing whatever. It is not merely the Catholic who regards them as having this full significance; though, of course, we are most ready to admit, or rather most earnest to maintain, that nowhere else is genuine Theism so purely exhibited as within the Catholic Church. But, as one instance out of a thousand, take, *e.g.*, the Rev. Dr. Martineau, a preacher, who is, alas! very widely indeed removed from Catholic Dogma. His truly admirable volumes called "Hours of Thought" inculcate a standard of human action not one whit below what we have just set forth.

Now, the more extreme and fanatical of the Phenomenistic Antitheists protest with excitement, and with a kind of fury, in the name of "suffering humanity," against such a view as this. "This life," they say, "is the only term of existence which we have any reason whatever to expect. And is this brief period of man's enjoyment to be poisoned and changed into a time of self-torture by the fantastical dream of an imaginary hereafter?* Humanity

* We must not be understood to admit for a moment what Antitheists here imply—to admit for a moment that religiousness is ordinarily adverse to earthly happiness. No doubt there is many an irreligious man far happier than many a pious man; so great is the power of temperament, and, again, of external circumstances. But we are confident that, in all ordinary cases, the same man, under the same external environment, is happier in proportion as he is more pious. At the same time, we admit that there are certain saintly souls whom God visits on earth with exceptional tribulation in order that their probation may be nobler and their future crown brighter.

On the other hand, let it be remembered how keen an anguish is inflicted on many minds by the notion that man has no knowledge of a life beyond the grave.

forbid! Let us eat and drink, for to-morrow we die. Those who promote such theories concerning the obligation of present obedience to a Deity and the ever-impending peril of future woe, are simply odious conspirators against the happiness of mankind."

In truth there are a certain number of violent thinkers who cleave to the "great cause" of man's earthly enjoyment with a fanaticism as heated and blind as any class of religionists ever exhibited towards the specialties of their sect. Of such men it is hardly to be expected, without a kind of miracle, that the most cogent adverse reasoning imaginable shall produce on them its due effect. Still, it is by no means all Antitheists who are so inaccessible to argument: on the contrary, many are fully convinced, indeed, of their own tenets, but without being so simply intolerant and contemptuous towards opponents. Then there are, perhaps, not a few who, while they are strongly impressed with the force of Antitheistic reasoning and find great difficulty in reconciling religion with their scientific convictions, shrink, nevertheless, from definitively taking their place in the irreligious camp, owing to their dread of the tremendous moral and social evils which would result from rejection of God.* Lastly, there are many who have ever been Theists and earnestly desire so to remain, who, nevertheless, for the sake of their own future security, wish to understand how the prevalent Antitheistic arguments can be met. Here, then, is a rough classification of those thinkers to whom our course of reasoning in future essays will be directly addressed.

* So a writer—manifestly himself an unbeliever—in the *Pall Mall Gazette* of Sept. 21, 1881. He says, "Faith in the supernatural has a wonderful power of adapting itself to scientifically established facts. Already the hesitations and admissions of those who have pushed scientific conclusions to the fullest, and the speculations of other men of science about the 'Unseen Universe,' might convince the most timid that the world has not seen the last of religion."

Of course, at this time of day we do not profess to have unearthed any novel arguments in defence of Theism: such a profession would be absurd enough. But there is a philosophical work of extreme importance which urgently needs being done. It is urgently needful that the recognized Theistic arguments be exhibited in such a shape, that their indubitable cogency shall be capable of being made immediately manifest to the particular thinkers whom we have in view. And, again, it is hardly less necessary that a philosophical method be brought before their attention, which, on one hand, shall commend itself to them as plainly reasonable; while, on the other hand, it may afford them the greatest attainable protection against their own reckless impetuosity. Such, and no less, is the task which we are venturing to undertake. We cannot hope, indeed, that we shall even approximately "rise to the height of our great argument:" on the contrary, no one feels more keenly than ourselves the incompleteness and manifold imperfection of what we do. But we hope, nevertheless, that we shall be able to submit suggestions of real importance, which more competent artificers may substantially accept and more successfully develop.

And there is another cognate task which naturally falls within the same scope. It would be a most serious mistake to suppose that the atheistic current of the day flows only among men of cultivated and scientific minds: though, even were this so, the calamity would hardly be less in regard to the future prospects of man. But, in truth, the uneducated class is already, to no very small extent, more or less imbued with the poison. On this head we will give a short extract or two from a very powerful article which appeared in the *Month* as far back as September, 1874:—

> The spread of infidelity [says the writer] among a large part of the generation now entering, or having entered, upon the full enjoyment and use of life, has reached the line at which

even morality becomes a sentiment rather than a law; conscience a phenomenon, rather than the voice of God sitting in judgment; Free Will and responsibility an imagination; the universe a physical system, self-evoked and self-regulated; the soul of man a mechanism; the future of man a blank; sin, original and actual, a fiction; the Atonement an impossible superstition. . . .

The advance of infidelity among the lower classes in our towns, the extreme activity with which the poison is spread in books, cheap newspapers, by lectures and the like, and the measures by which this activity should be met on the side of all who are for religion and for God, should be subjects of earnest thought and meditation.

The writer proceeds with more to the same effect, on the growing prevalence of irreligious tenets among the uneducated class. Now, of course, our argument will not bring us into contact with considerations of a practical and quasi-political kind, however deeply important, such, *e.g.*, as the organization of good educational schemes. But we do hope to speak in due course on relevant questions, within what may be called the internal and personal sphere; so far, at least, as they concern the verities of Natural Religion. I come across some uncultured person whom I find profoundly imbued with the fashionable infidelity. What course of thought and action can I recommend to him, which, on one hand, he will see to be reasonable, and in some sense obligatory; while, on the other hand, it will supply him with valid grounds for accepting Religious Truth? This question has a close relation with the general line of argument which we propose to ourselves; and we must not fail to bear it carefully in mind.

We do not happen to know any other living writer who can so serviceably assist us in our anxious enterprise as M. Ollé-Laprune.* He is a thinker, deeply penetrated with

* "De la Certitude Morale," par Léon Ollé-Laprune. Paris: Eugène Belin. 1880.

Catholic Truth; he has made philosophy, both ancient and modern, his special study; he has carefully, discriminatingly, and appreciatively examined the various phases of Antitheism; he never once transgresses the laws of courtesy and self-restraint; and, above all, he writes consistently in that tone of earnest piety which alone befits his most sacred theme. We do not, however, profess here either to follow his order of arrangement or to analyze the general course of his work. Our space will not permit this. We must pursue our own independent line of thought, and content ourselves with such extracts from M. Laprune as shall serve to illustrate it. We should add, however, that our own line of thought has been in many respects much influenced by his.

We begin with expressly commemorating one important work which he has done, to which, indeed, we have already referred. We mentioned four cognate doctrines, as jointly constituting the Creed of a genuine Theist. They are (1) the necessary character of Ethical Truth; (2) Freewill; (3) the Existence of God; (4) a Future Life of Reward or Punishment. M. Laprune, as far as we know, has been the first philosopher distinctly to insist on the fact that these four doctrines have the closest philosophical union; that in practice, under the circumstances of the present day, they stand or fall together; that the proof of each one adds indefinite force to the proof of all the rest. On the other hand, he still more emphatically urges (we are convinced, with great truth) that these four doctrines stand out in characteristic separation, as regards their rational treatment, from any other subject of investigation whatever.* He calls the complex of these four doctrines by the name "Moral Doctrine;" but, for reasons which will

---

* The exact meaning of this statement will presently appear. It does not ever so distantly imply that these doctrines are proved with less absolute certainty than others.

appear in due course, we prefer the name "Religious Doctrine." The term "Religious Doctrine," then, for the purposes of our present argument, we use as precisely signifying the complex of the four doctrines above mentioned; for we are prescinding entirely from Revelation and from the supernatural order. By the term "Theism" we designate that particular and central doctrine of the four—God's Existence. But we shall not preclude ourselves from continuing to use the term "genuine Theism," as expressing the *whole body* of "Religious Doctrine."

Before we enter on any argument, it will greatly conduce to clearness if we explain in one or two details the conclusions which we are in due course to advocate. And, firstly, we shall maintain, with M. Laprune and the general body of Christian philosophers, that the whole assemblage of "Religious Doctrine" admits of absolutely conclusive scientific establishment. We mean this—An explicit train of argument admits of being exhibited, resting on given truths of intuition and on given experienced facts as on its primary premisses. And in regard specially to these "truths of intuition," a course of psychological investigation is producible, which proves with certainty that they are really what they claim to be. Such train of argument, we add, is sufficient entirely to convince any reasonable and intellectually competent person—however adverse his original prepossessions—who shall choose to fix his mind on it, to study it with patient candour and with a sustained struggle of attention. Indeed, if this were not so, the profession of philosophical argument would be unmeaning. How far, indeed, it is probable that existent Antitheists will in fact *exercise* this patient candour and sustained struggle of attention—here is a different inquiry altogether, but one on which we shall in due course have something to add.

But we shall not be misunderstood, then, as in any way

disparaging the absolute conclusiveness of the philosophical argument, when we proceed to say that, according to God's merciful design, argument was not to have constituted any part of the original ground on which religious belief reposes.* Our readers must remember that we are not at this moment professing to *reason*, but merely to exhibit certain conclusions for which in due course we shall *give* our reasons. And what we hold on the present subject is this—Whenever men are obliged to *depend* on argument for their religious belief, this can only be because, whether or no through their own fault, they have failed to embrace and appropriate those more solid and penetrating proofs of Religious doctrine which God has offered in an implicit shape to mankind in general. This truth is so vitally important in its whole bearing on the Theistic controversy, that we must not fail to place before our readers in connection with it a most pregnant and beautiful passage of F. Kleutgen's. The passage is very long, but we are confident that no reader will find it tedious. We will but premise two brief remarks. Firstly, F. Kleutgen, is directly speaking of Theism proper; but his view of things will evidently apply no less to the whole of what we have called "Religious Doctrine." Secondly, the author implies throughout that there can be no invincible ignorance of God.† On this matter, however, we wish carefully to abstain from all expression of opinion, until we reach that part of our course in which it will be expressly and fully treated.

* Reasoning may be "explicit" or "implicit." It is explicit reasoning which we call "argument." This is, we think, the common usage; certainly it is Cardinal Newman's.

† The Editor thinks it right to mention in this connection that the author did not latterly hold with any confidence that circumstances might not exist under which ignorance of God would be invincible. He had at one time considered the theological authority against such a possibility so strong as to be conclusive. But more extensive reading led him to hold the more lenient opinion to which, as a matter of private judgment, he had ever inclined.—ED.

These, then, are F. Kleutgen's words:—

In many places Scripture declares, in the most express manner, that even for those to whom God has not manifested Himself by His Prophets or by His Son, there exists a revelation of God in His works, and even within the mind of men, whereby they can without any difficulty cognize God, their Creator and Maker, as well as His sovereign law. It is not necessary to point out that Scripture does not in this speak of any [supposable] first cause, but of the Living and True God, Who has created heaven and earth, and inscribed His law in the heart of man; and that, consequently, it speaks also of the moral order. Now, it says in the same passages that men who do not thus cognize their God are without excuse; that they are insensate; that they deserve God's wrath and all His chastisements. It necessarily follows, then, that this manifestation of God by His works is such, that man cannot fail by this means to cognize God with certitude, unless he commit a grave fault.

Assuredly this does not mean that it is philosophical researches, continued laboriously through obstacles and doubts, which can alone lead to knowledge of God. Very few men, in fact, are capable of these laborious researches: whereas Scripture speaks of all the heathens in general; and in the Book of Wisdom it is said expressly (xiii. 1), "All men are vanity who do not possess the knowledge of God." The sacred writer even adds that this knowledge, to which he gives the name of "sight" to express its clearness and certitude ["cognoscibiliter poterit Creator horum videri," v. 5], can be obtained with as much ease (and even more) as knowledge of this world; which certainly does not fail any one capable of the least reflection. ["Si tantum potuerunt scire ut possent æstimare sæculum, Quomodo hujus Dominum non facilius invenerunt," v. 9]. . . . It is easier, therefore, to know God, the Governor of the world, than to know enough of nature to admire its power and its beauty.

It necessarily follows, therefore, that there is a knowledge of God different from philosophical knowledge; a knowledge so easy to acquire and so certain, that ignorance and doubt on that head cannot be explained, except either by culpable carelessness or proud obstinacy. Such is also . . . the common doctrine of the Holy Fathers: they distinguish that knowledge of God which is obtained by philosophical research, from that which springs up spontaneously in every man at the very sight of creation. This latter kind of knowledge is called by them "a witness of Himself," which God gave to the soul at its creation; "an endowment of nature;" "an infused knowledge," inherent in every man without preliminary instruction; a knowledge which springs up in some sense of itself, in proportion as reason is developed; and which cannot fail, except in a man either deprived of the use of reason or else given up to vices which have corrupted his nature. And when the Fathers of the Church declare unanimously on this head that this knowledge is really found and established in all men, the importance of their testimony is better understood by remembering that they lived in the midst of heathen populations.

God has implanted in our reasonable nature everything which is necessary, that we may know Him, and know Him with facility. Now, He does not, after creation, withdraw Himself from creatures, but always remains near them; cooperating with them, exciting them to act, supporting and directing each one to its end conformably to its nature. If this is true of all creatures, how could this concurrence be refused to the most noble of all creatures, to those whom God has created for the very purpose of their knowing and loving Him? Man, indeed, does not arrive at his end, except by using the powers which God has given him; but the author of those gifts lends to man His concurrence, in order that he may make due use of them. Since that moral and religious life for which man was created is founded on a knowledge of the truths whereof we speak, God watches over man, in order that reason, as it is developed, may come to know them with facility and certainty. Observe, the question here is not of supernatural grace, but is [of the natural order]. . . .

What would not be the misery of man [if there were no reasonable certainty without philosophical argument]? It is easy to show those [ordinary] men who are capable of any reflection at all, that their knowledge of the truth is not scientific; that they do not deduce it [reflectively and explicitly] from the first principles of thought; and, consequently, they cannot defend it against the attacks of scepticism. If, then, as soon as we come to know that our knowledge is not scientific, the conviction of its truth were at once shaken—what, on that supposition, would be the lot of man? . . .

The fact is, indeed, not so: that consciousness which every one can interrogate within himself attests its denial; and at every period the voice of mankind has confirmed that denial. As soon as we arrive at the use of reason, the voice of conscience wakes within us; whether we choose or no, we must cognize the distinction between good and evil. [Again] just as it is absolutely impossible for us to doubt our own existence [in like manner], we are absolutely compelled to regard as real the external world; [to hold] that, further, there exists a Supreme Author of our being and of all other things; and that through Him there is a certain moral order. These also are truths which we cannot refuse to admit. No doubt we can do violence to ourselves in order to produce in ourselves the contrary persuasion, just as we may use efforts to regard the moral conscience itself as an illusion. But these efforts never succeed, or, at least, never succeed perfectly; and we feel ourselves even under an obligation of condemning the very attempt as immoral. The mind of man, in fact, is under the influence of truth, which has dominion over it, and which gives [man] certainty, even against his own wish. Truth manifests itself to our intelligence, and engenders therein the knowledge of its reality, even before we [explicitly] know what that truth is. Still, truth [I say] reigns over man and reveals itself to him— however great may be his resistance—as a sacred and sovereign authority, which commands him and summons him before its tribunal; and [standing] before that tribunal he is obliged to admit the immorality of even attempting to doubt. Just as he is bound to condemn the madness, I will not say of doubting, but of trying to doubt, the reality of the external world, so he is obliged to regard as an impiety [all] doubt of God's Existence and Providence. . . .

Nor can it be here objected that conscience, in the proper sense of the word, moral conscience, gives no certainty so long as its existence within us and its pronouncements are purely spontaneous. Of the conscience, more than of anything else, it may be said that it reveals to us its own truth; that it compels us to acknowledge an absolute good and a sovereign rule over our wills and actions, even though we know not its innermost nature, not only as really existing, but as an august and sacred power which is [in authority] over us. Whatever efforts man may make to overthrow and destroy his own intimate persuasion on the truthfulness of conscience, he will never succeed in doing so. Even though he seeks by every possible means to persuade himself that nothing obliges him to regard it as truthful, nevertheless he will always feel himself compelled to acknowledge its authority and even to condemn his own resistance to it.

It is true, indeed, that though conscience very often speaks against a man's inclinations [so loudly] as to confound, by its manifestation of its own truthfulness, all pride and all the sophistical dreams by which he might wish to stifle it,—still it does not *always* so speak and raise its voice, as to take from man the power of turning from it and refusing to listen. If he enters into himself and chooses to observe what passes within him, he will obtain that reflexive knowledge which, as we have said above, is required for actual certainty; he will know that he cannot prevent himself from acknowledging the truth of what the voice of conscience dictates. But it is in his power—if not always, at least often—to abstain from entering into himself and lending his ear to that voice. He has [often] the power of not hearing it, or of giving it so little attention that he withdraws himself from that influence which would make him certain. It is in this manner that, for a certain time at least, notwithstanding the habitual certainty * which nature gives him, he may remain undecided on the truthfulness of conscience. supposing that he has not yet acknowledged that truthfulness by philosophical reflection, or, again, that he does not seek to know it. But, even though we were not able to demonstrate by the intimate experience of every man that the doubt whereof we speak is contrary to the principles of morality, we ought, nevertheless, to be persuaded of that truth by the judgment of all mankind. Among civilized nations, in every time, the necessity of philosophical studies have been admitted, and those have been held in high esteem who devoted themselves thereto and who were regarded as sages. Nevertheless, though the nations, it is true, accepted at the hands of philosophers the solution of many questions, they have never ascribed to these men a decisive judgment on all truth without exception. As to those first truths on which all our convictions rest, humanity bears within itself the consciousness, or intimate persuasion, of knowing them with certainty. Philosophers may make these truths the subject of their speculations, but they are not allowed the right of pronouncing a definite judgment on these truths; and if their researches lead them to deny or doubt them, those

---

* By "habitual certainty," as he has explained just before, F. Kleutgen means to express the *proximate power* of actual certainty.

very persons who would otherwise be the disciples of these philosophers, rise up against them as judges and condemn them. Was there ever a nation which did not regard it as madness to doubt an external world? A nation which did not hold in horror a man so perverted as to acknowledge no truth superior to the senses, and reject all distinction between virtue and vice? Has not Atheism among all nations been accounted a crime? And, by the fact of seeing culpability in the denial of these truths, does not the world declare that they cannot possibly be unknown to men of goodwill? ("Philosophie Scolastique," nn. 226–232.)

F. Kleutgen, then, holds (1) that uncultured persons have full means of knowing with absolute certainty God's Existence; and (2) that God, by His Providence, watches over individuals one by one, impressing on their mind in due opportunity those implicit apprehensions and inferences which reasonably generate such certain knowledge. The same is Cardinal Franzelin's teaching ("De Deo," pp. 93–97). And it is this, add the same two great writers, which the Fathers mean when they unanimously assert that the knowledge of God is "divinely infused" into the human intellect.* And, for our part, we follow the late F. Dalgairns, in holding (see one of his *Contemporary Review* articles) that those proofs of God's Existence which are pressed by Him on man's attention in an implicit shape, are more subtle and profound, more penetrating, satisfying, and invigorating even than those which philosophical investigation brings to light.

In what follows our remarks are still primarily, but by no means exclusively, directed to Theism proper. Thinkers of every class will, we suppose, be ready to admit that, in all cases which need to be considered, belief in God's

* Cardinal Franzelin says that the knowledge of God is "common to all who have not quenched the light of reason" (p. 93); to all except those in whom "human nature is depraved" (p. 100). We do not, however, ourselves see how it *necessarily* follows, because some given person possesses the proximate power of cognizing God with certainty, that he sins gravely by not *exercising* that power.

Existence is accompanied by belief in the other three religious doctrines which we have named above. We proceed, then, to ask, of what kind are those proofs of Theism which are so salutarily impressed by God in an implicit shape on the human intellect? For our own part, we earnestly follow Cardinal Newman and F. Kleutgen, in assigning by far the principal place to those founded on man's moral nature and moral action. M. Laprune does the same. Nowhere have we happened to see so admirable an exposition as he has given, of that moral and educational training which implants a far deeper and more permanent conviction of Religious Doctrine than does any other possible method. We will give a quotation or two out of many which we should like to exhibit; only, in accordance with a previous remark, where M. Laprune uses the word "moral" we substitute "religious," and the italics are ours, not his :—

The transmission of [religious] truths cannot be effected at one stroke, by pure reasoning, coldly. They are communicated to the child by education; and if a man, entirely persuaded of their truth, wishes to imbue others with them, he must, in his turn, have recourse to persuasion. . . .

[In the matter of *instruction*] the child acquires the speculative knowledge which he needs by *a series of lessons* fitted to his intelligence. . . . Nothing of the kind takes place in *education*. This is a work *of every moment*, . . . it is the formation of the soul, a cultivation of the human being. . . . Nothing can be more various than its methods, or more elastic than its character: it accommodates itself to each need, to each circumstance; it adjusts itself to the thousand exigencies of man's living nature, and puts to its own use the thousand resources of that nature. Its work is to excite, direct, develop the conscience and the reason; and *preserve the moral atmosphere which is adapted to foster them*. In this labour—so incessant, delicate, difficult—its great art is to *obtain active co-operation from its recipient*. Its purpose is, not to act for him, but to *teach him to act for himself.* So we support and direct the infant, when we are teaching him to walk. . . . [Religious] education is an initiation; it advances by degrees, and addresses itself to the soul all round. . . . It labours to make [religious] truths grow into the very substance of the human being; to become the soul of his soul, and the life of his life (pp. 378–380).

Presently (p. 385) he quotes similar language from that illustrious philosopher, Maine de Biran.

It is necessary [for the securest and most certainly permanent conviction], that [religious] truths incorporate themselves in us and unintermittently penetrate us. There is a slow penetration of every day—an intro-susception of that truth which should be our guide throughout life—which effects that such truths become to our soul what sunlight is to our eyes, which enlightens us without our seeking it.

As we have already explained, we are not, indeed, here professing to *argue*; but we *are* professing to exhibit what we propose in due course to *maintain* by argument. We shall be asked, then, what we hold concerning the *reasonableness* of those religious convictions, which will be engendered by such a course of practical training as M. Laprune supposes ? As to their intensity and rootedness, there can be no second opinion: but how as to their *reasonableness?* On the one hand, we do not at all profess that an Antitheist will find reasonable ground for abandoning his error by merely contemplating that firmness of religious conviction which is generated in others by religious training. But, on the other hand, we shall maintain that, in the individual recipient of such training, the conviction thus acquired rests on entirely sufficient and conclusive grounds of reason. We should be inclined even to go farther, and to say that the Theism of those who lead consistently pious lives rests on firmer grounds of reason than does the Theism of any others whomsoever. We should add, indeed, that religious education may most possibly be very far less thorough-going and pervasive than that described by M. Laprune, and may yet be abundantly sufficient to generate reasonable certitude of Religious Truth.

It is this ethical argument, then, in favour of Theism, on which we lay our greatest stress. We hope in the next essay of our series to exhibit it scientifically, and to meet successively the various objections against it which Anti-theists will adduce. But there are other very powerful reasons also, which admit of being implicitly pressed by Almighty God on the human intellect as proof of His Existence. For instance, the principle of causation (see our essay thereon). This principle is deeply rooted in the minds of all adults : they have not so much as the power of gazing on this invisible world without cognizing that it must have some Self-Existent Being as its Author.* Further, the argument from design—the "teleological" argument, as it is now called—is one which appeals with extreme force to the uneducated; and we may add that recent scientific investigations have, we believe, strengthened rather than weakened its force. So also the analogous argument derived from the *order* of the universe. Then, again, there are various truths which are irresistibly borne in on the mind by contemplation of *beauty*. This may be called, perhaps, the "æsthetic" argument. Many minds, even otherwise uncultured, vaguely, but keenly, discern most precious realities through the veil of external beauty.

There are other arguments for Theism which we have not included in this catalogue, as they are not within the reach of uncultured men. Such is the general consent of mankind. Such, again, is the argument on which S. Augustine so repeatedly insists, and to which we are ourselves disposed to give a place only short of the highest. We refer to that founded on the demonstrated existence of

---

* No doubt—in this, as in so many other cases—uncandid persons, who cannot prevent themselves from "cognizing" this or that truth, may prevent themselves from "recognizing" it.

Necessary Truth. If there be Necessary Truth, there must be a Necessary Being, on Whom such Truth is founded.

So much, then, on those proofs of God's Existence, concerning which it is most intelligible to affirm, with F. Kleutgen, that He conveys them to the apprehension of the most uncultured men, and thereby gives such men full power of knowing Him. The controversialist, however, we need hardly say, is concerned with these proofs not in their implicit but in their explicit shape, as capable of being brought directly before the attention of Antitheistic philosophers. This will be our business in our future successive essays; but we had better at this point remind our readers what is our exact argumentative position. That which we have called "Religious Truth" consists of four doctrines:— (1) The necessary character of Ethical Truth; (2) Man's Freewill; (3) God's Existence; (4) the Soul's Immortality. The two first of these are required as premisses for the third; and they have received at our hands, we trust, sufficient treatment in the preceding portion of our course. The central one of all, we need hardly say, is God's Existence, on the argument for which we are to enter in our proximate essays. The argument for the Soul's Immortality requires for its efficacy the assumption of God's Existence, and, therefore, stands logically last in our list.

Meanwhile, what remains of our present essay shall be occupied with one particular thesis, applicable to these religious doctrines as a whole. On this, again, M. Laprune gives us very valuable assistance. But we will begin with a few comments of our own, calculated, we hope, to throw light on the position which he assumes.

And, first, as to the word "certitude," which is included in his title, and its correspondent term "certainty." If I am "certain" of some truth, it possesses "certainty" in regard to *me*, and I possess "certitude" in regard to *it*. Now, let our Catholic readers carefully observe that in what we shall here further say concerning "certainty" or "certitude," we shall entirely ignore "supernatural" certitude; we shall speak as though God had given men no revelation, nor raised them to the supernatural order. We entreat our Catholic readers to bear this in mind once for all, as otherwise they will grievously misapprehend what we are going to say. So much, then, being understood, we thus proceed. I possess "certitude" of some given truth always and only when I cognize grounds for its acceptance, which I recognize to be absolutely incompatible with its falsehood; and when, consequently—in recognized conformity with reason—I yield to it absolute assent. What do we here mean by "absolute" assent? We mean that special firmness of assent which is entirely incompatible with the co-existence of doubt.* We should say, nevertheless, that there are varying degrees of certitude; though this circumstance is not required by our argument, and we, therefore, omit its treatment. Then, there is another fact, also, which we do not forget, though we need not treat it on the present occasion. We refer to the fact that there exists in many minds very frequently what may be called "spurious" certitude; or, in other words, that they very often yield "absolute" assent to some proposition, when they are cognizant of no grounds whatever which in reason can warrant such assent.

Many authors write as though the word "certitude" had different meanings, accordingly as one speaks of "metaphysical," "physical," or "moral" certitude re-

---

* Certitude, it will be seen, is as entirely within the reach of a rustic as of a philosopher. I, being a rustic, am absolutely certain that A B has for some time past been my bitter enemy. I cognize a long series of facts, which, taken collectively, I recognize to be incompatible with the supposition of his not having been my bitter enemy. Make the grotesque hypothesis, that I suddenly become a philosopher. My grounds of certitude do not on that account become stronger, but I acquire a power which I did not possess before—of enumerating a sufficient number of those facts, and reflecting on the reasonableness of that certitude.

spectively. To us, on the contrary, it seems, in accordance with the reasoning of F. Palmieri, S.J., that the word "certitude" has precisely the same meaning in all three cases. Yet there is a very important sense in which we may prefix different adjectives to the word—viz. in order to express the *object-matter* on which certitude has been attained. As a metaphysician, I am certain that every event necessarily has a cause. As a physicist, I am certain that all diamonds are naturally combustible. It is a very convenient expression to say that I am "metaphysically" certain of the former truth, and "physically" of the latter. Why is this a convenient expression? Because my reasonable method of arriving at certitude in things metaphysical is so different from my reasonable method of arriving at certitude in things physical. I arrive at certitude in things physical by pursuing such experiments as those indicated in works on Inductive Logic. But I arrive at certitude in things metaphysical by carefully assuring myself that this or that mental phenomenon is my mind's authentic utterance of objective truth; by warily and cautiously carrying forward that truth to its legitimate consequences; and by other such appropriate methods. No two processes can be much more unlike than the two we have named; but I am "certain" of a metaphysical truth in the very same sense in which I am "certain" of a physical. In either case I cognize grounds for the acceptance of such truth, which I recognize as absolutely incompatible with the supposition of its falsehood.

We now take a further step. In the very same sense in which we speak of "metaphysical" and "physical" certitude respectively, we may properly enumerate *other* certitudes also: we may speak of "historical" certitude, *e.g.*, or "æsthetic" certitude. Those methods whereby I arrive at certitude in matters historical are very largely different from those whereby I arrive at certitude in matters metaphysical or physical; and those methods whereby I arrive at certitude in matters of taste and beauty are entirely different from any of the other three.* It is in this sense that M. Laprune may most suitably speak of "religious" certitude: because he holds—and we heartily agree with him—that the method whereby I arrive at certitude on religious doctrines has special characteristics of its own; characteristics which it is important that the philosopher shall carefully study.

Here we can at last give our reason for preferring the terms "Religious Truth," "religious certitude," to M. Laprune's terms, "Moral Truth," "moral certitude." The term "moral certitude" is so indissolubly associated, both in Catholic and non-Catholic theology and philosophy, with a totally different sense, that serious confusion, we think, would inevitably arise from M. Laprune's terminology.

So much on this purely verbal question, and we proceed with the course of our argument. What, then, are the special characteristics of that process whereby men reasonably arrive at certitude in the matter of Religious Truth? By far the most special characteristic of that process, we need hardly say, is one on which we have already insisted, viz. that by the constant practice of virtue and piety a deeper certitude is possessed of Religious Truth than is obtainable by any philosophical investigation whatsoever. So far M. Laprune and ourselves are entirely at one, and it is difficult to exaggerate the importance of what he and we thus hold in common.

But, further, M. Laprune lays down as one chief characteristic of religious certitude, that it is acquired by eliciting acts of "natural faith." Here we venture to differ from him, with some confidence, on the expediency of this expression, though we believe, as we shall presently point out,

* There *is* such a thing assuredly as æsthetic certitude. It is certain to me, *e.g.*, that Offenbach's music is less profound than Beethoven's, etc.

that we are in full accordance with the substance of what he intends to say. The recognized Catholic use of the word "faith" is most definite and intelligible. If I accept some proposition on human testimony, I thereby elicit an act of "human faith." If I accept some proposition on God's testimony, I thereby elicit an act of "divine faith." But if I accept some proposition on any other ground whatsoever, I do not thereby elicit any act of faith at all. We think that Sir W. Hamilton and other non-Catholic Theists have introduced a very unfortunate confusion by their vague use of the word "faith," and we think that the interests of true philosophy will be far better promoted by confining that word to its strict Catholic sense.*

One principal proposition which M. Laprune intends to express, when he says that men acquire certitude of Religious Truth by means of natural faith, is especially worthy of attention. In fact, it is the thesis to which we have above referred, as the proposed theme of our concluding remarks. Even where philosophically competent men are investigating Religious Truth by explicit argumentative methods, its acceptance, nevertheless, on the part of those who have hitherto repudiated it, will be due far more to active and conscientious exercise of the *will*, than to subtlety, vigour, perspicacity of the intellect. For our own part, we heartily subscribe to this proposition. What we have just mentioned is an especially distinctive characteristic of *religious* certitude, as compared with all other certitudes of the natural order.

And, first, we submit with much confidence, that—not on religious matters alone, but on all objects of human thought—the will's office, in the generation of legitimate certitude, is far more prominent than is often thought.

---

* We do not forget Ripalda and his *fides late dicta*. His was no mere question of words, but a very important question of doctrine. Its consideration, however, would be entirely external to our present theme.

Such a view as the following, *e.g.*, is maintained by several philosophers. "I am free," they say, "to use, or not to use, due diligence in collecting premisses, and in exhibiting to myself their due force; but there my power ceases." These philosophers speak, no doubt, exclusively of the natural order, and are not contemplating the case of divine faith. But, as regards the natural order, they consider me to be actually *necessitated* in the matter of ultimate assent. "If the premisses placed before my attention at this moment," they say, "are sufficient in reason to generate certitude, I am necessitated to be certain; if they are not sufficient, I have no power of eliciting genuine certitude at all: in neither case is there room for Freewill." Now, of course, we entirely concede that there can be no genuine certitude of the natural order, where the premisses are not sufficient to *warrant* certitude in the light of strict reason. But we are very far indeed from admitting that men are necessitated to accept as certain every proposition which reasonably *claims* such acceptance. On the contrary, we follow Cardinal Franzelin, who thus speaks in his work on "Faith in its relation to Reason" (ii. arts. 1–5): A truth, he says in effect, is "objectively certain" to me, if it be manifested to me by reasons which legitimately claim my absolute assent; and it is "subjectively certain" to me if I proceed, as I am in reason bound, to yield that assent. Sometimes, he adds, the objective certainty of a proposition is exhibited to me with such irresistible clearness as to necessitate my assent; such a proposition is not only "certain" to me, but "evident." Still, many propositions possess true objective certainty in my regard; while, nevertheless, their objective certainty is not so irresistibly clear to me as to extort my assent to them: these propositions are "certain" to me, but not "evident." Whereas, therefore, the other philosophers, to whom we have referred, use the words "certain" and "evident" as synonymous within the natural order—Cardinal Franzelin uses the word "evident" as denoting one particular class of "certain" propositions.*

Now, many persons will say, as a matter of course, that, whatever truth may otherwise be contained in this doctrine, there is one region of thought, at all events, within which it can have no possible place—the region of pure mathematics. But, on the contrary, it is from that very region that we shall adduce what we consider one of our most apposite illustrations. Let us first take a geometrical theorem: e.g. "the angle in a semicircle is a right angle." This theorem, we admit, as exhibited in Euclid, is "evidently" certain. Even here, no doubt, a continued exercise of Freewill is requisite, in order that I may carefully apply my mind to see the self-evidence of what I assume as axioms, and the validity of that reasoning which I base on those axioms. But, this process concluded, I have no longer the power of doubting the theorem. At the same time, there may still be important work for my Freewill to do in compelling my intellect fully to *realize* that theorem, which I have not the power to doubt. But now let us enter a more advanced portion of the mathematical region —the doctrine of infinitesimals. The Rev. Bartholomew Price, e.g., in his admirable work on that subject, lays down such propositions as these: "There may be infinite quantities infinitely greater than infinities;" "An infinity of the nth order must be infinitely sub-divided to produce an infinity of the $(n-1)^{th}$ order;" etc. ("Infinitesimal Calculus," pp. 16-20). Mr. Price would consider that the truth of these propositions is as demonstratively established as is any geometrical theorem: and we entirely agree with him. But am I, nevertheless—supposing I have mastered

---

* We would especially refer our readers to M. Laprune's second chapter, as containing a most admirable exposition of the part played by Freewill in the formation of genuine certitude.

the demonstration—*necessitated* to accept them? Surely not. I have the power of allowing myself to be so bewildered by the strangeness of such propositions, as to withhold that assent which the adduced arguments, nevertheless, as I see, reasonably claim. I laudably, therefore, exercise my Freewill, in exciting myself to have the courage of my convictions; in compelling my intellect to disregard even insoluble difficulties which may stand in the way of a demonstrated proposition.

And if this be so even within the sphere of rigid demonstration, how much greater scope is there for the laudable exercise of Freewill where there is far greater opportunity of self-deception! Take, *e.g.*, such instances as those on which Cardinal Newman's "Grammar" mainly turns, and which are within the adjudication of what he calls "the illative sense." A Whig historian shall be dealing with the Massacre of Glencoe; and facts stare him in the face which, taken together, conclusively prove that the King had an active share in the transaction. Nevertheless, our historian shall refuse to deal honestly with himself. It is not further facts that he needs for a true conclusion, nor yet clearer apprehension of the facts which he knows. What he needs is to deal honestly with himself by a laudable exercise of his Freewill. He *cognizes* premisses abundantly sufficient to claim absolute assent; but he refuses to *recognize* that they are sufficient.*

There is a large number of truths, then, which are "objectively" certain to me; but which I do not appropriate as "subjectively" certain, because my will fails in its

* Here a curious little psychological question may be asked. Have I the power of *recognizing*—of confessing to myself—that such or such premisses, known by me, reasonably claim my absolute assent to such or such conclusion; while, nevertheless, through indolence or the like, I fail to *elicit* such absolute assent? We are disposed to think the supposition a possible one; though, of course, in the vast majority of instances, pride would withhold me from such recognition.

proper duty. My will fails, we say, to contend duly against my prejudices or my indolence, and to enjoin on my intellect its one reasonable course. Now, the fact on which we would here lay special stress is this. In no other case is there anything like such urgent need for the will thus intensely and energetically to exert itself, as in the Antitheist's dealing with Religious Truth. For this statement we can at once give two reasons, and need mention no others. In the first place, Religious Truth is inexpressibly *startling* to him. Consider one who has long been in the habit of contemplating this world as the only cognizable sphere of action, and of regarding his fellow-men as the only persons with whom he can cultivate any kind of relation. To one so habituated the notion is bewildering beyond description, that this life is known with certainty to be no more than an infinitesimal part of his existence; that his relations with his fellow-men are comparatively of no importance, except in their bearing on his relations with an Invisible Eternal Being; lastly, that this Being created him, and, if He do not receive due obedience, will severely chastise him in a future life. Why, the mathematical theory of infinitesimals is immeasurably less startling and bewildering to a learner than are the doctrines here exhibited to such a one as we have here described. And we thus, indeed, come across a second truth, intended by M. Laprune when he says that religious knowledge is acquired by a kind of "faith." I find the dogmata of the Blessed Trinity and Transubstantiation most enigmatical, startling, and perplexing. But my reason shows me that they cannot be proved self-contradictory; and I know certainly on God's Word that they are true. I exercise, therefore, laudable firmness of faith, by enjoining on my intellect the acceptance of these enigmatical, startling, and perplexing dogmata. In a very similar way—when reason has proved to me the certainty of God's existence—I exercise firmness of religious assent by enjoining on my intellect the acceptance of that, if so be, enigmatical, startling, and perplexing truth. This "firmness of religious assent" is plainly very analogous to firmness of faith; though, as a matter of words, for ourselves we see great objections against calling it "faith" at all. It may be worth while to add that, in our humble judgment, there are Theistic truths cognizable by Reason, which are quite as enigmatical, startling, and perplexing as any disclosed by Revelation. To our mind, *e.g.*, the demonstrated doctrine of God's Simplicity, when duly pondered, is even more enigmatical, startling, and perplexing than is that of the Blessed Trinity.

Then, secondly, these religious doctrines are not only startling and perplexing to the confirmed Antitheist, but intensely repulsive. We have already dwelt on this, and will here only add one further remark. We are not wishing to speak objurgatorily but only to express our meaning, when we say that the ethical tenets on which our Antitheist acts are precisely in the number of those which a Christian would describe as the tenets of corrupt human nature—the tenets to which man's evil inclinations solicit him. Go back to the ages of faith. It was then the doctrine firmly held by all Christians—so firmly that the mass of them did not conceive any other as possible—that a man is really "virtuous" so far, and so far only, as he uses this life exclusively for his opportunity of serving God and gaining future bliss. Yet, notwithstanding this fact, there was an enormous multitude who "saw and approved" indeed "what is better," but "followed what is worse;" who made earthly objects the end of their existence. Now, the modern Antitheistic tenets precisely canonize what the mediævalists anathematized; they represent the interests of this life as those which alone demand attention from a wise and good man. If corrupt human instincts, as the

Christian calls them, were so influential even when the whole world accounted them detestable, how enormous will be their power in favour of a theory, which enables its advocate to pursue them without self-reproach! It requires a supremely energetic effort, in one enslaved by them, to recognize the certainty with which reason establishes a doctrine that condemns them.

You ask, says M. Laprune (p. 387), for more light; yet it is not the increase of proofs which you ought to desire, but the weakening of your passions. Subtle and delicate passions, I admit, for you are an upright man [*un honnête homme*]; secret pride, which prevents you from yielding truth its due; invisible weaknesses, which perhaps do not lead you to neglect your social duties, but which make you traitors to the Truth; attachments, injustices, negligences—small, I admit, but multiplied—such as constitute a perpetual falsification of your supposed good faith, a perpetual obstacle to the Truth.

Our readers will remember that the thesis with which we have been engaged is this: The acceptance of Religious Truth, we said, on the part of one who has hitherto repudiated it, will be due far more to active and conscientious exercise of the will, than to subtlety, vigour, perspicacity of the intellect. By what we have already urged, we shall have sufficiently established, we think, the *first* statement implied in this thesis; we shall have sufficiently shown what patient and sustained struggle of the will is necessary in order that an Antitheist may embrace Theism. The *second* statement implied in our thesis is that, whereas intense exercise of the will is thus requisite, subtlety, vigour, and perspicacity of the intellect are by no means equally needed. This statement can only be defended by showing that the Theistic arguments—if a man will duly contemplate them—are, in general, not such as to require rare intellectual powers for their appreciation. And this, of course, cannot be shown until we come to deal with those arguments one by one. Here we can only express our own firm conviction that such is the case ; and that the Theist, not being hampered by these tremendous adverse prejudices, can very readily and unmistakably see, when duly presented, the irresistible force of the Theistic argument.

Meanwhile, even at this stage of our investigation, we can give no unsatisfactory reply to one particular class of inquirers, who, we fancy, exist in considerable and rapidly increasing numbers. An inquirer of this kind uses such language as the following:—"You Theists," he says, "require me to believe in Theism as in an absolutely certain truth. In other words, whereas confessedly many of the greatest contemporary thinkers hold with complete confidence that man has no power of cognizing God's Existence, you require of me, not that I suspend my judgment, but that I contradict their statement as confidently as they utter it. Now, I am intellectually a very ordinary and commonplace person : how, therefore, can you expect that I should pit my own private judgment against the authority of these illustrious thinkers?"* Now, if this language is merely used as a cloak and pretext for moral and intellectual carnal-mindedness or indolence, of course there is no scope for adverse argument, but only for ethical reprobation. We are convinced, however, that the difficulty here expressed is not unfrequently genuine. It is not indeed by any means so perplexing to deal with as might at first appear ; because, as Butler says on another matter, whoever is able really to experience the difficulty, is able also to apprehend the reply to it. We hope, in each one of our future essays, to encounter expressly this particular phase of what may be called "Quasi-Antitheism." And on the present occasion we would draw our inquirer's

* We happen ourselves to know the particular case of a gentleman who in early life was a High-Church Anglican, but who gave up belief in God on the ground mentioned in the text. "Who am I," he asked, "that I should oppose my own personal prepossessions to the declaration of these great men?"

attention to three several facts, which, we consider, have been made abundantly manifest, by our preceding remarks, to any educated man of the most ordinary intelligence.

Firstly, it is manifest that, however conclusive and irresistible the Theistic arguments may be in themselves, there is no practical possibility of any Antitheist being convinced by them, unless he bring to their study a patient and sustained struggle of attention; unless he energetically labour to remove that mountain of prejudice which must otherwise intercept from him their view. Secondly, it is no less manifest to any man of ordinary knowledge and education who will exercise the simplest common sense and common observation, that these "illustrious thinkers" do nothing of the kind. On the contrary, they consistently preserve the most supercilious and disdainful attitude towards Religious Doctrine; nor do they show the faintest trace of a notion that they are under any kind of disadvantage in religious investigations. Never were there men more densely prejudiced, or more densely unaware of the circumstance. From the mere fact, therefore, that they account Theistic arguments worthless, there arises not the faintest presumption that those arguments may not be, as we of course are convinced they are, entirely irrefragable. And here comes in the *third* phenomenon, to which we just now referred; and which shows with quite extraordinary significance how perfunctory has been their examination of Theism. We mean that they always base their opposition to it on that extravagant tenet, which we have called "Phenomenism," and may here call "anti-Intuitionism." No one of the most ordinary education can read what we have said in the earlier part of our present essay without seeing the supreme absurdity of this tenet, as held by those who loudly proclaim themselves votaries of inductive science; or, indeed, as held by any one who admits that there is such a thing as human knowledge at all: and yet this transparently absurd tenet is advocated by these scientists without hesitation or shame. Surely these facts, taken in combination, are abundantly sufficient to show the most self-diffident man alive how utterly destitute these thinkers are of all claim on his intellectual deference in matters connected with religion.

Having so far addressed those particular inquirers who are frightened not by the arguments, but by the *name* of contemporary Antitheists, we now proceed rapidly to the conclusion of our present essay. Whenever those philosophers, with whom we have been controverting throughout, choose to take up the Theistic controversy as a matter of argument and not mere flippant sarcasm, they will be obliged to give up their transparently unsound contention that there is no such thing as a truth of intuition ; and will be obliged to content themselves with alleging that those particular intuitions which the Theist alleges are spurious. Here is a grave philosophical question on which issue may be joined with every prospect of fruitful result ; and it is only so far as Antitheists assume this attitude that the Theistic controversy can become a serious philosophical discussion.

In the first article of our series—following in the footsteps of F. Kleutgen—we set forth with one particular principle as the only possible, nay, the only conceivable, foundation of human knowledge. That principle is that whatever the human intellect, when its utterances are duly examined and interpreted, declares to be objective truth, is thereby certainly known as such. Metaphysics, then, is founded on Pyschology; for the question whether this or that proposition be objectively true depends on the question whether man's intellect genuinely avouches it. The human mind abounds in genuine utterances of objective truth, and precious results are attainable by examining and cataloguing its treasures. But there is always grave danger—so much we readily concede to Phenomenists—lest prejudice be mistaken for intuition; and this danger can only be met by vigorous and penetrating psychological inquiry. We submit that Intuitionist philosophers have not as yet in general given sufficient prominence to this psychological inquiry; that in dealing, *e.g.*, with the genuineness of this or that intuition, they have often not been at sufficient pains in sifting the relevant psychological phenomena. We hope to explain what we mean by this suggestion in our next essay. At all events this psychological examination of alleged intuitions will occupy a somewhat prominent place in our own reasonings.

And this criticism of Intuitionistic philosophers suggests a more general remark. Cardinal Newman says, somewhere, that he entirely refuses to be converted by "a smart syllogism." In a similar spirit speaks M. Laprune. Religious "Truth," he says, "when unknown or forgotten, despised, misconceived, is not brought into the mind by the all-powerful virtue of a syllogism. Neither the excellence of Truth nor the mind's dignity permits this" (p. 384). And, certainly, if it be true, as we have alleged, that, by the very fact of engaging in Theistic controversy, we summon the Antitheist to a supremely energetic act of will, one sees plainly that everything like flippancy or overbearingness of tone in the conduct of that controversy; or, again, any peremptory challenging of instantaneous assent and submission may probably be productive of most serious mischief. The sincere inquirer must be allowed his full time for patient consideration and healthy resolve.

To conclude. If, on the one hand, we have maintained that Theistic arguments are discerned as quite indubitably conclusive by those who will choose to give them prolonged and dispassionate consideration; on the other hand, what we have said will, we hope, powerfully illustrate the unspeakable blessedness of a religious education. It might seem difficult to exaggerate the blessedness of such education, even in the case of non-Catholics, who shall have been trained to regulate their whole course of life by those four doctrines, which we have included under the name of "Religious Truth." But happier—and quite indefinitely happier—is he who has been from infancy a child of that Church which infallibly preserves in their full purity the truths of Natural Religion, while supplementing them with a body of revealed dogmata that brings out those truths into ever-increasingly clearer and fuller light.*

* This essay is the last of the continuous series so often referred to in the text, purporting to exhibit the philosophical foundation of Theism. The scope of the remaining ones which follow, and the occasions upon which they were written, have been already spoken of in the Editor's introductory essay.—ED.

XIV.
SCIENCE, PRAYER, FREEWILL, AND MIRACLES.[*]

NOTHING can be clearer than that God desires mankind to cultivate experimental science. He has imprinted on nature fixed laws, which make it amenable to such science; and He has endowed man with an intellect capable of investigating those laws. Then, such investigation is morally advantageous to many; is a good intellectual discipline to all; and has issued, moreover, in the discovery of innumerable truths, which have promoted physical enjoyment and social comfort in a degree almost incredible. And the Church has ever thus interpreted God's Will. No one can maintain with the slightest plausibility that, even when her influence was greatest, she occupied any other attitude towards science[†] than that of respect and encouragement; still less that she viewed it with misgiving or suspicion. And yet, in full consistency with this avowal, we may and do regard it as a serious evil that the great triumphs of science have been achieved at a time like the present; at a time when—from causes easily to be traced, however deplorable—there has been so large and widespread a rebellion against the Church's authority over

[*] *Five Discourses on Miracles, Prayer, and the Laws of Nature.* By the REV. D. GILBERT, D.D. London: Farrell.
The Reign of Law. By THE DUKE OF ARGYLL. London: Strahan.
The Church and the World. Essay 16. *Science and Prayer.* By the REV. M. M'COLL. London: Longmans.

[†] In this essay we shall, for convenience' sake, use the word "science" in the sense which Englishmen so commonly give to it; as expressing physical and experimental science, to the exclusion of theological and metaphysical.

secular thought. It has resulted from this circumstance that science and theology have proceeded for centuries past, each in its own separate sphere, and each ignoring the other's existence. On the one hand, scientific men have continually assumed many a principle fundamentally irreligious, which they have not cared, however, to express and carry forward into its legitimate consequences. On the other hand, theologians have confined themselves to that high sphere which is exclusively their own, without troubling themselves to consider and correct what has been amiss in humbler regions of speculation. Such, we say, has been the state of things for many successive generations. But at length there are no doubtful signs that this chasm between the two different lines of thought is beginning to be bridged over, and that the temporary truce is to be succeeded by a vigorous war. Every one has observed how much greater interest is taken in matters theological, whether the interest of sympathy or of disgust, than was the case even twenty years ago. Scientific men are beginning to attack openly the foundations of religion; and correlatively no duty is at this moment more indispensably urgent on the theological faculty than to confront and encounter these malignant and formidable attacks.

Our present purpose is to consider what appears to us at once the most specious and the most fundamental of all those objections which have been brought against religion in the name of science. It cannot, indeed, be adequately treated, except in a volume, or rather in a series of volumes. All which we can hope to accomplish in an essay is to lay down principles in reply, which may recommend themselves both as true and as sufficient; and which may be more fully apprehended, and also carried out into due detail, by those Christian thinkers who are adequate to the task.*

* The present writer should confess at starting, what will, he fears, be manifest throughout, viz. that he labours under the great disadvantage of complete unacquaintance with all details of physical science. We should

We shall endeavour to state the objection in its full strength and extent, because nothing can be more injurious to the Church's cause than that her defenders should fail to apprehend the fatal malignity of that pestilence which is abroad. There are not a few scientific men, then, we fear, who, if they spoke out their full mind, would argue as follows :—

"The one principle implied in every scientific investigation of every kind is the principle of *phenomenal uniformity;* or, in other words, the principle that, in every case without exception, where there are the same phenomenal antecedents, the same phenomenal consequents will result. Let me suppose for a moment the contradictory of this; let me suppose, *e.g.*, that some deity had the power and the will to affect the fixed laws of nature; science would be an impossibility. I compose a substance to-day of certain materials, and find it by experiment to be combustible: I compose another to-morrow of the very same materials, united in the very same way and in the very same proportions, and I find the composition *in*combustible. If such a case were possible, the whole foundation of science would be taken from under my feet. Science from the first has assumed this phenomenal uniformity, as its first principle; nor could it have advanced one single step without that assumption. Those achievements, then, of physical science, which the most religious men cannot attempt to question, afford an absolutely irrefragable demonstration of that first principle which science has from the first assumed. No investigations, proceeding throughout on a false basis, could by possibility have issued in an innumerable multitude of unexperienced yet experimentally true conclusions.

add, however, that a Protestant gentleman of high scientific eminence has done us the very great favour of looking over our sheets.
[This was the late Professor De Morgan.]

"But now answer me candidly: how is this principle of phenomenal uniformity reconcilable—I will not say with Christianity—but with any practical system whatever of religion? I will begin with my weakest point of attack, and rise by degrees to my strongest. I will begin with the doctrine that prayer for temporal blessings is reasonable and may be efficacious. Your country is visited with famine or pestilence, and you supplicate your God for relief. Your only child lies sick of a dangerous fever; and, as a matter of course, you are frequent in prayer. You are diligent, indeed, in giving her all the external help you can; but your chief trust is avowedly in God. You entreat Him that He will arrest the malady and spare her precious life. What can be more irrational than this? Would you pray, then, for a long day in December? Would you pray that in June the sun shall set at six o'clock? Yet surely the laws of fever are no less absolutely fixed than those of sunset; and were the case otherwise, no science of medicine could by possibility have been called into existence. The only difference between the two cases is that the laws of sunset have been thoroughly mastered; whereas our knowledge as to the laws of fever, though very considerable, is as yet but partial and incomplete.* The 'abstract power of prediction,'—as Mr. Stuart Mill calls it —this is the one assumption, in every nook and corner of science. All scientific men take for granted—when they cease to do so they will cease to *be* scientific men—that a person of superhuman and adequate intelligence, who should know accurately and fully all the various combinations and properties of matter which now exist, could predict infallibly the whole series of future phenomena.

---

* "Ordinary Christians ask for fair weather and for rain, *but they do not ask that water may run up-hill;* while *the man of science clearly sees* that the granting of one petition would be *just as much an infringement of law* . . . as the granting of the other. Holding *the law* to be permanent, *he prays for neither*." (Professor Tyndall, quoted in *Church and World*, p. 230.)

He could predict the future course of weather or of disease with the same assurance with which men now predict the date of a coming eclipse. Pray God all day long—add fasting to your prayer if you like, and let all your fellow-Christians add *their* prayer and fasting to yours—in order that the said eclipse shall come a week earlier.: do you suppose you will be heard? Yet the precise date of an eclipse is not more peremptorily fixed by the laws of nature than is the precise issue of your daughter's fever. You do not venture to doubt speculatively this fundamental doctrine of science; in our various scientific conversations, my friend, you have always admitted it. But, like a true Englishman, you take refuge in an illogical compromise. You assume one doctrine when you study science; and another, its direct contradictory, when your child falls ill. And yet I am paying you too high a compliment: for you do not *profess* that this latter doctrine is *true;* you do not *profess* that your prayer to God is *reasonable,* or can possibly be *efficacious:* your only defence is that your reason is mastered and overborne by the combined effect of your religious and your parental emotion. As though you could please God—if, indeed, there be a Personal God at all—by acting in a manner which your reason condemns.

"Well, you tell me you see your mistake; you will henceforth pray for *spiritual* blessings, and for them alone. Why, you are still as unreasonable as you were before. Is not psychology, then, as truly a science as medicine? You never doubted that it was when you used to take such interest in the study of Reid and Hamilton. But if psychology *be* a science—if the conclusions, whether of Hartley and Mill or of Hamilton and M'Cosh, have more value than the inventions of a fortune-teller or the dreams of a madman—*mental* phenomena proceed on fixed laws, no less inflexibly than *physical.* What, then, can possibly be your meaning when you pray for what you call grace? when you supplicate for help against what you call temptation? for growth in what you call virtue? All these prayers imply in their very notion that your God is constantly interfering with the course of mental phenomena. To talk as you do, or, at least, to pray as you do, is equivalent to saying in so many words—not that this or that school of psychologians is in error, but that there is no science of psychology at all; that there are no fixed laws of mind to be discovered by any one whatever; that the real agency at work, in causing our various thoughts, volitions, and emotions, is the unceasing and arbitrary intervention of a Personal Creator and Sanctifier. Take your choice. Believe in science or believe in the efficacy of prayer. But at least do not assume an intellectual position so obviously contemptible, as that of seeking to combine the two.

"3. At least, you reply, you may exercise your *freewill* for good or for evil, however powerless your God may be to assist you in the combat. On the contrary, I rejoin, this figment of Freewill is even more directly unscientific than the superstition of prayer. The very foundation of all science, as every one well knows, is this great truth, that the same phenomenal antecedents are invariably succeeded by the same phenomenal consequents. Now, the notion of Freewill directly and, as it were, unblushingly contradicts this fundamental truth. When you say your will is free, your very meaning is that—the very same phenomenal antecedents being supposed, both physical and mental—you possess a real power of choosing *what* mental *consequent* shall ensue. How amazing—not that a priest-ridden Ultramontane or an ignorant rustic—but that you, an educated and scientific gentleman, can have been blind to so extravagant an inconsistency!

"4. After this it it hardly worth while to make one more remark, which I will not, however, omit. The Christian religion, in particular, is grounded on an allegation of *miracles*. But miracles, it is plain, constitute the same anti-scientific absurdity in the material world which Freewill constitutes in the mental. To believe the existence of miracles is, *ipso facto*, to disbelieve phenomenal uniformity; and to disbelieve phenomenal uniformity, is to reject the very possibility of science."

We have stated all this in its full extent, because we are very desirous that our readers should understand *what* the argument means, if it means anything at all. It would be most unjust to doubt that many scientific men, who carry it to a certain extent, would be appalled at the very thought of embracing that full conclusion in which it issues; and they may be greatly benefited, therefore, by being brought to understand what that full conclusion is. Moreover, as we have already said, it is of great moment that Christians in general, and Catholics in particular, should understand how tremendous is the danger lurking under a few plausible generalities; that they should see once for all how vain is all thought of concession and compromise; and that they should gird themselves for an internecine conflict. Lastly, we should be extremely glad if, by exhibiting the urgency of the crisis, we could induce competent Christian writers to enter more fully on the work of reply than they have hitherto done. There is no part, or hardly any part, of the true answer to these irreligious arguments which has not been already stated incidentally here or there by some Christian thinker; but we greatly desiderate a far more systematic, comprehensive, and emphatic consideration of the whole matter than has hitherto been afforded. Even were there far less than there is of vigour and conclusive argument in Dr. Gilbert's discourses, he would deserve our sincerest gratitude for drawing methodical attention to the subject. But he has done much more than this. He has failed indeed, we think, to grasp the full extent of that irreligious theory which Catholics have to encounter; but he has given many satisfactory, and some quite admirable, answers to the particular objections which he has considered.

We have seldom seen so disappointing a work as the Duke of Argyll's, which we have also named at the head of this essay. In saying this, however, we are very far indeed from intending simply to disparage it; on the contrary, it is the rare excellence of some individual passages which leads us to expect elsewhere what we do not find. Some of the defects which we lament are, no doubt, attributable to the volume's fragmentary character; and we certainly much regret that, instead of republishing a number of separate papers, the Duke did not take the trouble of working up his materials into one harmonious whole. Still, the intellectual faults exhibited, we cannot but think, lie deeper than the mere form of his production. There are many signs, indeed, in the volume of his possessing not only great fairness and justice of view, but also a real capacity for profound thought; yet the signs are not less conspicuous of his not having duly evoked into exercise this latter capacity. He impresses us as having given too large a proportion of his time to acquiring knowledge, and too small a proportion to digesting and reflecting on the materials thus obtained. The extent of his knowledge is certainly very remarkable, and many of his incidental observations display real originality and genius.

We cannot give a better specimen, both of the Duke's excellencies and of his defects, than his treatment of the first irreligious objection above recounted. We will begin, however, by soliciting our readers' most careful attention to his truly admirable remarks on the utter emptiness and baselessness of one cowardly intellectual subterfuge, to which resort has at times been attempted. Some writers have proclaimed the existence of a certain, as it were, impassable gulf between the respective realms of theology and secular science. It is by means of this subterfuge that minimizing Catholics would shirk the Church's authority throughout the whole sphere of secular speculation; and it is by the same means that many scientific men excuse themselves from the charge of injuring religion, when they admit irreligious principles into the sphere of their own science.

And so we see, says the Duke, the men of Theology coming out to parley with the men of science—a white flag in their hands, and saying, "*If you will let us alone, we will do the same by you.* Keep to your own province; do not enter ours. The reign of Law which you proclaim, we admit—outside these walls, but not within them: let there be peace between us." But this will never do. *There can be no such treaty dividing the domain of Truth. Every one Truth is connected with every other Truth in this great Universe of God.*

It is against a certain real danger, that some men would erect a feeble barrier by defending the position, that Science and Religion may be, and ought to be, kept entirely separate; that they belong to wholly different spheres of thought; and *that the ideas which prevail in the one province have no relation to those which prevail in the other*. This is a doctrine offering many temptations to many minds. It is grateful to scientific men who are afraid of being thought hostile to Religion. It is grateful to religious men who are afraid of being thought to be afraid of Science. To these, and to all who are troubled to reconcile what they have been taught to believe with what they have come to know, this doctrine forms a natural and convenient escape. *There is but one objection to it, but that is the fatal objection—that it is not true.*

The spiritual world and the intellectual world are not separated after this fashion; and the notion that they are so separated does but encourage men to accept in each ideas which will at last be found to be false in both. The truth is, that there is no branch of human inquiry, however purely physical, which is more than the word " branch " implies; none which is not connected through endless ramifications with every other— *and especially with that which is the root and centre of them all.* If He who formed the mind be one with Him who is the Orderer of all things concerning which that mind is occupied, *there can* be *no end to the points of contact* between our different conceptions of them, of Him, and of ourselves.

The instinct which impels us to seek for harmony in the truths of Science and the truths of Religion, is a higher instinct and a truer one than the disposition which leads us to evade the difficulty by pretending that there is no relation between them. For, after all, *it is a pretence and nothing more. No man who thoroughly accepts a principle in the philosophy of Nature which he feels to be inconsistent with a doctrine of Religion, can help having his belief in that doctrine shaken and undermined.* We may believe, and we must believe, both in Nature and in Religion, many things which we cannot understand; but *we cannot really believe two propositions which are felt to be contradictory.* It helps us nothing in such a difficulty to say that the one proposition belongs to Reason and the other proposition belongs to Faith. The endeavour to reconcile them is a necessity of the mind. We are right in thinking that *if they are both indeed true they can be reconciled, and if they really are fundamentally opposed they cannot both be true* (pp. 53–55).

It will have been observed with much interest, how frankly the Duke, in the course of this extract, admits theology to be "the root and centre of all" sciences. Such an opinion, indeed, cannot be avoided by any clear-headed man, who believes that there *is* such a science as theology, and who will look facts in the face. But, then, there are so many clear-headed men who do *not* believe that there is such a science as theology, and so many others who will *not* look facts in the face.

After this preliminary and most important introduction, the Duke states, with extreme force and candour, the anti-religious objection to which we referred above; and here again his language is so masterly and so clear that we cannot refrain from quoting it *in extenso*. He refers, then, to—

The conclusion to which the language of some scientific men is evidently pointing, that *great general Laws inexorable in their application*, and Causes in endless chain of invariable sequence, are the governing powers in Nature, and that they *leave no room* *for any special direction or providential ordering of events. If this be true, it is vain to deny its bearing on Religion. What, then, can be the use of prayer ? Can Laws hear us ? Can they change, or can they suspend themselves ?* These questions cannot but arise, and they require an answer. It is said of a late eminent Professor and clergyman of the English Church,[*] who was deeply imbued with these opinions on the place occupied by Law in the economy of Nature, that he went on, nevertheless, preaching high doctrinal sermons from the pulpit until his death. He did so on the ground that propositions which were contrary to his reason were not necessarily beyond his faith. The inconsistencies of the human mind are indeed unfathomable; and there are men so constituted *as honestly to suppose that they can divide themselves into two spiritual beings, one of whom is sceptical, and the other is believing.* But such men are rare— happily for Religion, and not less happily for Science. *No healthy intellect, no earnest spirit, can rest in such self-betrayal.* Accordingly we find many men now facing the consequences to which they have given their intellectual assent, and *taking their stand upon the ground that prayer to God has no other value or effect than so far as it may be a good way of preaching to ourselves.* It is a useful and helpful exercise for our own spirits, but it is nothing more. But how can they pray who have come to this? *Can it ever be useful or helpful to believe a lie ?* That which has been threatened as the worst of all spiritual evils, would then become the constant attitude of our "religion," the habitual condition of our worship. *This must be as bad science as it is bad religion* (pp. 58–60).

The Duke then proceeds, as our imaginary objector proceeded above, to show the impossibility of such a distinction as some have attempted to draw between physical and mental phenomena :—

The compromise now offered by some philosophers is this— that although the course of *external nature* is unalterable, yet possibly the phenomena of *mind and character* may be changed by the Divine Agency. But will this reasoning bear analysis? Can the distinction it assumes be maintained? Whatever difficulties there may be in reconciling the ideas of Law and of Volition, are difficulties which apply equally to the Worlds of

---

[*] We imagine that reference is here made to the late Rev. Baden Powell.

Matter and of Mind. *The Mind is as much subject to Law as the Body is.* The reign of Law is over all; and if its dominion be really incompatible with the agency of Volition, human or divine, then the Mind is as inaccessible to that agency as material things (p. 61).

This admirable statement of the difficulty raised our hopes to the highest pitch, and we fully expected to find the objection answered in the same satisfactory and masterly way in which it had been stated. In this hope we were disappointed. The previous extracts have shown, both how clearly the Duke is able to see the opposing argument and also how heartily he dislikes the conclusion to which it tends; but we close the volume in absolute uncertainty how he would himself reply to it.

Various other portions of the work will come before us, for the expression both of assent and dissent, as our discussion proceeds: but since the last chapter, on "the reign of Law in Politics," is wholly external to our present scope, we must not omit here to give it its due meed of praise. It is both original and powerful; and we are able more unreservedly to agree with it than with any other of the seven essays.

Mr. M'Coll's essay is written generally in the best possible spirit, and is not without incidental remarks of much force and vigour; yet on the whole he has neither done justice, we think, to the strength of his opponents' view, nor yet to the strength of his own. We regret also to find, towards the beginning, language savouring of that illogical attempt, which the Duke of Argyll so excellently rebukes, to deny all contact between the respective spheres of theology and secular science.

Science, says our author, not content with *toleration and good neighbourhood* on the part of the Church, aspires to dictate the articles of her creed, and prescribe her very forms of devotion. Of this aggressive disposition on the part of science the recent attack on special prayer is an instance. The prayer against the cholera and the cattle-plague *cannot be accused of encroaching on any of the rights and privileges of science.* It moves in another sphere, and is simply based on our recognition of a God whose Love is infinite, and whose Power is equal to His Love. It is strictly framed on Bacon's advice, " being kept within its own province," and not venturing on any " excursions into the limits of physical causes." Yet Natural Science, in so far as it is represented by Professor Tyndall, turns round upon us with a scowl, and tells us that, in the opinion of the great majority of sane persons, " we are little better than fools for believing that our prayers can avail to stop the progress of the pestilence " (p. 414).

Surely the Church does make an aggression—a most laudable and just one, doubtless, but still an aggression—on the domain of physical science, when she proclaims that prayer to God often alters the course of phenomena. Surely " the course of phenomena " is precisely the one object-matter of experimental science. How can it be said, then, that the Church exhibits "toleration and good neighbourhood" to that science, when she dogmatizes on its one object-matter? The " abstract power of predicting phenomena" is claimed as the very foundation of experimental science, by a large number of her most ardent votaries; and the Church, in teaching the efficacy of prayer, directly overthrows that foundation. Yet Mr. M'Coll says that theology " cannot " even " be *accused* of encroaching on any of the rights and privileges of science." Surely such an " accusation " is not only possible, but is thoroughly well founded; except, indeed, so far as the word " encroachment " implies an *undue* claim of control. She claims to control physical science, and her claim is a most just one. Consider the two following propositions:—Prop. 1: " There is an abstract power of scientifically predicting all future phenomena: " here is a *scientific* proposition, true or false. Prop. 2: " The future course of phenomena will be affected indefinitely by God's Intervention; whether He acts simply on His own inscrutable Will, or whether in answer to the prayer of Most Holy Mary, of Angels, of Saints, of men on earth: " here is a *theological* proposition, true or false. Mr. M'Coll speaks as though these two propositions respectively belonged to two spheres, which have no points of mutual contact. How strange! Why, one is the logical contradictory of the other. He who holds the former must reject the latter, and he who holds the latter must reject the former. To say that theology and science are mutually *independent*, seems to us the one position more obviously illogical and untenable than any other that can be devised. Sacred science must be granted superiority over secular; or else secular science will assume superiority over sacred. And if any Christian shrinks from claiming for theology such superiority, however pious and admirable may be his intentions, he is in fact betraying the cause which he wishes to serve.*

At the present day many, even among Catholics, are in the habit of conceding very readily that, in times past, "theologians intruded into the province of science;" and we cannot be surprised, therefore, that Mr. M'Coll, who is not a Catholic, has taken the accusation for granted (p. 412). It would certainly be over-bold to assert confidently a negative; but at least, before we admit the truth of so grave an accusation, we desire to see some attempt at demonstrating it. The only proof to which Mr. M'Coll refers, is the case of Galileo; and on that case we are perfectly confident, that the theologians were right in principle from first to last.†

So much, then, on the three works which we have named

* We have several times drawn attention to Pius IX.'s strong language in his Munich Brief, on the Church's authority over physical science.

† Galileo's case has been since treated at length, by the present writer, in the *Dublin Review* for April and July, 1871.

at the head of our article. For ourselves, as we have already said, we can aspire to nothing more than an exhibition of the merest skeleton and outline; which, should it meet with approval, might be filled up and expanded by those who are more fitted for the task both from natural qualifications and from scientific accomplishments.

We will beg our readers to look back at the four objections which we are to meet. They are directed respectively (1) against the efficacy of prayer for temporal blessings; (2) against the possibility of Divine Grace; (3) against Freewill; and (4) against Miracles. They are of very unequal force; and we consider the *last*, indeed, to be frivolous in the extreme. We will take them, however, in the order in which they have been stated. We admit, of course, at starting, what the Church has ever taught, viz. that God has impressed on each portion of matter certain intrinsic properties, and a certain definite unchanged agency of its own. Truth obliges us, indeed, further to maintain, that He has retained in His own hands the power of suspending or even reversing the action of such properties; yet, as regards the two first objections on our list, there is no necessity whatever for insisting on this qualification. On the contrary, we are fully prepared to concede for argument's sake, that He never does interfere with the properties of matter; that He never does reverse their natural agency; that the laws of nature are absolutely fixed, and the sequence of phenomena absolutely uniform. We contend that even were this hypothesis ever so unreservedly true, there would still be no cogency whatever in those irreligious arguments, which are adduced to sustain the two first objections above recited. Of these, we will treat the former in detail; and afterwards apply very easily to the second what will have been already said in reply to the first. The third and fourth shall afterwards be considered fully and carefully, on their respective grounds.

Let it be conceded, then, for argument's sake, that the whole material world proceeds unexceptionally on the basis of phenomenal uniformity; that the laws of nature are most absolutely fixed. Firstly, we say, it does not follow, or tend ever so distantly to follow, because they are *fixed* that they proceed independently of God's constant and unremitting "premovement."* Nay, secondly, we say that —putting aside all the evidences of revealed religion— physical phenomena alone, if duly considered, give even greater probability to the religious than to the irreligious conclusion. But if such Divine premovement be admitted, then the efficacy of man's prayer for temporal blessings is the dictate of reason no less truly than of faith. Since, however, it is essential that the reader shall carry with him a clear notion of what we mean by this Divine premovement, we trust he will pardon us much grotesqueness and some lengthiness of illustration. However grotesque may be the supposition we are going to make, we believe it will be found singularly adapted to the only purpose for which we use it—the purpose of enabling our readers to understand distinctly what we mean.

We begin, then, with imagining two mice, endowed, however, with quasi-human or semi-human intelligence, enclosed within a grand pianoforte, but prevented in some way or other from interfering with the free play of its machinery. From time to time they are delighted with the strains of choice music. One of the two considers these to result from some agency external to the instrument; but the other, having a more philosophical mind, rises to the conception of fixed laws and phenomenal uniformity.

* What we mean by this word will immediately appear. We do not say "premotion," because this word has a special sense in the Thomistic philosophy, totally distinct from that here intended. There is a certain "concursus" also, which Catholics consider to be constantly put forth by God, in default of which the whole creation would sink back into nothingness; but the "premovement" of which we speak in the text is a great deal more than this.

"Science as yet," he says, "is but in its infancy; but I have already made one or two important discoveries. Every sound which reaches us is preceded by a certain vibration of these strings. The same string invariably produces the same sound; and that louder or more gentle, according as the vibration may be more or less intense. Sounds of a more composite character result when two or more of the strings vibrate together; and here, again, the sound produced, as far as I am able to discover, is precisely a compound of those sounds which would have resulted from the various component strings vibrating separately. Then there is a further sequence which I have observed: for each vibration is preceded by a stroke from a corresponding hammer; and the string vibrates more intensely in proportion as the hammer's stroke is more forcible. Thus far I have already prosecuted my researches. And so much at least is evident even now, viz. that the sounds proceed not from any external and arbitrary agency—from the intervention, *e.g.*, of any higher will—but from the uniform operation of fixed laws. These laws may be explored by intelligent mice; and to their exploration I shall devote my life." Even from this inadequate illustration, you see the general conclusion which we wish to enforce. A sound has been produced through a certain intermediate chain of fixed laws; but this fact does not tend ever so distantly to establish the conclusion, that there is no human premovement acting continuously at one end of that chain.

Imagination, however, has no limits. We may very easily suppose, therefore, that some instrument is discovered, producing music immeasurably more heavenly and transporting than that of the pianoforte; but for that very reason immeasurably more vast in size and more complex in machinery. We will call this imaginary instrument a "polychordon," as we are not aware that there is any existing claimant of that name. In this polychordon, the intermediate links—between the player's premovement on one hand, and the resulting sound on the other—are no longer, two, but two hundred. We further suppose— imagination, as before said, being boundless—that some human being or other is unintermittently playing on this polychordon, but playing on it just what airs may strike his fancy at the moment. Well: successive generations of philosophical mice have actually traced one hundred and fifty of the two hundred phenomenal sequences, through whose fixed and invariable laws the sound is produced. The colony of mice, shut up within, are in the highest spirits at the success which has crowned the scientific labour of their leading thinkers; and the most eminent of these addresses an assembly. "We have long known that the laws of our musical universe are immutably fixed; but we have now discovered a far larger number of those laws than our ancestors could have imagined *capable* of discovery. Let us redouble our efforts. I fully expect that our grandchildren will be able to predict as accurately, for an indefinitely preceding period the succession of melodies with which we are to be delighted, as we now predict the hours of sunrise and sunset.* One thing, at all events, is now absolutely incontrovertible. As to the notion of there being some agency *external* to the polychordon—intervening with arbitrary and capricious will to produce the sounds we experience—this is a long-exploded superstition, a mere dream and dotage of the past. The progress of science has put it on one side, and never again can it return to disturb our philosophical progress."

This whole illustration will have made, we think, abundantly clear both the meaning, and the truth of that proposition for which we are contending. Two hundred absolutely fixed laws intervene between the player's pre-

---

* The polychordon, if the reader pleases, may be supposed to have a glass cover, through which the light penetrates.

movement and the resulting sound; but this fact does not tend ever so remotely to show that there is not an intelligent player, or that his premovement is not absolutely unremitting. And in like manner, though phenomenal laws the most strictly and rigorously uniform existed throughout the realm of nature, such a fact would not tend ever so remotely to show what irreligious men pretend: it would not tend ever so remotely to show that those laws are not at each moment directed, to this purpose or to that, by an *immediate and uncontrolled Divine Premovement*. God's real ends cannot be more inscrutable to us, according to the Christian's belief, than would be the end of a human performer to the mice within this supposed polychordon. Indeed, we do know so much as this, that His ends are those of Infinite Wisdom and Holiness. And as a player on the polychordon may readily be induced, at the smallest request of a little child, to produce this particular musical result rather than some other; so the heartfelt prayer of the humblest Christian may powerfully affect God's premovement of the physical world. We are not here arguing, be it observed, that the truth *is* so; we are but saying that the mere fact of phenomenal uniformity does not ever so remotely tend to show that the truth is *not* so.

We now, then, proceed to our second proposition. Even apart from any evidence of revealed religion, physical phenomena taken by themselves would make it, we maintain, more probable than not that God does unintermittently premove, in accordance with His inscrutable purposes, those fixed laws which pervade the external world. Before drawing out an argument which appears to us far more cogent than any other in behalf of this conclusion, we will enter on a preliminary matter of no inconsiderable importance. We will here, then, draw the attention of our readers to a thesis which occupies almost as much of the Duke of Argyll's volume as all his others put together, and which he certainly handles with signal power and success. It has not unfrequently been held that the investigation of *physical* causes interferes with the due appreciation of *final;* that the habit of exploring phenomenal *sequences* is greatly injurious to the habit of recognizing phenomenal *design.* Now, if by this be merely meant that many scientific men, through a certain deplorable narrowness and prejudice, close their eyes to a large number of undoubted facts, there is much truth, no doubt, in the allegation. But those who use such language generally mean much more than this. They seem to mean that the progress of physical science has really weakened the *evidence* derivable from nature, for the existence of design in the material world. No supposition can be more scientifically unfounded than this; and we wish we had space to quote all the masterly passages in which the Duke refutes it. We must confine ourselves, however, to two extracts, though the first will be of considerable length. The italics, of course, are our own.

And yet scientific men sometimes tell us that " we must be very cautious how we ascribe intention to Nature. Things do fit into each other, no doubt, as if they were designed; but all we know about them is that these correspondences exist, and that they seem to be the result of physical laws of development and growth." Very likely; but how these correspondences have arisen, and are daily arising, is not the question, and it is immaterial how that question may be answered. Do these correspondences exist, or do they not? *The perception of them by our mind is as much a fact as the sight or touch of the things in which they appear.* They may have been produced by growth—they may have been the result of a process of development, but it is not the less the development of a mental purpose. *It is the end subserved that we absolutely know. What alone is doubtful and obscure is precisely that which alone we are told is the legitimate object of our research,* viz. the means by which that end has been attained. Take one instance out of millions. The poison of a deadly snake—let us for a moment consider what this is. It is a secretion of definite chemical properties which have reference not only—not even mainly—to the organism of the animal in which it is developed, but specially to the organism of another animal which it is intended to destroy. Some naturalists have a vague sort of notion that, as regards merely mechanical weapons or organs of attack, they may be developed by use, that legs may become longer by fast running, teeth sharper and longer by much biting. Be it so: this law of growth, if it exist, is but itself an instrument whereby purpose is fulfilled. But *how will this law of growth adjust a poison in one animal with such subtle knowledge of the organization of another*, that the deadly virus shall in a few minutes curdle the blood, benumb the nerves, and rush in upon the citadel of life? *There is but one explanation—a Mind, having minute and perfect knowledge of the structure of both, has designed the one to be capable of inflicting death upon the other.* This mental purpose and resolve is *the one thing* which our intelligence perceives with direct and intuitive recognition. The method of creation, by means of which this purpose has been carried into effect, is utterly unknown.

Perhaps no illustration more striking of this principle was ever presented than in the curious volume published by Mr. Darwin on the "Fertilization of Orchids." It appears that the fertilization of almost all orchids is dependent on the transport of the pollen from one flower to another by means of insects. It appears, further, that the structure of these flowers is elaborately contrived so as to secure the certainty and effectiveness of this operation. Mr. Darwin's work is devoted to tracing in detail what these contrivances are. To a large extent they are purely mechanical, and can be traced with as much clearness and certainty as the different parts of which a steam-engine is composed. *The complication and ingenuity of these contrivances almost exceed belief.* "Moth-traps and spring-guns set on these grounds," might be the motto of the orchids. There are baits to tempt the nectar-loving Lepidoptera, with rich odours exhaled at night, and lustrous colours to shine by day; there are channels of approach along which they are surely guided, so as to compel them to pass by certain spots; there are adhesive plasters nicely adjusted to fit their proboscs, or to catch their brows; there are hair-triggers, carefully set in their necessary path, communicating with explosive shells, which project the pollen-stalks with unerring aim upon their bodies. There are, in short, an infinitude of adjustments, for an idea of which I must refer my readers to Mr. Darwin's inimitable powers of observation and description—adjustments all contrived so as to secure the accurate conveyance of the pollen of the one flower to its precise destination in the structure of another.

Now, there are two questions which present themselves when we examine such a mechanism as this. *The first is, What is the use of the various parts, or their relation to each other with reference to the purpose of the whole?* The second question is, How were those parts made, and out of what materials? *It is the first of these questions—that is to say, the use, objects, intention, or purpose of the different parts of the plant—which Darwin sets himself instinctively to answer first; and it is this which he does answer with precision and success.* The second question—that is to say, how those parts come to be developed, and out of what "primordial elements" they have been derived in their present shapes, and converted to their present uses—this is a question which Darwin does also attempt to solve, but the solution of which is *in the highest degree difficult and uncertain.* It is curious to observe the language which this most advanced disciple of pure naturalism instinctively uses when he has to describe the complicated structure of this curious order of plants. "Caution in ascribing intentions to nature" does not occur to him as possible. *Intention is the one thing which he does see, and which, when he does not see, he seeks for diligently until he finds it.* He exhausts every form of words and of illustration by which intention or mental purpose can be described. "Contrivance," "curious contrivance," "beautiful contrivance,"—these are expressions which recur over and over again. Here is one sentence describing the parts of a particular species: "The Labellum is developed into a long nectary, *in order* to attract Lepidoptera, and we shall presently give reasons for suspecting that the nectar is *purposely* so lodged that it can be sucked only slowly, *in order* to give time for the curious chemical quality of the viscid matter setting hard and dry." Nor are these words used in any sense different from that in which they are applicable to the works of man's contrivance—to the instruments we use or invent for carrying into effect our own preconceived designs. On the contrary, human instruments are often selected as the aptest illustrations both of the object in view and of the means taken to effect it. Of one particular structure Mr. Darwin says: "This contrivance of the guiding ridges may be compared to the little instrument sometimes used for guiding a thread into the eye of a needle." Again, referring to the precautions taken to compel the insects to come to the proper spot, in order to have the "pollinia" attached to their bodies Mr. Darwin says: "Thus we have the rostellum partially closing the mouth of the nectary, *like a trap placed in a run for game*—and the trap so complex and perfect!" But this is not all. The idea of special use, as the controlling principle of construction, is so impressed on Mr. Darwin's mind that, in every detail of structure, however singular or obscure, he has absolute faith that in this lies the ultimate explanation. If an organ is largely developed, it is because some special purpose is to be fulfilled. If it is aborted or rudimentary, it is because that purpose is no longer to be subserved. In the case of another species whose structure is very singular, Mr. Darwin had great difficulty in discovering how the mechanism was meant to work, so as to effect the purpose. At last he made it out, and of the clue which lead to the discovery he says: "The strange position of the Labellum perched on the summit of the column *ought to have shown me that here was the place for experiment.* I ought to have scorned the notion that the Labellum was thus placed *for no good purpose.* I neglected this plain guide, and for a long time completely failed to understand the flower" (pp. 35–42).

The laws of nature are employed in the system of nature in a manner precisely analogous to that in which we ourselves employ them. The difficulties and obstructions which are presented by one law in the way of accomplishing a given purpose, are met and overcome exactly on the same principle on which they are met and overcome by man, viz. by knowledge of other laws, and by resource in applying them—that is, *by ingenuity in mechanical contrivance.* It cannot be too much insisted on, that *this is a conclusion of pure science.* The relation which an organic structure bears to its purpose *in Nature* can be recognized as certainly as the same relation between a machine and its purpose *in human art.* It is absurd to maintain, for example, that the purpose of the cellular arrangement of material in combining lightness with strength, is a purpose *legitimately cognizable by science in the Menai Bridge,* but is not *as legitimately cognizable when it is seen in Nature,* actually serving the same use. The little barnacles which crust the rocks at low tide, and which to live there at all must be able to resist the surf, have the building of their shells constructed strictly with reference to this necessity. It is a structure all hollowed and chambered *on the plan which engineers have so lately discovered* as an arrangement of material by which the power of resisting strain or pressure is multiplied in an extraordinary degree. That shell *is as pure a bit of mechanics as the bridge*, both being structures in which the same arrangement is adapted to the same end (pp. 101, 102).

There is another evidence of design furnished by nature, on which writers like Paley have laid no stress at all; but which is, in truth, as argumentatively available as the former. "Mere *ornament or beauty*," says the Duke (p. 196), "is in itself an object, a purpose, and an end."

Some of the most beautiful forms in Nature, he proceeds, are the shells of the marine Mollusca, and many of them are the richest, too, in surface ornament. But, prodigal of beauty as the ocean now is in the creatures which it holds, its wealth was even greater and more abounding in times when there was no man to gather them. The shells and corals of the old Silurian Sea were as elaborate and as richly carved as those which we now admire: and the noble Ammonites of the Secondary ages must have been glorious things indeed. Even now there is abundant evidence that although Man was intended to admire beauty, beauty was not intended only for Man's admiration. Nowhere is ornament more richly given, nowhere is it seen *more separate from the use*, than in those organisms of whose countless millions the microscope alone enables a few men for a few moments to see a few examples (pp. 198, 199).

Our readers, we are sure, will thank us for putting before them a still more beautiful passage to the same effect from a long-forgotten article in the old *British Critic*. At the same time, we disclaim sympathy with its author's various hits against Paley's particular line of argument:—

There is no purpose of mere animal life that might not have been answered quite as well without such a thing as beauty or grandeur being in the number of created things. A very few and, weighed in some scales, very trifling changes, would have made the difference—a difference to them that are blessed with eyes that see and ears that hear, but no difference to the consistent utilitarian. *A very little change in the constitution and law of light would have made all nature of a dusky brown or a sickly yellow;* a very slightly different atmosphere would have excluded the sight and knowledge of the sun, moon, and stars, without utter exclusion of their light. Trees, shrubs, and herbs of the field might have been all one shape and hue: the earth a dead level, with just fall enough for rivers and canals. The natural geography of the globe might have run in lines of latitude and longitude like the boundaries in the United States. Let some one write a book on *the Catholicism of nature*—its rites and ceremonies—its symbols—*its infinite redundance of ornament—its boundless variety of form*—its ceaseless importunity of praise. Let him exclude from count all that may be brought under the head of "utility," and there will be a still *countless remainder of superfluous beauties*. His work will have a sort of Parallelism with Paley's more Protestant undertaking; but he need not fear encroaching on the province of that ingenious writer. On the contrary, he must purposely reject whatever can come under the Paleyan formula. His business will be with those features and qualities of the creation which are useless on mere physical principles; and only useful, and probably intentional, for their effect on the human soul, as *outwardly conspiring with its inward instincts to produce and cherish the sense of the beautiful, the awful, and the sublime* (Oct., 1841, pp. 468, 469).

Now, it would carry us entirely away from our course of argument, if we attempted here to consider how far natural phenomena, taken by themselves, would prove or even render probable the proposition that their Designer possesses the attribute of *Infinity*, or again of *Sanctity*. But we are here urging that, at all events, they make His *Existence* absolutely certain—the Existence of a real designing Mind. This is the one most certain of all lessons which physical science teaches; and this bears importantly on our present subject. The Creator originally fixed the laws of nature, with a view to certain momentous purposes; it is surely, then, far more probable than not that He *still* actively occupies Himself in the advancement of these purposes. It is far more probable, we say, that He still actively forwards those ends which He has at heart than that He rests content with such promotion of them, as was involved in the very fact of creation. A Creator, self-banished from active interference with the movements of His own work, is a possible indeed, but surely an almost incredible hypothesis.

We now proceed to the argument on which we are principally to dwell, as supporting belief in God's constant and unremitting premovement of natural laws. And we commence this argument by inquiring what is that imaginable conclusion of physical science which *would* disprove the doctrine we advocate. We answer most readily: *the abstract power of indefinite prediction.* Our imaginary objector took for granted that any person of superhuman and adequate intelligence, who should know thoroughly and accurately all the various properties and combinations of matter which now exist, could predict infallibly the whole series of future phenomena. If this hypothesis were established as true, there would at once result a final and absolute *disproof* of that great verity which we are defending; a final and absolute disproof of every notion that God does unintermittently premove the laws of nature. Let us suppose for a moment that we have no means of information on the subject, except physical science itself. Were this the case, so far as scientific investigations have added greater or less probability to the supposition that there exists an abstract power of indefinite prediction, precisely so far they would have added greater or less probability to the supposition that phenomena proceed independently of God's premovement. Here, then, we are at the very heart of that unspeakably momentous question which we are discussing.

Before going further, then, let us make it more clear and unmistakable that we have correctly stated the point at issue. And, firstly, when we speak of "indefinite prediction," what do we mean by this word "indefinite?" We use it as contra-distinguished from the word "brief." Let us go back for a moment to our imaginary polycordon.

It may well be supposed, considering the extraordinary complication which we ascribe to its machinery, that some ten minues, *e.g.*, shall elapse between the human premovement and its musical result. Philosophical mice, then—those who have investigated one hundred and fifty out of the two hundred intervening links—might be well able to predict quite infallibly, at least seven minutes beforehand, the coming melody. And so as to physical facts. We believe Sir H. Fitzroy was at last obliged to give up his attempted prognostication of weather from the mischievous or amusing blunders into which he constantly fell. Yet we can well suppose, as science advances, that a coming storm might be predicted with almost infallible accuracy, say twenty-four hours before the event. And yet it would none the less be true that, as man, according to our supposition, plays constantly on the polychordon, so God is constantly playing, so to speak, on the vast instrument of nature.

But now take a different type of musical instruments. The power of imagination, as we have more than once said, is boundless. Let us suppose, then, some huge instrument, constructed on the principle of a barrel-organ: set for ten years to a continuance of successive and never-recurring airs, and with mechanical provision for its constant movement throughout that period. Our philosophical mice, if shut up within such an instrument as this, might undoubtedly arrive at an indefinite power of predicting their future musical entertainment. If in five years' time they had successfully explored and studied the machinery, the last five years would furnish an uninterrupted fulfilment of their scientific predictions. And from such a circumstance they might most legitimately and irresistibly infer, not merely that their instrument, like the polychordon, acts on fixed laws; but also that, *un*like the polychordon, it is not affected by any arbitrary movement from without. There is no external player, they most logically infer, who unintermittently premoves the machinery for his own purposes. Undoubtedly, therefore, if any class of phenomena be abstractedly capable of indefinite scientific prediction, this class of phenomena is *not* premoved by Almighty God.

Here, then, is the vital and essential issue of our present investigation. How far, we inquire, has the course of science, taken by itself, added probability to the supposition that there is an abstract scientific possibility of indefinitely predicting the future course of all external phenomena? Most assuredly science has not approximated to *proving* such abstract possibility; but we really believe more than this. We believe that the march of scientific progress has been in such a direction that, on scientific grounds alone, the abstract possibility of such indefinite prediction is a more improbable hypothesis now than it was two centuries ago. For consider. What can be more amazing than the present rapid advance of scientific truth? " The enlargement of the circle of secular knowledge just now is simply a bewilderment; and the more so, because it has the promise of continuing, and with greater rapidity and more signal results." * The speculative and the practical results of science succeed each other with a rapidity which almost takes away one's breath. Suppose some inquirer of the seventeenth century, earnestly devoted to scientific pursuits, and possessing no firm grasp of religious truth—suppose such a man had been authoritatively told of the astounding development which science was to receive in this nineteenth century. If there is one augury rather than another which such an inquirer would most confidently have made, it would be that the sphere of *scientific prediction* must by this time have received an incredible enlargement. And yet what are the facts? The more astounding you consider the rapidity with which

* "Apologia," p. 401.

science advances, so much the more astounding must you consider one further fact. We mean the fact that this rapid advance *has not brought with it, in any one fresh department, any power whatever of indefinite prediction.* Astronomical facts were from the very first, to a large extent, capable of indefinite prediction; and science has no doubt in some degree enlarged the sphere of that capability. Science has enabled men, *e.g.*, to predict eclipses; the periodical return of comets; and certain other astronomical phenomena. But take such particulars as are relevant to the present inquiry, how widely different is the case! When did the Church ever pray against comets and eclipses? On the contrary, what *are* those temporal evils from which Christians have besought deliverance? Famine, disease, unseasonable weather, war, shipwreck, extreme poverty, and the like. There is not one of these, in regard to which there are the faintest signs that it will hereafter be capable of indefinite scientific prediction. The Church's supplications may still be put forth by the most scientific Catholic, with as simple faith and fervour as by the most ignorant of rustics. "Ut morbos auferat, famem depellat, aperiat carceres, vincula dissolvat, peregrinantibus reditum, infirmantibus sanitatem, navigantibus portum salutis indulgeat,"—these are blessings which a scientific Catholic of the nineteenth century, no less than of the first, recognizes without the slightest perplexity as obtainable from God through prayer. It is surely most remarkable that the whole of this has been, as it were, charmed ground, proof against all the incursions of advancing science.

Indeed, the contrast between astronomy and other sciences admits perhaps of being dwelt on more particularly. From the earliest periods mankind must have been struck with the broad difference of action between what we may call respectively *cosmical* and *earthly* phenomena: the former proceeding on a course so steady, equable, and amenable to calculation; the latter so apparently variable and capricious. By cosmical phenomena, we mean such as the hours of sunrise and sunset; of moonrise and moonset; the respective apparent position of the heavenly bodies, etc. By earthly phenomena we mean such as the weather; the violence and direction of the wind; the progress of disease; and others of a similar kind. The discovery of Copernicanism placed these two phenomenal classes in far more striking contrast. It appears that cosmical phenomena are produced by an incredibly vast machinery, in which this earth plays a very subordinate part; whereas earthly phenomena are due in great measure to agencies which act exclusively within the region of our planet. From the very first, therefore, there was a real presumption that these latter agencies were subject to a premovement, quite different in kind from any which influenced the former; and this presumption would be very greatly increased by the discoveries of Galileo and his successors. Now, it is most remarkable, and bears thinking of again and again, that the only power of indefinite prediction which science has ever procured concerns cosmical phenomena and not earthly. The spontaneous impression made even on the mind of savages, as we have already said, is that the march of cosmical phenomena is steady and equable, while the march of earthly phenomena is variable and incalculable. The effect of science has been only to make this contrast more striking and more unexceptional than it was before.*

Now, there is a further opinion, which, to say the least is theologically probable in a very high degree; and which, if admitted, will throw great light on this contrast between cosmical and earthly phenomena. It is the received-doctrine of the schools—it is far the more obvious implication of Scripture—that there are no rational and immortal

* See note at the end of this essay.

creatures, excepting only Angels and men. But if this be so, it would seem necessarily to follow that this planet, and no other, is the abode of rational and immortal creatures. Dr. Whewell's work on "the Plurality of Worlds" showed at the very least that physical science interposes no kind of obstacle to this belief; and we will, therefore, suppose it to be true. But if this proposition be accepted, you see at once how *a priori probable* it is that God should confine His constant premovement of physical sequences to that particular planet, which is inhabited by immortal beings; by those beings whom His Son has redeemed; by those beings who can plead for temporal blessings in that Son's availing Name.*

* A very eminent thinker, whose view of all these matters is diametrically opposed to our own, has most kindly given his attention to this essay since it has been in type. He here interposes an objection. He admits most fully the contrast between cosmical and earthly phenomena, as regards their respective capability (in the present state of science) of indefinite prediction. But he urges that a cause may most easily be assigned for this contrast, entirely distinct from any supposition of Divine premovement; viz. the fact that cosmical phenomena depend on causes comparatively simpler and fewer than those which produce earthly phenomena. It is nothing marvellous, he adds, that we can predict the result of causes which are few and simple, but *cannot* predict the result of those which are most numerous and complicated.

Here the first question to be considered is, whether such difference of causal complexity, however great, would in itself *suffice* to account for the contrast, admitted by our opponent, between those two classes of phenomena. On this question the present writer is wholly incompetent to form an opinion; but we submit it to the careful consideration of Catholic scientific men. For argument's sake, at all events, we will here concede that our opponent is so far in the right.

We frankly confess, then, that our *positive* argument from physical science, in behalf of Divine premovement, is very far less strong than it *would* have been had earthly phenomena resembled cosmical in the simplicity of their causation. Indeed, had this been so, their Divine premovement would have been (so to speak) a visible and palpable fact. But then it is not the general law of God's Providence that the truths of religion *shall* be visible and palpable facts; but, on the contrary, that they shall give occasion to the merit of faith. Let it be assumed, then, that God does premove earthly phenomena: and let the further very obvious supposition be also made, that He does not desire this premovement to be a visible and a palpable fact. On this supposition, He would act just as we maintain that He *has* acted. He would make earthly phenomena to proceed on so complex a chain of causation, that His assiduous premovement of them eludes direct observation.

At the same time, we would beg our readers distinctly to observe that this contrast between cosmical and earthly phenomena is no essential part of our argument. No scientific man in the world will maintain that science has *proved* any capability of indefinite prediction to exist, in the case of those temporal goods for which a Christian prays. Our argument, then—which is irrefragable and complete—may be thus drawn out. The Christian and Catholic religion has its own intrinsic motives of credibility; and such as may really be called peremptory and demonstrative. It is a most certain truth of that religion—it is declared so repeatedly in Scripture that it would be absurd even to attempt an enumeration of texts—that the most available of all methods for averting temporal calamities and for obtaining a healthy proportion of temporal goods, is prayer to God.* And it is an immediate inference from this truth, that God is constantly intervening in the course of nature, according to the inscrutable plans of His Providence. On the other hand, physical science has added strength to the proof otherwise existing of another and supplementary truth; viz. that external phenomena, putting aside the case of Miracles, which is afterwards to be considered, proceed uniformly and invariably on fixed laws. There is no inconsistency whatever, nor any approach to inconsistency, between these two truths; and the only reasonable course,

At last our opponent admits, with characteristic candour, that science in its present stage is unable to *disprove* the hypothesis of Divine premovement; and, as we state in the text, this is absolutely all which our argument requires.

[It may now be added without impropriety that this "very eminent thinker" was the late Mr. Mill.]

* See, *e.g.*, 2 Paralip. xv. 12, 13 :—" Nec [Asa] in infirmitate suâ quæsivit Dominum, *sed magis in medicorum arte confisus est:* dormivitque cum patribus suis." *Cf.* vv. 7-9 :—" In tempore illo venit Hanani propheta ad Asa regem Judæet dixit ei : ' Quia *habuisti fiduciam in rege Syriæ et non in Domino Deo tuo,* idcirco evasit Syriæ regis exercitus de manu tuâ. Nonne Æthiopes et Libyes multò plures erant quadrigis et equitibus et multitudine nimiâ quos cùm Domino credidisses tradidit in manu tuâ? Oculi enim Domini præbent fortitudinem his *qui corde perfecto credunt in Eum.*'"

therefore, is heartily to embrace them both. It is true, therefore, on the one hand, that the laws of external nature, with the above-named exception, are strictly invariable; but it is equally true on the other hand, that those laws are premoved and directed by God at every moment, according to the dictates of His uncontrolled and inscrutable Will. Philosophers who on theory refuse to pray, pursue a course no less simply unreasonable than any superstitious Christian, if such there were, who should be led, by his belief in the efficacy of prayer, to deny the possibility of physical science.

One final explanation. Our argument, be it observed, by no means requires us to deny any general uniformity which experience may indicate, in God's premovement of natural laws. It may be true, *e.g.*, that He more often sends rain in July than in June; and that the amount of rain which falls in one year is not very different from that which falls in another year. If scientific observation have established these facts, they are of course true: but, however true, they present no difficulty whatever to a Catholic or to any other Christian. Indeed, one would expect *à priori* much greater regularity of action from the All-Wise God, than from the human player on a musical instrument.

Let us now, then, consider the treatment given by our three authors, to that part of the general subject which has occupied us up to this point. Dr. Gilbert expresses most fairly and most forcibly, without one particle of exaggeration, the objection to which we have been hitherto replying.

Many of you may, no doubt, also remember how the futility, the uselessness of prayer is reported to have been pithily put by Lord Palmerston, in answer to the deputation which waited upon him for a public fast-day against the cholera. His answer is said to have been, " Never mind the fast day, but cleanse your drains."

From the positions taken by these men and their adherents, it follows not only that prayer against the cholera is useless, but that all prayer, where the laws of nature are concerned, is absurd, useless, puerile, if not positively wicked; so that, if you naturally suffer from indigestion, a thousand graces before meals will not save you from the consequences; if you naturally suffer from sleepless nights, *all the prayers of your friends will not procure as much sleep as a single drop of laudanum*; the prayer or the blessing of a parent on a child that is leaving his home, perhaps for ever, avails no more than the rustling of the wind; the prayers of a whole nation suffering from famine or pestilence affect God no more than the sorrowful sounds of the wild waves beating against the hard rocks; and finally, *as all temptations are mostly dependent upon an unequal distribution of the humours of the body, a night of prayer will not remove or even lessen one of them.*

With the efficacy of prayer, adds Dr. Gilbert, *the Bible stands or falls.* Hence the vast importance of the subject; it concerns not only the members of the one religion, but all who wish to be Christians, all who hold the Bible to be God's sacred Word (p. 4).

And further—

Besides the testimony of the Bible and Christianity, the instincts of our nature, no matter what our religion may be proclaim the efficacy of prayer (p. 10).

His own reply to the objection consists of three different particulars. Firstly, he adopts to some extent our own solution—the Divine premovement of natural laws. If *man*, he argues, can modify the laws of nature, how far more readily can this be done by God, the Author of those laws!

How countless are the modifications in natural causes produced by man! You cannot speak, you cannot walk, you cannot light a fire, without such modifications. There is not a word that passes from our lips that does not cause waves and pulsations of the air; there is not a keel that ploughs the surface of the sea that does not send an influence through the surrounding waters; there is not a man or beast that treads upon the earth that does not impart a motion to some of the particles thereof, and so modify the power or force of some of the waves of the air and of the sea, and of some of the particles of the land.

Now, as man is continually modifying natural causes, and is thereby curing disease, increasing the fertility of the land, and lessening accidents by land and sea, *allow God a similar power,* and though the laws of nature are immutable, every ordinary prayer can be heard (pp. 14, 15).

Our only comment, so far, would be, that he represents God's "modification of natural causes" as comparatively rare and exceptional; whereas to us it seems far more simple and straightforward to regard such intervention as unceasing. Such a view seems to us more accordant than any other with the language of Theology and Scripture; which surely represent God, not as occasionally interfering, but rather as ruling the events of each successive moment by His inscrutable and uncontrolled Will.

Secondly, Dr. Gilbert suggests (p. 16) that God may really disturb phenomenal uniformity, not in the way of what are commonly called miracles, but by altering the agency of "second causes out of sight." Such a course of Providence is undoubtedly possible in itself; and we believe we may safely defy scientific men to prove that God never adopts it. At the same time we do not ourselves see any necessity for the supposition, or any evidence of its truth.

But Dr. Gilbert's third suggestion shows, we think, that he has not fully mastered his opponent's view. He says that God may indirectly influence *matter* by directly influencing *mind.*

. . . Could not God, on a similar principle, suppress in man the feelings of anger, jealousy, and revenge, and every temptation? Could He not influence the mind of man, and so prevent him entering on a course of action which would bring ruin on himself and others? Could not God influence the mind of a captain so that he shall perceive a leakage in his vessel, or the mind of an engine-driver and he shall discover an impediment on the line of rails, and such influence shall save themselves and others from mutilation and even death? Could not God influence the mind of a physician, and, when he has ineffectually battled with some disease, suggest some combination of natural remedies which shall meet the peculiarities of the case? And so in numerous instances (p. 15).

Dr. Gilbert is answering certain arguments which purport to establish the impossibility of God's free and unfettered action on matter. But the very same arguments, if they had any weight at all, would be in every respect equally conclusive against the possibility of His exercising such influence on *mind*. Of course we most fully agree with Dr. Gilbert, that in both cases God does possess this power. We only say that our author cannot logically *assume* God's possession of this power over the mind, as a means of *explaining* how He may possess it over matter.

As to the Duke of Argyll, it is one singular instance of the strange incompleteness with which he has written, that we have found it impossible to decide with certainty whether he does or does not accept our doctrine of Divine premovement. He speaks, *e.g.*, of a "Supreme Will" "moving the hidden springs of nature" (p. 23); of a "Higher Will moving phenomena" (*ibid.*). He holds (p. 24) that Nature is a "plastic medium through which a Higher Voice and Will *are ever addressing us*." And all this seems directly available towards solving that difficulty, which, as we have already pointed out, he so forcibly and clearly states—the difficulty alleged against all belief in the efficacy of prayer. And yet it would appear that, after all, he does *not* make use of these considerations in answer to that difficulty; but, on the contrary, confines them to the particular case of *miraculous* intervention. He applies them in fact exclusively in that case to which, as we shall presently contend, they are entirely inapplicable.

Mr. M'Coll, so far as we are able to understand his argument, embraces the precise view which we have ourselves maintained. "Christianity," he says, "teaches the doctrine" "that God is behind the veil of Nature *working always*" (p. 429). But his argument, we think, required that he should have developed this view far more clearly and systematically than he has in fact done.

We have now, then, answered the first of those objections which we stated at the outset. In reply to the second, nothing more is needed than that we should transfer our argument from the macrocosm to the microcosm; from the realms of matter to the realms of mind. In this part of our reasoning we may fully admit, for argument's sake, that psychology is a science, in the very same full and unreserved sense in which mechanics and chemistry are such; that mental phenomena, no less than mechanical and chemical, succeed each other by a sequence which is absolutely fixed and invariable. The uniformity, however, of *material* phenomena is fully reconcilable with the doctrine of an unintermitting Divine premovement; and the same truth holds no less clearly in the case of *mental* phenomena also. Nor, again, does mental science, at all more than mechanical or chemical, afford the slightest indication that there exists that *abstract* scientific *possibility of indefinite prediction* which would alone disprove our doctrine. But now what is Divine Grace—so far as it is contemplated by the objection before us—except simply a Divine premovement of mental phenomena? * And if we may laudably and efficaciously pray for material benefits, with far more laudableness and efficacy may we pray for the priceless blessing of rich and more effectual Grace.

No one of our three authors has put forth a reply to this second objection; and Dr. Gilbert, indeed, as we have already observed, does not seem aware of its existence.

We are next to enter on Freewill: a far more anxious subject than those hitherto considered, as being so intimately connected with some of the most arduous and mysterious doctrines in Theology. We shall confine ourselves, however, strictly to what is absolutely necessary for

* The office of Grace, in *supernaturalizing* the soul and human action, is of course wholly external to the objection which we are here considering.

a due appreciation of the objection which we are to encounter.

The Church allows considerable latitude of opinion on the philosophical questions which concern Freewill. At the same time she fully permits her children to hold—what for ourselves, *i.e.* the present writer, we do hold—viz. that no view of Freewill is altogether satisfactory to the intellect, except that taken by the Jesuit theologians. These great thinkers—whether they embrace what is commonly called the Molinistic or the Congruistic system, whether they follow Lessius or Suarez—agree with each other in their definition of liberty. "Potentia libera est quæ, positis omnibus requisitis ad agendum, potest agere et non agere." To appreciate this definition, let us consider any given moment of human action. My soul possesses certain qualities, intrinsic and inherent; certain faculties, tendencies, habits, and the like: and it is solicited by various motives, having respectively their own special character, intensity, and direction. In order that my will may act, nothing more is necessary than that which now exists: "posita sunt omnia requisita ad agendum." My will cannot be considered *free*, say these theologians, unless at this very moment it has a real power, at least of either acting or abstaining from action. They consider, of course, that in the vast majority of cases it has *more* power than this; it has the power of acting with greater or less efficacy in this or that direction; but unless it have at least *so much* power as above described, it is not free at all.

We think that the least valuable part of the Duke of Argyll's work is that concerned with Freewill. He professes (p. 337) to oppose Mr. Stuart Mill, and to expose "a deceptive ambiguity" under which that philosopher's "doctrine seeks shelter;" but in fact, to our mind, it is Mr. Mill who is clear-headed, and the Duke who is misty and confused. His own view is precisely identical with

Mr. Mill's; and it is strange that he can have entertained any different notion. "The will of *the lower animals*," he says frankly (p. 331), "is *as free as ours*.... The only difference is that the will of the lower animals is acted upon by fewer and simpler motives." "Where all the conditions of mental action are constant, the resulting action will be constant too" (p. 338). "*If* we know *all* the motives which are brought by external things to bear upon his mind; and *if* we knew all the other motives which that mind evolves out of its own powers, and out of previously acquired materials, to bear upon itself; and *if* we knew the constitution of that mind perfectly;... *then* we should be able to" calculate "*with certainty* the resulting course of conduct" (p. 339).* Now, there is nothing to surprise one in the fact that the Duke of Argyll should hold that necessarian doctrine which is embraced by many powerful minds. But surely he displays much shallowness or thoughtlessness, when he says (p. 338) that his own view "is not only true, but something *very like a truism.*" We maintain that, on the contrary, it is directly subversive, not of Catholicity only, but of natural religion. Before arguing, however, for this proposition, we must make the reader more clearly understand what is the Duke's doctrine.

The view advocated, then, by Mr. Mill clearly, and by

* The Duke's text runs: "If we knew the constitution of the mind so *perfectly as to estimate exactly the weight it will allow to all the different motives operating on it.*" We have omitted these words in the text, as they might tend to distract attention from the Duke's meaning. They involve a *petitio principii*, since they imply in themselves the necessarian tenet. We precisely *deny*, of course, that the weight attached to motives *depends* exclusively on "the constitution of the mind." The mind, we maintain, whatever its constitution, has a certain power of deciding *for itself* what weight it shall attach to motives.

We have also placed the word "calculate" where the Duke says "predict." The meaning remains exactly the same. But we think it of great importance, for the sake of clearness, to preserve a broad verbal distinction between that "abstract possibility of indefinite *prediction*" on which we laid so much stress a few pages ago, and that abstract power of immediate *calculation* with which alone we are here concerned.

the Duke obscurely, is this : that in every single case the will's action is *abstractedly calculable*. Take an illustration from mechanics. A certain physical particle, possessing certain intrinsic qualities, is solicited at this moment by certain attracting forces. It is admitted by every one, that the movement immediately resulting is abstractedly calculable. In other words, any being who should possess adequate intelligence and infallible accuracy of thought; who should know with perfect precision the particle's intrinsic qualities ; who should know with equal precision the nature, the direction, the intensity, of the soliciting forces ;—could calculate with infallible certainty the movement immediately resulting. In like manner, say Mr. Mill and the Duke, let us suppose the mind of any given individual solicited at this moment by certain given motives. " Any being who should possess adequate intelligence and infallible accuracy of thought ; who should know with perfect precision that mind's intrinsic and inherent qualities ; who should know with equal precision the nature, the direction, the intensity, of the soliciting motives ;—could calculate with infallible accuracy the movement of will thence immediately resulting. Or, putting the same thing briefly, the will's movement at any moment is in the abstract capable of infallible calculation."

Now we, on our side, maintain that this tenet is subversive of that doctrine, concerning man's probation by means of Freewill,* which is at the very root, not of

---

* We purposely avoid saying that the Duke's tenet is inconsistent with the doctrine of Freewill in every imaginable shape, for the following reasons :— Jesus and Mary, when on earth, were truly endowed with Freewill: and yet Jesus and Mary—our Lord because He was God, and His Mother because of her singular grace—always elicited with infallible certainty that movement which was simply accordant with the Divine preference. So far, therefore, as they were concerned, the course of their will at any moment was abstractedly capable of infallible calculation. But then they were *not* on their probation. In like manner, we are not here concerned with the free will of Beati in Heaven, or of souls in Purgatory.

Catholicity only, but of natural religion. At this moment I am solicited by various motives; and it is my *probation* of this moment, how I shall comport myself under that solicitation. If I exert myself to please God better, my probation so far is advancing favourably; if otherwise, the reverse. But the very notion of my being on probation *at all*, implies that my will's action cannot be calculated beforehand; it implies that more than one course is, in the fullest and most unreserved sense, open to my free and unfettered choice. Let me once be persuaded, not speculatively alone, but practically and energetically, that my will's action at last can be no less infallibly calculated than the motion of a particle, I sink down paralyzed: religion becomes a mockery; and my Creator's profession of placing me under probation becomes (may He forgive the blasphemy!) a tyrannical insult. This is really one of those truths, which are so undeniable on the very surface, that their evidence is but obscured by any lengthened production of argument.

Our purpose in the present essay, as we have throughout explained, is purely defensive. Indeed, had we entertained any thought of *proving* those high religious truths with which we are occupied, we should have found it swell under our hands to a volume. We have now, indeed, pointed out that Freewill is an all-important religious truth; that it is a fundamental doctrine, not of Catholicity only, but of natural religion: but to enter upon a philosophical argument in its favour is entirely beyond our scope. What we have here to do is merely to answer the *objections* brought against it by such thinkers as Mr. Mill and the Duke of Argyll.

1. Mr. Mill in several parts of his works lays stress on the following:—"All Theists," he says in effect, "must admit that *God* at least does at each moment infallibly calculate the will's movement; and they must admit, there-

fore, that it is in the abstract *capable* of calculation." The reply to this is so obvious, that we have always wondered how this clear and powerful thinker can have been deluded by so transparent a fallacy. We totally deny, of course, that God does *calculate* the will's movement in the case of those under probation; on the contrary, His knowledge of that movement supposes, as its very foundation, the will's *free* exercise in this or that direction.* Nay, it is not strictly true to say that God *fore*sees acts at all, because He is external to time.

"Nothing to Him is present, nothing past,
But an Eternal Now doth ever last."

2. "There is no certainty," says the Duke (pp. 339, 340), "in the world of physics more absolutely certain than some certainties in the world of mind. We know that a humane man will not do a uselessly cruel action; we know that an honourable man will not do a base action." Well, there is a multitude of actions so cruel, and another multitude so base, that we may infallibly calculate of a humane and of an honourable man respectively, that he will not, until his character change, commit them. But such a statement has no value as grave reasoning. "Dolus latet in generalibus:" let us take a concrete case. I am a man, we will say, of really humane character. I am sitting comfortably at my fireside on a cold winter's day, with "The Last Chronicle of Barset" in my hands. Suddenly the news reaches me that a friend of mine has been immersed, while skating on a deep pond close to the house. You may calculate, no doubt, with infallible certainty, that I shall throw down my book and rush to the rescue. But take some case of an immeasurably more

* "Dei præscientia, ex doctrinâ Patrum, res *liberè* futuras *supponit.*" " In hypothesi quòd res futuræ sint, *eo ipso quòd futuræ sint*, Deus eas videre debet: *consequenter*, nempe ad *liberam* determinationem. . . . Cùm verum sit hominem se determinaturum ad talem vel talem actionem, *hoc ipso* Divinæ notitiæ subest."—" Perrone de Deo," nu. 393, 400.

frequent kind. I have been in the habit of reading to a poor cripple in the neighbourhood, who has nothing else to cheer him. The last two days I have been unavoidably prevented from going; and to-day also, if I do not start at once, I shall have no other opportunity. On the other hand, the outside air is cold; while the fire is warm, and Mr. Trollope, even for him, unusually amusing. Humanity draws me in one direction, comfort and amusement very strongly in another. Humanity solicits me to spend an hour in a cold draughty cottage, occupied in a very dull employment; comfort and amusement importune me to stay where I am. Under such circumstances, it is the Duke of Argyll's proposition, that the course which I shall adopt is as infallibly calculable as is the course of a physical particle solicited by divergent forces. Now, at all events, to allege, as the Duke alleges, that his proposition is *self-evident*, is a most startling paradox; a simple outrage on common sense : you can hardly exaggerate the violent absurdity of so speaking. But we should like uncommonly to know what possible ground the Duke has for alleging, we will not say that his proposition is *self-evident*, but that it is *true*. For ourselves, we take the liberty of affirming that it is entirely false; and we affirm this of it, because it is peremptorily condemned by religion and morality.

Now, it is precisely such cases as these which are of every-day occurrence, and on which man's probation mainly turns. The ordinary exhortation of a priest, or, for that matter, of any religious minister who is not a Lutheran or Calvinist, would be, we strenuously maintain, the only one consistent with sound philosophy. He would tell me that it is just on such an issue as this, that my upward or downward course might depend. If I choose the lower course, he will add, the course which I well know to be the less pleasing to my Creator, I begin the habit of fully deliberate imperfection; and on my next occasion of trial I shall find greater difficulty than at present, in freely making the better choice. Let me continue so acting for months and years, I shall be an immeasurably less humane man at the end of them than I am at present. On the other hand, if I correspond with grace and on every such occasion freely choose the better alternative, then, in the way even of natural consequence, my character will steadily rise; not to speak of the special benediction which I shall call down on myself, from my loving and approving God. Between these two alternatives, he will continue, I have now and on every such occasion the freest power of choosing. Such are the doctrines which a priest would practically impress on me as speculative truths. They belong to the very alphabet of natural religion, but they are doctrines which the Duke of Argyll by implication denies.

The sum, then, of our reply to this particular argument of the Duke's is simply this. Take any given man at any given moment. There are certain things so good, and certain things so bad, that we may infallibly calculate he will do neither the one nor the other. But then there is a large number of intermediate things, on which no such calculation is even abstractedly possible; and these are the very things on which his probation turns.*

3. Lastly, we are to consider that objection to Freewill which is most closely indentified with the direct purpose of our article. "If this doctrine of Freewill were true, and of probation by *means* of Freewill, then the course of mental phenomena is not in itself calculable; and if not, then psychology is no science at all. But such a conclusion is so paradoxical and so obviously false, as of itself to overthrow that theory from which it legitimately results." We

* The Duke of Argyll commented on these remarks in a subsequent edition of his work, and a reply to his comment was published in the *Dublin Review* for October, 1868, pp. 55, 56.

admit frankly in reply, that psychology is not as strictly scientific, throughout its whole extent, as mechanics or chemistry. But before replying to the objection which will be *founded* on that admission, we must consider how far the admission itself should extend. In other words, we will now consider to *what extent*, assuming the doctrine of Freewill, psychology fails of a strictly scientific character.

There are three different classes of mental phenomena: cognitions, volitions, emotions. Psychology, then, is divisible into five sections : the three former treating respectively these three classes in themselves, and the two latter treating them in their mutual relations. Of these five sections, the four former are absolutely unaffected by the doctrine of Freewill; and are therefore as strictly scientific as mechanics and chemistry. That section of psychology with which alone we are concerned, is that which treats the relation between cognitions and volitions ; between intellect and will. Even as regards this section of psychology, we need only look at one particular sub-section, viz. the theory of motives. Undoubtedly, granting Freewill, there can be no strictly scientific theory of motives. We are now, therefore, to inquire, how far this particular sub-section of psychology—the theory of motives—is deflected by the doctrine of Freewill from the rigorous character of a science.

We will here, then, lay down a proposition, which, beyond all possible question, is fully consistent with the doctrine of Freewill ; and which for our part we confidently embrace as true. My soul at some given moment possesses certain qualities intrinsic and inherent ; certain faculties, tendencies, habits, and the like. It is solicited, moreover, by certain motives, having their own special character, intensity, and direction. Our proposition is this. Under such circumstances, science, considered in its abstract perfection, may calculate infallibly the " spontaneous resultant," of those motives ; or, in other words, my will's "spontaneous impulse." Now, this proposition is indubitably consistent with Freewill, because I have the fullest power of *opposing* my will's spontaneous impulse. My thoughts are at this moment, perhaps, predominantly influenced by worldly or sensual motives. I may turn them, however, by an effort towards what is heavenly and divine ; but if I do *not* put forth some exertion, I follow as a matter of course my will's spontaneous impulse. How far I may *choose* to put forth such exertion—*this* is not abstractedly matter of calculation at all. I acquit myself more laudably under my probation, precisely in proportion as I more frequently and more energetically put forth effort in a good direction.* At the same time, it should be observed that in all ordinary cases the act of will, which results *in fact*, is found in *close vicinity* to the will's spontaneous impulse. It is only in the rarest and most exceptional cases—or rather, we may say, it never happens at all—that a man of ordinary piety will be found putting forth an act of heroic saintliness. In 999 cases out of 1000 a man's probation is carried to a successful issue by this more than by anything else, viz. by putting forward on repeated occasions a number of acts, which are *a little* higher than his spontaneous impulse. Nor does any exception to this general remark strike us at the moment, except those cases in which there is a violent temptation to mortal sin.

We maintain, then, that so far as regards, not the will's *actual movement*, but its *spontaneous impulse*, there is a theory of motives as strictly scientific, as abstractedly capable of scientific calculation, as any theory of mechanics or chemistry. But we further maintain that, in applying that theory to practice, allowance must always be made for

* The whole doctrine of preventing and assisting grace is of course *in fact* most intimately bound up with all this ; but our argument against necessarianism may be conducted legitimately without encumbering it with this further question.

the fact that in every instance the will has a real power of acting above the level of such spontaneous impulse. How far the will may *choose* to do so, is a matter incapable of calculation, and external to science altogether. And this circumstance precisely, neither more nor less, constitutes that one particular in which the doctrine of Freewill interferes with the strictly scientific character of psychology.

We are next, then, to inquire what arguments our opponents can adduce, for the purpose of showing that psychology has a more unreservedly scientific character than we have here assigned to it. Now, there are certain German writers, we believe, who have maintained that the fact of phenomenal uniformity can be established on pure *a priori* grounds; indeed, that it is not a mere *fact* at all, but as necessary a *truth* as the very axioms and theorems of geometry. We are wholly unaware, however, of the grounds on which they base so strange an assertion; nor do we know in what direction to look for those grounds.

But the writers with whom we are immediately concerned do not dream of putting forth any such peremptory pretension. We cannot take any more unexceptionable specimen of them than Mr. Mill; nor again can anything be more intelligible and simple than the position which he takes up. (See his "Logic," bk. iii. c. 3, and c. 21.) Scientific men, he says, ground their belief of phenomenal uniformity exclusively on their *observation* of that uniformity. Consequently, "the uniformity in the succession of events," and generally of phenomena, "must be received, not as a *law of the universe*, but of that portion of it only which is within the range of *our means of sure observation*." (Conclusion of c. 21.)

The present issue, then, is reduced to one which would appear very narrow and very easily decided. Can Mr. Mill, or any one else, allege any observed facts which vindicate for mental phenomena any greater uniformity of sequence than we have above assigned to them? Neither on Mr. Mill's part, nor on the Duke of Argyll's, have we observed the slightest *attempt* to adduce such facts. The doctrine of Freewill rests on philosophical arguments, which we do not profess here to adduce, but than which no stronger, as we confidently think, ever established a philosophical conclusion. We verily believe that in no other case has so strongly demonstrated a doctrine been opposed so confidently, we had almost said so superciliously, on grounds so frivolous, poverty-stricken, and meagre.

Take, for instance, Mr. Mill, a thinker of real genius and depth. With the single exception of that weak piece of reasoning above quoted, based on God's foreknowledge of human action, we are really not aware of one single argument, good, bad, or indifferent, which he has ever brought against the doctrine of Freewill.* He commonly contents himself with stating repeatedly and emphatically the *contradictory* tenet, that all mental phenomena proceed on an absolutely fixed and invariable sequence. He constantly speaks of this tenet, as though it were self-evident; and as though it sufficed, therefore, *by* such self-evidence, to disprove the dogma of Freewill. The Duke of Argyll, indeed, has adduced two reasons for the necessarian view; but they appear to us singularly feeble. One has been already noticed above; the other is rather implied in various places (see *e.g.* pp. 352, 363, 366) than directly stated. If the will were free, he says in effect, the science of politics would be impossible; for that science proceeds on an assumption that you may calculate the effect of this or that motive on the people's mind. We reply very easily. It results from what has been above said, that the "spontaneous impulse" of man's will under given circumstances is a matter in itself as simply capable of scientific calcula-

* This was published before the appearance of Mr. Mill's work on Sir W. Hamilton.

tion as is the motion of a physical point solicited by given attractions. And this truth is an abundantly sufficient basis for political science.

In fact it is obvious, as soon as stated, that you confer on men a moral benefit which no words can exaggerate, by placing them under the best motives; *i.e.* by placing them under motives the " spontaneous resultant " of which shall be morally good in the highest attainable degree. This principle, as we have seen, is most fully consistent with Freewill; and yet it is all which the politician can possibly need as a motive for action. Nor can any one dream that the Church has been blind or indifferent to this principle, who considers the unparalleled stress which she has ever laid, *e.g.*, on a good education : on the contrary it may rather be affirmed, that there is no philosophical doctrine in the world which has had so large an influence on her whole practical conduct. All that can be said on the other side is, that she has not exhibited that narrowness of thought which in this respect characterizes certain anti-Catholic philosophers. For, in remembering the unspeakable importance of good motives, she has not forgotten what may be called the opposite pole of sound doctrine, viz. the will's real power of choice, and God's probation of man by means of that power.

The objection, which remains to be considered, concerns *miracles*. Certainly, if the question of miracles were to be discussed in its full extent, it would require an essay to itself; but the mere answer to this particular objection may be given very briefly and easily. The objection, our readers may remember, is this:—" To assert the past or present existence of miracles is to deny that the laws of nature are absolutely fixed; and to deny this is to deny the very possibility of physical science." We admit the former of these two propositions, but deny the latter. We say that the interest of physical science is in no respect affected by the existence of miracles, because *these are always accompanied by visible symbols of Divine intervention*. And now to explain our meaning in this reply.

We cannot do better than repeat the argument which, at starting, we put into the mouth of our imaginary objector. "I compose a substance to-day of certain materials, and find it, by experiment, to be combustible; I compose another to-morrow, of the very same materials, united in the very same way, and the very same proportions, and I find the composition *in*combustible If such a case were possible, the whole foundation of science would be taken from under my feet." This allegation we consider incontrovertible; but then this is *not* the case of a *miracle*. Let us, then, vary our supposition. On the second occasion, when I enter my laboratory to make the desired experiment, I find a venerable man seated. He announces himself as commissioned by God to deliver me some authoritative message. "And now," he adds, "I will give you a proof that He sent me. You know, by experiment, that the substance in your hand is naturally combustible; but now place it in the same fire, or in one a thousand times fiercer, and it shall remain unscathed." If I find the fact to be so, I shall indeed have extremely strong ground for believing my visitor Divinely commissioned; but I shall have no ground whatever for doubting that the substance is naturally combustible. Nay, my conviction of this fact will be even strengthened. For my visitor assumed that it was *naturally* combustible by the very fact of treating its non-combustion as a *miracle*.

And the same answer may be made, however numerous may be the miracles wrought. The infidel Gibbon, when speaking of "the innumerable prodigies which were performed in Africa by the relics of S. Stephen," has this most shallow remark: "A miracle," he says, "in that age of superstition and credulity, lost *its name* and its merit, since it would scarcely be considered as a deviation from *the ordinary and established laws of nature."* Now, let us even make the wild and extravagant supposition that some given law of nature, in some given time and place, were far more frequently suspended by miracle than allowed to take its natural course. Let us imagine, *e.g.*, that England were again Catholic; and that every Englishman, by invoking S. Thomas of Canterbury, could put his hand into the fire without injury. Why, the very fact that in order to avoid injury he must invoke the Saint's name, would ever keep fresh and firm in his mind the conviction that fire does naturally burn. He would, therefore, as unquestioningly, in all his physical researches, assume this to *be* the natural property of fire, as though God had never wrought a miracle at all.

The Duke of Argyll says (p. 89, note), that "the question of miracles seems now to be admitted *on all hands* to be simply a question of evidence." We are extremely glad that the Duke can credit this; and we should be still more rejoiced if we could entirely credit it ourselves. For saying precisely this, Father Newman, a few years back, was assailed most violently, not by infidels and semi-infidels only, but by High-Church Anglicans; by the *Guardian* newspaper. However, *many* thinkers of the day must really admit this, or else the Duke could not possibly have thought that *all* admit it; and he quotes no less an authority than Professor Huxley, as counting it "unjustifiable" to "deny the possibility of miracles." The question of evidence, then, assumes singular importance; and we hope that both the Duke and the Professor will carefully study the evidence on which approved Catholic miracles rest. Dr. Gilbert has done great service by bringing this before the notice of Protestants.

Four miracles are required to be proved for beatification, and two more for canonization, and these must be proved *by eye- and not by ear-witnesses.*

In miracles where diseases have been cured, it is required: (1) that the disease must be of an aggravated nature, and difficult or impossible to be cured; (2) that it was not on the turn; (3) that no medicine had been used, or, if it had, that it had done no good; (4) the cure must be sudden; (5) the cure must be perfect; (6) there must have been no crisis. Could there be greater caution?

In the process of investigation no step is taken, no doubt propounded, without many of the members being present, and a printed report of each session being sent to those who are absent. Besides the cross-examinations, which are of a most scrutinizing character, it is the sole duty of one of the leading members, the Promotor Fidei, to make objections and, if possible, to disprove every reported miracle.

In cases of epilepsy thirteen years are required to elapse before miracles are approved, for fear of a relapse; in cases of hydrophobia and nervous diseases a longer period is necessary; whilst the opinions of physicians, surgeons, scientific men, and eye-witnesses, are taken down in writing.

Let me suppose that the miracle for investigation is the recovery of a person's sight. First of all, it has to be proved whether the person was born blind or became so afterwards; secondly, the duration of the blindness; thirdly, the cure in its most minute details; fourthly, the written opinion of the best scientific and medical men in Italy as to the cause of the blindness; fifthly, *whether it is possible to refer the miracle to natural causes;* sixthly, *whether the miracle was instantaneous;* . . . and, seventhly, whenever the physicians and scientific men cannot trace the cause of the blindness no decision is ever come to.

Indeed, so sifting and exhausting is the investigation, that Alban Butler tells us, on the authority of Daubenton, that an English Protestant gentleman, being present, and seeing the process of several miracles, said they were incontestable; but was utterly surprised at the scrupulosity of this scrutiny when told that *not one of those had been allowed by the Congregation of Rites to have been sufficiently proved.*

Perrone also asserts that he showed the process for certain miracles to a Protestant lawyer of some eminence, who was perfectly satisfied with the testimony and the reasoning, and declared that they ought to stand before any English jury, but was astonished when he was assured that the evidence was not considered *sufficient by the Congregation of Rites* (pp. 49, 50).

It may be well also to quote a passage written by F. Newman in the course of that discussion to which we have already referred, because it is precisely to the question of *evidence* that he directs his remarks :—

> Putting out of the question the hypothesis of unknown laws of nature (which is an evasion from the force of any proof), I think it impossible to withstand the evidence which is brought for the liquefaction of the blood of S. Januarius at Naples, and for the motion of the eyes of the pictures of the Madonna in the Roman States. I see no reason to doubt the material of the Lombard crown at Monza ; and I do not see why the Holy Coat at Trêves may not have been what it professes to be. I firmly believe that portions of the True Cross are at Rome and elsewhere, that the Crib of Bethlehem is at Rome, and the bodies of S. Peter and S. Paul also. I believe that at Rome, too, lies S. Stephen ; that S. Matthew lies at Salerno, and S. Andrew at Amalfi. I firmly believe *that the relics of the saints are doing innumerable miracles and graces daily*, and that it needs only for a Catholic to show devotion to any saint in order to receive special benefits from his intercession. I firmly believe that saints in their lifetime have before now *raised the dead to life, crossed the sea without vessels, multiplied grain and bread, cured incurable diseases*, and stopped the operation of the laws of the universe in a multitude of ways. ("Lectures on Catholicism in England," p. 298.)

Here, then, we bring to a close our treatment of that question which we began by raising. It must not be forgotten, however, that the Church teaches not a Divine only, but also a diabolical intervention in phenomena. Within certain limits fixed by God, evil spirits are permitted, on the one hand, to premove the laws of nature ; on the other hand, to violate those laws by certain portents, which, in some sense, simulate the character of Divine miracles. It is evidently impossible, without an intolerable lengthiness, here to enter on this important field of inquiry ;

but the preceding remarks will suffice to show the general view of it which we should be disposed to take.

We said at starting that we could only attempt to state, in the merest skeleton and outline, that reply which, as it seems to us, may be most conclusively given to one whole class of objections against religion; and that, too, a class immeasurably more specious and formidable than any other of those derived from experimental science. This class is more specious than any other, because the very foundation of experimental sciences is phenomenal uniformity; and because phenomenal uniformity seems on the surface directly contradictory to the Catholic doctrine on Prayer, on Grace, on Free Will, and on Miracles. As to the principles we have put forth in defence of this doctrine, we would say to any reader who is versed at once in theological and in experimental science—

"Si quid novisti rectius istis,
Candidus imperti ; si non, his utere mecum."

Nor are we without hope that some one, competent to the task, may complete them where they are defective ; may expand them into fulness ; may carry them out into detail ; and may illustrate them with a number of relevant scientific facts.

To conclude. Catholics and Christians generally are much too cowardly, we think, in presence of the so-called scientific world, and give far more weight to its view of things than is at all deserved. Scientific men exhibit a confidence, peremptoriness, sometimes superciliousness, which gives an impression of their having far more of argument at their back than really exists.* We should

* "Nothing is more common," says the Duke of Argyll most truly (p. 113) "than to find men who may be trusted thoroughly on the facts of their own science, but who *cannot be trusted for a moment on the place which these facts assume in the general system of truth*. Philosophy must include science, but science does not necessarily include philosophy."

run counter, indeed, to the Church's whole teaching, if we sought to repel them by denying either the truth or the value of experimental science; but we ought most carefully to distinguish between the *genuine* principles of such science, and others which so many of its votaries most gratuitously assume. Never, perhaps, was it so important as it is now to set forth the Church's rightful claim of authority over the whole field of secular science, so far as the latter directly or indirectly touches the truths of religion. Let Catholics make the Church's doctrine their one centre of thought; and let them so arrange the lessons of science, that in due subordination these may cluster around that centre. Studied on any other principle, secular science can only issue in mischief and deceit; it will be an *ignis fatuus*, and no true guiding light.

Nor again, in our humble judgment, do Catholics act wisely, who think of delaying their offensive measures against the enemy until science shall have directly and expressly attacked religion; for by that time the evil will have got to a far more unmanageable head. No: let them be prompt in assailing and exposing every irreligious principle which scientific men may assume, even though these latter are employing it principally or even exclusively in their own special and immediate sphere. False and evil principles have their own legitimate issue, and are ever most assuredly tending to that issue: whatever may be the present intention of this or that individual, who is unhappily their slave and victim.

ORIGINAL NOTE.—After this essay had gone to press, we lighted by the merest accident on the following letter from Professor Mansel to Dr. Pusey, quoted by the latter in his sermon on "The Miracles of Prayer," pp. 33-35. Its coincidence with what we have said is somewhat remarkable, because the present writer's view has been very long in his mind, and belongs to a far earlier date than Professor Mansel's letter :—

DEAR DR. PUSEY,—The following is a very rough statement of the matter on which I spoke to you this morning. I have not had time to think it over carefully, and I am by no means confident that my view will stand a critical examination.

The assumption that the existence of fixed laws of nature is incompatible with the intervention of special acts of God's Providence, and that science, in so far as it establishes the former, tends to overthrow our belief in the latter, appears to me to rest on a confusion between two very different kinds of natural law.

There are some sciences, such as astronomy, whose laws are to a great extent expressed in the form of statements of the *periodical recurrence* of certain phænomena. But there are other sciences, having also their fixed laws, in which the laws involve no statement of *time*. Thus it is a law of optics that, for the same medium, the sines of the angles of incidence and refraction are in an invariable ratio to each other; and it is a law of chemistry that elements combine in definite proportions: but these laws say nothing about the *time* when any given refraction or combination will take place.

Now, it is reasonable to infer, when a science has accumulated a certain number of laws of a given kind, that further progress in the science will discover more laws of the same kind: *e.g.* that when astronomy has discovered regular periods for the orbits of planets, similar discoveries may be made for comets; but it is illogical to go *per saltum* from one science to another, unless the laws already discovered in the latter science are of the same kind with those of the former. Chemistry or optics might be advanced by the discovery of new laws similar to the above, without any approach to a fixing of the time of phenomena such as exists in astronomy. It is even conceivable that the progress of a science might disturb the regularity of occurrence. If men were to acquire vast powers of producing atmospheric phænomena, the periodical recurrence of such phænomena would become more irregular, being producible at the will of this or that man. There is a remarkable note in Darwin's "Botanic Garden" (canto iv. l. 320), in which the author conjectures that changes of wind may depend on some minute chemical cause, which, if it were discovered, might probably, like other chemical causes, be governed by human agency. Whatever may be thought of the probability of this anticipation being realized, it is at least sufficient to suggest one reflection. If atmospheric changes may conceivably, without any violation of natural law, be brought under the control of man, *may they not now, equally without violation of natural law, be under the control of God?* And are we so fully informed of the manner of God's working with regard to these contingent phænomena of nature, as to know for certain that He can never exercise such a control for purposes connected with His moral government?

Is, then, our knowledge of the external conditions, say of health or disease, *likely to make a progress analogous to that of astronomy, or to that of chemistry?* We may discover that certain conditions of the atmosphere are regularly followed by certain states of health, as that certain chemical elements will produce certain results; but we do not thereby discover that those conditions must take place at a given time. Unless we have evidence that the law which manifests God's Will is a law of *periodical recurrence,* as in the case of the sun's rising, there is no more incongruity in praying for the removal of a pestilence than in asking a chemist to perform a particular operation. *We do not ask the chemist to violate the laws of chemistry, but to produce a particular result in accordance with those laws. Do we necessarily do more than this when we pray that God will remove from us a disease?*

If some changes of weather, or of health, had already become matter of certain prediction, like eclipses, we might reasonably presume that others would hereafter become equally certain. If we knew for certain the periodic times of fever, we might hereafter discover those of cholera; if we could now predict how many showers of rain will fall in the course of the present year, we might hereafter be able to make a similar prediction as regards thunderstorms. But has the progress of science in these matters hitherto been of *this kind?* If not, may not science advance indefinitely without in any way interfering with the duty of prayer? And has not the progress of the majority of sciences actually been of this kind?

Believe me yours very truly,
H. L. MANSEL.

Some of Dr. Pusey's own remarks also are well worth quoting:—

I may say freely that I do not see that anything more has been discovered than certain proximate causes and effects, or some larger physical laws, which, although they minister in their different ways to our well-being, yet, in their incalculable compass of variation, do not, in the least, account for those changes that most affect us. Thus, believing, as scientific men inform us, that the average quantity of rain which falls in the year in a given place does not much vary, and that the winds, from the different quarters, in each year blow in much the same proportions; yet they are not these general laws, which affect those things, upon which plenty or famine, health or disease, depend. A concentration of rain or its absence, uninjurious at other times, would ruin seed-time or harvest. Locusts, or perhaps cholera, may be brought at one time by winds which in other parts of the year, or in successive years, might be even beneficial. The growth of spring-corn in our climate depends, we are told, upon a nice adjustment of fine weather and showers. And yet some of us remember a spring when, scarcely any autumn corn having been sown (on account of the wetness of the season, which was continued or renewed in the spring), just at the very last we had exactly that succession of dry weather and rain which was needed. This was one only of several successive seasons in which, at the moment of extreme necessity, God gave us the weather which we needed. And yet they are, most of all, these minute variations which are, as yet, perfectly unaccountable by science. All the proximate cause and effects of conditions of the atmosphere are no more interrupted, *if, as most of us believe, they are regulated by the immediate Will of God directing and dispensing them*, than the inherent forces upon whose combination the going of a watch, or the motion of a steam-engine, or the discharge of cannon, depends, are *by the interposition of human will*, regulating those forces so that the watch or the steam-engine should go faster or slower, or the direction of the steam-engine or range of the cannon should be changed.

XV.

EXPLICIT AND IMPLICIT THOUGHT.*

THOSE who have studied the elaborate arguments drawn out in Catholic philosophical works to prove the Existence of God, may not unfrequently, perhaps, have been perplexed by the following difficulty. No one, of course, can know certainly that God exists, except on grounds of reason; and no one can make any act of *faith*, until he knows for certain that God exists. It is necessary, then, for all men without exception who would be saved, and not merely for philosophers, to know certainly God's Existence on grounds of reason. Yet to the enormous majority of mankind, such grounds of reason seem on the surface inaccessible. It would be very ludicrous child's play, that some given labourer, or farmer, or tradesman, or even hunting country gentleman, should explore such arguments for God's Existence as are found in Catholic philosophical works; especially if you suppose him to explore them on the principle of judging, for himself and by the perspicacity of his own intellect, how far they can be vindicated against the objections of Mill, of Huxley, or of Comte.

Such is the difficulty which must have occurred to many. And, considering its obviousness and plausibility, we have always been a good deal surprised that it has not

* *La Philosophie Scolastique exposée et défendue.* Par le R. P. KLEUTGEN. Paris: Gaume. 1869.
Sermons preached before the University of Oxford. By JOHN HENRY NEWMAN, B.D., Fellow of Oriel College. London: Rivingtons. 1843.

received more express treatment. But F. Kleutgen, in his great philosophical work, has handled the whole subject with such surpassing power, that instead of needing any apology, we shall on the contrary obtain our readers' gratitude, for placing before them a very long extract from this illustrious writer. We italicize a few sentences, to which we invite especial attention.

In many places Scripture declares in the most express manner that even for those to whom God has not manifested Himself by His prophets or by His Son, there exists a revelation of God in His works, and even within the mind of man, whereby *they can without any difficulty cognize God* their Creator and Maker, as well as His sovereign Law. It is not necessary to point out that Scripture does not in this speak of *any* [supposable] first cause; but of the Living and True God, Who has created heaven and earth, and inscribed His law in the heart of man: and that consequently it speaks also of the moral order. Now, it says in the same passages, that men who do not thus cognize their God are without excuse; that they are insensate: that they deserve God's wrath and all His chastisements. It necessarily follows, then, that this manifestation of God by His works is such that man cannot fail by this means to cognize God with certitude, unless he commit a grave fault. . . .

Assuredly this does not mean that it is *philosophical researches*, continued laboriously through obstacles and doubts, which can alone lead to knowledge of God. *Very few men, in fact, are capable of these laborious researches:* whereas Scripture speaks of all the heathens in general; and in the Book of Wisdom it is said expressly (xiii. 1), "all men are vanity who do not possess the knowledge of God." The sacred writer even adds that this knowledge, to which he gives the name of "sight," to express *its clearness and certitude* [" cognoscibiliter poterit Creator horum videri," v. 5], can be obtained *with as much ease—and even more— as knowledge of this world:* which certainly does not fail any one capable of the least reflection. ["Si tantum potuerunt scire ut possent æstimare sæculum, quomodo hujus Dominum non facilius iuvenerunt?" v. 9.] . . . *It is easier, therefore, to know God the Governor of the world, than to know enough of nature to admire its power and beauty.*

It necessarily follows, therefore, that *there is a knowledge of*

God different from philosophical knowledge; a knowledge so easy to acquire and so certain, that ignorance and doubt on that head cannot be explained, except either *by culpable carelessness or proud obstinacy.* Such is also . . . the common doctrine of the Holy Fathers. *They distinguished that knowledge of God which is obtained by philosophical research* from that which *springs up spontaneously* in every man at the very sight of creation. This latter kind of knowledge is called by them "a witness of Himself," which God gave to the soul at its creation; "an endowment of nature;" "an infused knowledge," *inherent in every man without preliminary instruction;* a knowledge which springs up in some sense of itself in proportion as reason is developed; and which cannot fail, except in a man either deprived of the use of reason or else given up to vices which have corrupted his nature. And when the Fathers of the Church declare unanimously on this head that this knowledge is really found and established in all men, the importance of their testimony is better understood by remembering that they lived in the midst of heathen populations.

God has implanted in our reasonable nature everything which is necessary, that we may know Him, and know Him with facility.* Now, he does not [after creation] withdraw Himself from creatures, but always remains near them, cooperating with them, exciting them to act, supporting and directing each one to its end conformably to its nature. If this is true of all creatures, *how could this concurrence be refused* to the most noble of all creatures, to those whom God has created *for the very purpose of their knowing and loving Him?* Man indeed does not arrive at his end, except by using the powers which God has given him; but the Author of those gifts lends to man his concurrence, in order that he may make due use of them. Since that moral and religious life *for which man was created* is founded on a knowledge of the truths whereof we speak, God *watches over man,* in order that reason, as it is developed, may come to know them with facility and certainty. Observe, the question here is not of supernatural grace, but is [of the natural order]. . . .

What would not be the misery of man [if there were no reasonable certainty without philosophical argument]? It is

---

*F. Kleutgen quotes from an opusculum of S. Thomas: "Dei cognitio nobis *innata* dicitur esse, in quantum *per principia nobis innata* de facili percipere possumus Deum esse."

easy to show those [ordinary] men who are capable of any reflection at all, that their knowledge of the truth *is not scientific;* that they do not deduce it [consciously and explicitly] from the first principles of thought, and consequently *they cannot defend it against the attacks of scepticism.* If, then, as soon as we come to know that our *knowledge is not scientific,* the *conviction of its truth* were at once shaken, what, on that supposition, would be the lot of man?

The fact is indeed not so; that consciousness which every one can interrogate within himself attests its denial; and at every period the voice of mankind has confirmed that denial. As soon as we arrive at the use of reason, *the voice of conscience awakes within us.** Whether we choose or no, *we must cognize the distinction between good and evil.* [Again] just as it is absolutely impossible for us to doubt our own existence, [in like manner] we are absolutely compelled to regard as real the external world; [to hold] that, further, there exists a Supreme Author of our being and of all other things; and that through Him there is a certain moral order.† These also are truths which we cannot refuse to admit. No doubt we can do violence to ourselves in order to produce in ourselves the contrary persuasion, just as we may use efforts to regard the moral conscience itself as an illusion. But *these efforts never succeed,* or, at least, never succeed perfectly; and we feel ourselves even under an obligation of *condemning the very attempt as immoral.* The mind of man, in fact, is *under the influence of truth which has dominion over it,* and which gives [man] certainty *even against his own wish.* Truth manifests itself to our intelligence, and engenders therein the knowledge of its reality, *even before we* [*explicitly*] *know* what that truth is. Still truth [I say] reigns over man and reveals itself to him, *however great may be his resistance* as a *sacred and sovereign authority* which commands him and *summons him before its tribunal.* And [standing] before that tribunal, he is obliged to admit the immorality of even attempting to doubt. Just as

---

* It is observable that here, and still more strongly in a later passage, F. Kleutgen uses the word "conscience," not as moral theologians speak of "conscientia," but to express man's natural power or faculty of knowing right and wrong.

† F. Kleutgen has spoken immediately before, and also speaks immediately afterwards, of "the moral conscience," the "distinction between right and wrong," as covering a *distinct* ground from this. By the present phrase, then, "a moral order," he plainly intends to express God's moral government of the world.

he is bound to condemn the madness, I will not say of doubting, but of trying to doubt, the reality of the external world, *so he is obliged to regard as an impiety* [*all*] *doubt in God's Existence and Providence.* . . .

Nor can it here be objected that conscience (in the proper sense of that word, moral conscience) gives us no certainty so long as its existence with us and its pronouncements are purely spontaneous. Of the conscience, more than of anything else (surtout), it may be said that *it reveals to us its own truth;* that it compels us to acknowledge *an absolute good and a sovereign rule over our wills and actions* (even though we know not its innermost nature), not only as really existing, but as *an august and sacred power which is* [*in authority*] *over us.* Whatever efforts man may make to overthrow and destroy his own intimate persuasion on the truthfulness of conscience, he will never succeed in doing so. Even though he seeks by every possible means to persuade himself that nothing obliges him to regard it as truthful, nevertheless, he will always feel himself compelled to acknowledge its authority, and even to condemn his own resistance to it.

It is true, indeed, that though conscience *often* speaks against a man's inclination [so loudly] as to confound (by its manifestation of its own truthfulness) all pride and all the sophistical dreams by which he might wish to stifle it, it does not *always* so speak and raise its voice as to take from man *the power of turning from it* and refusing to listen. If he enters into himself and chooses to observe what passes within him, he will obtain that reflex knowledge which, as we said above, is required for actual certainty; he will know that he cannot prevent himself from acknowledging the truth of what the voice of conscience dictates. But it is in his power, *if not always* at least often, to abstain from entering into himself and lending his ear to that voice. He has [often] the power of not hearing it, or of giving it so little attention that he withdraws himself from that influence which would make him certain. It is in this manner that, *for a certain time at least*, notwithstanding the habitual certainty * which nature gives him, he may remain undecided on the truthfulness of conscience, supposing that he has not yet acknowledged that truthfulness by philosophical reflection, or, again, that he does not seek to know it. But even though

---

* By "habitual certainty," as he has explained just before, F. Kleutgen means to express the *proximate power* of actual certainty.

we were not able to demonstrate by the intimate experience of every man that the doubt whereof we speak is contrary to the principles of morality, we ought, nevertheless, to be persuaded of that truth by the judgment of all mankind. Among civilized nations in every time the necessity of philosophical studies has been admitted, and those have been held in high esteem who devoted themselves thereto, and who were regarded as sages. Nevertheless, though the nations, it is true, accepted at the hands of philosophers the solution of many questions, they have never ascribed to these men a decisive judgment on all truth without exception. As to those first truths on which all our convictions rest, *humanity bears within itself the consciousness or intimate persuasion of knowing them with certainty.* Philosophers may make these truths the subject of their speculations; but they are not allowed the right of pronouncing a definite judgment on these truths; and if their researches lead them to deny or doubt them, those very persons who would otherwise be the disciples of these philosophers, rise up against them as judges and condemn them. Was there ever a nation which did not regard it as madness to doubt an external world? a nation which did not hold in horror a man so perverted as to acknowledge no truth superior to the senses, and reject all distinction between virtue and vice? Has not atheism among all nations been accounted a crime? And by the very fact of seeing *culpability* in denial of these truths, does not the world declare that they cannot possibly be unknown to men of good will? ("Phil. Schol.," Nos. 226, 227, 228, 229, 231, 232.)

Now, in order to appreciate F. Kleutgen's meaning in this singularly impressive passage, it must be remembered that he consistently and peremptorily refuses to credit the human intellect with any direct and *immediate* knowledge of God. According to F. Kleutgen—indeed, according to all orthodox Catholics—God is known to man only through His works; only through creatures. The doctrine, then, which F. Kleutgen lays down in the preceding passage, is to some extent represented by the two following theses.

Thesis I. A most real process of reasoning is constantly going on in the minds of men, quite distinct from any process of *philosophical* reasoning or *arguing;* and of a kind by no means available in *confutation of an opponent*. God watches with special care over mankind in their use of those intellectual faculties which He has given them, so as to assist them in arriving at the truth. Especially is this the case as regards their arriving at a true knowledge of Himself. He created them for the very purpose that they should know and love Him. He therefore uniformly provides—except, indeed, where man's grave culpability interposes an obstacle to His gracious operations—that they shall be led from those true premisses which legitimately establish His Existence, to the true conclusion itself, that He does exist.

Thesis II. Among the premisses available to all mankind, which legitimately establish His existence, two in particular may be mentioned. The first, and far the most important, is that moral voice within man's breast, which is ever testifying the necessary and eternal distinction between right and wrong, and which is ever summoning him to a virtuous life. This voice suffices by itself to prove with absolute certainty that there exists a certain necessary Supreme Rule of morality which obliges all reasonable beings, whatever that Rule may precisely be. But there is a second premiss, or rather combination of premisses, also available for all mankind, which conspires with the former in leading them to a knowledge of God. For this visible world is within their immediate cognizance; the principle of causation is accepted by them as axiomatic; and the inference is obvious and ready, to the Great First Cause.

As to this last-named inference from the visible world, F. Kleutgen rather incidentally alludes to it than directly expresses it. And though he would doubtless say that there are various other premisses also which bear their part in the great process of conviction, we do not observe that he has expressly referred to any others. At all events, it is to the moral voice that he again and again refers, as to the one immovable foundation of Theism. In this respect many readers of F. Newman will be almost startled by the singular resemblance to be found between these two great thinkers, whose philosophical history has been so entirely different. As an instance out of many which might be adduced, read F. Newman's " Occasional Sermons," from p. 84 to p. 87, and observe his profound agreement with what we have cited from F. Kleutgen.

Both these theses are of extreme importance; and it is perhaps almost difficult to know which is of the greater. Our present concern, however, will be exclusively with the first; and on this first thesis, indeed, there is a more startling resemblance between FF. Kleutgen and Newman, than even on the second. The latter half of that volume of F. Newman's which we have named at the head of this article, is occupied with a series of essays on the relation between faith and reason. These essays contain undoubtedly one or two incidental remarks, which F. Newman would not make now that he is a Catholic; and from which, indeed, he has carefully refrained since his conversion, when engaged on kindred topics. But F. Newman's fundamental thought is identical with F. Kleutgen's first thesis; and is expressed, indeed, in the very title of one essay, " Explicit and Implicit Reason." To exhibit this thought in its full light and its general bearing, would occupy at the very least a large volume: let us hope that either F. Kleutgen or F. Newman may hereafter be induced so to exhibit it ! Our present purpose is hardly more than the very elementary one of placing the truth before our readers in its simplest aspect, with the hope that Catholic philosophical thinkers may bear it in mind and ponder on its importance.

To reason is nothing else than to be led, by means of certain premisses which one knows, to a certain conclusion which legitimately follows from those premisses. Now, it is plain, from obvious and every-day instances, that great multitudes thus reason and with great accuracy, who never reflect on their premisses or put them into shape; and who would, in fact, cut a very poor figure, if ever they attempted such a task.

Let a person only call to mind the clear impression he has about matters of every day's occurrence, that this man is bent on a certain object, or that that man was displeased, or another suspicious; or that one is happy, and another unhappy; and how much depends in such impressions on manner, voice, accent, words uttered, silence instead of words, and all the many subtle symptoms which are felt by the mind, but cannot be contemplated; and let him consider how very poor an account he gives of his impression if he avows it and is called upon to justify it. (Newman, pp. 270, 271.)

Take some particular case. I am intimately acquainted with a certain relative: and some fine morning I have not been with him more than five minutes before I am perfectly convinced, and on most conclusive ground, that, for whatever reason, he is out of sorts with me. It is little to say that I could not so analyze my grounds of conviction as to make *another* see the force of my reasoning; I could not so analyze them, as that their exhibition shall be in the slightest degree satisfactory to *myself*. Especially in proportion as I am less philosophical and less clever in psychological analysis, all attempts at exhibiting my premisses in due form hopelessly break down. Yet none the less it remains true, both that my premisses are known to me with certainty, and that my conclusion follows from them irresistibly. There is an enormous number of past instances in which these symptoms *have* co-existed with ill-humour; there is no single known case in which they have existed *without* it; they all admit of being referred to ill-humour as effects to their cause; they are so heterogeneous that any other cause except ill-humour which shall account for them all is quite incredible, while it is no less incredible that they co-exist fortuitously, etc. Why, in all probability, the very Newtonian theory of gravitation does not rest on firmer and more irrefragable grounds. Yet to *analyze* all this or any part of it, to explain what is the peculiar character of these symptoms, in what they precisely differ from others which superficially resemble them, *how* they are referable to ill-humour as to a cause, or *why* it is incredible that they should co-exist fortuitously, —to express all this is utterly beyond the power of men who are not greatly versed in philosophy, and, indeed, of many who *are* so versed.

Another illustration :—

Consider the preternatural sagacity with which a great general knows what his friends and enemies are about, and what will be the final result, and where, of their combined movements,—and then say whether, if he were required to argue the matter in word or on paper, all his most brilliant conjectures might not be refuted, and all his producible reasons exposed as illogical (p. 210).

The *reasoning* on such matters of a really great general would be almost infallible, while his *arguments* might be below contempt.

The whole matter is so important that it is worth while to repeat illustrations even at the risk of wearying our readers. Take another case, then. A sharp-sighted and experienced seaman will tell you with the greatest confidence some fine evening, that there will be a violent storm before morning. It is often the case that the premises on which he rests this conclusion are amply sufficient to bear it out; that his reasoning is absolutely faultless; that nothing short of a miracle can falsify his prediction. But ask him to argue the matter, to tell you what are the precise phenomena on which he builds, to express accurately his reason for thinking that such phenomena denote the imminence of a storm, he will be nowhere.

Then, again, there is a well-known story of the advice given by a sagacious judge to magistrates possessing shrewd common sense, but an unpractised intellect. "Give your decisions confidently," he said, "but state no argument. Ten to one your decisions will be right, but a hundred to one your argument will be wrong." He did not mean, of course, that they would arrive at right decisions by guesswork or by inspiration. He meant that their reasoning would probably be sound, but their arguments almost certainly fallacious.

Once more. A singularly conscientious and upright man has a large family of sons, with whom he has lived from the first in habits of most familiar and affectionate intercourse. Hardly one of their convictions can be named which is so demonstratively established, which rests on reasoning so absolutely irresistible, as their conviction of his uprightness and conscientiousness. Though they were the best astronomers in Europe, it would not be one whit more absurd and irrational that they should reject Kepler's laws than that they should doubt their father's integrity of character. Yet, though first-rate astronomers, they may be very poor psychologians, and may be baffled in every attempt to draw out in shape their ground for this latter conclusion. Those grounds are, in fact, of that vague, impalpable, indefinite character, which eludes their grasp.

It is certainly true, then, of the enormous majority—we believe it to be true even of the most highly educated and philosophical—that for the most part they "advance forward" towards truth "on grounds which they cannot produce, and if they could, yet could not prove to be true; on latent grounds" which they certainly know, but have no power of expressly assigning. But we may take a step further. It happens again and again, not merely that men most reasonably hold this or that conviction without having analyzed its *grounds*, but that they hold it most reasonably, without even knowing, reflexly, of its *existence*. Here one single instance will suffice. There are certain persons, A, B, C, etc., with whom I have had various intimate relations, and whom I have seen in great and critical variety of circumstances. I am asked my opinion of A's character. The very question had never occurred to me; yet on interrogating my own consciousness, I find there stored up a complete answer to the question. I may find great difficulty in *expressing* my views of A's character, and, when I have done my best in that way, may be very dissatisfied with my success. But that view none the less *exists*, though I may fail in its expression; and it existed long before I had ever thought of its existence. It will at once be seen that there are numberless parallel instances to this.

Here another point is suggested, which deserves attention. How far more faithful is often the implicit representation of an object than the explicit! how far more correct and complete, *e.g.* is the view which I *observe within myself* of A's character, than any *expression* of that view which I find myself able to put forth! It will frequently happen, indeed, that I am utterly dissatisfied with the latter; that I feel bitterly how coarse an instrument is language for the exhibition of thought. F. Newman points this moral in reference to theology in a forcible passage. We italicize a few clauses.

No analysis is subtle and delicate enough to represent adequately the state of mind under which we believe, or the subjects of belief, as they are presented to our thoughts. The end proposed is that of delineating, or, as it were, painting what the mind sees and feels; now let us consider what it is to portray duly in form and colour things material, and we shall surely understand the difficulty, or rather the impossibility, of representing the outline and character, the hues and shades, in which any intellectual view really exists in the mind, or of giving it that substance and that exactness in detail in which consists its likeness to the original, or of sufficiently marking those minute differences which attach to the same general state of mind or tone of thought as found in this or that individual respectively. It is probable that *given opinions, as held by individuals,* even when of the most congenial views, *are as distinct from each other as their faces.* Now, how minute is the defect in imitation which hinders the likeness of a portrait from being successful! how easy is it to recognize who is intended by it, without allowing that really he is represented! Is it not hopeless, then, to expect that the most diligent and anxious investigation can end in more than in giving some very rude description of the living mind, and its feelings, thoughts, and reasonings? And if it be difficult to analyze fully any state, or frame, or opinion *of our own minds,* is it a less difficulty to delineate, as Theology professes to do, the works, dealings, providences, attributes, or nature *of Almighty God?* . . .

We are told, in human language, things concerning God Himself; concerning His Son and His Spirit; and concerning His Son's Incarnation, and the union of two natures in His One Person: truths which *even a peasant holds implicitly,* but which Almighty God, whether by His Apostles or by His Church after them, has vouchsafed to bring together and methodize, and to commit to the keeping of science. . . .

Now, all such statements are likely at first to strike coldly or harshly upon religious ears, when taken by themselves, for this reason, if for no other, that they express heavenly things under earthly images, which are infinitely below the reality (pp. 264, 265).

Curiously enough, unbelievers are in the habit of urging, that the Church's dogmatic definitions imply a far more precise and accurate apprehension of Divine Objects than men commonly possess. The fact, as F. Newman has argued in many places, is just the contrary. No amount of scientific statement can fully represent the distinct mental image, as implicitly possessed by an orthodox, well-instructed, and meditative believer.

On the whole, then, it is not too much to say that men are constantly occupied, the more constantly as their mind is more living and active, in observing premisses and thence inferring conclusions; and that every one holds, on more or less sufficient grounds, a very large number of fixed convictions, which have never been placed explicitly before his mind. Even as regards those who are most given to argument and philosophy, it does not seem too much to say that a very large number, even of their most influential convictions, remain in this latent and unrecognized state.

By such considerations as these F. Newman is led to the following weighty judgment :—

It is hardly too much to say, that almost all reasons formally adduced in moral inquiries *are rather specimens and symbols of the real grounds than those grounds themselves*. They do but approximate to a representation of the general character of the proof, which the writer wishes to convey to another's mind. *They cannot, like mathematical proof, be passively followed*, with an attention confined to what is stated, and with the admission of nothing but what is urged. Rather, they are hints towards, and samples of, the true reasoning; and demand an active, ready, candid, and docile mind, which *can throw itself into what is said*, neglect verbal difficulties, and pursue, and carry out principles. This is the true office of a writer, *to excite and direct trains of thought*; and this, on the other hand, is the too common practice of readers to expect everything to be done for them, to refuse to think, to criticize the letter, instead of reaching forwards towards the sense, and to account every argument as unsound which is illogically worded (pp. 271, 272).

Our readers, then, will have seen the essential distinction between *reasoning* and *argument*. To reason correctly, as we have already said, is to be led, through holding certain premises, to hold a certain conclusion which legitimately follows from those premises. But to *argue* quite correctly involves a great deal more : it involves, that you shall *analyze* your process of reasoning; that you shall *reflect* on what has gone on in your mind; that you shall enumerate quite exhaustively, and express quite accurately the various premisses on which you have relied.

And nothing is more easily supposable—we imagine few things are in fact commoner—than that the better reasoner may be the worse arguer. To fall back on one of our previous illustrations. A and B may have been intimately acquainted with some third person, and have enjoyed full means of knowing his character. It may well happen that A shall have formed, by implicit observation and reasoning, a far juster view of it than B has; while B nevertheless, from being much more logically and intellectually disciplined than A, may so thoroughly out-argue him as almost to make his view seem ridiculous.

On the other hand, it is argument, and not mere reasoning, which is the instrument of *philosophy*. Implicit thought, by the very fact of being implicit, not only remains, so to speak, each man's private property, but even in the individual mind may merely occupy its own isolated corner; it may fail grievously in influencing the judgment, on various important matters with which it is in fact connected. But it is the business of a philosopher, not only to *cognize* a truth, but to *recognize* it; to *know* that he knows it; to contemplate it; to express it; to combine it with other truths; to refer truths back to their common cause and origin. Nor must it be supposed, from anything we have said, that we have any wish to disparage the paramount importance of philosophy. Putting aside the Church's influence, we incline to think Mr. Mill hardly goes too far, when he says that the course of philosophy has more influence than all other causes put together, on the course of human thought. Certainly, however, we do think that the course of philosophy would be more satisfactory—that philosophy would be in a sounder and more healthy condition—if philosophers considered, more prominently than is their habit, the value and authority of that implicit reasoning which is in some sense external to their own sphere.

Nor, again, let it be supposed that we have any doubt

whatever of a Catholic's complete argumentative victory, under fair circumstances, over any opponent whomsoever. It may happen, undoubtedly, in some given time and place, that there may be very few Catholics who have received adequate philosophical training, and who have carefully studied the anti-Catholic theories. In such cases, the superiority of argument may possibly enough be on a different side from the superiority of reasoning. But where the combatants are intellectually on anything like equal terms, we are confident that on no field will the Church's triumph be more signal than on that of controversy and philosophy. Intellectual power and accomplishments being equal or nearly equal, it must at last be truth which determines the victory. Indeed, those anti-Catholics who are most peremptory and supercilious in expressing their argumentative contempt for Catholicity, are those very men whose arguments are the weakest, and who simply collapse when grappled with by some sounder thinker.

Still, after every such admission the fact remains, that the number of men is comparatively very small whose arguments in any way represent their reasonings; that the enormous majority either do not argue at all, or argue quite haphazard and at random. The question, therefore, is well worthy the attention of speculative men, whether there can be drawn out any practical "logic of implicit reasoning;" whether any practical rules can be laid down, which shall help towards guiding in true opinions that immense mass who must depend for their conclusions upon something entirely distinct from argument. We will not here attempt to enter otherwise on this question; but one remark frequently occurs in F. Newman's essays which is well worthy of consideration, because it leads, we think, to practical inferences of great importance. His opinion, then, is that almost all men are good (implicit) reasoners, when they are really earnest in their desire of attaining truth on the matter in hand. This is what accomplished arguers and philosophers are sometimes unwilling to think, but which seems to us true nevertheless.

.Nothing is more common among men of a reasoning turn than to consider that no one reasons well but themselves. All men of course think that they themselves are right and others wrong who differ from them; and so far all men must find fault with the reasonings of others, since no one proposes to act without reasons of some kind. Accordingly, so far as men are accustomed to analyze the opinions of others and contemplate their processes of thought, they are tempted to despise them as illogical. If any one sets about examining why his neighbours are on one side in political questions, not on another; why for or against certain measures of a social, economical, or civil nature; why they belong to this religious party, not to that; why they hold this or that doctrine; why they have certain tastes in literature; or why they hold certain views in matters of opinion;—it is needless to say that *if he measures their grounds by the reasons which they produce, he will have no difficulty in holding them up to ridicule or even to censure.* And so again as to the deductions made from facts which come before us. From the sight of the same sky one may augur fine weather, another bad; from the signs of the times one the coming in of good, another of evil; from the same actions of individuals one moral greatness, another depravity or perversity; one simplicity, another craft; upon the same evidence one justifies, another condemns. The miracles of Christianity were in early times imputed by some to magic, others they converted; the union of its professors was ascribed to seditious and traitorous aims by some, while others it moved to say, "See how these Christians love one another." The phenomena of the physical world have given rise to a variety of theories, that is, of alleged facts, at which they are supposed to point; theories of astronomy, chemistry, and physiology; theories religious and atheistical. The same events are considered to prove a particular providence, and not; to attest the divinity of one religion or another. The downfall of the Roman empire was to Pagans a refutation, to Christians an evidence of Christianity. . . .

Nor can it fairly be said that such varieties arise from deficiency of logical power in the multitude of men. . . . This is what men of clear intellects are not slow to imagine. Clear, strong, steady intellects, if they are not deep, will look on these differences in deduction chiefly as failures in the reasoning faculty, and will despise them or excuse them accordingly. . . .

But surely there is no greater mistake than this. For the experience of life contains abundant evidence that *in practical matters, when their minds are really aroused, men commonly are not bad reasoners. Men do not mistake when their interest is concerned.* They have an instinctive sense in which direction their path lies towards it, and how they must act consistently with self-preservation and self-aggrandisement. And so in the case of questions in which party spirit, or political opinion, or ethical principle, or personal feeling is concerned, *men have a surprising sagacity, often unknown to themselves, in finding their own place.* However remote the connection between the point in question and their own creed, or habits, or feelings, the principles which they profess guide them unerringly to their legitimate issues: and thus it often happens that in apparently different practices, or usages or expressions, or in questions of science, or politics, or literature, we can almost prophesy beforehand, from their religious or moral views, where certain persons will stand, and *often can defend them far better than they defend themselves.* . . .

All this shows that in spite of the inaccuracy of expression or, if you will, in thought which prevails in the world, *men on the whole do not reason incorrectly.* If their reason itself were in fault, they would reason each in his own way: whereas they *form into schools;* and that not merely from imitation and sympathy, but certainly from *internal compulsion,* from the *constraining influence* of their several principles. *They may argue badly, but they reason well;* that is, their professed grounds are no sufficient measure of their real ones (pp. 204, 205).

Here, then, in F. Newman's opinion, is one most principal security for good (implicit) reasoning: simplicity of intention. Let us give an instance.

Suppose, then, A and B are two merchants, equally well acquainted with matters of business. A, however, has far more " simplicity of intention " than B ; or, in other words, his heart is far more unreservedly devoted to money-getting. B has many literary and social tastes, while A cares for nothing but the main chance. Few men doubt that, this being the case, A will be a far better (implicit) reasoner than B, on the best mode of adding to his fortune. A thousand occasions of turning a penny will suggest themselves to one, which would never occur to the other; or, in other words, a thousand relevant premisses will actively energize in A's mind, which do not enter B's at all. And, moreover, when some particular question is raised of unusual commercial moment, B will be very far from bringing the same concentrated energy as A to its examination, and is much less likely, therefore, to arrive at a sound conclusion. In other words, two different phenomena present themselves. A's mind is far more constantly peopled than B's, with the implicit thought of relevant premisses; and (2) his implicit reasoning from those premisses will be far more accurate.

This principle may be very importantly applied in the sphere of morals and religion. We will assume F. Kleutgen's doctrine, that all men, who reach the age of reason, at once accept various moral truths as axiomatic; and that they are led quite inevitably—unless, indeed, through their own grave sin—to accept various further doctrines. They accept the doctrine, not only that there is an indefinitely large moral Rule of Life placed in authority over them, but also that that Rule is enforced by the Living God, Who created heaven and earth; that to please Him is the most important end of life; that through prayer they may obtain from Him greater strength for that purpose. Now, it is self-evident that, among all who admit this fundamental body of truths, those alone act reasonably who build their whole course of life predominantly on its consideration; who ever seek moral and religious truth with earnestness and simplicity of intention. In other words, a man acts more reasonably—whether he be educated or uneducated, speculative or unspeculative, matters not at all—the more constantly these primary religious doctrines occupy his mind as actively energizing premisses, carrying him forward (implicitly) to a larger and larger assemblage of practical conclusions. These men are infallibly certain of their original premisses; and the validity of their reasoning is largely secured by their purity and earnestness of intention. They may very possibly be the worst arguers, but they are quite certainly the best reasoners in the whole world. They fly towards moral and religious truth as on eagles' wings; they often discern with the precision of an instinct the path of duty under difficult circumstances; and are found to possess quite an extraordinary power of choosing rightly for themselves among a multitude of conflicting religious teachers.*

The same truth is exemplified in the case of Catholic dogmata. These were revealed not for the purpose of lying dormant in the mind, but on the contrary of motiving practical action. A Catholic, then, acts more reasonably and more acceptably to God in proportion as he labours to view, by the light of these dogmata, every phenomenon of daily life with which they are in any way connected. Or, in other words, in proportion as he lives more reasonably and virtuously, the more prominent among these verities will be actively energizing as (implicit) premisses in his mind, and will animate his whole view of society and of his fellow-men. This is equally so, just as in the former case, whether he be philosophically cultivated or otherwise; and it is in fact precisely these implicitly deduced conclusions which are commonly called " Catholic instincts." Again and again it is not less startling than edifying to find that some saintly Catholic sees his way, as if spontaneously, to complete harmony with the Church's mind on this or that

* Adest in intellectu humano inclinatio quædam naturalis a Sapientissimo Auctore indita, quâ . . . ad judicia practica, quæ vitam regendam respiciunt, proferenda pollemus. At id non cæce et sine motivo, sed ex objecti perspicientiâ sive immediatâ ut in primis principiis moralibus, sive mediatâ ut *in eorum deductionibus.* Deductiones autem ejusmodi . . . *a rudibus etiam fiunt.*—Liberatore, " Ethica," n. 31.

momentous question, on which many Catholics, far abler than himself, still wrangle or rebel.

Old Catholics sometimes good-humouredly laugh at converts, for having introduced into English Catholic talk the word "realize" in a special sense of their own. It must be admitted, however, that the idea intended is so important as to *need* a word for its expression; and this idea is greatly illustrated by what we have been just saying. One very important part of what a convert means when he speaks of "realizing" certain truths is the keeping those truths ever in one's mind as actively energizing premisses.

Again, from what has been said, you may see the importance of Catholics being surrounded, especially during the period of their education, with what is called "a Catholic atmosphere." Non-Catholics erroneously profess a most opposite theory, and allege that moral and religious truth is normally attained by a free and explicit comparison of conflicting arguments. We shall endeavour to expose this fundamental fallacy a few pages on; but our present concern is with a different objection. Liberals often ridicule this expression, "a Catholic atmosphere," as though it were a mere unfounded and unmeaning figure of speech, devised for the purpose of avoiding argument. We maintain, on the contrary, that never was there an expression more thoroughly philosophical. He is the best Catholic in his views and doctrines in whom Catholic dogmata are most constantly energizing as active implicit premisses. But no other way can be named in which the mind can be kept so constantly under the control of such premisses, as by the unconscious influence of others thoroughly possessed by them, with whom it is brought into efficacious contact. And this influence is most curiously parallel in character to those physical agencies which constitute an "atmosphere." Even were it true—which most certainly it is *not*—that the very few who are highly educated can be sufficiently influenced by argument and explicit statements,—at all events, for the vast majority it is this contagious sympathy which alone has power to imbue them with sound reasoning.

In these later remarks, we have been drawing various inferences from one particular statement which we had made. But a very large number of practical results follow from the *whole theory* which we have so briefly sketched, and we will conclude our essay by selecting a few out of their number.

1. F. Kleutgen's very pregnant remark will have been observed, that it is part of God's tender providence towards each individual soul to watch carefully over its implicit advance from truth to truth; and, moreover, that He exercises this office the more solicitously in proportion as the truth is of more vital importance to sanctification and salvation. Unbelievers often sneer at the Catholic's *prayers* that this or that person may be led to the Faith or to more orthodox views of doctrine. "Surely," they say, "truth is discovered by *argument;* and it will be much more to the purpose if you *argue* with him than if you *pray* for him." We reply that moral and religious truth is indubitably obtained by *reasoning,* but to a very small extent by *argument*; and in order to solid and effective reasoning, it is necessary that the relevant premisses be duly suggested and efficaciously impressed on the mind. What more suitable office than this to that Living Creator, who is the God of Truth? And what will move him more powerfully to still wider and more gracious interpositions than that sound so dear to His ears, the voice of prayer?

2. Another frequent gibe of unbelievers is founded on the fact that the great mass of Catholics are so strictly forbidden to read atheistical books. "The Church," say these critics, "virtually confesses that Theism cannot bear the light of reason; for if reason were on the side of

Explicit and Implicit Thought. 237

Theism, to reason Theists would eagerly appeal." There would undoubtedly be great force in this objection, if Catholics alleged that believers are commonly led to Theism by *argument*. And in the case, indeed, of philosophical *controversialists*, it *is* very important that they study atheistical works. But as to the great mass of men who are led to religious truth, indeed, by *reasoning*, but who cannot *argue*, how can you act more absurdly than by calling on them to examine both sides? to read treatises? to study adverse arguments? They have no *arguments* on their own side; how can they do justice to arguments on the other? Take the various illustrations of implicit reasoning which we gave a few pages back, and the self-evident truth of our statement will be abundantly manifest.

To make our point clearer to all our readers, let us fix our thoughts on one case in particular: the case in which a large family of sons are firmly convinced—and that on the most irrefragable ground, viz. a whole life's intimate experience—of their father's uprightness and conscientiousness. He occupies, we will suppose, an important position (diplomatic or otherwise), of which they know absolutely nothing beyond its existence. They are ignorant of its duties; of the circumstances under which those duties oblige; of the maxims of conduct which are appropriate to the situation: indeed, they are not sufficiently advanced in age and experience to understand these things if they tried. Their father meanwhile has certain bitter enemies, who bring against him a charge of unscrupulousness and dishonesty, based on his alleged malversation in this official sphere. What will be the duty of his sons in regard to these charges, and in regard to the arguments adduced in support thereof? Will they be bound to examine such arguments with scrupulous care and candour? How absurd! They are bound, of course, in reason and common sense, utterly to disregard and disbelieve the whole. Their knowledge of his singular conscientiousness rests on demonstrative evidence; while the adverse arguments turn on considerations, entirely external to their power of apprehension.

Yet some one of them may by possibility be so contemptibly weak as to lay stress on these allegations, and allow them to shake his firm confidence in his father. Evidently his conduct is unreasonable on the one hand, and immoral on the other hand: unreasonable because he does not choose to keep the strength of his convictions on a level with the strength of evidence on which they rest; and immoral because he fails egregiously and most inexcusably in filial duty. Those who have placed such arguments before him, and pressed them on his attention, have simply tempted him to sin. When so tempted, his reasonable course would have been to pray for strength; that he might remain faithful to the legitimate conclusions of his reason, and that he might laugh to scorn these dangerous argumentative temptations.

The application of all this is so obvious as to need no exposition. It should only be added that even Theistic controversialists, who examine atheistical arguments, do so purely with a view of understanding and answering them for the benefit of mankind, and in no degree whatever with a purpose of questioning their own convictions.*

3. Remarks very similar may be made on what is called the Church's "evidence of credibility." It is an admitted Catholic doctrine that no adult non-Catholic can reasonably enter the visible Church until he has been convinced on sufficient grounds of reason that she is, as she professes to

* We should be very sorry if we were understood by this to disparage the extreme importance of a controversialist labouring to seize accurately his opponent's precise point of view. The value of a controversial work is to be tested, not by the praise it receives from those who are already convinced, but by its efficaciousness in leading opponents to re-examine their grounds of conviction. But no opponents will ever be influenced by a controversialist who does not appreciate the real strength of their position.

be, an infallible teacher. Now, certainly a very extravagant and desolating paradox would be presented if by this were meant what would indeed be monstrous; viz. that Hodge the Protestant carter cannot rightly be received until he does justice to the various arguments contained in treatises "de verâ religione," and until he is prepared to vindicate those arguments against all exception. But a very large number of the most uneducated Protestants have access to this or that assemblage of implicit premisses, which abundantly suffice to establish the Church's credibility. And God on His side will never be wanting to impress such premisses on the mind of this or that given individual, and conduct him to a true conclusion.*

Here also, as in the former case, nothing can be wilder than to maintain that every ordinary believer is bound to be a controversialist; or that his grounds of belief cannot be sufficient in reason, unless he is able to display them advantageously in argument; or that he is at liberty to enter into temptation by studying anti-Catholic controversial books.

4. Lastly, we will apply the doctrine which we have been setting forth to illustrate the intense dislike—we might almost say horror—felt by all good Catholics for mixed education in every shape. There is hardly any Catholic instinct which non-Catholics find it so difficult to understand as this. We were a good deal amused lately by reading two different letters on the subject, which appeared the same day in the *Times* and *Pall Mall Gazette* respectively. The latter writer maintained that denominational education, as imparted to children *below the age of sixteen*, is a simple absurdity, however useful it may be *at*

---

* Mgr. Dechamps, the present illustrious Archbishop of Malines, has written one or two very interesting works on the question, what *is* that evidence of credibility which, in fact, legitimately persuades uneducated persons. We cannot, however, enter episodically on a matter which requires much careful adjustment and consideration.

a later age. The *Times* correspondent said just the contrary. His object was to defend Mr. Fawcett's Bill about Trinity College, Dublin; and his argument was that denominational education is *necessary up to the age of sixteen or seventeen*, but that afterwards its evils preponderate over its advantages. We will consider, then, these two cases, which may be considered the *extremes:* viz. (1) popular education as imparted to children of the masses; and (2) higher education as imparted to youths of the leisured class. The principles, applicable to these, may easily be applied by our reader for himself to all intermediate instances.

The *Pall Mall Gazette* correspondent grounds his argument on the undoubted fact that children can derive very little real knowledge from merely learning by heart catechism or creed. Never was there an objection more curiously suicidal. It is precisely *because* the mere learning catechism by heart can teach so little religion that a scheme of mixed popular education is of necessity so profoundly irreligious. We by no means undervalue the advantage of a child learning his Catechism by heart; for the knowledge of its text is most useful, as binding together and retaining in his memory the various doctrines he is taught. Still, Catechism is very far indeed from being the *chief* way in which he learns doctrine. The Church testifies a large body of revealed verities, which are intended most powerfully to influence the Catholic's whole interior life. What she aims at, then, in her education of a Catholic child is firstly, as a foundation—not necessarily that he shall be able *explicitly to state* these verities—but that he shall implicitly and intimately *apprehend* them; that he shall have formed in his mind the one true impression, on Father, Son, and Holy Ghost; on our Blessed Lady; on prayer; on the Sacraments, etc. Then, this foundation having been laid, the second great desideratum is that he

may learn the art (one may almost say the knack) of
"living to" these great verities; of imbuing his interior
life with them as with its animating principle; of ever preserving their thought in his mind, as of actively energizing
implicit premisses. We are not here to consider all the
various methods used by her for this great purpose. But
it is important to point out that the most important of all
is the "surrounding him with a Catholic atmosphere;"
the securing, that those under whose influence he is
brought, shall think and feel those very thoughts and
feelings with which she desires *him* to be implicitly but
most efficaciously imbued.

Even Protestants admit the truth of this principle;
and therefore it would be strange indeed if Catholics
were less possessed by it. We may adduce a citation made
by Cardinal Cullen from two great Protestant authorities.
"It is necessary," says M. Guizot, "that national education should be given and received in the midst of a
religious atmosphere, and that *a religious impression should
penetrate all its parts*. Religion is not a *study*, or an
exercise . . . it is a *faith* and a *law* which *ought to be
felt everywhere*." And the Royal Commissioners of 1861
give it as the view of "*the principal promoters* of education" that "*everything which is not mechanical* ought to
be made the occasion of giving religious instruction."

We now pass from one extreme to the other; from the
education of poor children to that of the leisured class
during the concluding years of their course. It is these
years which give to what has gone before its full meaning
and significance. Hitherto the student has acquired much
explicit religious and much explicit secular knowledge: the
characteristic work of the last period is blending the two
into one harmonious whole. He knows Christian doctrine
in itself; he has to be trained in the habit of measuring,
by its standard, the whole field of philosophy, history, and

literature. Here, then, just as in other cases, the verities taught by the Church are to fill his mind, as actively energizing implicit premises, colouring instinctively and spontaneously every detail of secular knowledge. As the soul in its indivisible integrity animates alike every separate part of the human frame, and, by thus animating it, blends it into one, so the highly educated Catholic welds the whole mass of his knowledge into one solid and consistent organism, by the implicit presence, throughout every separate portion, of the Church's unifying doctrinal system.

It is truly amazing, not that non-Catholics refuse to concur with this opinion, but that they so totally fail to apprehend it. Our readers must be acquainted with instances in which they gravely argue that a Protestant university is no unfit place of education for Catholics because the Catholics who go there do not in general actually apostatize. What the Church wishes in educating her children is certainly something more than that they shall not actually cease to be her children. She desires, not merely that they shall remain her children, but that they shall be her *better and more serviceable* children; not merely that they shall not *lose* the Faith, but that they shall foster and cherish it. A system under which they do no more than avoid losing it is no Catholic system at all. Let us suppose the case of a youth, who (1) on the one hand remains a Catholic, who does not cease to accept the Church's various definitions of faith; who (2) on the other hand has mastered and appropriated large portions from the field of philosophy, history, and literature; but (3) who has not in any way learnt the habit of viewing the various parts of this latter field under the light of Catholic doctrine and principle. Such a youth is a Catholic, and is a highly educated *gentleman*: what he utterly fails to be is a decently educated *Catholic*. It is only in proportion as the Church's doctrines have been actively energizing implicit premises throughout his course of secular study that he has been receiving a Catholic education at all. And whether any one is likely to learn such a habit, while living among Protestant companions and learning from Protestant teachers, we may safely leave it for men of common sense to determine. It is precisely these uncatholicly educated Catholics who are the Church's most dangerous enemies. If they apostatized, it would be an immeasurably greater calamity to *themselves*—but in many respects it would lessen, or even destroy, their power of injuring the Church. Instead of this, they will grow up a noxious school of disloyal, minimizing anti-Roman Catholics; Catholic in profession, but anti-Catholic in spirit; Catholics who combine the Church's naked dogmata with the principles of her bitterest enemies, and place the priceless gem of the Faith in a setting of the very basest metal; a constant cause of anxiety to ecclesiastical authorities; a canker eating into the Catholic body; a standing nuisance and obstruction.

Here we conclude. There is a relevant inquiry of extreme moment, on which we have said little or nothing. Philosophers who admit (what seems to us undeniably sound) the general theory laid down by FF. Kleutgen and Newman, have to explain what criterion is open to individuals, that they may assure themselves on the legitimacy of their implicit reasoning; how they are to distinguish between their well-grounded conclusions, on the one hand, and the dictates of prejudice, passion, caprice, on the other. This inquiry must occupy a very prominent place in any complete and methodical treatment of our theme; but nothing can have been further from our intention than to give that theme such a treatment. In fact, our purpose will have been answered, if we succeed in drawing the attention of speculative Catholics to a line of thought which hardly any other throughout the whole range of philosophy exceeds in importance.

XVI.
CERTITUDE IN RELIGIOUS ASSENT.*

F. NEWMAN deserves the warm gratitude of his co-religionists, were it only as being the first to fix Catholic attention on what is certainly the one chief stronghold of philosophical objectors against the Church; and he deserves still more gratitude for the singular power of argument and felicity of illustration which he has brought to his task. There are undoubtedly various incidental statements in his volume with which we are far from agreeing; but it is not our intention to say much of them on the present occasion. The series of able articles from the pen of F. Harper, now appearing in the *Month*, will doubtless in due course be collected in a separate publication; and their appearance in that state will give us the opportunity of expressing our own humble opinion on the points at issue. But we are at all events thoroughly in accordance with what we regard as F. Newman's central position; and to this part of his work we shall confine ourselves in what we are now going to say.

What, then, is that "chief stronghold of philosophical objectors against the Church," on which F. Newman has been the first to fix Catholic attention? This—that since the strength of assent, given to any proposition, should invariably be proportioned to the amount of evidence on which that proposition rests, no man loves truth for its

* *An Essay in Aid of a Grammar of Assent.* By JOHN HENRY NEW-MAN, D.D., of the Oratory. London: Burns, Oates, & Co.

own sake who does not labour, in every single matter of thought, to effect this equation between his strength of proof and his firmness of conviction. See, *e.g.*, F. Newman, pp. 155, 156; p. 167; p. 169, etc. Let us begin, then, with pointing out the powerful argument which an anti-Catholic could at once build up, if this foundation were conceded him.

"Catholics are taught to regard it as a sacred duty that they shall hold, most firmly and without a shadow of doubt, the truth of certain marvels which are alleged to have taken place nineteen centuries ago. As to examining the *evidence* for those truths, the great mass of Catholics are of course philosophically uncultured and simply incompetent to such a task. But even were they competent thereto, they are prevented from attempting it. Except a select few of them, they are all forbidden to read or knowingly to hear one syllable of argument on the other side. Under such circumstances, *proof* for their creed they can have none; any more than a *judge* can have proof who has only heard witnesses on one side, and them not cross-examined. So far from proportioning their assent to the evidence on which their doctrine rests, the assent claimed from them is the very highest, while the evidence afforded them is less than the least.

"But take even any one of the select few who are permitted to study both sides of the question. He will tell you quite frankly that his belief was as firm before his examination as it is now; nay, and that he regards it as a sin, which unrepented would involve him in eternal misery, if he allowed himself so much as one deliberate doubt on the truth of Catholicity. I place before him some serious difficulty, which tells against the most central facts of his religion: he had never heard of the difficulty before, and he is not now at all sure that he will be able to answer it. I should have expected, were it not for my knowledge of

Catholics, that the confidence of his conviction would be *diminished* by this circumstance; for, plainly, an unanswered difficulty is no slight abatement from the body of proof on which his creed reposes. But he says unblushingly that if he were to study for ten years without seeing how to meet the point I have suggested, his belief in his Church, whose claim of authority he recognizes as divinely authorized, would be in no respect or degree affected by the circumstance.

"Nor is it for themselves alone, but for all mankind, that Catholics prescribe this rebellion against reason. They maintain that every human being, to whom their Gospel is preached, is under an obligation of accepting with firmest faith the whole mass of Catholic facts—the miraculous Conception, Resurrection, Ascension, etc.; while it is simply undeniable that 999 out of every 1000 are absolutely incapable of appreciating ever so distantly the evidence on which these facts are alleged to repose.

"Nor, to do them justice, do they show the slightest disposition to conceal or veil their maxims. The Vatican Council itself has openly anathematized all those who shall allege that Catholics may lawfully suspend their judgment on the truth of Catholicity, until they have obtained for themselves scientific proof of its truth.*

"I have no general prejudice against Catholics; on the contrary, I think many of them possess some first-rate qualities. But while their avowed intellectual maxims are those above recited, I must regard them as external to the pale of intellectual civilization. I have no more ground on which I can argue with a Catholic than I have ground on which I can argue with a savage."

---

* Si quis dixerit parem esse conditionem fidelium, etc., ita ut Catholici justam causam habere possint fidem, quam sub Ecclesiæ magisterio jam susceperunt, assensu suspenso in dubium vocandi donec demonstrationem scientificam credibilitatis et veritatis fidei suæ absolverint, anathema sit."— "Dei Filius," c. 3, canon 6.

We shall have repeatedly, in our present essay, to comment on the principle set forth and applied to this objection; and it will be much more convenient, therefore, at once to give it a name. Perhaps we may be permitted to call it the principle of "equationism;" the principle which alleges that there is an obligation on every one who loves truth, of setting himself expressly to the task of effecting an "equation" between the strength of his convictions and the amount of proof on which they respectively rest. And to those Catholics who regard with suspicion the general tendency of F. Newman's volume, we would entreat them to consider how the objection of equationists, as above stated, can be otherwise met than by the substantial adoption of his doctrine. However, we have no kind of right to constitute ourselves his interpreters. Our purpose in the present essay is only to solve the above objection in our own way, making abundant use for that purpose of the invaluable materials which he has supplied. And we shall understand the doctrine of these equationists, not as one of their number might explain it when cross-questioned, but in the sense it must bear if it is to warrant the anti-Catholic objections just now recited.

We cannot proceed, however, one step in our task till we have made some explanation of our terminology. F. Newman uses the word "certitude" in a sense different from that usually given by Catholic philosophers. They divide certitude into two elements: as signifying, firstly, the reasonable absence of all doubt; and, secondly, a certain *degree* of positive adhesion to the truth embraced. F. Newman includes in the term only the *former* of the two elements; and in saying, therefore, that certitude has no *degrees* as regards the absence of doubt, he entirely concurs with them in their doctrine.* We shall ourselves, so far,

---

* Take Liberatore, for instance. "Quòd una [certitudo] alteri præstet, facile suadetur: si non attendas ad partem negativam, nimirum *exclusionem*

use the word "certitude" in F. Newman's sense. In p. 204, however, he draws a distinction between what he calls "material" and "formal" certitude; which we do not find useful for our own purpose, and which we shall therefore not adopt.* We shall speak of "certitude" existing in my mind as to any truth, whenever I undoubtingly assent to that truth on grounds which legitimately generate such undoubtingness; on grounds, we mean, which *conclusively establish* the truth in question. Undoubting assent itself we shall call "absolute assent;" whether it do or do not rest on fully adequate grounds. By "absolute assent," in other words, we understand an assent which is not only *unaccompanied* by doubt, but which is so firm as to *expel* doubt; to be *incompatible* with the presence of doubt. And we shall say that an absolute assent, resting on *in*adequate grounds, possess "*putative* certitude" only.

Here, however, before going further, we must interpose an explanation which has no bearing indeed on our argument, but which is necessary for the prevention of possible misunderstanding. No "certitude," in the sense we have given the word, can be *greater* than another; but it may be very much more *irresistible* than another. Wherever grounds for certitude exist, doubt is *unreasonable;* but in one case, very far more than another, it is *possible.* Suppose I have gone through Euclid I., prop. 47, and satisfied myself that the whole argument is cogent. I am as *certain* of that proposition as I am of the axiom that things equal to the same are equal to each other; but

dubii, quæ indivisibilis omnino est et *gradus non habet;* sed attendas ad partem positivam, nimirum intensitatem adhæsionis, etc."—"Logica," n. 11. Dmowski, again. "Omnis naturalis certitudo formaliter spectata est æqualis." Vol. i. p. 32.

* There is one part of F. Newman's view on which he himself lays very great stress, but which we have not yet been able to apprehend. It is his speaking of "assent" as in its nature "unconditional," and independent of the inferential act which may have led to it.

plainly it is far more *possible*, though not more *reasonable*, to doubt the former than the latter verity.

This, then, being laid down, we give two answers to the equationist doctrine: our answers, we believe, being substantially the same with F. Newman's. Firstly, there are no *degrees* of certitude; and consequently, when complete certitude is once obtained, additional *proofs* can add nothing to the certitude itself as regards all absence of doubt. For instance: to speak quite within bounds, by the time I was twenty-five years old, I possessed abundantly sufficient ground for complete certitude that there are such cities in the world as Paris and Vienna. Since that date my *proofs* for this conclusion have much more than doubled; but it is simply ludicrous to say that I should now be more than twice as certain of the fact as I was then. I was completely certain of it then; and I cannot be *more* than completely certain of it now.

Take another case. My father is a man of singularly spotless integrity; and I have lived continually with him, from my infancy down to the prime of life in which I now am. It is very long since I acquired a complete certitude of such being his character. Five years ago a heavy charge was brought against his morals; and he frankly told me that he was wholly unable for the moment to explain those suspicions which pressed against him so heavily. Indubitably there was at that time one argument of weight on the adverse side; and equationists must in consistency maintain, that my only reasonable course was to diminish *pro tanto* my confidence in his character. But though they are bound *in consistency* to maintain it, we do not dream that they *will* maintain it. On the contrary, the common voice of mankind declares that, had I so acted, I should have done what is no less intellectually unreasonable than morally detestable. It is intellectually unreasonable; because if I possess certitude of any truth, I thereby *also* possess certitude that apparent objections against it are worthless.

This latter illustration leads us to a second remark, which is of vital moment in the present discussion. It is in the highest degree noteworthy, how many of men's strongest, most important, and most reasonable convictions rest on *implicit* premisses. Nay, many truly momentous conclusions depend on premisses which are not only implicit, but in their present shape are no more than confused memories of the past. My conviction that Paris and Vienna exist, my conviction that my father is a man of spotless integrity, are both cases in point. To insist that in either of these cases I shall expressly labour to equate the strength of my conviction with the degree of its evidence, would be to take the surest means of rendering it utterly *dis*proportioned thereto. In either case premiss has for years succeeded premiss, each leaving its legitimate impression on my mind and then forgotten. How is it possible that I can labour to equate my conviction with its evidence, when that evidence, in its original and adequate shape, is wholly inaccessible, having left behind it but a vague record on my memory? In like manner, every acute and intelligent person, who has lived an active life among men, possesses, stored within him, all sorts of miscellaneous convictions on the fit way of dealing with mankind, the result of his past experience. These are, indeed, among his most valuable possessions, so far as this world is concerned; and yet it would be the merest child's play if he professed to remember the individual experiences which have gradually built them up. It is rather a hopeless task certainly for the thinker to aim at proportioning his conviction to its premisses, when these premisses, in their original and adequate shape, are no longer present to his mind.*

---

* We cannot, however, concur with F. Newman, if we rightly understand him (p. 160), that such a conviction is now "self-sustained in our minds."

Equationists, however, may hope to meet the *first* of our two objections by asking leave to amend their plea. They will no longer, perhaps, speak of proportioning the *degree* of conviction to the *degree* of evidence ; but will urge that every one should sedulously take heed that he holds no proposition with absolute assent for which he does not possess evidence abundantly sufficient. And their doctrine certainly deserves much more respectful consideration in its new shape than it deserved in its old.

We conclude, then, that, putting aside one or two exceptional instances on which there is no need to insist, it would *cæteris paribus* be *a great advantage*, if no one yielded more unreserved assent to any proposition than is warranted by the evidence he possesses.* But this is a most different proposition from saying, that all men should expressly *aim* at obtaining for themselves this advantage. Take an obvious illustration. It would be a great advantage *cæteris paribus*, putting aside one or two exceptional instances, if all men enjoyed excellent bodily health ; but it does not at all follow from this that men would act wisely in *pursuing* this object through every detail of their life. Such a course would lead to two evils : for, firstly, this minute care would so occupy their attention as indefinitely to weaken their energy in more important directions; and, secondly, the constant *endeavour* for bodily health would be injurious to bodily health. Now let us apply this illustration : and we will begin with far the less important reason of the two.

Firstly, then, we say, if all men were thus to busy themselves with pruning down their putative certitudes, they would disastrously diminish their energy in other more

On the contrary, we would submit that those confused memories of the past which now exist, are its reasonable and amply sufficient basis.

* If our readers are surprised that we should admit any " exceptional instances," we will mention, as one of their number, the assent given by a child of ten years old to his parent's trustworthiness. Would it really be universally an advantage, that this assent should not be more unreserved than his premisses warrant?

important directions. Let us take one case out of a thousand. No one will deny that *philanthropists* have done great service to mankind: yet how far stronger are their beliefs than their premisses warrant! . Each one holds implicitly an undoubting conviction that his own particular hobby is the one most important element of human happiness. Now, we ask which of the two following alternatives is more for the welfare of mankind? On the one hand, that he should proceed steadily in his admirable and disinterested efforts for benefiting his fellow-men? Or, on the other hand, that he should largely divert his energy from this noble course, to the far less congenial employment of lowering down his view on the importance of what he is about to the exact level warranted by evidence? Again, take a much graver case. I am fifteen years old; and I have a father, not of comparatively spotless excellence as in a former illustration, but of mixed character; by no means predominantly wicked, yet with serious faults. And for one reason or another it is very important for me to have a true implicit *impression* of that character. Would it on that account be desirable that I should apply myself directly to the study? labour to obtain all requisite candour? contend laboriously against my tendency, prompted by affection, to undervalue his defects?

But now, secondly, and much more importantly, however desirable it may be that putative certitudes should be pruned down, it continually happens that the worst possible means of *effecting* this object will be for the thinker himself to aim directly at its accomplishment. In the immense majority of cases men are absolutely incapable of any such effort. Take the whole class of labourers, farmers, tradesmen; or take a large number of hunting country gentlemen. They hold with absolute assent a large number of convictions; many resting on fully sufficient grounds, many on grounds more or less inadequate, many on no grounds at all.

Various influences may be brought to bear on these men by a more cultured mind, with the result of considerably diminishing this intellectual evil; but it is more like a bad joke than a grave suggestion, to advise that they shall be summoned to pass under review their various beliefs, and reject those which are insufficiently supported. The grave philosopher, who should urge this, could not get them to understand so much as what he means. And even if he could, they would be no more competent to the task than the said philosopher would himself be competent to the task of riding across country after the hounds. Each man has his speciality.

Then even as regards one of the most cultivated mind. Is it true that he has always the power of confronting his conclusion with the ground on which it rests, in order to estimate its reasonableness? Why, in many cases, as we have already pointed out, those grounds are no longer accessible in their original shape, having left behind them but a vague record on the memory. But further, even when his premisses are actually before him, they very often defy his power of analysis. F. Newman has illustrated this with exquisite felicity.

As by the use of our eyesight we recognize two brothers, yet without being able to express what it is by which we distinguish them, as at first sight we perhaps confuse them together, but on better knowledge, we see no likeness between them at all; as it requires an artist's eye to determine what lines and shades make a countenance look young or old, amiable, thoughtful, angry, or conceited, the principle of discrimination being in each case real, but implicit—so is the mind unequal to a complete analysis of the motives which carry it on to a particular conclusion, and is swayed and determined by a body of proof, *which it recognizes only as a body, and not in its constituent parts* (p. 285).

Take, as one instance, the case of medicine to which F. Newman refers at p. 325. A third-rate practitioner is one who forms his conclusions *theoretically:* who derives universal propositions from his acquaintance with treatises, and deals no otherwise with each particular case than by classing it under one or other of these universal propositions. The physician of *genius,* while availing himself to the utmost of past experience as recorded in treatises, at the same time studies each several case on its own merits and forms a conclusion based on the whole phenomena before him. Is that conclusion to be accounted *unreasonable,* until he is able to produce those phenomena one by one before his conscious observation ? Then, all the most important cures have been wrought by unreasonable men ; and the patient, if a " lover of truth," would rather have been left to die " secundùm artem." Turn, indeed, where you will externally to the region of pure mathematics, the same fact will meet your observation. The careful student of history, *e.g.*, will pronounce, with absolute confidence, that such or such a nation would be so or so affected by such or such a circumstance ; that such or such a change has been wrought in that nation's character since such or such a period. Is he able to exhibit in detail, for his own satisfaction, the precise premisses which have led him to these conclusions ? No one will think so. F. Newman again points to a different field of illustration. He gives extracts (p. 321) from a work with which we are not otherwise acquainted, on " the authorship of a certain anonymous publication as suggested mainly by internal evidence." We preserve F. Newman's italics. " Rumour," says this author—

> Speaks uniformly and clearly enough in attributing it to the pen of a particular individual. Nor, although a cursory reader might well skim the book without finding in it anything to suggest, etc., . . . will it appear improbable to the more attentive student of its internal evidence ; and the improbability will decrease more and more, in proportion as the *reader is capable* of judging and appreciating the *delicate, and at first invisible*

touches, which limit, to *those who understand them*, the individuals who can have written it to a very small number indeed. The utmost scepticism as to its authorship, *which we do not feel ourselves*, cannot remove it farther from him than to that of some one among his most intimate friends; so that, leaving others to discuss antecedent probabilities, etc. (p. 321).

On this passage F. Newman thus comments :—

Here is a writer who professes to have no doubt at all about the authorship of a book, which at the same time he cannot prove by mere argumentation set down in words. The reasons of his conviction are too delicate, too intricate; nay, they are in part invisible, except to those who from circumstances have an intellectual perception of what does not appear to the many. They are personal to the individual. This again is an instance, distinctly set before us, of the particular mode in which the mind progresses in concrete matter, viz. from merely probable antecedents to the sufficient proof of a fact or a truth, and, after a proof, to an act of certitude. (*Ib.*)

Criticism of this kind affords a large field for illustrating the proposition with which we are engaged. There are many passages, *e.g.*, of which a good scholar would pronounce with most absolute certitude that they were not written by Cicero or by Tacitus, as the case may be. Yet how hopeless his attempt of exhibiting, for his own inspection, the various premisses which make this conclusion legitimate ! *

Now, we do not for a moment deny that even the most philosophically cultured men often enough yield absolute assent to some propositions on insufficient evidence ; nor again do we deny that they may with great advantage put themselves through some course of intellectual discipline, with the view of diminishing this evil. Some of their conclusions, doubtless—though we believe that these are with most men comparatively few—have been entirely arrived at by *explicit* reasoning; *i.e.* by *argument*: and, it will certainly be very useful to confront these from time to time

* On this part of our theme, see our essay on "Explicit and Implicit Thought."

with the arguments on which they rest. Then, as to those far more numerous assents which rest mainly or partly on implicit premisses, it is often very important that a philosophically cultured lover of truth shall impartially examine every *argument*, whether favourable or adverse to them, with which he can become acquainted. And there is another remedy against prejudice which is also available to such minds; viz. that they labour to analyze their various opinions, compare them with each other, and compare them also with all cognizable phenomena. But after allowing all this, it still remains true, with the highly educated man no less than with the most uncultured, that the number of convictions is very considerable, for which he has no evidence capable of being placed distinctly before his mind. And it is also true, that there are not a few among the number which he intimately feels to rest on evidence super-superabundantly sufficient, nay in some cases simply irresistible; and which he could not eradicate without rending his whole moral and intellectual nature.

Let so much have been said on the philosophical principle of equationism, whether in its original or its amended shape. We will now proceed to consider those two fundamental theses on which the devout Catholic rests his whole hope for this life and the next: the truth of Theism, and the truth of Catholicity. We affirm that any ordinary Catholic, however uneducated, has access to superabundantly conclusive evidence for these truths. As regards Theism, we placed before our readers in a former paper a long and most striking passage to this effect from F. Kleutgen (pp. 422–425), which we hope they will read again in the present context. Nor can we do better here than supplement it with another, from a later portion of his great work, in which, as will be seen, he incidentally applies the same principle to the evidence of *Catholicity*. As in the former case, we italicize a few sentences to which we invite special attention; and we here and there add a word or two within brackets, to make clear what we conceive to be the author's meaning.

Our reasonable nature is so constituted that, with but little reflection, we are excited and constrained, not only by a spontaneous inclination of heart, but by a necessitated power of mind (esprit), to acknowledge the Existence of a Supreme and Absolute Being, Cause, and Sovereign Master of all things. And this necessity especially makes itself felt, when we vividly represent to ourselves our imperfection and dependence. Why? Partly no doubt because God at the same time *makes Himself felt within us by His moral law as an August Power to which we are subject;* but partly also because it is conformable to the laws of our intelligence, thus to conclude from things relative and dependent to the Absolute and Sovereign Being Who is their Cause. This is the explanation given long ago by the Fathers of the Church, as to the origin and knowledge of God which is natural to us. Nevertheless it may easily happen that the human understanding, in virtue of a law inherent in its nature, is led on from one truth to the knowledge of another, without [explicitly] going through those reasonings which, according to that very law, are the steps from premiss to conclusion; nay, even without reflecting on the fact that it *has* passed from premiss to conclusion at all.*

Now, to require that in the *scientific examination* of those convictions which rise up within us, it may be said, without our own agency [qui naissent en nous, on dirait, sans nous] no mention should be made of those intermediate considerations [which are the implicit stepping-stones from the first premiss to the last conclusion], and that attention should only be given to what is found in the spontaneous and, as it were, instinctive deductions of reason, this would be entirely to misunderstand the office of science. *How many truths are there, concerning moral duty, concerning nature and art, which a man of good judgment* [bon sens] *knows with perfect accuracy, without being distinctly cognizant how he passes in his successive judgments from one truth to another.*

---

* As we have translated this last clause rather freely, we subjoin the words of the authorized French translation:—"Sans qu'elle fasse les raisonnements qui, d'après cette loi même, nous font passer de l'une à l'autre, et même sans que nous ayons conscience de cette transition."

Now this distinct knowledge, which he does not possess and often cannot obtain, is precisely what we expect to derive from science, which, exhibiting the connection between divers cognitions, strengthens these spontaneous convictions; and not only defines their object more distinctly, but makes the knowledge of them clearer. Why, then, should not science take as the object of its researches *that knowledge of God which we instinctively possess*, in order to make clear on what principle we can legitimately reason, from the dependence of our own being, to the Existence, not of some generally conceived first cause, but of the Absolute and Independent Being [whom we call God]: in order thus to strengthen our convictions on His Existence and to arrive at a more intimate knowledge of His Nature? Do we not proceed in the same way when we desire to satisfy ourselves *on the foundations of the Christian Faith?* All that we have heard from infancy on the foundation and stability of our holy religion, suffices abundantly to convince us without much reasoning that God only can be its author. *It is true that in order to form this judgment we are assisted by the light of grace; but neither is that [instinctive] knowledge of God on which we have spoken obtained without Divine aids of the natural order.* Now, theology develops those reasons which we have for believing in the divinity of the Christian religion. . . . In the same way, philosophy is able and is bound to show that that method of reasoning from the world's existence to God's, to *which our intellect is spontaneously impelled*, is conformable to the clearly known laws of our thought" ("Phil. Scol.," n. 929).

If our readers will peruse, in connection with this striking passage, the extracts which we gave in our essay on "Explicit and Implicit Thought," they will find that F. Kleutgen's doctrine is such as the following; and it is the doctrine which we ourselves cordially embrace. All men have access to super-superabundant evidence for the truth of Theism; and all Catholics have access to super-superabundant evidence for the truth of Catholicity. Moreover, God in His tender love deals with men one by one; presses such premisses efficaciously on their attention; and strengthens their mind that they may draw the legitimate conclusion. Such assistance, in bringing home to men's mind the truth of Catholicity, is the work of supernatural grace; while such assistance in bringing home to men's mind the truth of Theism, appertains, says F. Kleutgen, not to supernatural grace, but to Divine aid of the natural order. We need not ourselves here consider in any way this distinction between natural and supernatural auxilia; which would lead us entirely beyond the bounds of philosophical disquisition: otherwise, as we have said, we are prepared heartily to defend F. Kleutgen's doctrine.

The criticism of this doctrine put forth by anti-Catholic philosophers on first hearing it, will probably be, not merely that it is *untrue*, but that it is *manifestly* and *on the surface* untrue; that it is obviously and undeniably inconsistent with phenomena. Our first task must be to meet this allegation; and to argue that the theory before us may be firmly held, without in any way contradicting obvious and ascertainable facts. For this purpose we would submit to our opponents the following considerations:—

1. We have already pointed out that certitude, in the sense we give that term, admits of no degrees; and consequently, that when premisses sufficient for certitude have once been accumulated, *additional* premisses cannot increase the undoubtingness of one who acts faultlessly on the principles of sound reason. We would now add, however, what must not be forgotten, that such additional premisses are often of invaluable service. A has a mind indefinitely more acute and profound than B; and may draw the legitimate conclusion at the first moment, so to speak, when it *becomes* legitimate. But B with the best intentions remains unconvinced; and it is only through the multitude of reasons which keep thronging in, that the fort of his reason, made as it is of somewhat impenetrable materials, can at length be stormed. The super-superabundance therefore of evidence, on which, as we consider, Theism and

Catholicity respectively rest, is a circumstance of great force towards the conviction of ordinary minds.

2. There is no more remarkable fact in psychology than the extraordinary number of operations which may be elicited by the human mind without its own consciousness. As regards the case of cultured persons, one illustration will suffice. We suppose such an experience as the following will be common to many of our readers. I am intensely interested in some author—say Gerdil—some of whose treatises are in Latin and some in French; two languages which I can read with about equal facility. Immediately on finishing one of these treatises I ask myself whether it was in Latin or in French; and I find myself entirely unable to answer. Now, how many operations have thus unconsciously passed through my mind! Firstly, the letters have been read, each one separately and all together; (2) the letters formed into words; (3) the words translated from a foreign language into English; (4) the construction of the sentences mastered so that the words shall group themselves in proper order; (5) the ideas expressed by the sentences conveyed to my understanding. Every single part of this long and complicated chain must by necessity have traversed my thoughts; for there is literally no connection between the letters which I read and the ideas which I receive, except by means of it: and yet it has left absolutely no trace on the memory.

But now this phenomenon is by no means confined to philosophically cultured intellects. Consider the extraordinary quickness with which some uneducated mariner will prognosticate, on some fine evening, that there will be a storm before next morn. He fixes his attention on a certain assemblage of phenomena; accurately distinguishes them from others with which they have a greater or less resemblance; brings to bear on them the confused memory of innumerable former occasions, on which he has observed appearances precisely similar; and draws the one conclusion legitimately resulting from his premisses. In fact, he has gone correctly through the various processes described in Mill's "Logic," with no more suspicion of the fact than if he had been all along fast asleep. Or take the rustic's firm conviction that such or such of his companions is honest and trustworthy and friendly to himself. How large a number of premisses must be intimately known, and how lengthy a chain of reasoning gone through, to warrant the conclusion! Yet again and again the rustic will arrive at such a conclusion with faultless certitude, and without the faintest suspicion that his mind has been engaged in any special exercise. To the same effect is an illustration which we gave in our last essay, and which is fully within the most uneducated man's compass. "I am intimately acquainted with a certain relative: and some fine morning I have not been with him more than five minutes before I am perfectly convinced, and on most conclusive grounds, that, for whatever reason, he is out of sorts with me. It is little to say that I could not so analyze my grounds of conviction as to make *another* see the force of my reasoning; I could not so analyze them, as that their exhibition shall be in the slightest degree satisfactory to *myself*. Especially in proportion as I am less philosophical and less clever in psychological analysis, all attempts at exhibiting my premisses in due form hopelessly break down. Yet none the less it remains true, both that my premisses are known to me with certainty, and that my conclusion follows from them irresistibly. There is an enormous number of past instances in which these symptoms *have* co-existed with ill-humour; there is no single known case in which they have existed *without* it; they all admit of being referred to ill-humour as effects to their cause; they are so heterogeneous, that any other cause except ill-humour which shall account for them all is quite incredible, while it is no less incredible that they co-exist fortuitously, etc. Why, in all probability the very Newtonian theory of gravitation does not rest on firmer and more irrefragable grounds." Yet it is not only true that I cannot *analyze* my process of conviction; I should naturally never dream of thinking that I have *gone through* any such process. The whole has as simply escaped my notice as though it had never been.

3. Nothing is more easily imaginable, than that the illative faculty—if we may borrow F. Newman's adjective—should be indefinitely strengthened by God for a special purpose. Another faculty, that of memory, will supply a ready illustration. Of course, it would be simply unmeaning to say that God so strengthens my memory as to give me knowledge of things which I never experienced; but it would be most intelligible that he should so stimulate it as to give me certain knowledge of every past thought, word, and act of mine, however transitory. In like manner, it would be simply unmeaning to say that God so assists my illative faculty as to enable me to draw confident conclusions from premisses which do not warrant certitude; and such a notion we entirely put aside. But it is most intelligible that He so elevates it in some particular process as to enable me to discern the legitimacy of certain inferences, which *are* legitimate, but which I should never by my natural strength of mind have *discerned* so to be. Or, putting the thing more generally, it is a most intelligible statement that God, for the sake of obtaining my assent to some momentous verity, (1) specially presses on my attention this, that, and the other premiss; and (2) so strengthens my illative faculty as to make me see, what otherwise I should *not* have seen, the full sufficiency of those premisses as establishing the verity in question.

We will next, then, apply what has been said to those cardinal doctrines, the truth of Theism and the truth of Catholicity. We begin with the former.

All mankind have access to premisses, the cumulative force of which is super-superabundantly sufficient for the proof of God's Existence. We reserve to a future article a consideration of what those premisses precisely are, and what their ratiocinative force. We will here but briefly enumerate one or two of their number. First and foremost we must mention those deducible from the testimony of the Moral Faculty.* So importunate and, at the same time, so authoritative are the utterances of man's moral voice, that no adult, except for his own grave fault, can be ignorant of their essential teaching. No one, we say, except for his own grave fault, can be ignorant of the truth that, as F. Kleutgen expresses it, there exists "an absolute good and a sovereign rule over our wills and actions;" "an august and sacred power which is [in authority] over us." But this truth is only part of what may be called man's natural stock of Theistic premisses; † of those premisses with which every one is familiar as he advances towards maturity. Thus the manifold and most unmistakable marks of order and design, visible in creation, sink deeply into his mind, and make their due impression. Other premisses, again, are supplied by the great principle of causation,‡ which is

---

* Pius IX. speaks of "præcepta [legis naturalis] *in omnium cordibus à Deo insculpta*" (Encycl. "Quanto conficiamur.")

† F. Newman seems to speak here and there (see *e.g.* p. 101) as though men had no conclusive proof of God's existence, except that derived from the moral voice within them. If he intends this, we much regret the statement; but if he intends no more than to give this particular argument the chief and most prominent place, he entirely agrees with F. Kleutgen. According to that great champion of scholasticism, as we have seen, all men are so created as to receive spontaneously, from the first dawn of reason, a certitude of God's Existence: and the very principal means by which He produces this result is the "making Himself *felt within us* by His moral law as an August Power to which we are subject."

‡ We deeply deplore F. Newman's language in pp. 63, 64, concerning the axiom of causation. It would appear, indeed, that he has here expressed himself somewhat hastily; for within six lines he represents the doctrine that "everything must have a cause" as identical with the doctrine that "nothing *happens* without a cause." But the first-named expression, as he himself points out, would include *God* as caused: whereas the other expression

as inevitably and as constantly, however unconsciously, recognized by the most uncultured rustic as by the profoundest philosopher. And these at last are but specimens and samples, though principal ones, of a class.

Such are the premisses which, as we maintain after F. Kleutgen, are pressed by God on the implicit attention of all adults; and which legitimately issue in a most firm and most reasonable conviction of His Existence. F. Kleutgen further points out a very significant fact. "When the Fathers of the Church," he says, "declare unanimously that knowledge of God is really found and established among all men, the importance of their testimony is better understood by remembering that they lived in the midst of heathen populations." This theme—the prevalence of implicit Theism among the most inveterate polytheists—is worthy of far more attention than we can here give it.

But it must never be forgotten how indefinitely higher and happier is the state of those who have been educated in explicit Theism, and who have practised the lessons of their education. Reverting to a former distinction—if in all men doubt of God's Existence is *unreasonable*, to these men it is, in some sense, *impossible*. Take that premiss on which F. Kleutgen lays by far his most prominent stress—the truth that there exists "an absolute good and a sovereign rule over our actions," "an august power which is over us." It is only in proportion as men act consistently and energetically on the dictates of their moral faculty, that this truth impresses itself on their minds with an evidence, which is not luminous only, but simply irresistible; and none but Theists can act thus consistently and energetically.* And this leads us to another most

excludes Him. As F. Harper explains (*Month*, December, 1870, p. 682), the axiom of causation which "grave authors seem to enunciate as an intuitive truth," is that every *new* existence or *changed* existence has a cause.

* This is one of the several momentous propositions which we are obliged in our present essay to assume, for want of space to argue them.

cogent and persuasive proof, which is the special property of what we may call practising Theists ; for they have experience of the singular assistance derived from *prayer* towards fulfilment of the moral law. Such evidences as we have just now recounted, we say, are accessible to every man, not in proportion as he is philosophically cultured, but in proportion as he has been zealous in obeying and serving that God, Whom from the first dawn of reason he has instinctively known.

So much on the truth of Theism. We now proceed to similar considerations on the truth of Catholicity. In doing so, however, we will invert our previous course, and *begin* with considering what evidences are available to those, however destitute they may be of mental culture, who have been trained from childhood in the Catholic religion. We must content ourselves, in this, as in other parts of our essay, with the merest skeleton outline of what we would say.

1. Firstly, there is no fact more profoundly impressed on the Catholic at every turn than that the Church claims emphatically to be God's one accredited messenger ; infallible in teaching and intolerant of rivals. All her allegations are in harmony with this claim. She professes that Apostles established their divine commission by miracles and by the fulfilment of prophecy; that they regarded one of their number as placed by God over the rest ; that that one has had a successor unintermittently through intervening centuries ; that the society which he governs is one in faith and communion, holy, Catholic, and, of course, Apostolic.*

---

* "Till these last centuries," says F. Newman (p. 372), "the Visible Church was, at least to her children, the light of the world, as conspicuous as the sun in the heavens; and the Creed was written on her forehead, and proclaimed through her voice, by a teaching as precise as it was emphatical ; in accordance with the text, 'Who is she that looketh forth at dawn, fair as the moon, bright as the sun, terrible as an army set in array?' It was not, strictly speaking, a miracle, doubtless; but in its effect, nay, in its circumstances, it was little less. Of course I would not allow that the Church fails in

The humblest Catholic knows that all his educated co-religionists are firmly convinced of these facts, as of undoubted historical truths.

2. On the other hand, there is no writing, nor any *other* society whatever which makes a parallel claim, which alleges itself to be God's one accredited messenger to mankind. Most certainly Scripture does not put forth any such claim in *its own* behalf.

3. Moreover, to put forth such a claim without foundation is nothing less than insolent blasphemy. The Catholic Church is necessarily either Vice-God or Anti-God ; * and this fact wonderfully simplifies the issue.

4. There is a certain type of morality, impressed on all Catholics in their various devotional books, their hagiologies, their catechisms, their religious practices ; a type which those who disapprove it commonly call the "ascetical." Reason rightly directed, we affirm, peremptorily declares that this is the one type conformable with eternal truth ; and the most uneducated Catholic, in proportion as he is devout, has had his reason thus rightly directed.

5. The various revealed dogmata, which in themselves are wholly inaccessible to reason, are nevertheless found by a believer to be in deep and mysterious harmony on many points with this true type of morality. To meditate on them and bring them in every possible way to bear on practical action, has a singular effect in elevating his mind towards the true moral standard. "The Catholic religion is true," says F. Newman (p. 205), among other reasons, "because it has about it an odour of truth and sanctity *sui*

this manifestation of the truth now, any more than in former times, though the clouds have come over the sun ; for what she has lost in her appeal to the imagination, she has gained in philosophical cogency, by the evidence of her persistent vitality."

* This is taken from a phrase of F. Newman's, who says that the Church, from her claims, must be either Vice-Christ or Anti-Christ.

generis, as perceptible to my moral nature as flowers to my sense, such as can only come from heaven."

6. Then, all who really hold the Catholic Faith are more or less keenly impressed with a sense of *sin*. If they labour to serve God, in proportion as they do so they feel profoundly their numberless faults; because clearness of moral perception grows far more quickly than consistency of moral action. On the other hand, if they retain the Faith *without* labouring to serve God, they see by the light of reason, no less than by the light of faith, that such omission is most sinful. All Catholics, then, really such, are impressed with a reasonable conviction that there can be no surer note of a divinely sent religion than its prominent recognition of human sinfulness. To our mind there is no greater excellence in F. Newman's volume than his repeated inculcation of this truth. But this note is a special characteristic of Catholicity in many different respects. Consider, *e.g.*, the dogma of the Atonement: how marvellously it appeals to man's sense of sin!

7. Emphatically also to be considered is the *experienced effect* of Catholicity, as assisting a believer in all increase of virtue and piety. As one instance out of many, consider that power of resisting the most importunate temptations which is obtained by Catholic prayer, by frequentation of the Sacraments, by the constant and tender worship of Mary Most Holy.

Now, all the reasons which we have mentioned are accessible to the most unintellectual Catholics; and they are reasons, moreover, which admit of being pressed home to the mind with special impressiveness by divine agency. In their legitimate effect, they are super-superabundantly sufficient to produce certitude; and our affirmation is that the Holy Ghost uses these and similar reasons for that very purpose in the soul of Catholics. From first to last undoubtedly the Catholic is perfectly free to *reject* that which he has such abundant reason for accepting; but in proportion as he surrenders the whole current of his life to the influence of his Faith, in that proportion the divine origin of that Faith is more vividly and efficaciously evidenced to his mind.

As to the reasons available for the conversion of un-cultured non-Catholics, we cannot even enter into that amount of detail which we gave to the last case; but we heartily concur with the whole of F. Newman's magnificent sermon—"Dispositions for Faith"—which stands fifth in the "Occasional" volume. For ourselves we can only make two, and those most general, observations. Firstly, in proportion as externs are brought more closely into contact with the Church, they are enabled more clearly to discern such *notes* of the Church as we have already mentioned. Secondly, we are most strongly disposed to concur with what F. Newman has consistently advocated, we may say, through his whole theological life; viz. that by far the most hopeful course for an extern (speaking generally, and allowing for exceptions) is to act energetically, under the guidance of his moral faculty, on what is placed before him as moral truth by his parents and teachers.* These are his words in the volume before us—

> Of the two I would rather have to maintain that we ought to begin with believing everything that is offered to our acceptance, than that it is our duty to doubt of everything. This, indeed, seems the true way of learning. In that case we soon discover and discard what is contradictory; and error having always some portion of truth in it, and the truth having a reality which error has not, we may expect that when there is an honest purpose and fair talents, we shall somehow make our way forward, the error falling off from the mind, and the truth developing and occupying it. Thus it is that the Catholic religion is reached, as we see, by inquirers from all points of the

---

* If this be admitted, here will be a second exception to the general truth, that it is in itself a great advantage for men to hold no conclusion more strongly than is warranted by its evidence.

compass; as if it mattered not where a man began, so that he had an eye and a heart for the truth (pp. 371, 372).

Now, the purpose of our essay is, as our readers will remember, to consider a certain "chief stronghold of philosophical objections against the Church," which we set forth at starting. And we suppose we may assume, without express argument, that if Catholics have really such super-superabundant ground for their belief as we have affirmed, a thoroughly satisfactory answer is furnished by such a fact to the philosophical objection. The whole question, therefore, turns on the issue whether the account we have given of Catholic evidence is substantially true.

Hitherto we have been merely arguing that, at all events, it cannot be *disproved;* that it contains nothing inconsistent with phenomena. No such inconsistency, so far as we see, can be even alleged, except by assuming that such processes as we suppose to have traversed a Catholic mind, must, if they really did so, have left behind them some record on the memory. But the illustrations we have given amply refute any such attempted argument. Indeed, there is perhaps no one point in which psychologians of the present day have so outstripped their predecessors as in their very strong doctrine on the multitude and importance of implicit mental processes.*

We have proved, then, we trust, to philosophical non-Catholics, that our theory is not inconsistent with phenomena; but can we further prove to them that it is *true?* Even if we could not prove this to *them*, this theory might nevertheless be cognizable by *Catholics* as true, and might, therefore, be obligatory on their action. Let us revert to our familiar illustration. I have the firmest conviction of

* We should add, however, that the doctrine itself cannot possibly be stated with greater clearness than it was by Lugo two centuries back. "Hæc est virtus intellectûs et voluntatis, ut uno actu brevissimo et subtilissimo attingant compendiosè totam illam seriem motivorum," etc. "De Fide," d. i, n. 98. See also n. 87 and n. 91.

my father's integrity. I may be utterly unable to make my friends *sharers* in this conviction; but I am none the less bound to act on it *myself*, and should be greatly culpable if I did otherwise. The application is obvious. Catholics are responsible for their conduct to their Creator, and not to their non-Catholic fellow-creatures.

But we say much more than this. We say that the only question really at issue is, whether the historical and philosophical arguments, adduced by educated Catholics for the truth of their religion, be really conclusive. *This*, of course, is a question entirely external to the present essay, and we are obliged to *assume* the affirmative answer.* But what we wish here to say is this. Whatever arguments suffice to convince an educated man that the Catholic religion is *true*, should suffice *also* to convince him that uneducated Catholics have full *evidence* of its truth. There are two reasons for this, either sufficient.

1. Suppose an educated man to become convinced that Catholicity is true. He thereby becomes convinced that, wherever the Gospel is duly preached, all men are under an obligation of accepting what the Church teaches; and that her Gospel is more especially directed to the uneducated and poor. If, then, it is their *duty* to accept what the Church teaches, they must have sufficient evidence to make such acceptance *reasonable*.

8. Then again. Suppose an educated man becomes convinced that Catholicity is true, he thereby becomes convinced that the Church is infallible in faith and morals. But no one ever questioned that she prescribes to her

---

* F. Newman does not hesitate to say ("Lectures on the Present Position of Catholics in England," Preface, p. viii.) that "the proof" of Catholicity "is irresistible, so as even to master and carry away the intellect directly it is stated." We rather fancy him, however, here to assume as *granted*, that Christianity in one shape or another is of divine origin, and that the facts narrated in the New Testament are substantially true. So understood, we thoroughly concur with his statement.

children that very course of conduct set forth in the philosophical objection against which our whole argument has been directed. If an educated man, then, becomes convinced that Catholicity is true, he thereby becomes convinced that this very course of conduct is conformable to right reason. But it is *not* conformable to right reason, unless an uneducated Catholic has access to such implicit evidence as we have alleged. The inference is obvious.

In saying, however, what we have said, we have had no thought of doubting that an educated Catholic will often find it of great importance to enter on an explicit investigation* of Catholic evidences in this or that direction. Here, again, we are brought to a very important theme, which it is impossible to handle in our brief remaining space; and we can but state most briefly the opinions which we should humbly advocate. On the one hand, we cannot but think that the implicit grounds of belief, possessed by educated and uneducated alike, and pressed on the attention of all by divine grace, will ever remain the strongest and most satisfying basis of conviction.† · On the other hand, an

---

* F. Newman (p. 184) draws a very important distinction between "investigation" and "inquiry."

† So F. Newman. "The grounds on which we hold the divine origin of the Church, and the previous truths which are taught us by nature—the being of a God, and the immortality of a soul—are felt by most men to be *recondite and impalpable, in proportion to their depth and reality*. As we cannot see ourselves, so we cannot well see intellectual motives which are so intimately ours, and which spring up from the very constitution of our minds" (pp. 328, 329). And he thus concludes the fifth of his "Occasional Sermons," to which we have already referred. "This is a day in which much stress is laid upon the *arguments* producible for believing Religion, Natural and Revealed; and books are written to prove that we ought to believe, and why. These books are called Natural Theology and Evidences of Christianity; and it is often said by our enemies, that Catholics do not know why they believe. Now, I have no intention whatever of denying the beauty and the cogency of the arguments which these books contain; but I question much, whether in matter of fact they make or keep men Christians. I have no such doubt about the argument which I have been here recommending to you. Be sure, my Brethren, that the best argument, better than all the books in the world, better than all that astronomy, and geology, and physiology, and all other sciences, can supply; an argument intelligible to those who cannot read as

educated Catholic will often be tempted to doubt, however unreasonably, the conclusiveness of these grounds, unless he has learned to see how strongly reinforced they are by *explicit* reasoning, derived from every branch of human thought and study. Moreover, as we need hardly add, it is of vital moment that a sufficient number of able Catholic thinkers shall be, for controversial purposes, thoroughly acquainted with the vast variety of arguments adducible for the truth of Catholicity.

In the essay which we here conclude, we have not unfrequently verged on the confines of various delicate philosophical questions, which we have thought it better to avoid. It seems to us abundantly plain that the view we have put forth is substantially true so far as it goes; while it is, nevertheless, constantly ignored by anti-Catholic disputants. If we can obtain the concurrence of such persons to the truth of what has here been said, we shall be in a far more favourable position for treating the more anxious and difficult questions which remain behind.

well as those who can; an argument which is 'within us;' an argument intellectually conclusive, and practically persuasive, whether for proving the Being of a God or for laying the ground for Christianity; is that which arises out of a careful attention to the teachings of our heart, and a comparison between the claims of conscience and the announcements of the Gospel" (pp. 98, 99).

XVIII.

THE EXTENT OF FREEWILL.

THE ground we have taken up in the Freewill controversy, as our readers will remember, has been this. Determinists maintain that the same uniformity of sequence proceeds in the phenomena of man's will, which otherwise prevails throughout the phenomenal world; that every man at every moment, by the very constitution of his nature, infallibly and inevitably elicits that particular act to which the entire circumstances of the moment, external and internal, dispose him. We have argued in reply, that, whereas undoubtedly each man during far the greater part of his waking life is conscious of a "spontaneous impulse" which is due to his entire circumstances of the moment, and results infallibly therefrom, he finds himself by experience, nevertheless, able again and again to *resist* that impulse. He is able, we say, to put forth at any given moment what we have called "anti-impulsive effort;" and to elicit again and again some act indefinitely different from that to which his spontaneous impulse solicits him.

Here our position stands at present: and it contains all which is necessary, in order that the fact of Freewill may possess its due efficiency in our argument for Theism. Nevertheless, in order to complete the scientific treatment of Freewill, a supplementary question of great importance has to be considered; a question, moreover, which Dr. Bain expressly challenged us to face. During how large a period of the day, in what acts, under what conditions, is any given human being able to exercise this gift of Freewill? And we are the rather called on not to shrink from this question, because the very course of reasoning which we have been obliged to adopt against the Determinists— unless it be further developed and explained—might be understood, we think, to favour a certain tenet, with which we have no sympathy whatever ;. a tenet which we cannot but regard as erring gravely against reason, against sound morality, and against Catholic Theology. The tenet to which we refer is this: that my will is only free at those particular moments when, after expressly debating and consulting with myself * as to the choice I should make between two or more competing alternatives, I make my definite resolve accordingly. This tenet is held, we incline to think, more or less consciously by the large majority of non-Catholic Libertarians; and even many a Catholic occasionally uses expressions and arguments of which we can hardly see how they do not imply it. Now, we are especially desirous that *Catholics* at all events shall see the matter in what we must account its true light. Our present essay, then, may in some sense be called intercalary.† We shall not therein be addressing Determinists at all, or proceeding in any way with our assault on Antitheism, except, of course, so far as such assault is indirectly assisted by anything which promotes philosophical unanimity and truth among the body of orthodox believers. It is Catholics alone whom we shall directly and primarily address; and, indeed, as regards the theological reasoning, which will occupy no very small portion of our space, we cannot expect it, of course, to have any weight *except* with

* We purposely avoid the word "deliberating," because it has led, we think, to much confusion of thought.

† The editor has thought it better, from this circumstance, to place it at the end of the volume rather than in its original place in the series on Theism.—ED.

Catholics. But we hope, as we proceed, to deal with each successive question on the ground of philosophical, no less than theological, argument. Nor will our philosophical arguments imply any other controverted philosophical doctrines, except only those which we consider ourselves to have established in our previous essays. We consider, therefore, that our reasoning has a logical claim on the attention, not of Catholics only, but of those non-Catholics also who are at one with us on the existence of Freewill, and on the true foundation of Ethical Science. Still, as we have said, our direct and primary concern will be throughout with Catholics.

The tenet which we desire to refute, as we have already explained, is this: that a man is only free at that particular moment when, after expressly debating and consulting with himself as to the choice he shall make between two or more competing alternatives, he makes his definite resolve in one or other direction. The thesis which we would oppose to this, as we said in answer to Dr. Bain's inquiry, may be expressed with sufficient general accuracy by affirming that each man is free during pretty nearly the whole of his waking life. The controversy, which may be raised between these two widely different views, is our direct controversy on the present occasion; and the thesis we have just named is our direct thesis. But it will be an absolutely necessary preliminary task to exhibit what we may call a map of man's moral nature and moral action. This preliminary task will occupy half of our essay; and when it is finished, we shall have gone, we consider, considerably more than half-way towards the satisfactory exposition and defence of our direct thesis itself. Moreover, we hope that this preliminary inquiry will be found by our readers to possess some interest, even apart from the conclusion for the sake of which we introduce it. It will be necessary, indeed, to discuss incidentally one or two points, which have been warmly debated in the schools; and we have need, therefore, at starting to solicit the indulgence of our readers for any theological error into which we may unwarily fall. At the same time, we shall do our very best to avoid any such error. And, at all events, we shall confidently contend in due course, that, as regards the direct point at issue— the extent of Freewill—we are substantially following the unanimous judgment of standard Catholic theologians. Without further preface, then, we embark on our preliminary undertaking.

I. We begin with the beginning. It is held as a most certain truth by all Libertarians, both Catholic and other, that no human act of this life can be formally either virtuous or sinful, can be worthy either of praise or blame, unless it be a *free* act; and only so long as it *continues* free. On this truth we have spoken abundantly on earlier occasions, and here need add no more. Whenever, therefore, in the earlier part of this essay, we speak of acts as "virtuous" or "sinful," we must always be understood as implying the hypothesis that they are at the moment free. How far this hypothesis coincides with fact—how large a part of human voluntary action is really free, this is the very question on which, before we conclude, we are to set forth and defend what we account true doctrine. Meanwhile, let it be distinctly understood, that where there is no liberty, acts may be "materially" virtuous or sinful; but they cannot be "formally" so, nor deserve praise or blame.

II. "Nemo intendens ad malum operatur." There is no attractiveness whatever to any one in wrong-doing *as such*; no human being does—or, from the constitution of his nature, can—do wrong precisely because it *is* wrong. This is the absolutely unanimous doctrine of Catholic theologians and philosophers. It deserves far fuller exposition than we have here space to give it; but a very few words will suffice to show how clearly experience testifies its certain and manifest truth. Take the very wickedest man in the whole world, and get him to fix his thoughts carefully on such topics as these: "How exquisitely base and mean to ruin the friend that trusts me!" "How debasing, polluting, and detestable is the practice of licentiousness!" "How odious and revolting are acts of envy and malignity!" Will it be found that such considerations spur him on to evil actions? that the baseness, meanness, odiousness of an evil action is an additional motive to him for doing it? On the contrary, he knows to the very depth of his heart how fundamentally different is his moral constitution. He knows very well that if he could only be got to dwell on such a course of thought as we have just suggested, he would assuredly be reclaimed; and for that very reason he entirely refuses to ponder on the wickedness of his acts. It is their pleasurableness, not their wickedness, which stimulates him to their performance.

III. Accordingly, it is the universal doctrine of Catholic theologians and philosophers, that all ends of action which men can possibly pursue are divisible into three classes: "bonum honestum;" "bonum delectabile;" "bonum utile." Let us explain what we understand by this statement. Virtuousness,* pleasurableness, utility, these are the only three ends, which men can possibly pursue in any given action. Whatever I am doing at any particular moment, I am doing either (1) because I account it "virtuous" so to act; or (2) because I seek "pleasurableness" in so acting; or (3) because I regard the act as "useful," whether to the end of virtuousness or of pleasurableness; or (4) from an intermixture of these various motives. This is plainly the case: because I have not so much as the physical power of doing what is wicked

---

* For our own part—and with great deference to those excellent and thoughtful Catholics who think otherwise—the more we reflect, the more confidently we hold that "virtuousness" is an entirely simple idea.

because it is wicked; and the only motive, therefore, which can possibly prompt my wrong action is the pleasurableness which I thence expect to derive.

Or let us put the same truth in a different shape. My "absolute" end * of action must in every case, by the very necessity of my mental constitution, be either virtuousness, or pleasurableness, or the two combined: but there are various "intermediate" ends at which I may aim, as being "useful" to the attainment of my "absolute" ends.

At the same time, it is abundantly clear on a moment's consideration that if this division is to be exhaustive, under the term "pleasurableness" must be included not bodily pleasurableness alone, but intellectual, æsthetical, or any other; the delight of reading a beautiful poem, or of gazing on sublime scenery, or of grasping a mathematical, philosophical, theological demonstration. Then again the malignant, the envious, the revengeful person finds delight in the sufferings of his fellow-men. Lastly, it is further clear that "pleasurableness" includes very prominently "negative" pleasurableness, viz. the escape from pain, grief, ennui.

We have spoken on an *intermixture* of ends; but a few more words must be added to elucidate that subject. On some occasion, under circumstances entirely legitimate, I largely assist some one who has fallen under heavy misfortune. Let us first suppose that I do this exclusively because I recognize how virtuous it is to render such assistance. Yet the act may cause me intense pleasure—the pleasure of gratifying my compassion—because of God's merciful dispensation, which has so largely bound up pleasurableness with the practice of virtue. So far is clear. But now it is abundantly possible—indeed, it probably

---

* We purposely avoid saying "ultimate" end, because we are inclined to think that much confusion has arisen from the different senses which have been given to the term "finis ultimus."

happens in a very large number of cases—that this pleasurableness may be part of the very end which motives my external act. If this be so, the more convenient and theologically suitable resource is, we think, to account the will's movement as consisting of two different simultaneous acts. Of these two acts, the one is directed to virtuousness, to pleasurableness the other : the one, as will be seen in due course, is virtuous ; the other, as will also be seen, *may* indeed be inordinate, and so sinful, but *need* not be sinful at all.

Something more should also be said on that special end of action, virtuousness. It is laid down by various theologians (see Suarez, " De Gratiâ," l. 12, c. 9, n. 1; Mazzella, " De Virtutibus Infusis," n. 1335) that acts truly virtuous, though done without thought or even knowledge of God, are referred to Him nevertheless "innately," "connaturally," " by their own weight." And Suarez gives a reason for this ("De Ultimo Fine," d. 3, s. 6, n. 6). Such an act, he says, is pleasing to God ; and is *capable* of being referred to Him, even though in fact not so referred.* This explanation must be carefully borne in mind ; because otherwise various theological statements, on the obligation of referring human acts to God, might be importantly misunderstood. Then, going to another particular, S. Thomas (*e.g.* 2ª 2ᵃᵉ q. 23 a. 7, c.) speaks of virtuousness as "*verum bonum*," in contrast with "bonum *apparens*." He contrasts again " bonum incommutabile " with " bonum commutabile : " a matter on which much amplification might be given, had we the space.

Here, moreover, to avoid serious misconception, we must carefully consider the particular case of what may be called " felicific " possessions. There is a large number of such possessions, which it is entirely virtuous and may sometimes even be a duty for me to pursue or desire, not as

* See also d. 2, s. 4, n. 5.

means to any ulterior end, but simply as an integral portion of my happiness.* So theologians speak of "caritas erga nos," or "amor nostri"—either of which phrases we may translate "self-charity"—as designating one particular virtue: the virtue of promoting my own true happiness. Immeasurably the foremost, among these possible felicific possessions, stand, we need hardly say, my own permanent happiness, considered as a whole and not as confined to its earthly period. But there are very many others also. Such are, *e.g.*, my permanent earthly happiness; bodily health; equable spirits; competent temporal means; happy family and social relations; a good reputation among my fellow-men; a sufficient supply of recreations and amusements; intellectual power; poetical taste; sufficient scope for the exercise of such power and such taste, and generally for what modern philosophers call "self-development," etc. Now, as regards all these except the first, it appertains no doubt to higher perfection, as Suarez observes,†

* We here use the word "happiness" and its co-relative "felicific" in what we take to be its ordinary use throughout non-theological writings. Theologians no doubt, as we shall explain in due course, use the word "felicitas" in a fundamentally different sense. But we suppose that, in ordinary parlance, "my own happiness" always means "my own sum of enjoyment." No doubt the word suggests far more prominently the higher, more subtle, more mental sources of enjoyment, than those which are lower and more animal; but the probable reason of this is, that cultured persons—who in the last resort fix linguistic usage—recognize the former class as being indefinitely more pervasive, permanent, satisfying, than the latter.

† In the Foundation of the Exercises "such indifference of affection is recommended towards created things not prohibited, as that we should not rather seek health than sickness, nor prefer a long life to a short one. But at once this objection occurs: viz. that health and life are among those things which a man is bound by precept to preserve and seek by such methods as are virtuous and becoming. Consequently [so the objection proceeds] such indifference is not *laudable*, as would be exhibited in not seeking health rather than sickness."

[Reply.] "The good of life and [again] of health is no doubt among those things which may be desired for their own sake; that is, as being of themselves suitable to nature and necessary to a certain integrity thereof, for the sake of which [integrity] they are virtuously desired without relation to any ulterior end. Therefore, a man's affection may, without any sin, not be entirely indifferent concerning those goods considered in themselves. Never-that a man desire them only so far as they may be instruments of virtue. Still they may virtuously be loved and, if so be, pursued for no ulterior end, but merely as constituent parts of my happiness, and as the objects of self-charity. Yet it might appear on the surface that, in pursuing my own happiness, I cannot conceivably be aiming at any other end except that of mere *pleasurableness;* and this is a misconception, which it is important to clear up. A very few words will enable us to do so.

Let us take, as a particular instance, the blessing of health. I am lying on my sick-bed, in pain of body and depression of mind. I recognize that I may quite virtuously aim at the recovery of my health, not merely as a means for more effectively serving God, or more successfully gaining my own livelihood, or the like, but simply as an integrating part of my happiness. Accordingly I pursue this virtuous end of self-charity. As a matter of conscience, I adopt regularly the prescribed remedies, however distasteful at the moment; and I fight perseveringly against my natural tendency towards availing myself of those immediate gratifications which may retard my recovery. What is my end in such acts? Precisely the *virtuousness* which I recognize to exist, in pursuing health as an integral part of my earthly happiness. I am grievously tempted, for the gratification of present (negative) pleasurableness, to neglect my more permanent happiness; and I recognize it as virtuous to resist such gratification. It is extremely probable indeed that these acts, directed to virtuousness, will be simultaneously accompanied by other acts, tending to (negative) pleasurableness as their end; wherein I eagerly

theless, it appertains to *greater perfection* that we love not these goods except as they are instruments of virtue. . . . And the same thing may be said concerning all those goods which are such that, though they may be rightly loved for their own sake, nevertheless a man has it in his power to make a good or bad use of them. For in regard to *virtues*—of which a man *cannot* make a bad use—such indifference is not lauaable." (Suarez, " De Religione Societatis Jesu," l. 9, c. 5, n. 11.)

desire to be free from all this suffering and weariness of soul. But this is no more than a phenomenon, which, as we just now explained, continually occurs in the case of other virtuous acts, and is by no means confined to these acts of self-charity. Now, however, take an opposite picture. In my state of sickness I am a very slave to (negative) pleasurableness; I give myself up without restraint to my present longing for escape from my present anguish; I wantonly retard my recovery, by shrinking from immediate pain; I do nothing on principle, but everything on impulse. Here certainly none of my acts are directed to virtuousness, but all to (negative) pleasurableness. There is this fundamental and most unmistakable contrast between the two cases. In the former, the thought that I act *virtuously* by aiming at my recovery is constantly in my mind, prompting me to correspondent action; whereas in the latter case such thoughts of virtuousness are only conspicuous by their absence. And exactly the same kind of contrast may be drawn, as regards my method of pursuing those other felicific possessions which admit of being pursued at all. At the same time, it should not be forgotten that my desire itself of a felicific possession may very easily indeed become inordinate and therefore sinful: as will be explained towards the conclusion of our essay.

IV. We have been speaking of those ends at which a human being can aim. It is plain, however, that an end, which has once been "explicitly" intended, may continue vigorously to influence my will, though it is no longer explicitly in my mind. When such is the fact, theologians say that it is "virtually" pursued. And the fact here noted is of such very pervasive importance in the whole analysis of man's moral action, that we are most desirous of placing it before our readers as emphatically and as accurately as we can. Let us give, then, such an illustration as the following. I start for the neighbouring town on some charitable mission, and, as it happens, there are a great many different turns on my road, which I am quite as much in the habit of taking as that particular path which leads me securely to the town. I have not proceeded more than a very little way, before my mind becomes so engaged with some speculative theme that I entirely lose all explicit remembrance of the purpose with which I set out. Nevertheless, on each occasion of choice, I pursue my proper path quite as a matter of course, and so arrive safely at my journey's end. It is very plain that my original end has in fact been influencing me throughout; for how otherwise can we possibly account for the fact, that in every single instance I have chosen the one right course? Will you say that my *habit* of going to the town accounts for it? Not at all; because we have supposed that there is no one of the alternative paths which I have not been quite as much in the habit of pursuing as that which leads to the town. My original end, then, has motived my act of walking quite as truly and effectively, after I have ceased explicitly to think about that end, as it did when it was most conspicuously present on the very surface of my mind. But whereas, during the few first minutes of my walk, my pursuit of that end was " explicit," during the later period it has been changed from " explicit " into " virtual."

So much on the word " virtual." Dr. Walsh, the President of Maynooth, in his recent work " De Actibus Humanis " (nn. 71–81),* most serviceably recites the

* If it be not impertinent for one in our position to express even a favourable judgment on the labours of such an authority, we would say how inestimably valuable this volume appears to us. Extremely valuable for its own sake, when we consider how full it is both of unusual learning and singularly fresh and independent thought; but still more valuable as an augury of more extended treatment being hereafter given to the "De Actibus," than has in recent times been the case. It has always seemed to us a very unfortunate circumstance, that the "De Actibus" has of late been exclusively treated as a part of Moral Theology. We would submit that its dogmatic importance also, as introductory to the "De Gratiâ," is very great. But a result, we think, of the circumstance to which we are adverting,

various psychological theories, adopted by various Catholic theologians for the elucidation of this term. He thus, however, sums up (n. 81) the conclusions on which all are agreed: "An intention," they say, "which has previously been elicited, inflows 'virtually' into the [subsequent] action so long as the agent, being sui compos and acting humanly—although he be not [explicitly]* thinking of his previous intention—nevertheless is in such disposition of mind, that, if asking himself or asked by others what he is doing, and why, he would at once [supposing him rightly to understand what passed in his mind]† allege his previous intention, and answer: 'I do this for the sake of that.'" Elsewhere (n. 669) Dr. Walsh quotes with approval, from S. Bonaventure, an equally excellent definition. "Acts," says the saint, "are then said to be 'virtually' referred" to some end, "when the preceding intention" of pursuing that end "is *the true cause* of those works which are afterwards done."

As to the psychological theories recited by Dr. Walsh, with very sincere deference to his judgment, we cannot ourselves but adhere to Lugo's, which he rejects in n. 77. That great theologian holds, that whenever the "virtual" intention of some end motives my action, an "actual" intention thereof is really present in my mind, though but implicitly. And we would submit, that the very definition of the word "virtual" given by Dr. Walsh substantiates the accuracy of this analysis. Take an instance. I foresee

has been that those portions of the treatise which are not wanted for the Confessional, have been left unduly in the background.

We hope largely to avail ourselves of Dr. Walsh's labours in what follows. And we would also do what we can towards drawing attention to three papers on "Probabilism," from the same writer's pen, which appeared in the "Irish Ecclesiastical Record." We should venture to describe them as forming quite an epoch in the study of Moral Theology.

* We add the word "explicitly" because Dr. Walsh avowedly includes Lugo's theory in his summary, and Lugo holds that in all such cases there is *implicit* thought of the end previously intended.

† We add this qualification on our own responsibility.

that in half an hour's time I shall very probably be disappointed of some enjoyment, which I earnestly desire. I well know how grievous is my tendency to lose my temper under such a trial; and, accordingly, I at once resolve to struggle vigorously against this tendency should the occasion arrive. This resolve is founded on some given virtuous motive, or assemblage of virtuous motives: in order to fix our ideas, let us suppose that it is founded exclusively on my pondering the virtuousness of *patience*. The occasion does arrive in due course, and my previous explicit intention now " virtually " influences my successful resistance to temptation. It is Lugo's doctrine, that, supposing such to be the case, my will is *now* influenced by the virtuousness of patience no less really and genuinely than it was half an hour ago, when I made my holy resolve. The only difference, he considers, between the two cases is, that then I thought of that virtuousness "explicitly," whereas now I do but think of it "implicitly." This conclusion seems to us certainly true; and we would thus argue in its favour.

Dr. Walsh lays down as the unanimous judgment of theologians, that, in the supposed circumstances, if I ask myself *why* I resist the temptation, my true answer will be, "I do this for the sake of that; " or, in other words, "I resist the temptation for the sake of carrying out my previous resolve." But my previous resolve was, by hypothesis, founded exclusively on the virtuousness of patience; and, therefore, my present resistance is founded on the selfsame motive. That motive was, then, indeed present to my mind explicitly, and now it is present no more than implicitly. But the motive of action in either case must surely be the very same.

Or, take S. Bonaventure's explanation of the word "virtual." The preceding resolve, he says, has been "the true cause" of my present action. But who will say that my explicit resolve to practise one given virtue has, when occasion arises, been the "true cause" of my practising, *not* that virtue, but some other?*

We do not deny that, according to Lugo's doctrine, a "virtual" intention may very frequently motive an act without having been preceded by a corresponding "explicit" intention at all. But we do not see any difficulty in this conclusion. And, indeed, we should point out that, for our own purpose, the preceding paragraphs have not been strictly necessary. If indeed we were building on theological statements concerning "virtual intention," it would be strictly necessary to inquire what theologians *mean* by that term. But our own argument is logically untouched, if we simply say that, in what follows, we ourselves at least shall consistently use the term "virtual intention," as simply synonymous with "implicit."

We wish we had space to pursue this whole theme of "virtual" or "implicit" intention, at a length worthy of its pre-eminent importance; but we must find space for an illustrative instance. Some considerable time ago, men of the world were in the habit of using much indecent language in mutual conversation; while, nevertheless, they thought it thoroughly ungentlemanly so to speak in the presence of ladies. We will suppose two gentlemen of the period to be talking with each other, while some lady is in the room, occupied, we will say, in writing a letter. They are wholly engrossed, so far as they are themselves aware, with the subject they are upon—politics, or the Stock Exchange, or sporting. They are not explicitly thinking of the lady at all; and yet, if they are really gentlemen, her presence exercises on them a most real and practical influence. It is not that they fall into bad language and then apologize; on the contrary, they are so restrained by

* In which of its many senses S. Bonaventure here uses the word "cause," there is no need to inquire.

her presence that they do not dream of such expressions. Yet, on the other hand, no one will say that the freedom of their thought and speech is explicitly perceived by them to be interfered with. Their careful abstinence, then, from foul language is due indeed to an intention actually present in their mind; the intention, namely, of not distressing the lady who is present. Yet this intention is entirely implicit; and they will not even become aware of its existence, except by means of careful introspection. And this, we would submit, if we may here anticipate our coming argument, is that kind of practical remembrance and impression concerning God's intimate presence, which it is of such singular importance that I preserve through the day. What I need, we say, is a practical remembrance and impression, which shall really inflow into my thoughts and powerfully influence them; while, nevertheless, it shall be altogether implicit, and shall therefore in no perceptible degree affect my power of applying freely and without incumbrance to my various duties as they successively occur. And this indeed is surely the very blessing which a Catholic supplicates, when he prays each morning that "a pure intention may sanctify his acts of the day."

But this very prayer itself is sometimes perverted into what we must really call a mischievous superstition. A certain notion seems more or less consciously to be in some person's mind, of which it is absolutely necessary to show the entire baselessness, if we would exhibit a conspectus of man's moral action with any kind of intelligibleness and availableness. The Catholic is taught to pray in the morning, that a pure intention may sanctify his actions of the day as they successively take place. But a notion seems here and there to exist that these successive actions have *already* been sanctified by *anticipation* in his morning oblation of them. This strange notion assumes two different shapes, and issues accordingly in one or other of two importantly distinct tenets. One of these tenets we will at once proceed to consider; while the other will find a fit place for discussion a few pages further on.

Some persons, then, have apparently brought themselves to think that if in the morning I offer to God all my future acts of the day, I thereby secure beforehand the virtuousness of all those which are not actually evil in object or circumstance. I secure this virtuousness, they think, because by my morning's good intention I secure that the same good intention shall virtually motive them when they actually occur. But, as Billuart demands (Walsh, n. 668), "if any one, who has in the morning offered his acts to God, be afterwards asked, when he is dining or walking, *for what reason* he dines or walks, who will say that such a man can truly answer, 'I am doing so in virtue of my intention made this morning'?" And the following passage, from F. Nepveu, S.J., is so admirably clear on the subject that we can add nothing of our own to its unanswerable argument.

"When this intention is so far removed from the time of action as happens if one is contented with offering one's actions in the morning, there is reason to fear that this intention will gradually become fainter and even come entirely to an end, . . . so that it shall not *inflow at all* into the action. Moreover— since we have a profound depth of self-love—unless we bestow great attention on ourselves and much vigilance on all our [interior] movements, it is difficult to prevent the result, that there escape from us a thousand . . . movements of vanity, sensuality, desire to please mankind and ourselves; in fact, a thousand human respects, which are *so many retractations* of our morning intention, and therefore destroy it entirely." ("L'Esprit de Christianisme," pp. 95, 96.)

V. In order that some given act be virtuous, theologians commonly require that its virtuousness be directly intended, though such intention, of course, need be no more than "virtual." Dr. Walsh says (n. 397) that this proposition is maintained by all theologians, except a very few (paucissimos); and its truth is most manifest on grounds of reason. Take an illustration. I am very desirous, for some special purpose, of conciliating the favour of my rich neighbour, A. B. Among other things which I do to please him, I repay him a small sum he had lent me; and I make him a present of some picture, to which he took a fancy when he was paying me a visit. My one motive for both these acts is precisely the same; viz. my desire to be in his good books. Suppose it were said that—whereas the second of these two acts may be indifferent—the first, at all events, is virtuous under the head of justice, because the repayment of a debt is an act of that virtue : every one would see that such a statement is the climax of absurdity.

On the other hand, as Dr. Walsh proceeds to point out, it is by no means requisite, in order to the virtuousness of an act, that its virtuousness be at the moment the *absolute end* of my action. Suppose I give alms to the deserving poor, in order that I may gain a heavenly reward. Here the virtuousness of almsgiving is directly intended, for it is that very virtuousness which is my *means* towards my retribution; yet this virtuousness is, by hypothesis, desired only as a means, and not as the absolute end of my action. Most persons will at once admit that such an act is a truly virtuous act of almsgiving. On the other hand, suppose I give alms merely in order that my outward act may become known and help me to a seat in Parliament, it would be, as we have said, the climax of absurdity to allege that my act of almsgiving is virtuous as such.

There is one class of actions, however, which claims further attention. Suppose I do some act entirely for the sake of pleasurableness; but, before doing it, I carefully ponder whether the act be a morally lawful one, being resolved otherwise to abstain therefrom. Dr. Walsh (n. 623) refers to this case, and quotes Viva on it; but we do not think that Viva quite does justice to such an act as he supposes. He holds that such an act is neither virtuous nor sinful, but indifferent. We think he would have been much nearer the truth had he said that it is virtuous. But the true account of the matter, we think, is as follows. In this, as in so many other cases, the will's movement may be decomposed into two simultaneous acts. One of these acts is, "I would not do what I am doing were it opposed to morality;" and this is obviously most virtuous. As to the other act—the mere pursuit of pleasurableness— under such circumstances, we submit, it is neither virtuous nor sinful, but indifferent.

This will be our appropriate place for considering the *second* tenet, concerning the matutinal oblation of my day's acts, to which we have already referred. According to the *first* tenet on this subject—the tenet which we have already criticized—this oblation secures the result, that my morning intention shall really motive all my subsequent acts of the day, one by one, which are not actually evil in object or circumstances. This is, to be sure, a most singular notion; but some persons seem to hold another, indefinitely *more* amazing. They seem to hold that, even though the morning intention do *not*, in fact, motive these acts, nevertheless it makes them intrinsically virtuous. This allegation seems to us so transparently unreasonable that we feel a real perplexity in divining how any one, even of the most ordinary thoughtfulness, can have dreamed of accepting it. We quite understand that God, by His free appointment, may bestow gifts upon a human being, in consideration of what is not virtuous in him at all; as, *e.g.*, in an infant's reception of Baptism, or the Martyrdom of the Holy Innocents. And we understand the doctrine, held, we fancy, by many Protestants, that some act, not intrinsically virtuous, is often extrinsically acceptable to God. But we really do not see how it is less than a contradiction in terms to say that a given act is made intrinsically virtuous, by a certain circumstance which is no intrinsic part of it whatever. Yesterday afternoon I elicited a certain act; and this afternoon I elicit another, which is precisely similar to yesterday's in every single intrinsic circumstance without exception. Yet the act of yesterday afternoon, forsooth, was virtuous, whereas the act of this afternoon is otherwise; because yesterday *morning* I made an oblation of my day's acts, and this morning I made no such oblation. You may as well say that my evening cup of tea is sweet because I put a lump of sugar into the cup which I drank at breakfast. Lugo gives expression to this self-evident principle, by taking the particular case of temperance at meals. You and I are both at dinner; our will is directed (suppose) in precisely the same way to precisely the same ends, and our external acts also are precisely similar. Yet it shall be judged that you are eating virtuously and I otherwise, because *in the morning* you referred your acts to God and I did not. No doubt your morning's oblation may have given you great *assistance* in making your present act intrinsically virtuous, by facilitating your present reference of that act to a good end. But the act is intrinsically affected by what is intrinsic, not by what is extrinsic. And so Lugo points out, assuming the theological principle, that no act is meritorious which is not intrinsically virtuous. "He who in the morning refers all his acts to God, if afterwards, when at dinner, he is in just the same state of mind as though he had *not* elicited that matutinal intention, and if his action of eating does not *arise* from that matutinal intention or from some other good and virtuous one,—that man no more merits through his present act than he would if he had never formed such preceding intention at all." ("De Penitentiâ," d. 7, n. 39.) Sporer states the same proposition very earnestly and emphatically, adding that such is the common doctrine of theologians. He does not mention indeed so much as one on the opposite side. ("De Actibus," n. 22.)

On this profoundly practical doctrine, we cannot better conclude our remarks than by citing the noble passage from Aguirre, with which Dr. Walsh concludes his volume (nn. 690–692). It refers, however, as our readers will observe, not to a virtuous intention generally, but to that particular virtuous intention which motives an act of *sovereign love*.

Wherefore before all things I admonish—and entreat all theologians to inculcate and preach as a most wholesome doctrine—that each man endeavour, with the whole earnestness and fervour of his mind, to practise continuously and assiduously (so far as this fragile and mortal life permits) the exercise of referring explicitly himself and all his thoughts, affections, words, and works to God, loved for His own sake. For he should not be content if once or [even] at various times in the day he do this; but he ought frequently to insert [explicitly into his daily life] that sacrifice of mind which is far more acceptable to God than all other homages in the matter of the moral virtues.

VI. Passing now to another matter—how are we to measure the *degree* of virtuousness or sinfulness, in virtuous and sinful acts respectively? It is evident that this consideration must proceed, in the two respective cases, on principles fundamentally different: for in a virtuous act its virtuousness must of necessity be directly intended; whereas in a sinful act its sinfulness cannot by possibility be intended at all as an absolute end. We will take the two classes therefore separately.

As to virtuous acts—it is held, we suppose, by all theologians that, cæteris paribus, an act is more virtuous in proportion as it is directed to virtuousness with greater vigour and efficacy.* We have said " cæteris paribus,"

* We find it somewhat hard to find out in what sense theologians use the word "intensio." Do they use it to express "vigour," "efficacity"? or do they rather use it to express "effort"? The two ideas are very distinct.

because one kind of virtuousness may be higher than another. A comparatively remiss act, *e.g.*, of sovereign love, being really such, may be more virtuous than a far more vigorous act of some particular virtue; of justice, or temperance, or beneficence.

As regards the degree of evil in evil acts—we incline to think that theologians have given far too little methodical attention to the subject. For ourselves, we submit that any given act is more morally evil, in proportion as its pursuit of pleasurableness is more *inordinate*: more *morally unprincipled*, if we may so speak; in proportion as the act is more widely removed from subjection to God's Will and the Rule of Morals; in proportion as the transgressions of God's Law are more grievous, which such an act would, on occasion, command. In proportion as this is the case, its agent is said to "place his ultimate end in creatures" more unreservedly and more sinfully. However, to set forth in detail—still more to defend—what we have stated, would carry us a great deal too far.*

But at last is it true, that *all* acts are either virtuous or the reverse? In other words, are there, or are there not, individual acts which are neither morally good nor bad, but "indifferent"? This is the famous controversy

---

Consider, *e.g.*, a *blow*, possessing some certain fixed degree of intrinsic force or efficacity, just sufficient, let us say, to overcome a certain definite obstacle. A very strong man will deal forth such a blow without any "effort" or trouble whatever. A weaker man must put forth some exertion for the purpose. A still weaker must exert his whole strength. A child, even if he does exert his whole strength, finds himself unable to accomplish it. In like manner, two different acts, elicited by two different persons, may be directed to some given virtuous end with approximately equal "firmness," "tenacity," "vigour," "efficacity;" and yet one may cost the agent quite immeasurably more "effort" than the other. Is it "vigour," "efficacity," or, on the other hand, "effort," which theologians call "intensio"? We incline to think that commonly, yet not quite universally, they use the word in this *latter* sense. But we should be very glad of light on the subject from some competent quarter.

* Something more, however, is said on the subject towards the end of our essay.

between Thomists and Scotists; which Dr. Walsh (nn. 588-673) treats with quite singular completeness and candour, insomuch that his whole discussion presents, to our mind, one of the most profoundly interesting studies we ever fell in with. He has established, we think, quite triumphantly, that acts may be directed to pleasurableness as to their absolute end without being on that account sinful. We will briefly express our own opinion on the whole matter, by submitting (1) that very many acts are directed to pleasurableness as to their absolute end, yet without any vestige or shadow of inordination; and (2) that though such acts are commonly not virtuous, there is no ground whatever for accounting them sinful.*

* We cannot, however, follow Dr. Walsh in his view (nn. 674-688) of S. Thomas's doctrine on this subject. He considers S. Thomas to teach (see n. 675) that acts may be actually virtuous and referable to God which are not directed to virtuousness as such. For our own part, we altogether agree with F. Murphy of Carlow College—who contributed to the "Irish Ecclesiastical Record" of Dec. 16, 1880, a very appreciative review of Dr. Walsh's volume—that the latter writer "has not established his view of S. Thomas's teaching." "In nearly every one of the passages cited," adds F. Murphy, "or in the immediate context, S. Thomas most distinctly mentions *ends* which every Thomist would denominate good." This remark does not, indeed, apply to *all* the passages cited by Dr. Walsh in n. 683, note, where the Angelic Doctor describes virtue as consisting in a mean. But as regards all these passages without exception, we submit that S. Thomas is quite manifestly *supposing* throughout a real aim at virtuousness on the agent's part. "I am desiring to pursue the course of virtue, and I inquire therefore (in this or that individual case) what is the true *mean* wherein virtue consists." For ourselves, with very great deference to Dr. Walsh—the only passages which we can consider to need any special attention, are the two from the "De Malo," cited in nn. 686, 687. On these passages we would submit the following reply to Dr. Walsh's argument.

F. Mazzella has considered them (along with several others from S. Thomas) in his important volume "De Virtutibus Infusis," n. 1350; and he by no means understands them as Dr. Walsh does. According to Dr. Walsh, S. Thomas teaches in them (1) that an act, not directed to virtuousness as such, may nevertheless be free from inordination and referable to God; then (2) that such an act, if elicited by one in habitual grace, is meritorious of supernatural reward. According to F. Mazzella, what S. Thomas teaches is, that an act, otherwise faultless, which is directed indeed to impersonal virtuousness (bonum honestum) as its end, but which is neither explicitly nor virtually referred to God—that such an act, if elicited by one in a state of grace, is meritorious of supernatural reward. Now, this latter doctrine may or may not

VII. Here, in order to prevent possible confusion of thought, it will be better to recapitulate four propositions, among those which we have been advocating in the course of our essay.

(1) By the very constitution of man's nature, every act of the human will is by absolute necessity, during its whole continuance, intrinsically directed, whether explicitly or virtually, to virtuousness, or to pleasurableness, or to some intermixture of the two, as to its absolute end. But it may pursue of course intermediate ends, as "useful" towards those ends which are absolute.

be theologically true; it may or may not be S. Thomas's ordinary doctrine; but at all events it is fundamentally different from that which Dr. Walsh ascribes to the Angelic Doctor, and is entirely unexceptionable so far as regards any ground of natural reason. And we submit that, without travelling one step beyond the two articles to which Dr. Walsh refers, we can establish conclusively the correctness of F. Mazzella's interpretation. We turn, then, to the earlier article of the two: "De Malo," q. 2, a. 5, c. We italicize a few words

"If we speak of an individual moral act," says S. Thomas, "every particular moral act is of necessity either good or bad, because of some circumstance or other. For it cannot happen that an individual act be done without circumstances, which make it either right or wrong (rectum vel indirectum). For if any thing be done when it should (oportet), and where it should, and as it should, such an act is ordinate and good; but if any one of these fail, the act is inordinate and bad. And this should most of all be considered in the circumstance of *the end*. For what is done because of *just necessity and pious utility*, is done laudably, and the act is good. But what is destitute of just necessity and pious utility is accounted 'otiose,' . . . and an 'otiose' word—much more an 'otiose' act—is *a sin*" according to Matt. xii. 36.

Nothing, then, can well be more express than S. Thomas's statement, that every act not directed to a virtuous end is "inordinate" and "a sin." We have already said in the text that we cannot ourselves here follow the Angelic Doctor, because we admit a very large number of indifferent individual acts. But S. Thomas's meaning is surely indisputable. No doubt, later theologians would say that acts done for the sake of impersonal virtuousness are "innately," "connaturally," "by their own weight," referred to God; whereas S. Thomas speaks of them as not referred to God at all. But F. Mazzella points out (n. 1350) that S. Thomas and many others of the older theologians were not in the habit of using the more modern language on this head. And of course it is nothing *more* than a question of language.

We hope our readers will pardon this digression. The question is a vitally practical one, and it is of much importance clearly to understand what is S. Thomas's doctrine thereon.

(2) No act is virtuous unless it directly aims at virtuousness as such; and of course, therefore, it remains virtuous only so long as that aim continues. But such aim need not be explicit: sufficient if it be virtual.

(3) Acts which are explicitly or virtually directed to pleasurableness as to their absolute end, are either "inordinate" or not. If they are, they are sinful; if they are not—and if they are not otherwise faulty in object or circumstances—they are commonly indifferent.*

(4) The morning oblation of my acts to God is a most auspicious and effective commencement of a well-spent day. It is the first link of a potentially continuous chain; and most powerfully tends to effect that those acts be successively directed to virtuousness, when they come to be elicited in due course. But if an act be not *in fact* so directed, all the morning oblations in the world cannot suffice to make it virtuous. Nay, if I offer my acts to God every hour of every day, such oblation could not infallibly secure that my acts be virtuous during the interval. That my act of eleven o'clock is offered to God, does not infallibly secure that my act of ten minutes past eleven be intrinsically directed to virtuousness; and if it be not so directed, it is not virtuous.

VIII. This will be our most convenient place for exhibiting the well-known distinction between "Liberty of exercise" and "Liberty of specification." I do not at this moment possess Freewill *at all*, if I do not possess at least the power of *acting* or *abstaining* from action as I shall please.† If I have so much power of choice as this and no

* We say "commonly," because we wish to avoid the speculative controversy, whether an act can be virtuous which is directed indeed to virtuousness as to an intermediate end, but to mere pleasurableness as to its absolute end. The exact meaning we give to the word "inordinate" is explained towards the end of our essay. And we there also treat of two certain condemned propositions, not unfrequently alleged in controversy against the doctrine which we follow.

† So in the well-known Catholic Definition, "potest agere et *non agere*."

more, I have at least "Liberty of exercise." But as regards the very great majority of my free acts, I do possess more power than this; I possess the power, not only of either acting or abstaining from action, but of acting in this or that given *direction* as I shall please. We have deferred to this place our notice of the fundamental distinction here set forth, because by far its best illustration will be found in what now follows.

IX. All Catholic theologians and philosophers hold that the thought of "beatitude," and again of "generic goodness [bonum in communi]" imposes on the will necessity of *specification*. Whether, on the other hand, such thought do or do not impose necessity of *exercise*, this is disputed; and Suarez for one answers in the negative. See, *e.g.*, Metaph. d. 19, s. 5. But it is very important carefully to examine the true signification of that common dictum, on which all are agreed; because it has at times, we think, been mischievously misunderstood. Firstly, then, as to beatitude.

Let us suppose that an imaginary state of privilege be proposed to me as possible, in which, on the one hand, I shall enjoy a very large amount of mental and physical enjoyment: while, on the other hand, I shall be entirely free from suffering of every kind; in which accordingly there shall be absolutely no pain of ungratified wish, or of remorse, or of self-discontent. But let us further suppose that this state of privilege should involve no exemption from sin; that I should be involved in habits of pride, vainglory, sensuality, and indeed general indifference to God's Will. We are not here meaning for an instant to imply that such a state of privilege is possible, consistently with the constitution of human nature; or, again, consistently with God's methods of government: but still the supposition contains no contradiction in terms, and may therefore intelligibly be made. Would the thought of such a privilege as this impose on my will necessity of specification? God forbid! Manifestly I have abundant proximate power to elicit an act, whereby I shall repudiate and detest such a possible prospect; and I am bound indeed by strict obligation to abstain from all complacency in the thought of it.

On the other hand, let an imaginary state of privilege be proposed to me as possible, in which I shall be exempt, not only from sin, but from all moral imperfection; in which I shall elicit continuous and vigorous acts of theological and other virtues; but in which, nevertheless, I shall be a victim to severe continuous suffering, both mental and physical. No one will doubt that I have full power, to say the least, of earnestly deprecating such a future.

But now, lastly, let us suppose that an imaginary state of privilege is proposed to me as possible, in which secure provision shall be made both for unmixed virtuousness and unmixed pleasurableness; in which there shall neither be moral imperfection, nor yet pain and suffering. Such a state of privilege would be termed by Catholic theologians a state of "beatitude," in the widest range they give to that term. We may call it "generic" beatitude; and it is distinguished from more definite beatitudes, as the genus is distinguished from the species. Thus, there is a certain definite Beatitude, which God has proposed to mankind in raising them to the supernatural order: this is "supernatural" Beatitude, and its special characteristic is the Beatific Vision. There is another definite beatitude, which God would have proposed to mankind had he left them in the state of pure nature: see Franzelin on "Reason and Faith," c. 3, s. 4. There is again, perhaps, another, which will be enjoyed by the souls in Limbus. But these, and any further number of more definite beatitudes, are but different cases of that beatitude which we have called "generic." It is plain, moreover, that all these several beatitudes agree with each other in their *negative* characteristic; viz. that they exclude all moral imperfection and all suffering: whereas they may differ indefinitely on the positive side, as regards the kind or degree of virtuousness and pleasurableness which they respectively contain.* But it is on generic beatitude, and not on any of these particular beatitudes, that we are here principally to speak.

We say, then, in accordance with all Catholic theologians and philosophers, that the thought of generic beatitude imposes on my will necessity of specification. A moment's consideration will show the obvious certainty of this truth. If, when thinking of beatitude, I am not under necessity of specification, I have the power of preferring to it some other object. But what can such object possibly be? By the very constitution of my nature I am physically unable to pursue or desire any absolute end, except only virtuousness and pleasurableness; while both virtuousness and pleasurableness are included in beatitude, without any admixture whatever of their contraries. There is much, then, in the thought of that privilege to attract me, and absolutely nothing to repel me. It may be objected, indeed, that the thought of *virtuousness* is *repulsive* to many persons, because they have learned to associate it with the thought of irksomeness. But those who are thus minded are not really contemplating beatitude at all; they are not con-

---

* We need hardly remind our readers that, even within each one of these more definite beatitudes, there is a large inequality of individual endowment. One person in heaven, *e.g.*, enjoys indefinitely more of Supernatural Beatitude than another.

But it is remarkable, as a matter of theological expression, that the soul of Christ—notwithstanding its unspeakable suffering—is always spoken of as having been "Beata" from the very moment of its creation, on account of its possessing the Beatific Vision. And this circumstance indeed furnishes another instance of the fact on which we are especially insisting, viz. that the theological term "beatitude" is very far indeed from synonymous with the English word "happiness" as commonly used. The sense ordinarily given by theologians to the term "beatitude" is, we submit with much confidence, substantially identical with that exhibited in our text.

templating a state from which all irksomeness is as stringently excluded as all sin. A similar objection, indeed, may be put in a much stronger shape, but answered at once on the same identical principle. It may be said that the thought of Supernatural Beatitude itself is very far from imposing on men's will necessity of specification. There are many excellent Catholics who entirely take for granted, indeed, that the Beatitude of heaven is one of unspeakable delight; and who yet, as regards their own *conception* of that Beatitude, would vastly prefer some happiness more nearly resembling their earthly enjoyments. Nay, it may, perhaps, even be said that—excepting eternal punishment itself—few imaginable prospects of a future life would be more formidable to them than the promised heaven as invested with that shape in which their imagination depicts it: so intimately does their imagination associate the thought of continually gazing on God with the notion of something dreary, weary, monotonous. Some men are most assuredly under no necessity of specification, in the desire, as they exhibit it, of future Beatitude. But then this is only because their *picture* of that Beatitude fundamentally differs from its original; because their intellect and imagination fail adequately to realize how peremptorily the Beatific Vision will exclude the most distant approximation to dreariness, weariness, monotony. Their case, therefore, presents no difficulty whatever, even on the surface, in the way of our accepting the theological statement that the thought of true beatitude, supernatural or natural, imposes on my will necessity of specification. A more plausible objection, however, to that statement is the following.

Beatitude—so the objector may urge—is presented to my mind in a certain concrete shape; and I may easily enough desire *greater* virtuousness or *greater* pleasurableness than happens to be included in that presentation.

To this objection, however, also, the reply is not far to seek. (1) I do not the less desire beatitude in the very shape in which it is presented to my intellect, because I *also* desire something more. And (2) that "something more" is not something *different* from beatitude, but beatitude itself in higher kind or greater degree. We need hardly add, that those who shall be in the actual enjoyment of beatitude, will necessarily be preserved from all emotions of discontent or repining.

Suarez, however, and several other theologians, add that the thought of beatitude does *not* impose on my will necessity of *exercise*. When that thought presents itself, I am free to abstain, they think, from deliberately eliciting any correspondent act of will whatever. But we need not enter on this controversy, which is of most insignificant importance.

So much on "beatitude;" and very little more need be added on the similar term "generic goodness." Goodness, in the sense here relevant, is simply "that which is able to attract the human will;" "that which can be made an end of human action or desire." Goodness, therefore, as has already been explained, is exhaustively divided into (1) "virtuousness;" (2) "pleasurableness;" (3) "utility" towards either of the two former ends. But this fact, though otherwise of great importance, is entirely beside the present question, and need not here be taken into account. Our argument is simply this. If it were true that the thought of generic goodness does not impose on my will necessity of specification—this statement would precisely mean, that I have the power to pursue or desire some other end, in preference to pursuing or desiring goodness. But this supposition is a direct contradiction in terms; because "goodness," by its very definition, includes every end which man is *able* to pursue or desire. The thought, then, of "generic goodness" may or may not impose on my acts necessity of exercise; but most certainly does impose on them necessity of specification.

X. We are thus led to consider a common theological statement, than which hardly any other perhaps in the whole science needs more careful examination and discrimination. Words are often used by the greatest theologians, which seem on the surface to mean (1) that the thought of "felicity" imposes on the will of all men necessity of specification; nay (2) further, that whatever else they desire, they desire only as a *means* to felicity; (3) lastly, and most amazingly of all, that this is a truth quite obvious on the surface of human nature. Now, if such language as this be understood in the sense it may well present to an ordinary reader, we should say for our part that such a doctrine, concerning man's desire of felicity, might with far greater plausibility be called self-evidently *false* than self-evidently true. Is it self-evidently impossible, then, that even in the smallest matter I can prefer virtuousness to happiness, if I suppose the two to clash? Is it self-evidently impossible that I can obey God because of His just claims on me, without thinking of my own felicity at all? Is it self-evidently impossible, that I can act justly to others, except as a means to my own enjoyment? Is every sinner under the impression that sin is his best road to happiness? Or, in other words, is every sinner necessarily an implicit heretic? But we need not pursue the picture into further details. We may be very certain that this is not what can have been meant by theologians. Our purpose here is to explain what they *intend* by language, which admits of such gross misapprehension.*

Firstly, then, we would point out, that the word "felicity" is always used in Theology as synonymous with

---

* On what seems to us the true doctrine concerning men's desire of happiness, and again, on their obligation of pursuing that happiness, we would refer to Dr. Ward's "Philosophical Introduction," pp. 402-423.

"beatitude;" and that thus its sense is importantly different from that of the English word "happiness," as commonly used. This latter word (as we have already incidentally said) commonly expresses "my sum of *enjoyment*," quite distinctly from the question of virtuousness or sin. But S. Thomas, *e.g.*, defines "beatitude" as "perfect and sufficing good" (1ª 2ᵃᵉ q. 5, a 3, c.): would he describe happiness, irrespective of virtuousness, as "perfect and sufficing good"? In the very next article, indeed, he expressly answers this question; for he says that "felicity" on earth, so far as it can be attained, "*principally* consists in virtuous action [in actu virtutis]." Other theologians speak similarly. Arriaga, *e.g.*, divides "felicity" into "moral" and "physical:" the former signifying virtuousness, and the latter enjoyment ("De Beatitudine Naturali," n. 27). Theologians, then, do not say that man's motive of action is always desire of his own *happiness*. At the utmost, they say no more than that it is always desire of his own *beatitude; i.e.* desire of a certain complex blessing, which includes the virtuous no less than the pleasurable.

These remarks, however, of themselves by no means meet the full difficulty of the case. For a very large number of the greatest theologians say, not only that the thought of beatitude imposes on my will necessity of specification, but also that my desire of beatitude is the one primary source of all my actions. Yet, objectors will ask on hearing such a statement, can this be maintained? Is it really true that all human acts are motived by desire of beatitude? The impure man indulges in forbidden pleasure; the envious or malevolent man rejoices in his neighbour's suffering; the irreligious man detests God's Law, as imposing on him an intolerable yoke. Is it really true, that these three men first form to themselves a picture of beatitude in any sense of that term; and that their respective sins are motived by their desire of such beatitude? Or even in the case of a good man, is it really true that every act of grateful loyalty to his Redeemer, of obedience to his Creator, of zeal for the salvation of souls, is preceded, either explicitly or implicitly, by a mental picture of his own beatitude? To all these questions we reply, that no such inferences are necessarily involved in the theological dictum, that "men do everything for the sake of beatitude." A large number of the greatest theologians interpret the dictum as simply meaning this: "Every one of my acts," they say, "is directed to the attainment of some good or other, be it virtuous or pleasurable. But the sum of all such good constitutes beatitude; therefore every one of my acts is interpretatively referred to beatitude, because it is actually referred to a solid portion thereof." *

We conclude, that there is no one absolute end whatever of all human action; but, on the contrary, that as many absolute ends are possible as there are possible exhibitions, whether of the virtuous or the pleasurable. No doubt God is *by right* my one exclusive Ultimate End; or, in other words, I act more perfectly in proportion as I come nearer to a state in which all my acts are ultimately referred to Him, whether explicitly, virtually, or connaturally. (On the last adverb see our preceding n. III.) But, as a matter of *fact*, it need hardly be said that the number of human actions is enormously great which are motived quite otherwise.

XI. We now arrive at the last of our necessary preliminaries. Those acts on which our argument will principally turn are those which are "perfectly voluntary." Here, therefore, we must explain what we mean by "per-

---

* Dr. Ward, in his "Philosophical Introduction," pp. 410–415, quotes passages to this effect from Suarez, Vasquez, Viva; but he might have added indefinitely to the number of his authors.

fectly voluntary." Two conditions are necessary, in order that an act may have that attribute. The will must be in a certain given state; and the act itself must possess certain given characteristics. We will consider successively these two conditions.

Firstly, then, the will must be in a certain given state. It must be "sui compos;" or, as we may translate the expression, "self-masterful." This condition is so familiar to the experience of all, that a certain general description of it will amply suffice. We may say, then, that my will at this moment is "self-masterful," if I possess the proximate power of regulating my conduct by steady and unimpassioned resolve. This condition is, of course, unfulfilled if I am asleep, or intoxicated, or in a swoon, or otherwise insensible. Or (2) so violent a storm of emotion may be sweeping over my soul, that I have no proximate power to prevent this emotion from peremptorily determining my conduct. Or (3) I may be in what may be called a state of invincible reverie; I may be so absorbed in some train of reflection, that nothing can disturb my insensibility to external objects, except some, as it were, external explosion. During such periods my will entirely fails of being "self-masterful." At other periods, again, it may fail of being *entirely* "self-masterful:" I may be *half* asleep; or *half* intoxicated; or my emotions or my reverie may leave me no more than a most partial and imperfect power of proximately regulating my conduct by steady and unimpassioned resolve. All this is so clear, that we need add nothing further thereon.

But it is of great importance to our direct theme that we set forth systematically how fundamental is the distinction in idea, between my will being "self-masterful," and being "free." Nothing is more easily conceivable than that at the moment I have on one hand full proximate power of regulating my conduct by steady and unimpassioned resolve; while yet, on the other hand, that this resolve, should I form it, be inevitably determined for me by what a Determinist would call "the relative strength of motives." In fact, Determinists hold just as strongly as Libertarians, the broad and momentous distinction of idea which exists between the will being "free" on one hand, and on the other hand no more than "self-masterful."

Here, then, is the first condition necessary, in order that my act be "perfectly voluntary," my will must at the moment be entirely "self-masterful." On the other hand, when we say that some given act is "perfectly voluntary," we mean that it is (1) "explicit;" and (2) what we will here call "mature."* Let us consider these two elements successively. The latter is very easily explained; but the former will need our careful attention.

In order to make clear what is meant by "explicit" acts—and again by "explicit" thoughts—our best plan will be to pursue a course somewhat resembling that (see our preceding n. IV.) whereby Dr. Walsh explains what is meant by "virtual." If we ask any given man what he is doing at any given moment, he will pretty certainly be ready with an answer. "I am conning my brief, for to-morrow's sitting," says the lawyer. "I am trying a new kind of steam-plough," says the farmer. "I am pursuing the fox," says the sportsman. "I am standing in expectance of buyers," says the shopman. "I am watching this furnace," says the stoker. "I am attending to my opponent's speech, that I may answer it," says the M.P. "I am driving down to my man of business," says the country gentleman. And so on indefinitely. In all these cases, of course, there may be other acts of will or intellect simultaneously proceeding; but the prompt answer given to our

* We do not forget that some theologians use the phrase "perfectly voluntary" as synonymous with "free." But we think our own sense of the term is much the commoner, and also much more appropriate and convenient.

question shows, to use a very intelligible expression, what is *on the surface* of each man's mind. Now an " explicit " act means precisely an act " which is on the surface of my mind."

For the sake of illustration, let us pursue the last instance which we gave. I am driving down to my man of business. This may most properly be called an " act," because it began with an order I gave to my coachman, which I can revoke at any moment. As I proceed, I look dreamily from my carriage window at the various objects which present themselves : these objects summon up an indefinite number of associations, in regard both to the present and the past ; silent processes of thought ensue and an ever-varying current of emotion ; acts of repentance, of yearning, of complacency, of grief, of anxiety, follow each other in rapid succession. Still no one of these so rises to the *surface* of my thoughts that it would furnish my spontaneous answer to a friend, who should ask me what is my present employment. By careful mental analysis, I may observe a very large number of the thoughts, emotions, volitions, which are peopling my mind ; but still none of these thoughts, emotions, volitions, furnish spontaneously my reply to the proposed question. They are mental phenomena, of which I am truly " conscious " indeed, but which nevertheless are " implicit " phenomena.

On the other hand, my mental procedure may be quite different from this. As I drive along, I concentrate my energies on the examination of some scientific problem ; on pressing various data to their legitimate conclusion ; on harmonizing the various truths which I have already acquired. Under these circumstances, if I were asked what is my present employment, I should spontaneously answer that I am occupied in this scientific investigation. This scientific investigation, then, is my " explicit " act; and my carriage drive has sunk into the position of " implicitness."

Or it may be, again, that *both* acts are on the surface of my mind and explicit; so that my spontaneous answer to the question, "What is my present employment?" would enumerate both of the two. And what we have said on this particular instance is applicable to ten thousand other cases, in which one or two "explicit" acts may be accompanied by an indefinite number of "implicit" thoughts or acts simultaneously proceeding.

But it is not only that the explicit act is often *accompanied* by implicit acts or thoughts: one important *element* of the explicit act itself—we refer to its end or motive—is much more commonly implicit. Go back to our barrister studying his brief. What is the animating motive which impels him to this labour? Perhaps he is merely prompted by that virtuousness or pleasurableness or union of the two, which he recognizes in the due performance of his routine duties. Perhaps he is stimulated by prospects of ambition; by the thought of rising to fame and eminence. Perhaps he is aiming at the due permanent support of wife and children. Perhaps, again, these various ends are simultaneously, in whatever proportion, inflowing into his work. Lastly, if he is a devout and interior Christian, the thought of God's approval may probably enough supply his absolute end of action; though various intermediate links *conduce* to this absolute end. But whatever be the absolute end which he is effectively and continuously pursuing, only at rare intervals will it become explicit. For the most part, the study of his brief so exclusively occupied the surface of his mind, that no other thought can share that prerogative. Nay, his end of action may even *vary* from time to time, without his being aware of the fact; though of course he *might* become aware of it by sufficiently careful introspection.

So much, then, on explicit acts; but one further explanation must most carefully be borne in mind. Explicit acts need not be "reflected on." Explicit acts, as we have explained, are acts which are on the surface of my mind; but they need not be direct objects of my explicit thought. What the barrister explicitly contemplates is his brief with its contents; he does not in general explicitly contemplate his *study* of that brief. Let us briefly elucidate this important distinction.

The great majority of my thoughts, whether explicit or implicit, have for their object somewhat external to my mind. I am contemplating my chance of success at the bar; or the probable price of money in the immediate future; or Mr. Gladstone's Irish land bill; or the beauty of this poetry, or music, or scenery; or the mysteries of God and Christ. But if I am psychologically disposed, a certain small number of my thoughts will have for their object my own mental phenomena. These thoughts may be called "reflexive;" because in eliciting them I "turn back" my attention on myself.* Acts of the will, then, which are the *object* of these reflexive thoughts, may be called acts "reflected on." They are not only "explicit," but something more; they are actually at the moment *reflected on* by me as such.

We must here introduce two explanations of terminology. Firstly, Catholic theologians often speak of "full advertence to an act," or "to the substance of an act." As we understand the matter, they precisely mean by this that the act is what we have called "explicit." Most certainly they do not necessarily mean that the act is "reflected on," and that there is a reflexive thought in my mind which has such act for its object.

What we have said concerning "full advertence to an act" or "the substance of an act," applies of course equally

* They are called by Catholic writers, "actus reflexi;" but, curiously enough, the term "reflex acts" is commonly used by contemporary philosophers in a sense quite extremely opposite.

to virtuous and sinful acts. It must be carefully distinguished from that "full advertence" to the "malitia" of a sinful act, which so many theologians, rightly or wrongly, maintain to be required for commission of mortal sin. On the latter we shall speak before we conclude.

Our second terminological explanation refers to the word "consciousness." Sometimes this word is used as though I were not "conscious" of any except "explicit" acts; nay, sometimes as though I were not "conscious" of any acts except those "reflected on." We think that a different usage from this is far more appropriate and convenient. We shall say that *every* act elicited by my soul is one of which I am "conscious." We may obviously divide this term—consistently with our previous remarks—into consciousness "implicit," "explicit," and "reflected on." But we are disposed to think that no one, or hardly any one, *consistently* used the word "consciousness" in a sense different from ours. When by introspection I have come to observe the existence in my mind of some given implicit act or thought, we think almost every one will say that I detect simultaneously, not only the act or thought itself, but also my—hitherto latent—"consciousness" of that act or thought. So much on the "explicitness" of acts. But, as we have said, in order that they be "perfectly voluntary," it is further necessary that they be "mature." When any thought whatever of the virtuous or the pleasurable is proposed to me by my intellect, my will in the first instant is attracted to the end so proposed, without itself having, if we may so speak, any voice in the matter. Even after the first instant, a further period elapses before my will has had opportunity to put forth its *full* power in the way of acceptance or repudiation. It is not, then, until this *second* period has come to an end, that the act becomes what we have called "mature." It is when an "explicit" act has become "mature," that theologians call it "perfectly deliberate." For our own part, as we have already said, we think it better to avoid the word "deliberate" as much as possible; because we are disposed to think that the particular question which is our direct theme in this article, has been indefinitely obscured by an equivocal use of that term.

No act, therefore, is "perfectly voluntary," unless my will at the moment possess full self-mastery; nor unless the act itself be (1) explicit and (2) mature. If an act (1) is "implicit" or (2) merely "inchoate," it belongs to a different category.

We have now sufficiently prepared our way for treating our direct theme, the extent of Freewill. Concerning our own doctrine, at this early stage of our argument we need say no more than this. According to our view of the matter—whereas throughout the day I am almost continuously engaged in one perfectly voluntary act or other —all these acts are not voluntary only, but also perfectly free. They possess this liberty, not only at starting, but uninterruptedly during their whole course; insomuch that I am my own master, and responsible for my course of action, during pretty nearly the whole of my waking life. We do not mean, indeed, that my action at any given moment is always either formally virtuous or formally sinful; because, as we have already explained, we recognize the existence of many acts which, even materially, are indifferent. But we do say that, speaking generally, there is not any absence of *liberty*, which would prevent such acts from being formally virtuous or sinful during their whole continuance. This is the doctrine which in due course we are to illustrate and defend. But we must first dispose of that most divergent tenet to which we have so often referred, and which it is the direct purpose of our essay to assail.

There is a large number, then, of firmly convinced Libertarians, especially in the non-Catholic world, who are earnestly opposed to our doctrine, and who consider that a man's possession of Freewill is a more or less exceptional fact in his daily life. They hold that I do not possess Freewill, except at those particular moments in which I have expressly consulted and debated with myself between two or more competing alternatives, and have just made a choice accordingly. "Shall I resist this evil thought," I have just asked myself, "or shall I not resist it?" "Shall I adopt this course of life, which promises better for my spiritual interests and worse for my secular, or shall I adopt that other, which promises better for my secular interests and worse for my spiritual?" I have just made my choice between these two alternatives, and in making it I was free. But when this express self-debate and self-consultation have come to an end, then, according to these philosophers, my Freedom of Will has also for the time ceased.

This theory has always impressed us as most extraordinary; and we have been in the habit of thinking that it has largely originated in an equivocal sense of the word "deliberate." Men constantly say, and with undoubted truth, that no act can be perfectly free, unless it be "perfectly deliberate;" *i.e.* unless it be "explicit" and "mature." But the *verb* "to deliberate" is often used as synonymous with to "debate and consult with one's self;" and this sense, though fundamentally different from the former, is not so entirely heterogeneous from it as to prevent the possibility of confusion. A "deliberate act" comes almost unconsciously to be taken as meaning "an act which has been deliberated on," and thus a notion has grown up that no other kind of act is really free. But whatever may be the origin of the tenet which we criticize, we do not deny that its advocates may adduce one argument at least in their own favour, which is not entirely destitute of superficial plausibility. I cannot be free at this moment in eliciting any given act—so far all Libertarians are agreed —unless I have the proximate power at this moment either to do it, or to abstain from doing it, as I may please. But—so the argument may proceed—I have not this proximate power, unless I have been just now expressly *consulting* with myself between these two alternatives. We shall not fail in the sequel to give this reasoning due attention.

Such, however, being our opponents' argument, they are obviously led to a further conclusion, from which indeed, we believe, they by no means shrink. Even at the period of my internal debate and self-consultation, I have been no otherwise free than as regards the particular alternatives which have competed for my acceptance. Let us suppose, *e.g.*, that I have long since firmly resolved to pursue a systematically inimical course against some one who has offended me. At this moment I debate with myself, not at all whether I shall desist from my injurious machinations, but only whether I shall adopt this particular *method* of aggression or some other. Our opponents would hold that my resolve of assailing him is not at the moment a free resolve at all; because on *that* question I have been holding with myself no express consultation whatever. I am only free just now, they consider, in my election of the *particular* mine which I shall spring against him. This is a most obvious result of their theory; nor are we aware that they at all disavow it.

As we are throughout primarily addressing Catholics, we will begin by briefly considering this tenet in its theological aspect. And, firstly, let us consider its bearings on our Blessed Lady's Freewill. Theologians point out in detail how continuous throughout each day were her merits, while she remained on earth; and how unspeakably elevated a position she has thereby attained in heaven. Now, if her merits were continuous, her exercise of Freewill must have been continuous also. Yet how often did she debate and consult with herself on the choice which she should make between two or more competing alternatives? Never, we suppose, except in those comparatively most rare instances, when she did not certainly know what course at some given moment God preferred her to take. All the acts, *e.g.*, wherein, faithful to grace, she avoided imperfection, were destitute of liberty, and destitute therefore of merit. For no Catholic will, of course, dare to say that she ever debated and consulted with herself whether she should or should not elicit some given action, known by her as the less perfect alternative.

But the theological objection is even immeasurably graver in the case of Jesus Christ. It is simply impossible that even once, while upon earth, He should have debated and consulted with Himself between two or more competing alternatives. This supposition, we say, is simply impossible, because at every moment He knew, in the Beatific Vision, what act His Father desired at His hands; and most assuredly did not debate or consult with Himself whether or no He should elicit that act accordingly. Consider in particular His freely-accomplished death for the salvation of mankind. Did He debate and consult with Himself whether He should die? But if He did not, then, according to our opponents, He was not *free* in dying; and man's redemption remains unaccomplished. We do not indeed at all forget how many difficulties the theologian encounters in mutually harmonizing the various truths connected with our Lord's Freewill in dying. But any one who has studied the discussions on this question will have thus only received a stronger conviction than he could well obtain in any other way, how absolutely unheard of and undreamed of among theologians is that theory on the supposed limits of Freewill, which it is our direct purpose to attack.

And we are thus led to express theological citations on the subject. We will select a very few out of the large number adducible; but they shall be amply sufficient to show beyond the possibility of doubt how profoundly at variance is this theory with the voice of standard Catholic theologians.

There is no more authoritative writer just now on Moral Theology than F. Gury; and his treatise has, of course, received great additional importance since F. Ballerini has chosen it for his text-book. Now, in the seventeenth edition of Gury's work, on which Ballerini founded his own of 1861, occurs the following singularly express statement:—
"Although," says Gury, "the Free and the Voluntary are mutually distinguishable in the abstract [in se distinguantur], in man during his earthly course [in homine viatore] they are in reality not distinguished, because man, during his earthly course, while sui compos, *never acts under necessity.*" According to this statement, then, all human acts are free, except, *e.g.*, when the agent is asleep, or otherwise incapable of truly voluntary action. And F. Ballerini made on this no adverse comment whatever.

In his edition of 1875 we find F. Gury's words slightly modified. They now run thus:

"Although the Free and the Voluntary are distinguished in the abstract—as is plain from the Definition of the two—nevertheless in those acts in which man on this earth tends to his end, they are, in fact, never separated; for whenever any act is voluntary, it is free, and *vice versâ*. The reason is, because, as S. Thomas says, in those acts which are directed to [man's] ultimate end, nothing is found so bad as to contain no admixture of good; and nothing so good as to suffice in all respects [for satisfaction of desire]. Now, the only thing which the will has not the power to abstain from willing is that which has the unmixed quality of good [completam boni rationem habet]; such is perfect beatitude, or [man's] ultimate end, for the sake of which all [other] things are desired."

Here, it will be seen, F. Gury is making a distinction, which he had not made in his earlier editions, between those acts, on one hand, which men perform as *conducive* to their ultimate end, and those acts, on the other hand, in which they aim immediately at that ultimate end itself. It will be further seen that, as regards these latter acts, Gury regards them as subject to necessity of exercise no less than to necessity of specification. But as regards that vast number of perfectly voluntary actions which are directed immediately to some other end than that of my own beatitude, Gury pronounces that they are certainly free. Yet the enormous majority of such actions during the day are indubitably elicited without express self-debate and self-consultation.

Ballerini, in his edition of 1878, cites at length the passage of S. Thomas to which Gury refers; and then adds this remark: "Which doctrine—accordant as it is no less with Right Reason than with the Catholic Faith—shows plainly in what light a certain recent philosophy is to be regarded, which, under the title of 'The Limits of Human Liberty,' introduces without any ground [inaniter invehit] innumerable acts, in which [forsooth] man on earth (being otherwise sui compos) is supposed to be *necessitated.*" What the "modern philosophy" *is*, here so severely censured by F. Ballerini, we confess ourselves entirely ignorant; but we should say from his context that it must be some *Catholic* philosophy. Ballerini himself, at all events, is plainly full of suspicion as to any philosophy which would circumscribe "human liberty" by undue "limits."

Let us now pass to standard theologians of an earlier period; or rather to Suarez, who, as will be immediately seen, may stand as representing them all. Suarez, then, holds ("De Oratione," l. 2, c. 20, n. 5) that those acts of love, which holy men elicit *in a state of ecstasy*, are free:

sometimes with liberty of specification, always with liberty of exercise. No one will say that holy men in a state of ecstasy expressly debate and consult with themselves whether they shall continue their acts of love or no. And presently (n. 8) Suarez adds: "It is *the common axiom of theologians* that, externally to the Beatific Vision, the will is not necessitated in exercise by force of any object which is but abstractively known, however perfectly, *i.e.* which is not known in the Beatific Vision." According to Suarez, then, it is the common axiom of theologians that no object necessitates the human will, except only God as seen face to face in heaven. It might indeed be a matter of reasonable inquiry how far so simply universal a statement—concerning *the whole body* of theologians—is consistent with the fact that many theologians consider the will to be even under necessity of *exercise*, when the thought of beatitude is proposed *in this life*. There is no reason, however, for *us* to undertake such inquiry. We need nothing for our own purpose, except to show how unheard of among theologians is the particular notion which we are directly combating; and this fact is most abundantly evident from our citations.

We should add that Suarez ("De Bonitate et Malitiâ Actionum Humanarum," d. 5, s. 3, nn. 22-35; "De Gratiâ," l. 12, c. 21) makes plain how admitted a truth it is with theologians, that an act protracts its formal virtuousness or sinfulness—in other words, preserves its freedom—during the whole of its continuance.*

---

* The discussions in Moral Theology, concerning the "number" of sins, sometimes, we incline to fancy, produce a certain misapprehension. It is sometimes perhaps unconsciously supposed that if, during some given period, A's sins are more numerous than B's of the same kind, A may presumably be considered to have sinned more grievously than B during the same period. But the very opposite inference is quite as commonly the true one. A perhaps interrupts his sinful action from time to time, and again renews it; while B. continues his evil course unintermittently and unrelentingly. We need hardly point out that, in such a case, gravity of the sinful action being

From the ground of theological authority we now proceed to the ground of reason. And, in arguing with our present opponents, we are to take for granted the truth of those doctrines, and the validity of those arguments, which they hold and adduce in common with ourselves. Now, in our articles against Determinism, we laid very great stress on that ineradicable conviction of their own Freewill, which is common to all mankind; a conviction which is the more remarkable because so very few can look at their own habitual conduct with satisfaction, if they choose carefully to measure it even by their own standard of right. All Libertarians agree with us on this matter, and lay stress on the fact to which we refer as furnishing, even though it stood alone, a conclusive proof of Freewill. They say—no less than we say—that on such a subject the common sense and common voice of mankind are an authority against which there lies no appeal. In arguing, then, against *them* we have a right to assume the principle to which they themselves assent; we have a right to assume the peremptory authority due, on this subject, to the common judgment of mankind. We now, therefore, proceed to maintain that, when our opponents' theory is embodied in concrete fact and translated into every-day practice, the very doctrine of Determinism is less repulsive to the common sense and common voice of mankind than is *their* doctrine on the limits of Freewill. We will explain what we mean by a short succession of instances.

We will begin with one, to which we just now referred in a different connection. Let us suppose that I have long

equal, B formally commits far more of mortal sin than A, precisely *because* A's sins are more " *numerous.*" The number of instants during which A merits increased eternal punishment is much smaller than the number of instants during which B does so. Yet B's sinful instants make up what in the Confessional is only counted as one sin, while A's, from the very fact of their having been interrupted, count as many. On the other hand, we do not forget that, as Suarez somewhere observes, the fresh starting of a mortally sinful act involves a certain special malitia of its own.

resolved on a course of grave enmity against some one who has offended me, and that I have long with entire consistency acted on that resolve. It has become, indeed, an inveterate habit with me—a first principle, as it were, of conduct, so to act; and as to raising the question with myself, whether I shall or shall not continue in the same groove, I should as soon raise the question with myself, whether I shall or shall not continue to support my children whom I tenderly love. At this moment, however, I am debating and consulting between two different *methods* of assailing my foe, which suggest themselves; and I am calculating which of the two will inflict on him the heavier blow. Under these circumstances, our opponents must say that I am free indeed in my choice between these two evil machinations, but that I am strictly *necessitated* to carry out my original resolve of injuring him in what way I can. I am strictly necessitated at this moment so to act—if our opponents' theory be accepted—because at this moment I have been as far as possible from consulting and debating with myself on this particular question. But if I am necessitated so to act, I cannot of course incur any formal sin thereby. In other words, I no more commit formal sin at this moment by pursuing his ruin to the bitter end, than I commit formal sin by giving my daughter a new bonnet in proof of my affection.

Those Catholics, who are more or less implicated in the theory which we are opposing, sometimes seek to evade the force of our objection by a singular reply. They reply, that, under the supposed circumstances, though my earnest resolve of crushing my enemy be not *directly* free, yet it is free " in causâ; in its cause." They argue, therefore, that they can consistently call my present resolve formally sinful, because they consider that resolve to be "*free in its cause.*" But what is meant by this recognized theological expression? There is no doubt whatever about its meaning. My resolve, they must mean to say, was "directly" free at its outset, because then I did debate and consult with myself whether I should or should not form it. Moreover, at that time of outset I was well aware that, if I formed such a resolve, the issue would in all probability be a long continuance of my revengeful action. Consequently, they urge, I *then* incurred the formal guilt of my subsequent evil machinations. Well, the whole of this is entirely true; but then it is no less entirely irrelevant. Indeed, their making such an answer is but an unconscious attempt to throw dust into the eyes of their critic. For we are not now discussing with our opponents the moral quality of that evil action—now so long past—which I elicited in forming my detestable resolve. We are discussing with them the moral quality of my *present* evil volition; wherein I apply myself to the vigorously *carrying out* that earlier resolve, without any pause of self-debate and self-consultation. And their theory must compel them to admit that this volition is destitute of liberty, and exempt, therefore, from sin. According to their tenet, we say, I am as exempt from formal sin in continuing my settled plan of revenge, as though I were engaged in hymning the divine praises, or in spiritually assisting a sinner on his death-bed.

As an opposite picture, before we proceed to the case of saintly Catholics, let us take a more ordinary specimen of human virtue. Let us look, *e.g.*, at such a person as the excellent Elizabeth Fry ; and such a work as her reformation of the Newgate female prisoners. "The pleasures which London affords to the wealthy, were at the disposal of her leisure. But a casual visit paid to Newgate in 1813 revealed to her the squalor and misery of the wretched inmates. She succeeded in forming a society of ladies, who undertook to visit the female prisoners. The most hardened and depraved evinced gratitude ; and those who had hitherto been unmanageable, became docile under her gentle treatment."* One cannot suppose that she entered on this noble enterprise without much planning, self-debate, self-consultation: and in the *planning* it, our opponents will say that she was free. But when her heart and soul became absorbed in her glorious work—when she no more dreamed of debating with herself whether she should discontinue it, than of debating with herself whether she should include dancing lessons in her course of instruction—then, forsooth, her Freewill collapsed. Thenceforward there was no more formal virtue in her noble labours, than if instead thereof she had spent her husband's money in equipages and dress, and had enjoyed in full "the pleasures which London offers to the wealthy."

In truth, on this amazing theory, there can be no such thing as confirmed laudableness or confirmed reprehensibleness of conduct. When my habit of virtue or of sin is confirmed, I no longer of course commonly *debate* or *consult* with myself whether I shall act in accordance with its promptings; and, not being free therefore on such occasions, I cannot by possibility act either laudably or reprehensibly.

Then consider the devout and interior Catholic, who labours day by day and hour by hour that his successive acts be virtually and energetically referred to God. He may spare himself the pains, if our opponents' theory hold, as far as regards any supposed laudableness which can thence accrue. If indeed he were weak-kneed and half-hearted in his spiritual life, if he were frequently *debating* and *consulting* with himself whether he should trouble himself at all with referring his acts to God, then he might no doubt from time to time elicit acts formally virtuous. But it is far otherwise with a fervent Catholic. Again and again he is too much immersed in the thought of *God*, to think reflexively about *himself*. He dwells on the mysteries of

* Slightly abridged from Walpole's "History of England," vol. i. p. 202.

Christ; he makes corresponding acts of faith, hope, and love; he prays for the Church; he prays for his enemies; he prays for the various pious ends which he has at heart; and his thoughts are entirely filled with such holy contemplations. Who will be absurd enough to say that this holy man has all this time been expressly *debating* with himself, whether he shall or shall not cease from his prayers and meditations? Yet, except so long as such debate continues, he possesses forsooth no liberty; and his prayers are no more formally good and meritorious than if he were in bed and asleep.

Surely such a view of things as we have been exhibiting, is one which would inexpressibly shock any reasonable man who should contemplate it in detail. And yet we cannot for the life of us see how the consequences which we have named fail to follow in their entirety from that theory on the limits of Freewill, which we so earnestly oppose. Now, on a question so profoundly mixed up with every man's most intimate experience, it is not too much to say that the universal testimony of mankind is a conclusive proof of truth. Moreover, as we have already pointed out, the adverse testimony of mankind is a consideration which inflicts a blow of quite singular force on those particular thinkers, with whom we are just now in controversy. They press the adverse testimony of mankind, as conclusive against Determinists; and we in our turn press it, as even more conclusive against themselves.

Such is the first reply, which we adduce against our opponents. Our second is the following:—The main argument, it will be remembered, by which we purported to establish Freewill, was based on man's experienced power of putting forth anti-impulsive effort. We here assume that our present opponents agree with us on the validity of our reasoning on this head; because of course it was in our earlier papers, and not in this, that the proper opportunity occurred for vindicating the efficacy of our earlier argument. So much, then, as this we may consider to be common ground between our present opponents and ourselves: viz. that whenever I put forth "anti-impulsive effort," in that moment at all events I possess Freewill. Let us proceed, then, to point out how very frequently it happens, that I am putting forth, perhaps very successfully, these anti-impulsive efforts on occasions when I do not dream of *debating* and *consulting* with myself whether I shall put them forth. I have received, *e.g.*, some stinging insult; I have offered it to God; I have firmly resolved, by His grace, steadfastly to resist all revengeful emotions thence arising. I make this resolve once for all: and I no more dream of *debating* with myself whether I shall continue to act on it, than of debating with myself whether I shall in due course eat my dinner. Yet how frequent at first, perhaps almost unintermitting, are my anti-impulsive efforts. Again and again, while I am engaged in my daily occupations, the thought of the insult I have received sweeps over my soul like a storm, awakening vivid emotions in correspondence. As every such successive emotion arises, I exert myself vigorously to oppose its prompting. But the most superficial glance will show that such exertion is very far oftener than not put forth spontaneously, unhesitatingly, eagerly; without any admixture whatever of self-debate and self-consultation. Nay, it is precisely in proportion as this may be the case—in proportion as the element of self-debate and self-consultation is more conspicuously absent—in such very proportion that particular argument for my possessing Freewill becomes more obviously irresistible, which is based on the promptitude and vigour of my anti-impulsive effort.

Thirdly, another consideration must not be omitted, which does not indeed rise in the way of argument above the sphere of probability, but which, within that sphere, is surely of extreme weight. There is no question on which the infidels of this day profess themselves more profoundly agnostic, than this: What is the meaning, the drift, the significance of man's life on earth? Is life worth living? And if so, on what grounds? Theistic Libertarians most justly claim it as an especial merit of their creed, that it supplies so intelligible and effective an answer to this question. This life, they say, is predominantly assigned by God to man, as a place of probation; such that on his conduct here depend results of unspeakable importance hereafter. Yet, according to those particular Libertarians with whom we are now in controversy, a man's probation is at last confined to certain rare and exceptional passages of his earthly existence. Even of that normal period, during which his will is most thoroughly self-masterful, active, energetic, supreme over emotion—during which he devises and carries out his chief schemes, develops his most fertile resources, manifests and moulds his own most distinguishing specialties of character,—very far the larger portion is entirely *external* to this work of probation, which one would expect to find so pervasive and absorbing. During far the greater portion of this period, we say, our opponents are required by their theory to account him destitute of Freewill; unworthy, therefore, of either praise or blame; incapacitated for either success or failure in his course of probation.

It is quite impossible that a theory, so paradoxical and startling, could have found advocates among men undeniably able and thoughtful, had there not been at least some one superficially plausible argument adducible in its favour. We have already said that there *is* one such argument; and we have no more imperative duty in our present essay than fairly to exhibit and confront it. We will suppose an opponent then to plead thus:

"I am not free at this moment, unless I have the proximate power at this moment, either to do what I do or to abstain from doing it. But I cannot have this proximate power of choice, unless I have what may be called a 'proximate warning;' nor can I have this, unless I have expressly in my mind the two alternatives between which I am to choose. I promised my daughter that, the next time I went to the neighbouring town, I would bring her back some stamped note-paper. Well, here I am, close to the stationer's shop; but I have clean forgotten all about my promise. No one will say that, under these circumstances, I have proximate power of choice as to getting the note-paper. Why not? Because I have received no *proximate warning*. Let the remembrance of my promise flash across my mind, this affords the condition required. In like manner, if I am expressly debating and consulting with myself at this moment whether I shall do this act or abstain from it, here is my proximate warning. But if I am not thus expressly debating and consulting, then I have no proximate warning at all, nor proximate power of choice."

Now, in replying to this, we will confine our discussion to perfectly voluntary acts. Our contention, as a whole, is that all perfectly voluntary acts are perfectly free; and that all imperfectly voluntary acts have a certain imperfect freedom of their own. But assuredly no one who is convinced of the former doctrine will stumble at the latter; and we need not trouble ourselves, therefore, with specially arguing in its favour. Then, for our own part, we follow Suarez in thinking that even as regards men's desire of beatitude, however accurately they may apprehend that blessing, they possess therein full liberty of *exercise*.* And accordingly we hold, as just set forth, that all perfectly voluntary acts in this life, without exception, are perfectly free. This, then, being understood, the sum of the answer we should give to the argument above drawn out is this,

* This particular question seems to us so devoid of practical importance, that there is no necessity of giving reasons for our opinion.

and we submit our view with profound deference to the judgment of Catholic theologians and philosophers: I possess an *intrinsic continuous sense* of my own Freewill, and this sense amply suffices to give me the proximate warning required for proximate power of choice. Now, therefore, to exhibit this statement in greater detail, and to defend it by argument.

It is commonly said by Libertarians, whether Catholic or non-Catholic, that man's Freewill is a simple and unmistakable fact of experience. Arriaga, *e.g.*, considers it to be so immediate an object of perception that you can, as it were, touch it with your hand (quasi manu palpare). And, indeed, a very common expression is that men are "conscious" of their own Freewill. Mr. Stuart Mill objected to this use of language. "We are *conscious*," he said, "of what *is*, not of what *will* or *can* be." In one of our previous essays we admitted that, on the verbal question, we are disposed here to agree with Mr. Mill,* though he had himself in a former work, by his own confession, used the word "consciousness" in the very sense to which he here objected. He had used the word as expressing "the whole of our familiar and intimate knowledge concerning ourselves." However, we willingly accepted Mr. Mill's second thoughts in repudiation of his first thoughts; and we have throughout abstained from using the word "consciousness" in the sense to which he objected. "We will ourselves," we added, "use the word 'self-intimacy' to express what is here spoken of." We will not, then, say that I am "conscious" of my own Freewill, but that I have a "self-intimate continuous sense thereof." So much on the question of words; and now for the substance of what we would say.

How is this self-intimate continuous sense engendered

---

* We have spoken on the meaning of this word "conscious" in a previous page.

of the power which I have over my own actions? Let us first consider, by way of illustration, another self-intimate continuous sense of power which I also indubitably possess: my sense of my power over my own limbs. When I was first born, I was not aware of this power; but my unintermittent exercise thereof has gradually given me a self-intimate continuous sense of my possessing it. A student, let us suppose, has been sitting for three hours on the edge of a cliff at his favourite watering-place, immersed in mathematics. A little girl passes not far from him, and falls over the cliff, to the great damage of her clothes, and some damage of her person. Her mother reproaches the mathematician for not having prevented the accident, though probably enough he may have quite a sufficient defence at his command. But suppose what he does say were precisely this: "I could not reach your child without *moving;* and in the hurry of the moment I really did not remember that I had the *power* of moving. I must tell you that it was full three hours since I last had moved my legs; and you cannot be surprised, therefore, that my remembrance of my possessing the *power* to move them was none of the freshest." The mother would feel that he was here adding insult to injury. Had she scientific words at her command, she would energetically press on him the fact that his sense of his power over his limbs is not a fitful, intermittent sense, liable to temporary suspension; but, on the contrary, is such a continuous, self-intimate sense as would have most amply sufficed had he possessed any genuine inclination to move.

Now, as to the still more important power which I possess—the power of resisting my will's spontaneous impulse—my experience of it, no doubt, did not begin for (say) a year or two after I had habitually experienced my power over my limbs. But when once it did begin, it was called into almost as frequent exercise. If I received a good moral and religious education, that very statement means that I was repeatedly summoned to the exercise of anti-impulsive effort in the interests of religion and morality. If I received *no* such education, the circumstances of each moment nevertheless brought with them after their own fashion a lesson, entirely similar as regards our present argument. My life would have been simply intolerable had I not a thousand times a day energetically resisted my will's spontaneous impulse in order to avert future suffering and discomfort, or in order to avoid the displeasure of those among whom I lived. This proposition we assume, from our previous essays on the subject. In accordance, then, with the well-known laws of human nature, I acquired by degrees, as I grew up, a self-intimate continuous sense that I have the *power* of resisting at pleasure my spontaneous impulse; or, in other words, that my Will is Free. My notion of acting *at all* with perfect voluntariness has become indissolubly associated with my notion of acting *freely*. I have a self-intimate continuous sense that I am no slave to circumstances, whether external or internal; that I have true control over my own conduct; that I am responsible for my own voluntary acts. The very consciousness that I am acting *voluntarily* carries with it the sense that I am acting *freely*. This self-intimate sense suffices to give me proximate warning at each instant of perfectly voluntary action; and so suffices to give me a true proximate power of choice, whatever I may be about at the moment, between continuing to do it and abstaining therefrom.

Before going further, let us examine what we have now said by the test of plain facts; and let us once more resort to our old illustration of the revengeful man. I am firmly resolved to inflict on my enemy whatever suffering I can; for such, indeed, is my rooted and inveterate principle of conduct; but I am debating with myself what *method* of aggression will just now be most conducive to my end. Now, we say this. If I believe in Freewill at all, and if I choose to think about the matter at all, I cannot possibly persuade myself that the doctrine of "limited" Freewill here holds good. I cannot possibly persuade myself that I am free indeed at this moment in my choice between these *particular* machinations; but that my *general* resolve of crushing him is a *necessitated* act, for which I incur no present responsibility. We really do not think that any one capable of self-introspection would here even dream of any statement contrary to ours, except under extremest pressure of a paradoxical theory. But if I cannot possibly persuade myself that my resolve is necessitated—this is merely to say, in other words, that I invincibly recognize within myself the proximate power of choosing at this moment to abandon such resolve.

In truth, the cases are by no means rare in which it is most obvious on the surface—in which no one can by possibility doubt—that I have most abundant proximate power of choice without any debate or self-consultation. The whole psychology of *habit*, as we have already implied, is here directly to our purpose. I have acquired a deeply-rooted habit of forgivingness, and receive a stinging insult. Spontaneously and instinctively, as soon as my will obtains even a very moderate degree of self-mastery, I select between the two alternatives of succumbing or not succumbing to my violent emotion. I select the virtuous alternative; I fight successfully God's battle in my soul; I should be utterly ashamed of myself if I condescended to self-debate and self-consultation. It is precisely because I do *not* so condescend that I have *more* proximate power, not less, of making my effective choice between the two alternatives.

It may be said, no doubt, that this sense of proximate power, given me by an acquired habit, is not *continuous;*

for it is only at comparatively rare intervals that any one given acquired habit has occasion of exhibiting its efficacy. Still, other instances are easily found in which my self-intimate sense of proximate power does continue unintermittently. Consider, *e.g.*, my self-intimate sense of the power which I possess to talk correct English, or to practise correct spelling. Consider a groom's self-intimate continuous sense that he possesses the power of riding, or a law-clerk's that he possesses the power of writing legibly. Again, a very conspicuous instance of what we mean is afforded by the phenomena of gentlemanliness. One who has lived all his life in thoroughly gentlemanly society has a continuous self-intimate sense of his power to comport himself like a gentleman throughout every event of the day. Or let us adduce a very different illustration. Suppose I am suffering under some affection in the neck, which makes this or that posture intensely painful. At first it does not happen so very unfrequently that I accidentally assume the posture and incur the penalty. But as time advances, I obtain by constant practice the desired knack of so moving myself as to avoid pain; and the possession of that power is speedily followed by my self-intimate continuous *sense* of its possession.

The sum, then, of what we have been saying is this. On one hand, the self-intimate continuous sense of possessing this or that proximate power is by no means an uncommon fact in human nature. On the other hand, it is established by due introspection, and easily explicable also by recognized psychological laws, that men do possess this self-intimate continuous sense of their proximate power, either to acquiesce in their spontaneous impulse of the moment, or to resist it. In other words, they possess a self-intimate continuous sense of Freewill; a sense which at every moment gives them proximate warning of their responsibility.

Such, we are convinced, is substantially true doctrine concerning the extent of Freewill; and we only wish we had space to enter on its more complete and detailed exposition. One theological objection, however, occurs to us as possessing a certain superficial plausibility, an objection founded on that very doctrine which we alleged against our opponents, viz. the doctrine of our Blessed Lady's interior life. If men's self-intimate sense of liberty is founded on their repeatedly experienced power of resisting spontaneous impulse, how, it may be asked, can *she* have acquired it who was never even once called on or permitted to resist spontaneous impulse? But the answer is obvious enough. Those most noteworthy characteristics, which so conspicuously distinguished her interior life from that of ordinary mortals, did not arise, we need hardly say, from the fact that her nature differed from theirs; but from a cause quite different. They rose from the fact that, over and above that perfection of natural and supernatural endowments with which she started, God wrought within her a series of quite exceptional Providential operations— operations which preserved her infallibly from sin, from concupiscence, from moral imperfection, from interruption of her holy acts and affections. If this continuous sense of Freewill, therefore, were required for the formal virtuousness of her acts, it is included in the very idea of God's dealings wth her, that He either directly infused this sense into her soul, or otherwise secured for her its possession. And if it be further inquired how her possession of Freewill was consistent with the fact that her unintermittently virtuous action was infallibly secured, nothing on this head need be added to the most lucid explanation given by Suarez and other theologians. For our own purpose, however, we should further explain that, though she possessed Freewill, as did our Blessed Lord, we do not for a moment mean to imply that she was in a state of *probation.* And we should also add, once for all, that what remarks we have further to make in this essay will not be intended as including our Blessed Lady within their scope, but only as applying to other human persons.

We have now completed all which strictly belongs to our direct theme, and must once more express that we put forth all our remarks with diffidence and deference, submitting them to the judgment of Catholic theologians and philosophers. But we would further solicit the indulgence of our readers while we touch, as briefly as we can, two further subjects, which are in somewhat close connection with our theme, which throw much light on it, and which are in some sense necessary as its complement. No one can more regret than we do the unwieldy length which thus accrues to our essay. But the course of our series will not bring us again into contact with the two subjects to which we refer; and if we do not enter on them now, we shall have no other opportunity of doing so. We cannot attempt indeed to do them any kind of justice, or to set forth in detail the arguments which seem to us adducible for our doctrine concerning them. Still, we are very desirous of at least stating the said doctrine; in hope that other more competent persons may correct and complete whatever is here mistaken or defective.

The first of these two subjects concerns the relation between Freewill and Morality. And at starting let us explain the sense of our term, when we say that, during certain periods, a man has a "prevalent remembrance" of this or that truth. A merchant, *e.g.*, is busily occupied at this moment on 'Change. There are certain general principles and maxims of mercantile conduct which he has practically learned by long experience, of which he preserves a "prevalent remembrance" throughout his period of professional engagement. This does not mean that he is actually *thinking* of them all the time; but that he has acquired a certain quality of mind, in virtue of which, during his mercantile transactions, these various principles and maxims are proximately ready to step, as it were, into his mind on every appropriate occasion. Or to take a very different instance. A fox-hunter, while actually in the field, preserves a "prevalent remembrance" of certain practical rules and sporting axioms—on the practicability, *e.g.*, of such or such a fence—which again and again saves him from coming to grief. Now, this "prevalent remembrance" may in some cases, instead of being confined to particular periods, become "pervasive" of a man's whole waking life. Let us take two instances of this, similar to two which we have already given in a somewhat different connection. The thoroughly gentlemanly man enjoys all day long a "pervasive remembrance" of the general laws and principles which appertain to good breeding. And one who for many years has had a malady in his neck, possesses all day long a "pervasive remembrance" of what are those particular postures which would give him pain. This does not mean either that the gentlemanly man, or again the neck-affected man, never for one moment forgets himself; but it does mean that the instants of such forgetfulness are comparatively very few.

This terminology being understood, we submit the following proposition. As all men on one hand, throughout all their long periods of perfectly voluntary action, possess a self-intimate sense of their Freewill; so on the other hand, during the same periods, they preserve a "pervasive remembrance" of two cardinal truths. These two truths are (1) that virtuousness has a paramount claim on their allegiance; and (2) that pleasurableness, whether positive or negative, will incessantly lead them captive, whenever they do not actively resist it. We have already said that we have no space here for anything like a due exhibition of the arguments adducible in support of our statement; and as regards, indeed, the *second* of our two cardinal truths, we suppose every one will be disposed readily enough to accept it. As regards the *former* of our truths —that virtuousness has a paramount claim on men's allegiance—we have, of course, nothing to do here with proving that it *is* a truth. This task we consider ourselves to have abundantly performed on more than one earlier occasion, and we would refer especially to our essay on "Ethics in its bearing on Theism." Again, we are not for a moment forgetting, that men differ most widely from each other, on the surface at least, as to what are those particular acts and habits, which *deserve the name* of "virtuous." Still, we have maintained confidently, on those earlier occasions, that the idea "virtuousness," as found in the minds of all, is one and the same simple idea; and that virtuousness, so understood, is really recognized by all men, as having a paramount claim on their allegiance. What we are *here* specially urging is that, throughout their period of perfectly voluntary action, all men, even the most abandoned, preserve a "pervasive remembrance" of this truth.

We have already explained how entirely impossible it is on the present occasion, to attempt any adequate exhibition of the arguments adducible for our doctrine; but such considerations as the following are those on which we should rely. Firstly, let it be observed how indefinitely large is the number of moral judgments which succeed each other in every one's mind throughout the day. "I am bound to do what I am paid for doing." "K behaved far better than L under those circumstances." "M is really an unmitigated scoundrel." "No praise can be too great for N's noble sacrifice." "How base it was of O to tell me those lies!" "What cruel injustice I received at the hands of P!" It is not merely men that live by moral rule, and look carefully after their consciences, who are quite continually thus speaking; but the general rough mass of mankind. Even habitual knaves and cheats are no less given than honest people, to censure the conduct of others as being unjust, oppressive, mendacious, or otherwise immoral. "There is" moral "honour" and moral dishonour "among thieves." The notion of right and wrong, in one shape or other, is never long absent from any one's thoughts; even his explicit thought. Then, secondly, let those psychical facts be considered which have led ethical philosophers of the intuitionist school to insist on "the still small voice of conscience;" the instinctive efforts of evil men to stifle that voice; the futility of such efforts; etc.* We are entirely confident that such statements are most amply borne out by experienced psychical facts, though we cannot here enter on the investigation.

If the doctrine be accepted which we have here put forth, assuredly it throws most important light on man's moral constitution. My self-intimate sense of Freewill, we have already seen, gives me unintermittent information of my responsibility for my acts, one by one. But now further, the Moral Voice, which speaks so constantly within me, in emphatic correspondence with that information, gives me full proximate warning, by what *standard* I am to measure those acts. On one hand, I am *free* to choose; while on the other hand, I *ought* to choose virtuously. The claims of virtuousness, the attractions of pleasurableness— these are, as one may say, the two poles between which my moral conduct vibrates. Either motive of action is

* So, as one instance out of a thousand, F. Kleutgen speaks. "Conscience," he says, "does not *always* so speak and raise its voice as to take from man the power of turning from it and *refusing to listen*." "It is *often* in man's power to abstain from entering into himself and *lending his ear* to that voice," etc. We quoted the whole of F. Kleutgen's very remarkable passage in our essay on Implicit and Explicit Thought.

legitimate within its sphere, but one of the two rightfully claims supremacy over the other. And my self-intimate sense of Freewill unfalteringly reminds me that I am here and now justly reprehensible and worthy of punishment, so far as I rebel against the higher claim, under solicitation of the lower attractiveness.

The second subject on which we desire to touch is a certain thesis concerning the kind and degree of advertence required for mortal sin. That tenet concerning the extent of Freewill, which it has been our direct purpose to oppose, is very seldom, if indeed ever, applied by Catholics to their appraisement of *virtuous* actions. One never hears, *e.g.*, that a holy man's prayer is necessitated, and therefore destitute of merit, because he has not been just debating and consulting with himself whether he shall or shall not continue it. But there are two classes of occasion, we think, on which the tenet of limited Freewill does at times, consciously or unconsciously, find issue. One of these is when the Catholic defends Freewill against Determinists; under which circumstances he is sometimes tempted by the exigencies of controversy to minimize his doctrine: and on this matter we have now sufficiently spoken. The other occasion is, when question is raised concerning the advertence required for mortal sin. Here, then, alone would be ample reason for our wishing not to be entirely silent on this grave theological question. But, by a curious coincidence, there is another reason, altogether distinct, which makes it pertinent that we enter on this particular subject. For the thesis to which we have referred, if consistently carried out, would place in a quite extraordinarily and preposterously favourable light the moral position of those Infidels who are our immediate opponents throughout our present series of essays.

Some Catholics, then, seem to hold that no mortal sin

can be formally committed, unless (1) the agent explicitly advert to the circumstance, that there is at least grave doubt whether the act to which he is solicited be not mortally sinful; and unless (2), after having so adverted, he resolve by a perfectly voluntary choice on doing it.*
Now, we admit most heartily that here is contained an admirable practical rule, as regards a large class of persons whom Moral Theology is especially required to consider. Take a Catholic who is ordinarily and normally averse to mortal sin, and who regularly frequents the Confessional. Such a man may be certain that some given past act, which tends to give him scruple, was not formally a mortal sin, unless, at the time of doing it, he explicitly adverted to the circumstance, that there was grave doubt at least whether the act were not mortally sinful. But the thesis of which we are speaking seems sometimes laid down—not as supplying a test practically available in certain normal cases, but as expressing a necessary and universal truth. If this be the thesis really intended, our readers will readily understand our meaning, when we said just now that it seems intimately connected with that tenet of limited Freewill which we have been so earnestly opposing. In the first place, there is on the surface a very strong family likeness between the two theories. Then further, we are really not aware of any reasoning by which the "explicit advertence" theory can be defended, unless its advocates assume the tenet of limited Freewill. But, however this may be, we would entreat theologians duly to consider some few of the consequences which would result, if the "explicit advertence" thesis were accepted. We will begin with the case of those antitheistic Infidels, who are at this time so increasing in number and aggressiveness.

* Such seems the obvious sense of Gury's exposition, "De Peccatis," n. 150. S. Alphonso and Scavini use far more guarded language. Suarez gives a most thoughtful treatment of the matter—"De Voluntario," d. 4, s. 3. But we have no space for citing the dicta of theologians.

The Antitheist, then, would not be accounted capable of mortal sin at all. What Catholics call "sin" is something most definite and special. "Sin," in the Catholic's view, is separated by an absolutely immeasurable gulf from all other evils whatever; insomuch that all other evils put together do not approach to that gravity, which exists in even one venial sin. But the whole body of Antitheists (we never heard of one exception) entirely deny that there can be any such "malitia" as this, in any possible or conceivable act. It is simply impossible, then, as regards any act in the whole world which the Antitheist may choose to commit, that he shall, before committing it, have asked himself whether it were mortally sinful. And consequently, according to the thesis we are criticizing, it is simply impossible that any act in the whole world, which he may choose to commit, can be formally a mortal sin.

Consequently no such thing is possible to any human being, as gravely culpable ignorance of God. Ignorance of God, according to Catholic doctrine, cannot be gravely culpable unless it result from the formal commission of mortal sin; and Antitheists, according to this thesis, are *unable* formally to commit mortal sin. Now, we are very far from wishing here to imply any special doctrine, concerning invincible ignorance of God: few theological tasks, we think, are just now more urgent than a profound treatment of this whole question. But that there is not, and cannot possibly be, any ignorance of God which is *not* invincible, this our readers will confess to be a startling proposition. We submit, however, that it follows inevitably from the thesis before us.

From Antitheists let us proceed to Theistic non-Catholics. Suarez quotes with entire assent S. Augustine's view that the two causes which, immeasurably more than any other, keep back a non-Catholic from discerning the

Church's claims, are (1) pride and (2) worldliness.* Yet in regard to these two classes of sins, which, in the judgment of S. Augustine and of Suarez, spread so subtle a poison through man's moral nature, and so signally dim man's spiritual discernment, how can the thesis which we are opposing account them mortally sinful at all? What proud man ever *reflected* on his pride? What worldly man on his worldliness? Suppose, *e.g.*, a man considered himself to reflect on the fact that he is eliciting a mortally sinful act of pride—all men would be at once sure that it is his very *humility* which deceives him. He who is at this moment committing what is materially a mortal sin of pride, most certainly does not dream that he is so doing; and still less does he explicitly advert to the circumstance. Or consider some other of the odious characters to be found in the non-Catholic world. Take, *e.g.*, the typical revolutionary demagogue. He is filled with spite and envy towards those more highly placed than himself. He consoles himself for this anguish by inhaling complacently the senseless adulation of his dupes. He gives no thought to their real interest, though he may persuade himself that the fact is otherwise, but uses them as instruments for his own profit and aggrandizement. How often does this villain *reflect* on his villainy from one year's end to another? God in His mercy may visit him with illness or affliction; but otherwise the thought never occurs to him that he is specially sinful at all. Yet would you dare to deny, that during a large part of his earthly existence he is formally committing mortal sin? And remarks entirely similar may be made on the whole catalogue of those specially

* "Heresy is found in a man after two different fashions, viz. either as himself author of the heresy, or as persuaded by another. And it does not arise after the former fashion, except either from pride or from too great affection for earthly and sensible objects, as Augustine says. But he who is drawn by another into heresy either imitates [the heresiarch himself] in pride and worldliness, or else is deceived ignorantly and through a certain simplicity." ("De Amissione Innocentiæ," c. 2, s. 17.)

odious offences which are built on fanaticism and self-deception.

And now, lastly, we would solicit theologians to consider how such a thesis as we are considering will apply even to those Catholics who absent themselves from the Confessional and are confirmed sinners. Look at our old case of the revengeful man. My resolve of injuring my enemy in every way I can has become, by indulgence, a part, one may say, of my nature; and I am at this moment immersed in some scheme for inflicting on him further calamity. I have been profoundly habituated, these several years past, to set the Church's lessons at defiance, and to commit mortal sin without stint or scruple. In consequence of this, I no more explicitly advert to the fact that I am sinning mortally in my revengeful resolves, than I explicitly advert to the fact that I am passing through certain streets, on my daily trodden road from my office to my home. Now, there is no Catholic, we suppose, who will not admit that I continue to be formally committing a large number of mortal sins during all this protracted course of vindictiveness. But how can such an admission be reconciled with the thesis which we are opposing?

Now take an importantly different instance. I am just beginning an habitually wicked life. I secretly retain some large sum, which I know to be some one else's property; or I enter into permanent immoral relations with another person. I cannot get the fact out of my head, and so I am always reflecting on my sinfulness; while I still cannot make up my mind to amend. I formally, therefore, commit mortal sin at pretty well every moment of my waking life. Time, however, goes on; and in due course I become so obdurate that I do not reflect for a moment, from week's end to week's end, on the circumstance that I am setting God's Law at defiance. Let us briefly contrast these two periods. Suppose, *e.g.*, I make my definitive resolution of remaining in sin on March 12, 1871, and since that day have not once made any real effort to reform. Then compare the moral life which I led on March 13, 1871, with that which I led on March 13, 1881. On the earlier day I was, beyond the possibility of doubt, formally committing mortal sin almost every moment of the day, during which I was not asleep or tipsy; because I was constantly reflecting on my wicked life, and purposing to continue it. Now, my acts of March 13, 1881, taken one by one, are assuredly far more wicked than those of March 13, 1871. Suarez ("De Peccatis," d. 2, s. 1, n. 3) lays down as the commonly admitted doctrine, that "the deformity of mortal sin consists in this—that through such sin the sinner virtually and interpretatively loves the creature more than he loves God." But if, in my acts of March 13, 1871, I was virtually and interpretatively loving the creature more than I loved God, who will doubt that in those of March 13, 1881, I am doing this same thing very far more signally and unreservedly? And if the former acts, therefore, were mortally sinful, much more are these latter. Yet, according to the adverse thesis, these latter acts are not mortally sinful at all; because my detestable obduracy is now so confirmed, that I do not even once explicitly advert to the circumstance, how wicked is my course of life.

Such are a few instances which we would press on the attention of theologians, as exhibiting results which ensue from the thesis we deprecate; and many similar ones are readily adducible. We submit with much deference, that a satisfactory solution of the whole difficulty cannot be found, unless that doctrine be borne in mind which we just now set forth, concerning (1) men's self-intimate sense of Freewill; and (2) the constant urgency of the Moral Voice speaking within them. But before entering directly on this argument, we will distinctly express two propositions, which otherwise it might possibly be supposed that we do not duly recognize. First, there cannot possibly be mortal sin in any act which is not "perfectly voluntary;" and we have fully set forth in our preceding n. xi. how much is contained in this term "perfectly voluntary." Secondly, no one can commit mortal sin, except at those times in which he possesses full proximate power of suspecting the fact. When we come, indeed, to treat the particular case of anti-theistic Infidels, we shall have to guard against a possible misconception of this statement; but to the statement itself we shall entirely adhere. So much, then, having been explained, we will next try to set forth, as clearly as is consistent with due brevity, the principles which, as we submit, are truly applicable to the moral appreciation of such instances as we have just enumerated.

We begin with the revengeful Catholic, who is well aware indeed of the circumstance that his vindictive machinations are mortally sinful; but who is so obdurate in his sin, that he gives no explicit advertence to their sinful character. If those doctrines which we advocate are admitted—concerning this self-intimate sense of Freewill, and the constant monitions of his Moral Voice—he has evidently, during almost the whole period occupied by these revengeful machinations, full proximate power of explicitly adverting to their sinfulness. There may be occasional moments of invincible distraction; and at those moments, we admit, his formal commission of mortal sin temporarily ceases: but these surely cannot be more than exceptional, and recurring at rare intervals. And such as we have here given, would be substantially, we suppose, the account given by all Catholic thinkers; for all Catholics surely will admit that his successive machinations are for the most part, even if there be any exceptional moment, imputed to the agent as mortally sinful.

We now come to the second instance. A Catholic, we have supposed, has plunged into some mortally sinful mode of life: at first he has been tormented all day long by remorse of conscience; but, in due course of obduration, has entirely ceased to reflect on his deplorable state. Now, in order to solve both this and the other difficult cases which we just now set forth, it is necessary, we think, not only to bear in mind the doctrines which we have already exhibited concerning men's self-intimate sense of Freewill and the monitions of their Moral Voice, but another doctrine also entirely distinct. We may call this the doctrine of "inordination." It is one on which recent theologians, we venture to submit, have not sufficiently insisted,* but which is of most critical importance on such questions as we are now discussing. It has been expressed and illustrated with admirable force by the late F. Dalgairns, in that chapter of his work on "The Blessed Sacrament," which is called "Communions of the Worldly;" a chapter which we earnestly hope our readers will study as a whole in the present connection. We can here only find room for a very few of the relevant passages.

Christianity holds as a first principle that God is to be loved above all things, in such a sense that if a creature appreciatively loves any created thing more than God, he commits a mortal sin. (Second edition, p. 359.)

When the affection for an earthly object or pursuit for a long time together so engrosses the soul as to superinduce an habitual neglect of God and a continued omission of necessary duties, then it is very difficult for the soul to be unconscious of its violation of the First Commandment, or, if it is unconscious, not to be answerable to God for the hardness of heart which prevents its actual advertence. (*Ibid.*)

We will suppose a merchant to be entirely engrossed in the acquisition of riches. No one will say that to amass wealth is

* All theologians admit that no divine precept can possibly be violated except through the sinner's inordinate attachment to creatures. But we venture to think that the tendency has of late been to dwell too exclusively on the violation of precept, and not to exhibit in due prominence the attachment to creatures. S. Thomas's treatment of such matters is emphatically different, we think, in its general tone.

in any way sinful. It has never come before him to do anything dishonest in order to increase his property, and he has never formed an intention to do so. Nevertheless, if his heart is so fixed on gain that his affection for it is greater than his love of God—even though he has formed explicitly no design of acting dishonestly—he falls at once out of the state of grace. Let him but elicit from his will an act by which he virtually appreciates riches more than God, that act of preferring a creature to God, if accompanied with sufficient advertence, is enough of itself to constitute mortal sin. . . . The First Commandment is as binding as the Seventh, and a man who does not love God above all things is as guilty as the actual swindler or thief." (*Ibid.*, p. 360.)

And in p. 371 F. Dalgairns adduces theological authority for his doctrine. We should be disposed to express it thus. Any one, we should say, is at this moment materially committing mortal sin if he is eliciting, towards this or that pleasurable end, some act of the will so inordinate that, by force of such acts, he would on occasion violate a grave precept of God, rather than abandon such pleasure. And he formally commits mortal sin, if he elicits such an act while he possesses full proximate power to suspect its being mortally sinful.

Or let us exhibit our doctrine in the concrete. No one, as has been so repeatedly pressed in this essay, can possibly offend God, except for the sake of this or that pleasure; and every one, therefore, who commits mortal sin is ipso facto preferring some pleasure to God. At this moment I am gravely calumniating an acquaintance, in order to gratify my vainglory by being more highly thought of than he is. Here are two concomitant mortal sins; related to each other, as respectively the "commanding" and "commanded" act ["actus imperans;" "actus imperatus"]. The "commanding" act is my mortal sin of vainglory; the "commanded" act is my mortal sin of calumny. But how comes the former to be a mortal sin? There is no sin whatever in my mere desire of being highly

thought of by my fellow-men. True; but that desire is
"gravely inordinate"—" a mortal sin of vainglory "—if
it be such, as to command what is objectively a mortal sin
rather than lose the pleasure at which it aims.* But now
observe. I may, the next minute, altogether forget the
particular man whom I have been calumniating; and the
"commanded" mortal sin may thus come to an end. But
this is no reason in the world why my "commanding"
mortal sin, my sin of vainglory, should change its character.
If it were mortal sin before, and if there be no change in
its intrinsic attributes, it continues to be mortal sin now.
Wherein does its mortally sinful character consist? In this:
that *by force* of my present act, I should on occasion gravely
offend God, rather than lose the pleasure at which I am
aiming; or, in other words, that, by eliciting my present
act of vainglory, I appreciatively prefer to God the being
highly thought of by my fellow-men.

Here, then, we are able to explain what we mean by
the "inordinate" desire of pleasurableness. The particular
given act, wherein I desire the pleasure which ensues from

* "If love of riches so increase that they be preferred to charity—in such
sense that, for the love of riches, a man fear not to act in opposition to the
love of God and his neighbour—in this case avarice will be a mortal sin.
But if the inordination of the man's love [for riches] stop within this limit,
in such sense that, although he loves riches too much, nevertheless he do not
prefer the love of them to the love of God, so that he do not will, for their
sake, to do anything against God and his neighbour, such avarice will be a
venial sin." (S. Thomas, $2^a\ 2^{ae}$ q. cxviii. a. 4.)

"Inordination of fear is sometimes a mortal sin, sometimes a venial. For
if any one is so disposed that, on account of that fear whereby he shrinks
from danger of death or from some other temporal evil, he would do something prohibited or omit something commanded in the Divine Law—such
fear is a mortal sin." (*Ibid.* q. cxxv. a. 3.)

"If the inordination of concupiscence in gluttony imply aversion from a
man's Ultimate End [accipiatur secundum aversionem à Fine Ultimo], so
gluttony will be a mortal sin. Which happens, when a man cleaves to the
pleasurableness of gluttony as to an end, on account of which he despises
God, being prepared to violate the Precepts of God in order to obtain such
gratifications." (*Ibid.* q. cxlviii. a. 2.)

F. Ballerini says ("On Gury," vol. i. n. 178) that S. Thomas's "Secunda
Secundae" "ought never to be out of the Confessor's hands."

good opinion of my fellow-men, may be of three different characters, which it is extremely important mutually to distinguish. It may (1) be such that, by force of such act, I would rather gravely offend God than lose the pleasure in question; in which case the act is "gravely inordinate," and—at least materially—a mortal sin. Or it may (2) be such that, by force of such act, I would offend God *venially*, though not gravely, rather than lose the pleasure, in which case the act is "venially inordinate" and "venially sinful." Or, lastly, however strong my act of desire may be, yet it may not be such that, by force of it, I would offend God *in any way* rather than lose the pleasure. In this latter case the act is not "inordinate" at all; not properly called "vainglory" at all; nor, as we should say, possessing any element whatever of sin.*

It will be remembered, also, that that "gravely in-

---

* In the early part of our essay we referred with entire assent to Dr. Walsh's argument in favour of the doctrine here assumed, that an act may be directed to pleasurableness as to its absolute end, yet without inordination. But there are two condemned propositions, often cited against this doctrine, which we ought expressly to notice. They are the 8th and 9th, condemned by Innocent XI. ("Denz," nn. 1025, 1026), "Comedere et bibere," etc., "Opus conjugii," etc. On the former of these we need do no more than refer to Dr. Walsh's remarks from n. 638 to n. 641, with which we unreservedly concur. On the latter, what we would say is substantially what Viva says. The constitution of lapsed human nature being what it is, there is one most definitely marked out class of pleasurable ends, which tend to exercise so special and abnormal influence over a man's will, that his pursuit of them will quite infallibly be "inordinate" (in our sense of that term), unless it be kept in check by being subordinated to some virtuous end. Now, it is obvious that those who, like ourselves, affirm this, may utterly repudiate the proposition condemned by Innocent XI., and yet entirely hold that general doctrine concerning indifferent acts, which we have exhibited in our text. It may be well to add that F. Ballerini ("On Gury," vol. ii. n. 908) has some valuable remarks concerning the virtuous ends which may be pursued in that particular class of acts to which we refer.

Another theological remark. The distinction which we have made between the "inordinate" and "non-inordinate" pursuit of a pleasurable end is closely connected, if, indeed, it be not identical, with the recognized theological distinction between pleasure being sought as the "finis *positivè* ultimus" and "*negativè* ultimus" respectively. See Dr. Walsh, n. 479; and Ballerini, "On Gury," vol. i. n. 28.

ordinate" act, which is materially a mortal sin, is not one formally, unless the agent possess full proximate power of suspecting this fact.

In our view, it is almost impossible to exaggerate the momentousness of this whole doctrine, for the true moral appreciation, whether of those outside the Church, or of obdurate sinners within her pale. To avoid prolixity, however, we will only consider it in detail as applicable to the obdurate Catholic whom we were just now describing. He has sunk into so abject and degraded a moral condition that he appreciatively prefers pretty nearly *every* passing pleasure to God. There is hardly any gratification at all to his taste, from which he would abstain rather than gravely offend God. In other words, as the day proceeds, almost every act which he elicits is gravely inordinate and mortally sinful.

The only question to be further raised concerning him is whether these repeated gravely inordinate adhesions to pleasure are in general formally, no less than materially, mortal; or, in other words, whether he have full proximate power of suspecting their true character. And of this, as a general fact, there can, we conceive, be no fair doubt. We are throughout supposing him not to have abandoned the Faith. It is plain that a Catholic, who for years has absented himself from the Confessional, who is living in what he fully knows to be the persistent and unrelenting violation of God's Laws, has an abiding sense all day long, how degraded and detestable is his mode of acting. He feels all day long that he "is drinking in sin like water," though he would, of course, be unable to express in theological terms his protracted course of evil.

Some of our readers may be disposed at first sight to regard this view of things as startling and paradoxical, because of the large number of instants during which it accounts such men to be formally committing mortal sin.

But, to our mind, it is precisely on this ground that any *other* view ought rather to be considered startling and paradoxical, as we pointed out a page or two back. The unrepentant *novice* in sin, before his conscience became obdurate, was most indubitably committing mortal sin during pretty nearly the whole of his waking life. It would surely be startling and paradoxical indeed if his acts *ceased* to be mortally sinful, merely because, through a course of unscrupulous indulgence, he has come to treat his indifference to God's Commandments as a simple matter of course, to which, therefore, he gives no explicit advertence.*

This doctrine of "grave inordination" is, as we just now said, entirely applicable to solving the other difficulties we have mentioned; to appreciating the sins of pride and worldliness, so widely found among non-Catholic Theists; to appreciating the various sins of fanaticism and self-deception; and, lastly, to appreciating also the moral position of antitheistic Infidels. It would occupy, however, considerable space duly to develop and apply the doctrine for this purpose, and we must therefore abandon all attempt at doing so. In regard, indeed, to the last-named

* It might be thought, at first sight, that there is some similarity between the doctrine which we have submitted in the text concerning obdurate sinners, and that advocated by Pascal in his Fourth Provincial Letter. But in truth the full doctrine which we would defend is the very extreme contrary to Pascal's. The direct theme of his Fourth Letter—as laid down in the title—is "Actual Grace;" and he reproaches the Jesuits for maintaining that "God gives man actual grace under every successive temptation." For our own part, not only we cleave most firmly to the doctrine here denounced by Pascal, but we are disposed to go further. We are strongly disposed to accept the Fifteenth Canon of the Council of Sens, and to affirm that "not even a moment passes" while a man is *sui compos*, "in which God does not stand at the door" of his heart, "and knock" by His supernatural grace.

We need hardly say that the Council of Sens was not Ecumenical, but Suarez speaks of its Decrees as possessing very great authority. Of course this is not the place for a theological discussion concerning the frequency of Actual Grace, but our readers will observe the close connection of our *theological* doctrine with the doctrine which we have defended in the text, on the constant urgency of man's Moral Voice in the *natural* order.

class, a certain theological point needs to be considered; because it may be suggested that since mortal sin derives its characteristic malignity from its being an offence against God, those who deny His Existence cannot possibly commit it. This whole matter, however, has been amply discussed by theologians, since a certain proposition was condemned concerning "Philosophical Sin." For our own part, therefore, we will but briefly express our own adhesion to those theologians—of whom Viva may be taken as a representative instance—who hold that the recognition of acts as being intrinsically wicked is ipso facto a recognition of them as being offences against the paramount claims of God as rightful Supreme Legislator; and that this recognition suffices for their mortally sinful character.

Otherwise, what we have generally to say about these Antitheists is this. We assume the truth of our own doctrine as exhibited in the preceding pages. But if this doctrine be true, if God have really granted to all men a self-intimate sense of Freewill, if He have really endowed them with an ineffaceable intuition of right and wrong, if He is constantly pleading within them in favour of virtue, He has, by so acting, invested them with a truly awful moral responsibility. And it is perfectly absurd to suppose that a set of rebels can evade that responsibility by the easy process of shutting their eyes to manifest facts.

In concluding our lengthy discussion, we must once more say how entirely we submit all that we have suggested to the judgment of theologians. We indulge the hope, however, that, even where we may have unwarily fallen into error, we shall nevertheless have done good service by obtaining for some of the points we have raised more prominent and scientific consideration than, we think, they have hitherto received.

THE END.

PRINTED BY WILLIAM CLOWES AND SONS, LIMITED,
LONDON AND BECCLES.

A LIST OF

KEGAN PAUL, TRENCH, TRÜBNER, & CO.'S (LTD.)

PUBLICATIONS.

Paternoster House,
Charing Cross Road,
February 26, 1892.

A LIST OF
KEGAN PAUL, TRENCH, TRÜBNER, & CO.'S PUBLICATIONS.

NOTE.—*Books are arranged in alphabetical order under the names or pseudonyms of author, translator, or editor. Biographies "by the author of" are placed under the name of the subject. Anonymous works and "selections" will be found under the first word of the title. The letters I.S.S. denote that the work forms a volume of the International Scientific Series.*

A. K. H. B., From a Quiet Place: some Discourses. Cr. 8vo. 5s.

ABEL, CARL, Linguistic Essays. Post 8vo. 9s. (*Trübner's Oriental Series.*)
  Slavic and Latin: Lectures on Comparative Lexicography. Post 8vo. 5s.

ABERCROMBY, Hon. RALPH, Weather: a popular Exposition of the Nature of Weather Changes from day to day. With 96 Figures. Second Edition. Cr. 8vo. 5s. (*I.S.S.*)

ABRAHAMS, L. B., Manual of Scripture History for Jewish Schools and Families. With Map. Cr. 8vo. 1s. 6d.

ACLAND, Sir HENRY, Bart., Science in Secondary Schools. Cr. 8vo. 1s. 6d.

ADAMS, ESTELLE, Sea Song and River Rhyme, from Chaucer to Tennyson. With 12 Etchings. Large cr. 8vo. 10s. 6d.

ADAMS. Johns Hopkins University Studies in History and Politics. Edited by HERBERT B. ADAMS. Nine Annual Series, and nine Extra Volumes. 8vo. £10. 10s. Also sold separately.

ADAMS, W. H. DAVENPORT, The White King; or, Charles the First, and Men and Women, Life and Manners, &c., in the first half of the 17th Century. 2 vols. 8vo. 21s.

ÆSCHYLUS. The Seven Plays in English Verse. Translated by Prof. LEWIS CAMPBELL. Cr. 8vo. 7s. 6d.

AHLWARDT, W., The Diváns of the Six Ancient Arabic Poets—Ennábiga, 'Antara, Tharafa, Zuhair, 'Alquama, and Imruulquais. With a complete list of the various readings of the text. 8vo. 12s.

AHN, F., Grammar of the Dutch Language. Fourth Edition, revised and enlarged. 12mo. 3s. 6d.
  Grammar of the German Language. New Edition. Cr. 8vo. 3s. 6d.
  Method of Learning German. 12mo. 3s. Key, 8d.
  Manual of German Conversation; or, Vade Mecum for English Travellers. Second Edition. 12mo. 1s. 6d.
  Method of Learning French. First and Second Courses. 12mo. 3s.; separately, 1s. 6d. each.
  Method of Learning French. Third Course. 12mo. 1s. 6d.
  Method of Learning Italian. 12mo. 3s. 6d.
  Latin Grammar for Beginners. Thirteenth Edition. Cr. 8vo. 3s.

AINSWORTH, W. F., Personal Narrative of the Euphrates Expedition. With Map. 2 vols. Demy 8vo. 30s.

A 2

AIZLEWOOD, J. W., **Warbeck.** A Historical Play. Cr. 8vo. 6s.

Albanaise Grammaire, à l'usage de ceux qui désirent apprendre cette langue sans l'aide d'un maître. Par P. W. Cr. 8vo. 7s. 6d.

ALBÊRÛNÎ'S **India:** an Account of the Religion, Philosophy, Literature, Geography, Chronology, Astronomy, Customs, Laws, and Astrology of India, about A.D. 1030. Arabic text, edited by Prof. E. SACHAU. 4to. £3. 3s.

ALEXANDER, Major-Gen. G. G., **Confucius, the Great Teacher.** Cr. 8vo. 6s.

ALEXANDER, S., **Moral Order and Progress:** an Analysis of Ethical Conceptions. Second Edition. Post 8vo. 14s. (*Philosophical Library.*)

ALEXANDER, WILLIAM, D.D., **Bishop of Derry, St. Augustine's Holiday,** and other Poems. Cr. 8vo. 6s.

The Great Question, and other Sermons. Cr. 8vo. 6s.

ALEXANDROW, A., **Complete English-Russian and Russian-English Dictionary.** 2 vols. Demy 8vo. £2.

ALLEN, C. F. ROMILLY, **Book of Chinese Poetry.** Being the collection of Ballads, Sagas, Hymns, and other Pieces known as the Shih Ching, metrically translated. 8vo. 16s.

ALLEN, GRANT, **The Colour-Sense:** its Origin and Development. An Essay in Comparative Psychology. Post 8vo. 10s. 6d. (*Philosophical Library.*)

ALLEN, MARY L., **Luncheon Dishes;** comprising Menus in French and English, as well as Suggestions for Arrangement and Decoration of Table. Fcp. 8vo. cloth, 1s. 6d.; paper covers, 1s.

Five-o'clock Tea. Containing Receipts for Cakes, Savoury Sandwiches, &c. Eighth Thousand. Fcp. 8vo. 1s. 6d.; paper covers, 1s.

ALLIBONE, S. A., **Dictionary of English Literature and British and American Authors,** from the Earliest Accounts to the Latter Half of the 19th Century. 3 vols. Roy. 8vo. £5. 8s. SUPPLEMENT, 2 vols. roy. 8vo. (1891), £3. 3s.

ALLIES, T. W., **A Life's Decision.** Cr. 8vo. 7s. 6d.

ALTHAUS, JULIUS, **The Spas of Europe.** 8vo. 7s. 6d.

AMBERLEY, Viscount, **Analysis of Religious Belief.** 2 vols. 8vo. 30s.

AMOS, Professor Sheldon, **History and Principles of the Civil Law of Rome:** an Aid to the Study of Scientific and Comparative Jurisprudence. 8vo. 16s.

Science of Law. Seventh Edition. Cr. 8vo. 5s. (*I.S.S.*)

Science of Politics. Third Edition. Cr. 8vo. 5s. (*I.S.S.*)

ANDERSON, DAVID, **'Scenes' in the Commons.** Cr. 8vo. 5s.

ANDERSON, J., **English Intercourse with Siam in the Seventeenth Century.** Post 8vo. 15s. (*Trübner's Oriental Series.*)

ANDERSON, WILLIAM, **Practical Mercantile Correspondence:** a Collection of Modern Letters of Business, with Notes. Thirtieth Edition, revised. Cr. 8vo. 3s. 6d.

ANDERSON, W., and TUGMAN, J. E., **Mercantile Correspondence:** a Collection of Letters in Portuguese and English, treating of the System of Business in the principal Cities of the World. 12mo. 6s.

Antiquarian Magazine and Bibliographer, The. Edited by EDWARD WALFORD and G. W. REDWAY. Complete in 12 vols. 8vo. £3 net.

APEL, H., **Prose Specimens for Translation into German.** With copious Vocabularies and Explanations. Cr. 8vo. 4s. 6d.

APPLETON, J. H., and SAYCE, A. H., **Dr. Appleton:** his Life and Literary Relics. Post 8vo. 10s. 6d. (*Philosophical Library.*)

ARAGO, ÉTIENNE, **Les Aristocraties: a** Comedy in Verse. Second Edition. 12mo. 4s.

ARBUTHNOT, Sir A. J., Major-Gen. Sir Thomas Munro: a Memoir. Cr. 8vo. 3s. 6d.

ARCHER, WILLIAM, William Charles Macready. Cr. 8vo. 2s. 6d. (*Eminent Actors.*)

ARISTOTLE, The Nicomachean Ethics. Translated by F. H. Peters. Third Edition. Cr. 8vo, 6s.

ARMITAGE, EDWARD, Lectures on Painting. Delivered to the Students of the Royal Academy. Cr. 8vo. 7s. 6d.

ARNOLD, Sir EDWIN, Grammar of the Turkish Language. With Dialogues and Vocabulary. Pott 8vo. 2s. 6d.

Death—and Afterwards. Reprinted from the *Fortnightly Review* of August 1885, with a Supplement. Eleventh Edition. Cr. 8vo. cloth, 1s. 6d.; paper covers, 1s.

In My Lady's Praise: Poems Old and New, written to the honour of Fanny, Lady Arnold. Third Edition. Imperial 16mo. parchment, 3s. 6d.

India Revisited. With 32 Full-page Illustrations. Second Edition. Cr. 8vo. 7s. 6d.

Indian Idylls. From the Sanskrit of the Mahâbhârata. Second Edition. Cr. 8vo. 7s. 6d.

Indian Poetry. Containing 'The Indian Song of Songs' from the Sanskrit, two books from 'The Iliad of India,' and other Oriental Poems. Fifth Edition. 7s. 6d. (*Trübner's Oriental Series.*)

Lotus and Jewel. Containing 'In an Indian Temple,' 'A Casket of Gems,' 'A Queen's Revenge,' with other Poems. Third Edition. Cr. 8vo. 7s. 6d.

Pearls of the Faith, or Islam's Rosary. Being the Ninety-Nine Beautiful Names of Allah. Sixth Edition. Cr. 8vo. 7s. 6d.

Poems, National and Non-Oriental, with some new Pieces. Cr. 8vo. 7s. 6d.

The Light of Asia, or The Great Renunciation. Being the Life and Teaching of Gautama. Presentation Edition. With Illustrations and Portrait. Sm. 4to. 21s. Library Edition, cr. 8vo. 7s. 6d. Elzevir Edition, 6s. Cheap Edition (*Lotos Series*), cloth or half-parchment, 3s. 6d.

The Secret of Death: being a Version of the Katha Upanishad, from the Sanskrit. Fourth Edition. Cr. 8vo. 7s. 6d.

The Song Celestial, or Bhagavad-Gîtâ, from the Sanskrit. Fifth Edition. Cr. 8vo. 5s.

With Sa'di in the Garden, or The Book of Love: being the 'Ishk,' or third chapter of the 'Bostân' of the Persian poet Sa'di, embodied in a Dialogue. Third Edition. Cr. 8vo. 7s. 6d.

Poetical Works. Uniform Edition, comprising—The Light of Asia, Lotus and Jewel, Indian Poetry, Pearls of the Faith, Indian Idylls, The Secret of Death, The Song Celestial, With Sa'di in the Garden. 8 vols. Cr. 8vo. 48s.

ARNOLD, THOMAS, and SCANNELL, T. B., Catholic Dictionary. An account of the Doctrine, Discipline, Rites, Ceremonies, &c., of the Catholic Church. Fourth Edition Revised. 8vo. 21s.

ASTON, W. G., Grammar of the Japanese Spoken Language. Fourth Edition. Cr. 8vo. 12s.

Grammar of the Japanese Written Language. Second Edition. 8vo. 28s.

ATKINSON, EMILY, A Few Impressions from the Poems of Robert Browning. 27 full-page Plates from Pencil Drawings, with smaller Sketches and Text. 4to. 21s.

AUBERTIN, J. J., A Flight to Mexico. With 7 Full-page Illustrations and a Railway Map. Cr. 8vo. 7s. 6d.

Six Months in Cape Colony and Natal. With Illustrations and Map. Cr. 8vo. 6s.

A Fight with Distances. With Illustrations and Maps. Cr. 8vo. 7s. 6d.

Camoens' Lusiads. Portuguese Text with Translation. Second Edition. 2 vols. Cr. 8vo. 12s.

AUGIER, ÉMILE, Diane: a Drama in Verse. Third Edition. 12mo. 2s. 6d.

Autumn Manœuvres (of 1871), Retrospect of the. With 5 Plans. 8vo. 5s.

AXON, W. E. A., The Mechanic's Friend. A Collection of Receipts and Practical Suggestions relating to Aquaria, Bronzing, Cements, Drawing, Dyes, Electricity, Gilding, Glass-working, &c. Numerous Woodcuts. Second Edition. Cr. 8vo. 3s. 6d.

AZARIAS, Brother, Aristotle and the Christian Church: an Essay. Sm. cr. 8vo. 3s. 6d.

BADER, CHARLES, Natural and Morbid Changes of the Human Eye, and their Treatment. 8vo. 16s. Atlas of Plates, in portfolio. Medium 8vo. 21s. Text and Atlas together, £1. 12s.

BADHAM, F. P., Formation of the Gospels. Cr. 8vo. 2s. 6d.

BAGEHOT, WALTER, The English Constitution. Sixth Edition. Cr. 8vo. 7s. 6d.
    Lombard Street. A Description of the Money Market. Ninth Edition. Cr. 8vo. 7s. 6d.
    Essays on Parliamentary Reform. Cr. 8vo. 5s.
    On the Depreciation of Silver, and Topics connected with it. 8vo. 5s.
    Physics and Politics; or, Thoughts on the Application of the Principles of 'Natural Selection' and 'Inheritance' to Political Society. Ninth Edition. Cr. 8vo. 5s. (*I.S.S.*)

BAGENAL, PHILIP H., American Irish and their Influence on Irish Politics. Cr. 8vo. 5s.

BAGOT, ALAN, Accidents in Mines: their Causes and Prevention. Cr. 8vo. 6s.
    Principles of Colliery Ventilation. Second Edition, greatly enlarged. Cr. 8vo. 5s.
    Principles of Civil Engineering as applied to Agriculture and Estate Management. Cr. 8vo. 7s. 6d.

BAIN, ALEX., Education as a Science. Seventh Edition. Cr. 8vo. 5s. (*I.S.S.*)
    Mind and Body. The Theories of their Relation. With 4 Illustrations. Eighth Edition. Cr. vo. 5s. (*I.S.S.*)

BAKER, Major EDEN, R.A., Preliminary Tactics. An Introduction to the Study of War. For the use of Junior Officers. Cr. 8vo. 6s.

BAKER, IRA, Treatise on Masonry Construction. Royal 8vo. 21s.

BAKER, Sir SHERSTON, Bart., Laws relating to Quarantine. Cr. 8vo. 12s. 6d.

BALDWIN, Capt. J. H., Large and Small Game of Bengal and the North-Western Provinces of India. With 20 Illustrations. Sm. 4to. 10s. 6d.

BALFOUR, F. H., The Divine Classic of Nan-Hua. Being the Works of Chuang Tsze, Taoist philosopher. 8vo. 14s.
    Taoist Texts, ethical, political, and speculative. Imperial 8vo. 10s. 6d.
    Leaves from my Chinese Scrap-Book. Post 8vo. 7s. 6d.

BALL, JOHN, Notes of a Naturalist in South America. With Map. Cr. 8vo. 8s. 6d.

BALL, Sir ROBERT, The Cause of an Ice Age. Cr. 8vo. 2s. 6d. (*Modern Science Series.*)

BALL, V., Diamonds, Coal, and Gold of India: their Mode of Occurrence and Distribution. Fcp. 8vo. 5s.

BALLANTYNE, J. R., Elements of Hindi and Braj Bhakha Grammar. Compiled for the East India College at Haileybury. Second Edition. Cr. 8vo. 5s.
    First Lessons in Sanskrit Grammar. Fourth Edition. 8vo. 3s. 6d.
    Sankhya Aphorisms of Kapila. With Illustrative Extracts from the Commentaries. Third Edition. Post 8vo. 16s. (*Trübner's Oriental Series.*)

BALLIN, ADA S. and F. L., **Hebrew Grammar.** With Exercises selected from the Bible. Cr. 8vo. 7s. 6d.

BANCROFT, H. H., **Popular History of the Mexican People.** 8vo. 15s.

BANKS, Mrs. G. LINNÆUS, **God's Providence House.** Cr. 8vo. 6s.

BARING-GOULD, S., **Germany, Present and Past.** New and Cheaper Edition. Large cr. 8vo. 7s. 6d.

BARLOW, J. W., **The Ultimatum of Pessimism.** An Ethical Study. 8vo. 6s.

BARNES, WILLIAM, **Poems of Rural Life in the Dorset Dialect.** New Edition. Cr. 8vo. 6s.

BARRIÈRE, THEODORE, and CAPENDU, ERNEST, **Les Faux Bonshommes.** A Comedy. 12mo. 4s.

BARTH, A., **Religions of India.** Translated by the Rev. J. WOOD. Second Edition. Post 8vo. 16s. (*Trübner's Oriental Series.*)

BARTLETT, J. R., **Dictionary of Americanisms**: a Glossary of Words and Phrases colloquially used in the United States. Fourth Edition. 8vo. 21s.

BASU, K. P., **Students' Mathematical Companion.** Containing Problems in Arithmetic, Algebra, Geometry, and Mensuration, for Students of the Indian Universities. Cr. 8vo. 6s.

BASTIAN, H. CHARLTON, **The Brain as an Organ of Mind.** With 184 Illustrations. Fourth Edition. Cr. 8vo. 5s. (*I.S.S.*)

BAUGHAN, ROSA, **The Influence of the Stars**: a Treatise on Astrology, Chiromancy, and Physiognomy. Second Edition. 8vo. 5s.

BAUR, FERDINAND, **Philological Introduction to Greek and Latin for Students.** Translated and adapted from the German by C. KEGAN PAUL and E. D. STONE. Third Edition. Cr. 8vo. 6s.

BAYNES, Canon H. R., **Home Songs for Quiet Hours.** Fourth and Cheaper Edition. Fcp. 8vo. 2s. 6d.

BEAL, S., **Catena of Buddhist Scriptures.** From the Chinese. 8vo. 15s.

Romantic Legend of Sakya Buddha. From the Chinese-Sanskrit. Cr. 8vo. 12s.

Buddhist Literature in China. 8vo. 10s. 6d.

Life of Hiuen-Tsiang. By the Shamans HWUI LI and YEN-TSUNG. With an Account of the Works of I-Tsing. Post 8vo. 10s. (*Trübner's Oriental Series.*)

Si-Yu-Ki: Buddhist Records of the Western World. Translated from the Chinese of HIUEN-TSIANG (A.D. 629). With Map. 2 vols. post 8vo. 24s. (*Trübner's Oriental Series.*)

Texts from the Buddhist Canon, commonly known as Dhammapada. Translated from the Chinese. Post 8vo. 7s. 6d. (*Trübner's Oriental Series.*)

BEAMES, JOHN, **Outlines of Indian Philology.** With a Map showing the Distribution of Indian languages. Enlarged Edition. Cr. 8vo. 5s.

Comparative Grammar of the Modern Aryan Languages of India: Hindi, Panjabi, Sindhi, Gujarati, Marathi, Oriya, and Bengali. 3 vols. 8vo. 16s. each.

BEARD, CHARLES, **Martin Luther and the Reformation in Germany.** 8vo. 16s.

BECQUER, GUSTAVO ADOLFO, **Poems.** Rendered into English Verse by MASON CARNES. Sm. cr. 8vo. 2s. 6d.

BEDE, The Venerable, **Historia Ecclesiastica Gentis Anglorum.** 8vo. 5s.

BELL, A. M., **Elocutionary Manual.** Fifth Edition Revised. 12mo. 7s. 6d.

BELLOWS, JOHN, **French and English Dictionary for the Pocket.** Containing the French-English and English-French Divisions on the same page; Conjugating all the Verbs; Distinguishing the Genders by Different Types; giving Numerous Aids to Pronunciation, &c. Fifty-first Thousand of the Second Edition. 32mo. morocco tuck, 12s. 6d.; roan, 10s. 6d.

Tous les Verbes. Conjugations of all the Verbs in French and English. Second Edition. With Tables of Weights, Measures, &c. 32mo. 6d.

8 *Kegan Paul, Trench, Trübner, & Co.'s Publications.*

BENEDEN, P. J. van, Animal Parasites and Messmates. With 83 Illustrations. Fourth Edition, Cr. 8vo. 5s. (*I.S.S.*)

BENEDIX, RODERICK, Der Vetter. Comedy in Three Acts. 12mo. 2s. 6d.

BENFEY, THEODOR, Grammar of the Sanskrit Language. For the Use of Early Students. Second Edition. Roy. 8vo. 10s. 6d.

BENSON, A. C., William Laud, sometime Archbishop of Canterbury. With Portrait. Cr. 8vo. 6s.

BENSON, MAY ELEANOR, At Sundry Times and in Divers Manners. With Portrait and Memoir. 2 vols. cr. 8vo. 10s. 6d.

BENTHAM, JEREMY, Theory of Legislation. Translated from the French of Etienne Dumont by R. HILDRETH. Seventh Edition. Post 8vo. 7s. 6d.

BENTLEY, W. H., Dictionary and Grammar of the Kongo Language. As Spoken at San Salvador, West Africa. 8vo. 21s.

'BERNARD,' From World to Cloister; or, My Novitiate. Cr. 8vo. 5s.

BERNSTEIN, Prof., The Five Senses of Man. With 91 Illustrations. Fifth Edition. Cr. 8vo. 5s. (*I.S.S.*)

BERTIN, GEORGE, Abridged Grammar of the Languages of the Cuneiform Inscriptions. Cr. 8vo. 5s.

BEVAN, THEODORE F., Toil, Travel, and Discovery in British New Guinea. With 5 Maps. Large cr. 8vo. 7s. 6d.

BHIKSHU, SUBHADRA, Buddhist Catechism. 12mo. 2s.

BILLER, EMMA, Ulli: the Story of a Neglected Girl. Translated from the German by A. B. DAISY ROST. Cr. 8vo. 6s.

Bible Folk Lore: a Study in Comparative Mythology. Cr. 8vo. 10s. 6d.

BINET, A., and FERE, C., Animal Magnetism. Second Edition. Cr. 8vo. 5s. (*I.S.S.*)

BLADES, W., Biography and Typography of William Caxton, England's First Printer. 8vo. hand-made paper, imitation old bevelled binding, £1. 1s. ; Cheap Edition, cr. 8vo. 5s.

Account of the German Morality Play, entitled, 'Depositio Cornuti Typographici.' As performed in the 17th or 18th Centuries. With facsimile illustrations. Sm. 4to. 7s. 6d.

BLASERNA, Prof. P., Theory of Sound in its Relation to Music. With numerous Illustrations. Fourth Edition. Cr. 8vo. 5s. (*I.S.S.*)

BLEEK, W. H. I., Reynard the Fox in South Africa, or, Hottentot Fables and Tales. Post 8vo. 3s. 6d.

BLOOMFIELD, The Lady, Reminiscences of Court and Diplomatic Life. New and Cheaper Edition, with Frontispiece. Cr. 8vo. 6s.

BLUMHARDT, J. F., Charitabali, The; or, Instructive Biography. By ISVARA-CHANDRA VIDYASAGARA. With Vocabulary of all the Words occurring in the Text. 12mo. 5s. Vocabulary only, 2s. 6d.

BLUNT, WILFRID SCAWEN, The Wind and the Whirlwind. 8vo. 1s. 6a.
The Love Sonnets of Proteus. Fifth Edition. Elzevir 8vo. 5s.
In Vinculis. With Portrait. Elzevir 8vo. 5s.
A New Pilgrimage, and other Poems. Elzevir 8vo. 5s.

BOGER, Mrs. E., Myths, Scenes, and Worthies of Somerset. Cr. 8vo. 10s. 6d.

BOJESEN, MARIA, Guide to the Danish Language. 12mo. 5s.

BOSANQUET, BERNARD, Knowledge and Reality. A Criticism of Mr. F. H. Bradley's 'Principles of Logic.' Cr. 8vo. 9s.

Introduction to Hegel's Philosophy of Fine Art. Cr. 8vo. 5s.

Kegan Paul, Trench, Trübner, & Co.'s Publications. 9

BOWDEN, Fr. CHARLES HENRY, Life of B. John Juvenal Ancina. 8vo. 9s.

BOWEN, H. C., Studies in English. For the use of Modern Schools. Tenth thousand. Sm. cr. 8vo. 1s. 6d.
English Grammar for Beginners. Fcp. 8vo. 1s.
Simple English Poems. English Literature for Junior Classes, 3s. Parts I. II. and III. 6d. each. Part IV. 1s.

BOYD, P., Nágánanda ; or, the Joy of the Snake World. From the Sanskrit of Sri-Harsha-Deva. Cr. 8vo. 4s. 6d.

BRACKENBURY, Major-General, Field Works : their Technical Construction and Tactical Application. 2 vols. Sm. cr. 8vo. 12s. (*Military Handbooks.*)

BRADLEY, F. H., The Principles of Logic. 8vo. 16s.

Brave Men's Footsteps : a Book of Example and Anecdote for Young People. By the editor of 'Men who have Risen.' Illustrations by C. DOYLE. Ninth Edition. Cr. 8vo. 2s. 6d.

BRENTANO, LUJO, History and Development of Gilds, and the Origin of Trade Unions. 8vo. 3s. 6d.

BRETSCHNEIDER, E., Mediæval Researches from Eastern Asiatic Sources : Fragments towards the Knowledge of the Geography and History of Central and Western Asia, from the 13th to the 17th century, with 2 Maps. 2 vols. Post 8vo. 21s. (*Trübner's Oriental Series.*)

BRETTE, P. H., THOMAS, F., French Examination Papers set at the University of London. Part I. Matriculation, and the General Examination for Women. Cr. 8vo. 3s. 6d. Key, 5s. Part II. First B.A. Examinations for Honours and D. Litt. Examinations. Cr. 8vo. 7s.

BRIDGETT, T. E., Blunders and Forgeries : Historical Essays. Cr. 8vo. 6s.
History of the Holy Eucharist in Great Britain. 2 vols. 8vo. 18s.

BROOKE, Rev. STOPFORD A., The Fight of Faith : Sermons preached on various occasions. Sixth Edition, cr. 8vo. 5s.
The Spirit of the Christian Life. Third Edition. Cr. 8vo. 5s.
Theology in the English Poets : Cowper, Coleridge, Wordsworth, and Burns. Sixth Edition. Post 8vo. 5s.
Christ in Modern Life. Seventeenth Edition. Cr. 8vo. 5s.
Sermons. Two Series. Thirteenth Edition. Cr. 8vo. 5s. each.
Life and Letters of F. W. Robertson. With Portrait. 2 vols. Cr. 8vo. 12s. Library Edition, 8vo. with portrait, 12s. Popular Edition, cr. 8vo. 6s.

BROWN, C. P., Sanskrit Prosody and Numerical Symbols Explained. 8vo. 3s. 6d.

BROWN, HORATIO F., Life on the Lagoons. With 2 Illustrations and Map. Cr. 8vo. 6s.
Venetian Studies. Cr. 8vo. 7s. 6d.

BROWN, Rev. J. BALDWIN, The Higher Life : its Reality, Experience, and Destiny. Seventh Edition. Cr. 8vo. 5s.
Doctrine of Annihilation in the Light of the Gospel of Love. Fourth Edition. Cr. 8vo. 2s. 6d.
The Christian Policy of Life : a Book for Young Men of Business. Third Edition. Cr. 8vo. 3s. 6d.

BROWN, J. P., The Dervishes ; or, Oriental Spiritualism. With 24 Illustrations. Cr. 8vo. 14s.

BROWNE, EDGAR A., How to Use the Ophthalmoscope. Third Edition. Cr. 8vo. 3s. 6d.

BROWNING, OSCAR, Introduction to the History of Educational Theories. Second Edition. 3s. 6d. (*Education Library.*)

BRUGMANN, KARL, Comparative Grammar of the Indo-Germanic Languages. 2 vols. 8vo. Vol. I. Introduction and Phonology, 18s. Vol. II. Morphology (Stem-Formation and Inflexion), Part 1, 16s.

BRUN, L. LE, Materials for Translating English into French. Seventh Edition. Post 8vo. 4s. 6d.

BRYANT, SOPHIE, Celtic Ireland. With 3 Maps. Cr. 8vo. 5s.

BRYANT, W. CULLEN, Poems. Cheap Edition. Sm. 8vo. 3s. 6d.

BRYCE, J., Handbook of Home Rule: being Articles on the Irish Question. Second Edition. Cr. 8vo, 1s. 6d.; paper covers, 1s.

Two Centuries of Irish History. 8vo. 16s.

BUDGE, E. A., History of Esarhaddon (Son of Sennacherib), King of Assyria, B.C. 681-668. Translated from the Cuneiform Inscriptions in the British Museum. Post 8vo. 10s. 6d. (*Trübner's Oriental Series.*)

Archaic Classics: Assyrian Texts, being Extracts from the Annals of Shalmaneser II., Sennacherib, and Assur-Bani-Pal, with Philological Notes. Sm. 4to. 7s. 6d.

BUNGE, Prof. G., Text-Book of Physiological and Pathological Chemistry, for Physicians and Students. Translated from the German by L. C. WOOLDRIDGE. 8vo. 16s.

BUNSEN, ERNEST DE, Islam; or, True Christianity. Crown 8vo. 5s.

BURDETT, H. C., Help in Sickness: where to go and what to do. Cr. 8vo. 1s. 6d. **Helps to Health.** Cr. 8vo. 1s. 6d.

BURGESS, JAMES, The Buddhist Cave-Temples and their Inscriptions, containing Views, Plans, Sections, and Elevation of Façades of Cave-temples; Drawings of Architectural and Mythological Sculptures; Facsimiles of Inscriptions, &c.; with Descriptive and Explanatory Text, and Translations of Inscriptions. With 86 Plates and Woodcuts. Royal 4to. half-bound, £3. 3s. [*Archæological Survey of Western India.*]

Elura Cave-Temples and the Brahmanical and Jaina Caves in Western India. With 66 Plates and Woodcuts. Royal 4to. half-bound, £3. 3s. [*Archæological Survey of Western India.*]

Reports of the Amaravati and Jaggayyapeta Buddhist Stupas, containing numerous Collotype and other Illustrations of Buddhist Sculpture and Architecture, &c., in South-eastern India; Facsimiles of Inscriptions, &c., with Descriptive and Explanatory Text; together with Transcriptions, Translations, and Elucidations of the Dhauli and Jaugada Inscriptions of Asoka. With numerous Plates and Woodcuts. Royal 4to. half-bound, £4. 4s. [*Archæological Survey of Southern India.*]

BURNELL, A. C., Elements of South Indian Palæography, from the 4th to the 17th century: an Introduction to the Study of South Indian Inscriptions and MSS. Enlarged Edition. With Map and 35 Plates. 4to. £2. 12s. 6d.

BURNEY, Capt., R.N., The Young Seaman's Manual. Cr. 8vo. 7s. 6d.

BURNS, ROBERT, Selected Poems of. With an Introduction by ANDREW LANG. Elzevir 8vo. vellum, 7s. 6d.; parchment or cloth, 6s. (*Parchment Library.*)

BURY, RICHARD DE, Philobiblon. Edited by E. C. THOMAS. Cr. 8vo. 10s. 6d.

BUTLER, F., Spanish Teacher and Colloquial Phrase-Book. 18mo. half-roan, 2s. 6d.

BUXTON, Major, Elements of Military Administration. First part: Permanent System of Administration. Small cr. 8vo. 7s. 6d. (*Military Handbooks.*)

BYRNE, Dean JAMES, General Principles of the Structure of Language. 2 vols. 8vo. 36s.

Origin of Greek, Latin, and Gothic Roots. 8vo. 18s.

CABLE, G. W., Strange True Stories of Louisiana. 8vo. 7s. 6d.

CAIRD, MONA, The Wing of Azrael. Cr. 8vo. 6s.

CALDERON'S Dramas. Translated by DENIS FLORENCE MACCARTHY. Post 8vo. 10s.

Kegan Paul, Trench, Trübner, & Co.'s Publications. 11

CALDWELL, Bishop R., Comparative Grammar of the Dravidian or South Indian Family of Languages. Enlarged edition, 8vo. 28s.
CALL, WATHEN MARK WILKS, Final Causes: a Refutation. Cr. 8vo. 5s.
CALLEJA, CAMILO, Principles of Universal Physiology. Cr. 8vo. 3s. 6d.
General Physiology, or Physiological Theory of Cosmos. Cr. 8vo. 6s.
Theory of Physics: a Rectification of the Theories of Molar Mechanics, Heat, Chemistry, Sound, Light, and Electricity. Cr. 8vo. 5s.
CAMERINI, E., L'Eco Italiano: a Guide to Italian Conversation, with Vocabulary. 12mo. 4s. 6d.
CAMERON, Miss, Soups and Stews and Choice Ragoûts. Cr. 8vo. cloth, 1s. 6d.; paper covers, 1s.
CAMOENS' Lusiads. Portuguese Text, with Translation, by J. J. AUBERTIN. Second Edition. 2 vols. Cr. 8vo. 12s.
Campaigns of the Civil War (American). 12 vols., and Supplement. With Maps and Plans. 12mo. 5s. each vol.
CAMPBELL, Prof. LEWIS, Sophocles. The Seven Plays in English Verse. Cr. 8vo. 7s. 6d.
Æschylus. The Seven Plays in English Verse. Cr. 8vo. 7s. 6d.
Candid Examination of Theism. By PHYSICUS. Second Edition, post 8vo. 7s. 6d. (*Philosophical Library.*)
CANDOLLE, ALPHONSE DE, Origin of Cultivated Plants. Second Edition. Cr. 8vo. 5s. (*I.S.S.*)
CARLYLE, THOMAS, Sartor Resartus. Elzevir 8vo. vellum, 7s. 6d.; parchment or cloth, 6s. (*Parchment Library.*)
CARNES, MASON. Poems by Gustavo Adolfo Becquer, rendered into English Verse. Sm. cr. 8vo. 2s. 6d.
CARPENTER, W. B., Principles of Mental Physiology, with their Applications to the Training and Discipline of the Mind, and the Study of its Morbid Conditions. Illustrated. Sixth Edition. 8vo. 12s.
Nature and Man. With a Memorial Sketch by J. ESTLIN CARPENTER. Portrait. Large cr. 8vo. 8s. 6d.
CARREÑO, Metodo para aprender a Leer, escribir y hablar el Inglés segun el sistema de Ollendorff. 8vo. 4s. 6d. Key, 3s.
CARRINGTON, H., Of the Imitation of Christ. By THOMAS À KEMPIS. A Metrical Version. Cr. 8vo. 5s.
CASSAL, CHARLES, Glossary of Idioms, Gallicisms, and other Difficulties contained in the Senior Course of the 'Modern French Reader.' Cr. 8vo. 2s. 6d.
CASSAL, CH., and KARCHER, THEODORE. Modern French Reader. Junior Course. Tenth Edition. Cr. 8vo. 2s. 6d. Senior Course. Third Edition. Cr. 8vo. 4s. Senior Course and Glossary in 1 vol. Cr. 8vo. 6s.
Little French Reader: extracted from the 'Modern French Reader.' Third Edition. Cr. 8vo. 2s.
CATLIN, GEORGE, O-Kee-Pa: a Religious Ceremony; and other Customs of the Mandans. With 13 coloured Illustrations. Small 4to. 14s.
The Lifted and Subsided Rocks of America, with their Influence on the Oceanic, Atmospheric, and Land Currents, and the Distribution of Races. With 2 Maps. Cr. 8vo. 6s. 6d.
Shut your Mouth and Save your Life. With 29 Illustrations. Ninth Edition. Cr. 8vo. 2s. 6d.
CHAMBERLAIN, Prof. B. H., Classical Poetry of the Japanese. Post 8vo. 7s. 6d. (*Trübner's Oriental Series.*)
Simplified Japanese Grammar. Cr. 8vo. 5s.
Romanised Japanese Reader. Consisting of Japanese Anecdotes and Maxims, with English Translations and Notes. 12mo. 6s.
Handbook of Colloquial Japanese. 8vo. 12s. 6d.
Things Japanese. Second, Revised Edition. Cr. 8vo. 7s. 6d.

CHAMBERS, J. D., Theological and Philosophical Works of Hermes Trismegistus, Christian Neoplatonist. Translated from the Greek. 8vo. 7s. 6d.

CHAUCER, G., Canterbury Tales. Edited by A. W. POLLARD. 2 vols. Elzevir 8vo. vellum, 15s. ; parchment or cloth, 12s. (*Parchment Library.*)

CHEYNE, Canon T. K., The Prophecies of Isaiah. With Notes and Dissertations. 2 vols. Fifth Edition, Revised. 8vo. 25s.

Job and Solomon ; or, The Wisdom of the Old Testament. 8vo. 12s. 6d.

The Book of Psalms ; or, the Praises of Israel. With Commentary. 8vo. 16s.

The Book of Psalms. Elzevir 8vo. vellum, 7s. 6d. ; parchment or cloth, 6s. (*Parchment Library.*)

The Origin and Religious Contents of the Psalter. The Bampton Lectures, 1889. 8vo. 16s.

CHICHELE, Mary, Doing and Undoing. Cr. 8vo. 4s. 6d.

CHILDERS, R. C., Pali-English Dictionary, with Sanskrit Equivalents. Imp. 8vo. £3. 3s.

CHRISTIAN, JOHN, Behar Proverbs, Classified and arranged according to subject matter, with Notes. Post 8vo. 10s. 6d. (*Trübner's Oriental Series.*)

CLAIRAUT, Elements of Geometry. Translated by Dr. KAINES. With 145 Figures. Cr. 8vo. 4s. 6d.

CLAPPERTON, JANE HUME, Scientific Meliorism and the Evolution of Happiness. Large cr. 8vo. 8s. 6d.

CLARKE, HENRY W., History of Tithes from Abraham to Queen Victoria. Cr. 8vo. 5s.

CLARKE, JAMES FREEMAN, Ten Great Religions: an Essay in Comparative Theology. 2 vols. 8vo. 10s. 6d. each.

CLAUSEWITZ, General CARL von, On War. Translated by Colonel GRAHAM. Fcp. 4to. 10s. 6d.

CLEMENT, C. E., and HUTTON, L., Artists of the Nineteenth Century and their Works. Two thousand and fifty Biographical Sketches. Third Edition, revised. Cr. 8vo. 15s.

CLERY, Gen. C. FRANCIS, Minor Tactics. With 26 Maps and Plans. Eleventh Edition, revised. Cr. 8vo. 9s.

CLIFFORD, W. KINGDON, Common Sense of the Exact Sciences. Second Edition. With 100 Figures. Cr. 8vo. 5s. (*I.S.S.*)

CLODD, EDWARD, Childhood of the World : a Simple Account of Man in early times. Ninth Edition. Cr. 8vo. 3s. Special Edition for Schools, 1s.

Childhood of Religions. Including a simple account of the birth and growth of Myths and Legends. Ninth Edition. Cr. 8vo. 5s. Special Edition for Schools, 1s. 6d.

Jesus of Nazareth. With a brief Sketch of Jewish History to the time of His birth. Second Edition. Revised throughout and partly re-written. Sm. cr. 8vo. 6s. Special Edition for Schools, in 2 parts, 1s. 6d. each.

COGHLAN, J. COLE, D.D., The Modern Pharisee and other Sermons. Edited by the Very Rev. H. H. DICKINSON, D.D. New and Cheaper Edition. Cr. 8vo. 7s. 6d.

COLEBROOKE, H. T., Miscellaneous Essays, with Biography by his son, Sir T. E. COLEBROOKE. 3 vols. 8vo. 42s.

COLERIDGE, Hon. STEPHEN, The Sanctity of Confession. A Romance. Cr. 8vo. 5s.

Demetrius. Cr. 8vo. 5s.

Fibulae. Poems. Sm. cr. 8vo. 4s. 6d.

COLERIDGE. Memoir and Letters of Sara Coleridge. Edited by her Daughter. Cheap Edition. With Portrait. Cr. 8vo. 7s. 6d.

Kegan Paul, Trench, Trübner, & Co.'s Publications. 13

COLLETTE, C. H., Life, Times, and Writings of Thomas Cranmer, D.D., the First Reforming Archbishop of Canterbury. 8vo. 7s. 6d.

Pope Joan. An Historical Study, from the Greek of Rhoïdis. 12mo. 2s. 6d.

COLLINS, MABEL, Through the Gates of Gold : a Fragment of Thought. Sm. 8vo. 4s. 6d.

Light on the Path. Fcp. 8vo. 1s. 6d.

COMPTON, A. G., First Lessons in Metal-Working. Cr. 8vo. 6s. 6d.

COMPTON, C. G., Scot Free : a Novel. Cr. 8vo. 6s.

COMTE, AUGUSTE, Catechism of Positive Religion, from the French, by R. CONGREVE. Third Edition, revised and corrected. Cr. 8vo. 2s. 6d.

Eight Circulars of Auguste Comte. Fcp. 8vo. 1s. 6d.

Appeal to Conservatives. Cr. 8vo. 2s. 6d.

Positive Philosophy of Auguste Comte, translated and condensed by HARRIET MARTINEAU. 2 vols. Second Edition. Post 8vo. 25s.

Subjective Synthesis ; or, Universal System of the Conceptions adapted to the Normal State of Humanity. Vol. I., containing the System of Positive Logic. 8vo. paper covers, 2s. 6d.

CONTE, JOSEPH LE, Sight : an Exposition of the Principles of Monocular and Binocular Vision. Second Edition. With 132 Illustrations. Cr. 8vo. 5s. (*I.S.S.*)

CONTOPOULOS, N., Lexicon of Modern Greek-English and English-Modern Greek. 2 vols. 8vo. 27s.

Modern-Greek and English Dialogues and Correspondence. Fcp. 8vo. 2s. 6d.

CONWAY, M. D., Emerson at Home and Abroad. With Portrait. Post 8vo, 10s. 6d. (*Philosophical Library.*)

CONWAY, R. S., Verner's Law in Italy : an Essay in the History of the Indo-European sibilants. 8vo. 5s.

COOK, KENINGALE, The Fathers of Jesus. A Study of the Lineage of the Christian Doctrine and Traditions. 2 vols. 8vo. 28s.

COOK, LOUISA S., Geometrical Psychology ; or, The Science of Representation. An Abstract of the Theories and Diagrams of B. W. Betts. 16 Plates. 8vo. 7s. 6d.

COOKE, M. C., British Edible Fungi : how to distinguish and how to cook them. With Coloured Figures of upwards of Forty Species. Cr. 8vo. 7s. 6d.

Fungi : their Nature, Influences, Uses, &c. Edited by Rev. M. J. BERKELEY. With numerous Illustrations. Fourth Edition. Cr. 8vo. 5s. (*I.S.S.*)

Introduction to Fresh-Water Algæ. With an Enumeration of all the British Species. With 13 Plates. Cr. 8vo. 5s. (*I.S.S.*)

COOKE, Prof. J. P., New Chemistry. With 31 Illustrations. Ninth Edition. Cr. 8vo. 5s. (*I.S.S.*)

Laboratory Practice. A Series of Experiments on the Fundamental Principles of Chemistry. Cr. 8vo. 5s.

COOMARA SWAMY, MUTU, The Dathavansa : or, The History of the Tooth Relic of Gotama Buddha. Pali Text. 8vo. 10s. 6d. English Translation, 6s.

Sutta Nipata ; or, Dialogues and Discourses of Gotama Buddha. Translated from the original Pali. Cr. 8vo. 6s.

CORDERY, J. G., Homer's Iliad. Greek Text, with Translation. 2 vols. 8vo. 14s. Translation only, cr. 8vo. 5s.

CORY, W., Guide to Modern English History. Part I. 1815-1830. 8vo. 9s. Part II. 1830-1835, 8vo. 15s.

COTTA, BERNHARD von, Geology and History. A Popular Exposition of all that is known of the Earth and its Inhabitants in Prehistoric Times. 12mo. 2s.

COTTON, H. J. S., New India ; or, India in Transition. Cheap Edition, paper covers, 1s.

COTTON, LOUISE, Palmistry and its Practical Uses. With 12 Plates. Cr. 8vo. 2s. 6d.

COWELL, E. B., Short Introduction to the Ordinary Prakrit of the Sanskrit Dramas. Cr. 8vo. 3s. 6d.

Prakrita-Prakasa; or, The Prakrit Grammar of Vararuchi, with the Commentary (Manorama) of Bhamaha. 8vo. 14s.

COWELL, E. B., and GOUGH, A. E., The Sarva-Darsana-Samgraha; or, Review of the Different Systems of Hindu Philosophy. Post 8vo. 10s. 6d. (*Trübner's Oriental Series.*)

COWIE, Bishop, Our Last Year in New Zealand, 1887. Cr. 8vo. 7s. 6d.

COX, SAMUEL, D.D., Commentary on the Book of Job. With a Translation. Second Edition. 8vo. 15s.

Salvator Mundi; or, Is Christ the Saviour of all Men? Fourteenth Edition. Cr. 8vo. 2s. 6d.

The Larger Hope: A Sequel to 'Salvator Mundi.' Second Edition. 16mo. 1s.

The Genesis of Evil, and other Sermons, mainly Expository. Fourth Edition. Cr. 8vo. 6s.

Balaam: an Exposition and a Study. Cr. 8vo. 5s.

Miracles: an Argument and a Challenge. Cr. 8vo. 2s. 6d.

COX, Sir G. W., Bart., Mythology of the Aryan Nations. New Edition. 8vo. 16s.

Tales of Ancient Greece. New Edition. Sm. cr. 8vo. 6s.

Tales of the Gods and Heroes. Sm. cr. 8vc. 3s. 6d

Manual of Mythology in the Form of Question and Answer. New Edition. Fcap. 8vo. 3s.

Introduction to the Science of Comparative Mythology and Folk-lore. Second Edition. Cr. 8vo. 7s. 6d.

COX, Sir G. W., Bart., and JONES, E. H., Popular Romances of the Middle Ages. Third Edition. Cr. 8vo. 6s.

COX, W. L. PAIGE, Present Day Counsels. Cr. 8vo. 5s.

CRAVEN, Mrs., A Year's Meditations. Cr. 8vo. 6s.

CRAVEN, T., English-Hindustani and Hindustani-English Dictionary. New Edition. 18mo. 4s. 6d.

CRAWFURD, OSWALD, Portugal, Old and New. With Illustrations and Maps. New and Cheaper Edition. Cr. 8vo. 6s.

Sylvia Arden. With Frontispiece. Cr. 8vo. 1s.

CRUISE, F. R., Notes of a Visit to the Scenes in which the Life of Thomas à Kempis was spent. With numerous Illustrations. 8vo. 12s.

CUNNINGHAM, Major-Gen. ALEX., Ancient Geography of India. I. The Buddhist Period, including the Campaigns of Alexander and the Travels of Hwen-Thsang. With 13 Maps. 8vo. £1. 8s.

CURTEIS, Canon, Bishop Selwyn of New Zealand and of Lichfield: a Sketch of his Life and Work, with further gleanings from his Letters, Sermons, and Speeches. Large cr. 8vo. 7s. 6d.

CUST, R. N., Linguistic and Oriental Essays. Post 8vo. First Series, 10s. 6d.; Second Series, with 6 Maps, 21s.; Third Series, with Portrait, 21s. (*Trübner's Oriental Series.*)

DANA, E. S., Text-Book of Mineralogy. With Treatise on Crystallography and Physical Mineralogy. Third Edition, with 800 Woodcuts and Plate. 8vo. 15s.

DANA, J. D., Text-Book of Geology, for Schools. Illustrated. Cr. 8vo. 10s.

Manual of Geology. Illustrated by a Chart of the World, and 1,000 Figures. 8vo. 21s.

The Geological Story Briefly Told. Illustrated. 12mo. 7s. 6d.

DANA, J. D., and BRUSH, G. J., System of Mineralogy. Fifth Edition. Roy. 8vo. £2. 2s.

Manual of Mineralogy and Petrography. Fourth Edition. Numerous Woodcuts. Cr. 8vo. 8s. 6d.

DANIELL, C. J., Industrial Competition of Asia: an Inquiry into the Influence of Currency on Commerce in the East. 8vo. 12s.
DANTE'S Treatise 'De Vulgari Eloquentiâ.' Translated, with Notes, by A. G. F. Howell, 3s. 6d.
Divina Commedia. Translated by F. K. H. Haselfoot. 8vo. 16s.
The Banquet (Il Convito). Translated by Katharine Hillard. Cr. 8vo. 7s. 6d.
DARMESTETER, ARSENE, Life of Words as the Symbols of Ideas. Cr. 8vo. 4s. 6d.
D'ASSIER, ADOLPHE, Posthumous Humanity: a Study of Phantoms. From the French by H. S. Olcott. With Appendix. Cr. 8vo. 7s. 6d.
DAVIDS, T. W. RHYS, Buddhist Birth-Stories; or, Jataka Tales. The oldest Collection of Folk-lore extant. Being the Jātakatthavannanā. Translated from the Pali Text of V. Fausboll. Post 8vo. 18s. (*Trübner's Oriental Series.*)
The Numismata Orientalia. Part VI. The Ancient Coins and Measures of Ceylon. With 1 Plate. Royal 4to. Paper wrapper, 10s.
DAVIDSON, SAMUEL, D.D., Canon of the Bible: its Formation, History, and Fluctuations. Third Edition. Sm. Cr. 8vo. 5s.
Doctrine of Last Things. Sm. Cr. 8vo. 3s. 6d.
DAVIDSON, T., Compendium of the Philosophical System of Antonio Rosmini-Serbati. Second Edition, 8vo. 10s. 6d.
DAVIES, G. CHRISTOPHER. Rambles and Adventures of Our School Field Club. With 4 Illustrations. New and Cheaper Edition. Cr. 8vo. 3s. 6d.
DAVIES, J., Sānkhya Kārikā of Iswara Krishna: an Exposition of the System of Kapila. Post 8vo. 6s. (*Trübner's Oriental Series.*)
The Bhagavad Gītā; or, the Sacred Lay. Translated from the Sanskrit. Post 8vo. 8s. 6d. (*Trübner's Oriental Series.*)
DAVITT, MICHAEL, Speech before the Special Commission. Cr. 8vo. 5s.
DAWSON, GEORGE, Prayers. First Series, Edited by his Wife. Tenth Edition. Sm. 8vo. 3s. 6d.
Prayers. Second Series. Edited by George St. Clair. Second Edition. Sm. 8vo. 3s. 6d.
Sermons on Disputed Points and Special Occasions. Edited by his Wife. Fifth Edition. Sm. 8vo. 3s. 6d.
Sermons on Daily Life and Duty. Edited by his Wife. Fifth Edition. Sm. 8vo. 3s. 6d.
The Authentic Gospel. Sermons. Edited by George St. Clair. Fourth Edition. Sm. 8vo. 3s. 6d.
Every-Day Counsels. Edited by George St. Clair. Cr. 8vo. 6s.
Biographical Lectures. Edited by George St. Clair. Third Edition Large cr. 8vo. 7s. 6d.
Shakespeare; and other Lectures. Edited by George St. Clair. Large Cr. 8vo. 7s. 6d.
DAWSON, Sir J. W., Geological History of Plants. With 80 Illustrations. Cr. 8vo. 5s. (*I.S.S.*)
DEAN, TERESA H., How to be Beautiful: Nature Unmasked. A Book for every Woman. Fcp. 8vo. 2s. 6d.
DELBRUCK, B., Introduction to the Study of Language: the History and Methods of Comparative Philology of the Indo-European Languages. 8vo. 5s.
DENNIS, J., Collection of English Sonnets. Sm. Cr. 8vo. 2s. 6d.
DENNYS, N. B., Folk-Lore of China, and its Affinities with that of the Aryan and Semitic Races. 8vo. 10s. 6d.
DEWEY, JOHN, Psychology. Large Cr. 8vo. 5s. 6d.
DEWEY, J. H., The Way, the Truth, and the Life: a Handbook of Christian Theosophy, Healing and Psychic Culture. 10s. 6d.

16 *Kegan Paul, Trench, Trübner, & Co.'s Publications.*

DIDON, Father, Jesus Christ. 2 vols. 8vo. 21s.
DILLON, W., Life of John Mitchel. With Portrait. 2 vols. 8vo. 21s.
DOBSON, AUSTIN, Old World Idylls, and other Verses. With Frontispiece. Elzevir 8vo. 6s.
  At the Sign of the Lyre. With Frontispiece. Elzevir 8vo. 6s.
DOMVILE, Lady M., Life of Alphonse de Lamartine. Large Cr. 8vo. 7s. 6d.
DONOVAN, J., From Lyre to Muse : a History of the Aboriginal Union of Music and Poetry. Cr. 8vo. 3s. 6d.
  Music and Action ; or, the Elective Affinity between Rhythm and Pitch. Cr. 8vo. 3s. 6d.
D'ORSEY, A. J. D., Grammar of Portuguese and English. Adapted to Ollendorff's System. Fourth Edition. 12mo. 7s.
  Colloquial Portuguese ; or, the Words and Phrases of Every-day Life. Fourth Edition. Cr. 8vo. 3s. 6d.
Doubter's Doubt about Science and Religion. Cr. 8vo. 3s. 6d.
DOUGLAS, Prof. R. K., Chinese Language and Literature. Cr. 8vo. 5s.
  The Life of Jenghiz Khan. Translated from the Chinese. Cr. 8vo. 5s.
DOWDEN, EDWARD, Shakspere : a Critical Study of His Mind and Art. Ninth Edition. Large post 8vo. 12s.
  Shakspere's Sonnets. With Introduction and Notes. Large post 8vo. 7s. 6d.
  Shakspere's Sonnets. Edited, with Frontispiece after the Death Mask. Elzevir 8vo. vellum, 7s. 6d. ; parchment or cloth, 6s. (*Parchment Library.*)
  Studies in Literature, 1789-1877. Fifth Edition. Large post 8vo. 6s.
  Transcripts and Studies. Large post 8vo. 12s.
  Life of Percy Bysshe Shelley. With Portraits. 2 vols. 8vo. 36s.
DOWNING, C., Fruits and Fruit Trees of America : or, the Culture and Management of Fruit Trees generally. Illustrated. 8vo. 25s.
DOWSON, JOHN, Grammar of the Urdū or Hindūstāni Language. Second Edition. Cr. 8vo. 10s. 6d.
  Hindūstāni Exercise Book. Passages and Extracts for Translation into Hindūstāni. Cr. 8vo. 2s. 6d.
  Classical Dictionary of Hindu Mythology and History, Geography and Literature. Post 8vo. 16s. (*Trübner's Oriental Series.*)
DRAPER, J. W., The Conflict between Religion and Science. 21st Edition. Cr. 8vo. 5s. (*I.S.S.*)
DRAYSON, Major-General, Untrodden Ground in Astronomy and Geology. With Numerous Figures. 8vo. 14s.
Dreamland and Ghostland : an Original Collection of Tales and Warnings from the Borderland of Substance and Shadow. 3 vols. 6s. each.
DRUMMOND. Maria Drummond : a Sketch. Post 8vo. 2s.
DUFFY, Sir C. GAVAN, Thomas Davis : the Memoirs of an Irish Patriot, 1840-46. 8vo. 12s.
DUKA, THEODORE, Life and Works of Alexander Csoma de Körös between 1819 and 1842. With a Short Notice of all his Works and Essays, from Original Documents. Post 8vo. 9s. (*Trübner's Oriental Series.*)
DUNN, H. P., Infant Health : the Physiology and Hygiene of Early Life. Sm. Cr. 8vo. 3s. 6d.
DUSAR, P. FRIEDRICH, Grammar of the German Language. With Exercises. 2nd Edition. Cr. 8vo. 4s. 6d.
  Grammatical Course of the German Language. 3rd Edition. Cr. 8vo. 3s. 6d.
DUTT, ROMESH CHUNDER, History of Civilisation in Ancient India, based on Sanskrit literature. Cr. 8vo. Vol. I. Vedic and Epic Ages, 8s. Vol. II. Rationalistic Age, 8s. Vol. III. Buddhist and Pauranik Ages, 8s.

Kegan Paul, Trench, Trübner, & Co.'s Publications. 17

DUTT, TORU, A Sheaf Gleaned in French Fields. 8vo. 10s. 6d.
Ancient Ballads and Legends of Hindustan. With an Introductory Memoir by EDMUND GOSSE. 18mo. cloth extra, gilt top, 5s.

EASTWICK, E. B., The Gulistan; or, Rose Garden of Shekh Mushliu-'d-Din Sadi of Shiraz. Translated from the Atish Kadah. 2nd Edition. Post 8vo. 10s. 6d. (*Trübner's Oriental Series.*)

EDGREN, H., Compendious Sanskrit Grammar. With a Brief Sketch of Scenic Prakrit. Cr. 8vo. 10s. 6d.

EDKINS, J., D.D., Religion in China. Containing a Brief Account of the Three Religions of the Chinese. 3rd Edition. Post 8vo. 7s. 6d. (*Philosophical Library* and *Trübner's Oriental Series.*)
Chinese Buddhism: Sketches Historical and Critical. Post 8vo. 18s. (*Trübner's Oriental Series.*)

EDMONDS, HERBERT, Well-spent Lives: a Series of Modern Biographies. New and Cheaper Edition. Cr. 8vo. 3s. 6d.

EDWARDS, EDWARD, Memoirs of Libraries, together with a Practical Handbook of Library Economy. Numerous Illustrations. 2 vols. roy. 8vo. £2. 8s.
Libraries and Founders of Libraries. 8vo. 18s.
Free Town Libraries: their Formation, Management, and History. With Brief Notices of Book Collectors. 8vo. 21s.

EGER, GUSTAV, Technological Dictionary in the English and German Languages. 2 vols. roy. 8vo. £1. 7s.

Eighteenth Century Essays. Edited by AUSTIN DOBSON. With Frontispiece. Elzevir 8vo. vellum, 7s. 6d.; parchment or cloth, 6s. (*Parchment Library.*) Cheap Edition, fcap. 8vo. 1s. 6d.

EITEL, E. J., Buddhism: its Historical, Theoretical, and Popular Aspects. Third Edition, revised, 8vo. 5s.
Handbook for the Student of Chinese Buddhism. Second Edition. Cr. 8vo. 18s.

Electricity in Daily Life: a Popular Account of its Application to Every-day Uses. With 125 Illustrations. Sq. 8vo. 9s.

Elegies and Memorials. By A. and L. Fcp. 8vo. 2s. 6d.

ELLIOTT, EBENEZER, Poems. Edited by his Son, the Rev. EDWIN ELLIOTT, of St. John's, Antigua. 2 vols. crown 8vo. 18s.

ELLIOTT, F. R., Handbook for Fruit Growers. Illustrated. Sq. 16mo. 5s.
Handbook of Practical Landscape Gardening. Illustrated. 8vo. 7s. 6d.

ELLIOT, Sir H. M., History, Folk-lore, and Distribution of the Races of the North-Western Provinces of India. Edited by J. BEAMES. With 3 Coloured Maps. 2 vols. 8vo. £1. 16s.
History of India, as told by its own Historians: the Muhammadan Period. From the Posthumous Papers of the late Sir H. M. ELLIOT. Revised and continued by Professor JOHN DOWSON. 8 vols. 8vo. £8. 8s.

ELLIOT, Sir W., Coins of Southern India. With Map and Plates. Roy. 4to. 25s. (*Numismata Orientalia.*)

Encyclopædia Americana. 4 vols. 4to. £8. 8s.

English Comic Dramatists. Edited by OSWALD CRAWFURD. Elzevir 8vo. vellum, 7s. 6d.; parchment or cloth, 6s. (*Parchment Library.*)

English Lyrics. Elzevir 8vo. vellum, 7s. 6d.; parchment or cloth, 6s. (*Parchment Library.*)

English Odes. Edited by E. GOSSE. With Frontispiece. Elzevir 8vo. vellum, 7s. 6d.; parchment or cloth, 6s. (*Parchment Library.*)

B

English Sacred Lyrics. Elzevir 8vo. vellum, 7s. 6d.; parchment or cloth, 6s (*Parchment Library.*)

English Poets (Living). With Frontispiece by WALTER CRANE. Second Edition Large cr. 8vo. Printed on hand-made paper, vellum, 15s.; cloth, 12s.

English Verse. CHAUCER TO BURNS. TRANSLATIONS. LYRICS OF THE NINETEENTH CENTURY. DRAMATIC SCENES AND CHARACTERS. BALLADS AND ROMANCES. Edited by W. J. LINTON and R. H. STODDARD. 5 vols. cr. 8vo. 5s. each.

EYTON, ROBERT, The Apostles' Creed: Sermons. Cr. 8vo. 3s. 6d.

The True Life, and Other Sermons. Cr. 8vo. 7s. 6d.

The Lord's Prayer: Sermons. Cr. 8vo. 3s. 6d.

A Rash Investment: Sermon on Salvation Army Scheme of Social Reform. Fcp. 8vo. 1s.

FABER, E., The Mind of Mencius; or, Political Economy founded upon Mora Philosophy. A systematic digest of the doctrines of the Chinese philosopher, Mencius. Original text Classified and Translated. Post 8vo. 10s. 6d.

FAUSBOLL, V., The Jataka, together with its Commentary: being Tales o the Anterior Birth of Gotama Buddha. 5 vols. 8vo. 28s. each.

FERGUSSON, T., Chinese Researches: Chinese Chronology and Cycles. Cr. 8vo. 10s. 6d.

FEUERBACH, L., Essence of Christianity. From the German, by MARIAN EVANS. Second Edition. Post 8vo. 7s. 6d. (*Philosophical Library.*)

FICHTE, J. GOTTLIEB, New Exposition of the Science of Knowledge. Translated by A. E. KROEGER. 8vo. 6s.

Science of Knowledge. From the German, by A. E. KROEGER. With an Introduction by Prof. W. T. HARRIS. Post 8vo. 10s. 6d. (*Philosophical Library*.

Science of Rights. From the German by A. E. KROEGER. With an Introduc tion by Prof. W. T. HARRIS. Post 8vo. 12s. 6d. (*Philosophical Library.*)

Popular Works: The Nature of the Scholar; The Vocation of the Scholar; The Vocation of Man; The Doctrine of Religion; Characteristics of the Presen Age; Outlines of the Doctrine of Knowledge. With a Memoir by W. SMITH. Post 8vo. 2 vols. 21s. (*Philosophical Library.*)

FIFE-COOKSON, Lieut.-Colonel, Man and the Deity: an Essay in Verse. Smal 8vo. 2s.

The Empire of Man. Sm. 8vo. 2s. 6d.

FINN, ALEXANDER, Persian for Travellers. Oblong 32mo. 5s.

FITZARTHUR, T., The Worth of Human Testimony. Fcp. 8vo. 2s.

FITZGERALD, R. D., Australian Orchids. Part I., 7 Plates; Part II., 10 Plates Part III., 10 Plates; Part IV., 10 Plates; Part V., 10 Plates; Part VI. 10 Plates. Each Part, coloured, 21s.; plain, 10s. 6d. Part VII., 10 Plates Vol. II., Part I., 10 Plates. Each, coloured, 25s.

FITZPATRICK, W. J., Life of the Very Rev. T. N. Burke. With Portrait 2 vols. 8vo. 30s.

FLETCHER, J. S., Andrewlina. Cr. 8vo. cloth, 1s. 6d.; paper covers, 1s.

The Winding Way. Cr. 8vo. 6s.

FLINN, D. EDGAR, Ireland: its Health Resorts and Watering Places. With Frontis piece and Maps. 8vo. 5s.

FLOWER, W. H., The Horse: a Study in Natural History. Cr. 8vo. 2s. 6d (*Modern Science Series*.)

FORNANDER, A., Account of the Polynesian Race: its Origin and Migrations and the Ancient History of the Hawaiian People. Post 8vo. Vol. I., 7s. 6d. Vol. II., 10s. 6d. Vol. III., 9s. (*Philosophical Library.*)

FORNEY, MATTHIAS N., Catechism of the Locomotive. Second Edition. revised and enlarged. Fcp. 4to. 18s.

Kegan Paul, Trench, Trübner, & Co.'s Publications. 19

FOTHERINGHAM, JAMES, Studies in the Poetry of Robert Browning. Second Edition. Cr. 8vo. 6s.

FRASER, Sir WILLIAM, Bart., Disraeli and His Day. Second Edition. Post 8vo. 9s.

FRAZAR, DOUGLAS, Practical Boat Sailing: a Treatise on Management of Small Boats and Yachts. Sm. cr. 4s. 6d.

FREEBOROUGH, E., and RANKEN, C.E., Chess Openings, Ancient and Modern. Revised and Corrected up to the Present Time from the best Authorities. Large post 8vo. 7s. 6d.

FREEBOROUGH, E., Chess Endings. A Companion to 'Chess Openings, Ancient and Modern.' Edited and Arranged. Large post 8vo. 7s. 6d.

FREEMAN, E. A., Lectures to American Audiences. I. The English People in its Three Homes. II. Practical Bearings of General European History. Post 8vo. 8s. 6d.

French Lyrics. Edited by GEORGE SAINTSBURY. With Frontispiece. Elzevir 8vo. vellum, 7s. 6d.; parchment or cloth, 6s. (*Parchment Library.*)

FREWEN, MORETON, The Economic Crisis. Cr. 8vo. 4s. 6d.

FRIEDLÄNDER, M., Text-Book of Jewish Religion. Second Edition revised. Cr. 8vo. 1s. 6d.

The Jewish Religion. Cr. 8vo. 5s.

FRIEDRICH, P., Progressive German Reader. With copious Notes. Cr. 8vo. 4s. 6d.

FRITH, I., Life of Giordano Bruno, the Nolan. Revised by Prof. MORIZ CARRIERE. With Portrait. Post 8vo. 14s. (*Philosophical Library.*)

FRŒMBLING, F. OTTO, Graduated German Reader: a Selection from the most popular writers. With a Vocabulary. Tenth Edition. 12mo. 3s. 6d.

Graduated Exercises for Translation into German: Extracts from the best English Authors, with Idiomatic Notes. Cr. 8vo. 4s. 6d.; without Notes, 4s.

GARDINER, LINDA, His Heritage. With Frontispiece. Cr. 8vo. 6s.

GARDNER, PERCY, The Numismata Orientalia. Part V. The Parthian Coinage. With 8 Plates. Royal 4to. Paper wrapper, 18s.

GARLANDA, FEDERICO, The Fortunes of Words. Cr. 8vo. 5s.

The Philosophy of Words: a popular introduction to the Science of Language. Cr. 8vo. 5s.

GASTER, M., Greeko-Slavonic Literature, and its Relation to the Folklore of Europe during the Middle Ages. Large Post 8vo. 7s. 6d.

GAY, JOHN, Fables. Edited by AUSTIN DOBSON. With Portrait. Elzevir 8vo. vellum, 7s. 6d.; parchment or cloth, 6s. (*Parchment Library.*)

GEIGER, LAZARUS, Contributions to the History of the Development of the Human Race. From the German by D. ASHER. Post 8vo. 6s. (*Philosophical Library.*)

GELDART, E. M., Guide to Modern Greek. Post 8vo. 7s. 6d. Key, 2s. 6d.

Simplified Grammar of Modern Greek. Cr. 8vo. 2s. 6d.

GEORGE, HENRY, Progress and Poverty: an Inquiry into the Causes of Industrial Depressions, and of Increase of Want with Increase of Wealth ; the Remedy. Fifth Edition. Post 8vo. 7s. 6d. Cabinet Edition, cr. 8vo. 2s. 6d. Cheap Edition, limp cloth, 1s. 6d.; paper covers, 1s.

Protection or Free Trade: an Examination of the Tariff Question, with especial regard to the interests of labour. Second Edition. Cr. 8vo. 5s. Cheap Edition, limp cloth, 1s. 6d.; paper covers, 1s.

Social Problems. Fourth Thousand. Cr. 8vo. 5s. Cheap Edition, limp cloth, 1s. 6d.; paper covers, 1s.

GERARD, E. and D., A Sensitive Plant: a Novel. With Frontispiece. Cr. 8vo. 6s.

B 2

GIBB, E. J. W., The History of the Forty Vezirs; or, The Story of the Forty Morns and Eves. Translated from the Turkish. Cr. 8vo. 10s. 6d.

GILBERT. Autobiography, and other Memorials of Mrs. Gilbert. Edited by JOSIAH GILBERT. Fifth Edition. Cr. 8vo. 7s. 6d.

GLANVILL, JOSEPH, Scepsis Scientifica. Edited, with Introductory Essay, by JOHN OWEN. Elzevir 8vo. 6s.

GLOVER, F., Exempla Latina: a First Construing Book, with Notes, Lexicon, and an Introduction to Analysis of Sentences. Second Edition, Fcp. 8vo. 2s.

GOETHE'S Faust. Translated from the German by JOHN ANSTER. With an Introduction by BURDETT MASON. With illustrations (18 in black and white, 10 in colour) by FRANK M. GREGORY. Grand folio, £3. 3s.

GOLDSMITH, Oliver, Vicar of Wakefield. Edited by AUSTIN DOBSON. Elzevir 8vo. vellum, 7s. 6d.; parchment or cloth, 6s. (*Parchment Library.*)

GOODENOUGH. Memoir of Commodore J. G. Goodenough. Edited by his Widow. With Portrait. Third Edition. Cr. 8vo. 5s.

GOODYEAR, W. A., A Treatise on the Assaying of Lead, Copper, Silver, Gold, and Mercury. From the German of TH. BODEMANN and BRUNO KERL. Illustrated with Plates. Cr. 8vo. 6s. 6d.

GORDON, Major-General C. G., Journals at Khartoum. Printed from the original MS. With Introduction and Notes by A. EGMONT HAKE. Portrait, 2 Maps, and 30 Illustrations. 8vo. 21s. Cheap Edition, 6s.

Last Journal: a Facsimile of the last Journal received in England from General Gordon, reproduced by Photo-lithography. Imp. 4to. £3. 3s.

GORDON, Sir H. W., Events in the Life of General Gordon, from the Day of his Birth to the Day of his Death. With Maps and Illustrations. Second Edition. 8vo. 7s. 6d.

Gospel according to Matthew, Mark, and Luke (The). Elzevir 8vo. vellum, 7s. 6d.; parchment or cloth, 6s. (*Parchment Library.*)

GOSSE, EDMUND, Seventeenth Century Studies: a Contribution to the History of English Poetry. 8vo. 10s. 6d.

New Poems. Cr. 8vo. 7s. 6d.

Firdausi in Exile, and other Poems. Second Edition. Elzevir 8vo. gilt top, 6s.

On Viol and Flute: Lyrical Poems. With Frontispiece by L. ALMA TADEMA, and Tailpiece by HAMO THORNYCROFT. Elzevir 8vo. 6s.

Life of Philip Henry Gosse. By his Son. 8vo. 15s.

GOSSIP, G. H. D., The Chess-Player's Text-Book: an Elementary Treatise on the Game of Chess. Numerous Diagrams. 16mo. 2s.

GOUGH, A. E., Philosophy of the Upanishads. Post 8vo. 9s. (*Trübner's Oriental Series.*)

GOUGH, EDWARD, The Bible True from the Beginning: a Commentary on all those portions of Scripture that are most questioned and assailed. Vols. I. to V. 8vo. 16s. each.

GOVER, C. E., Folk-Songs of Southern India. Containing Canarese, Badaga, Coorg, Tamil, Malayalam, and Telugu Songs. 8vo. 10s. 6d.

GOWER, Lord RONALD, My Reminiscences. Miniature Edition, printed on handmade paper, limp parchment antique, 10s. 6d.

Bric-à-Brac. Being some Photoprints illustrating Art Objects at Gower Lodge, Windsor. With Letterpress descriptions. Super roy. 8vo. 15s.; extra binding, 21s.

Last Days of Marie Antoinette: an Historical Sketch. With Portrait and Facsimiles. Fcap. 4to. 10s. 6d.

Notes of a Tour from Brindisi to Yokohama, 1883–1884. Fcp. 8vo. 2s. 6d.

Rupert of the Rhine: a Biographical Sketch of the Life of Prince Rupert. With 3 Portraits. Cr. 8vo. buckram, 6s.

Stafford House Letters. With 2 Portraits. 8vo. 10s. 6d.

GRAHAM, WILLIAM, The Creed of Science: Religious, Moral, and Social. Second Edition, revised. Cr. 8vo. 6s.
The Social Problem, in its Economic, Moral and Political Aspects. 8vo. 14s.
Socialism New and Old. Second Edition. Cr. 8vo. 5s. (I.S.S.)
GRAY, J., Ancient Proverbs and Maxims from Burmese Sources; or, The Niti Literature of Burma. Post 8vo. 6s. (Trübner's Oriental Series.)
GRAY, MAXWELL, In the Heart of the Storm. With Frontispiece by GORDON BROWNE. Cr. 8vo. 6s.
The Reproach of Annesley. Fifth Edition. With Frontispiece. Cr. 8vo. 6s.
Silence of Dean Maitland. Eighth Edition. With Frontispiece. Cr. 8vo. 6s.
Westminster Chimes, and other Poems. Sm. 8vo. 5s.
GREEN, F. W. EDRIDGE, Colour Blindness and Colour Perception. With 3 Coloured Plates. Cr. 8vo. 5s. (I.S.S.)
GREG, W. R., Literary and Social Judgments. Fourth Edition. 2 vols. Cr. 8vo. 15s.
The Creed of Christendom. Eighth Edition. 2 vols. post 8vo. 15s. (Philosophical Library).
Enigmas of Life. Seventeenth Edition. Post 8vo. 10s. 6d. (Philosophical Library).
Enigmas of Life. With a Prefatory Memoir. Edited by his WIFE. Nineteenth Edition. Cr. 8vo. 6s.
Political Problems for our Age and Country. 8vo. 10s. 6d.
Miscellaneous Essays. Two Series. Cr. 8vo. 7s. 6d. each.
GREY, ROWLAND, In Sunny Switzerland: a Tale of Six Weeks. Second Edition. Sm. 8vo. 5s.
Lindenblumen, and other Stories. Sm. 8vo. 5s.
By Virtue of His Office. Cr. 8vo. 6s.
Jacob's Letter, and other Stories. Cr. 8vo. 5s.
GRIFFIN, Sir Lepel, The Rajas of the Punjab: History of the Principal States in the Punjab, and their Political Relations with the British Government. Royal 8vo. 21s.
GRIFFIS, W. E., The Mikado's Empire. Book I. History of Japan from B.C. 660 to A.D. 1872. Book II. Personal Experiences, Observations, and Studies in Japan, 1870-1874. Second Edition, illustrated. 8vo. 20s.
Japanese Fairy World: Stories from the Wonder-Lore of Japan. With 12 Plates. Square 16mo. 3s. 6d.
GRIFFITH, R. T. H., Birth of the War-God: a Poem from the Sanskrit of KÁLIDASÁ. Second Edition. Post 8vo. 5s. (Trübner's Oriental Series).
Yúsef and Zulaikha: a Poem by JAMI. Translated from the Persian into English verse. Post 8vo. 8s. 6d. (Trübner's Oriental Series.)
GRIMLEY, H. N., The Prayer of Humanity: Sermons on the Lord's Prayer. Cr. 8vo. 3s. 6d.
Tremadoc Sermons, chiefly on the Spiritual Body, the Unseen World, and the Divine Humanity. Fourth Edition. Cr. 8vo. 6s.
The Temple of Humanity, and other Sermons. Cr. 8vo. 6s.
GRIMSHAW, R., Engine Runner's Catechism. A Sequel to the Author's 'Steam Engine Catechism.' Illustrated. 18mo. 8s. 6d.
GUBERNATIS, ANGELO DE, Zoological Mythology; or, The Legends of Animals. 2 vols. 8vo. £1. 8s.
GUICCIARDINI, FRANCESCO, Counsels and Reflections. Translated by N. H. Thomson. Cr. 8vo. 6s.
GURNEY, ALFRED, The Vision of the Eucharist, and other Poems. Cr. 8vo. 5s.
A Christmas Faggot. Sm. 8vo. 5s.
Voices from the Holy Sepulchre, and other Poems. Cr. 8vo. 5s.
Wagner's Parsifal: a Study. Second Edition. Fcp. 8vo. 1s. 6d.
Our Catholic Inheritance in the Larger Hope. Cr. 8vo. 1s. 6d.

HADDON, CAROLINE, The Larger Life: Studies in Hinton's Ethics. Cr. 8vo. 5s.

HAECKEL, Prof. ERNST, The History of Creation. Translation revised by Professor E. RAY LANKESTER, with 20 plates and numerous figures. Third Edition. 2 vols. Post 8vo. 32s.

The History of the Evolution of Man. With numerous Illustrations. 2 vols. Post 8vo. 32s.

A Visit to Ceylon. Post 8vo. 7s. 6d.

Freedom in Science and Teaching. With a Prefatory Note by Prof. T. H. HUXLEY. Cr. 8vo. 5s.

HAGGARD, A. C. P., Strange Tale of a Scarabæus, and other Poems. Cr. 8vo. 3s. 6d.

HAGGARD, H. RIDER, Cetywayo and His White Neighbours; or, Remarks on Recent Events in Zululand, Natal, and the Transvaal. Third Edition. Cr. 8vo. 6s.

HAGGARD, W. H., and **LE STRANGE, G.,** The Vazir of Lankuran: a Persian Play. With a Grammatical Introduction, Translation, Notes, and Vocabulary. Cr. 8vo. 10s. 6d.

HAHN, T., Tsuni-‖ Goam, the Supreme Being of the Khoi-Khoi. Post 8vo. 7s. 6d. (*Trübner's Oriental Series.*)

HALDEMAN, S. S., Pennsylvania Dutch: a Dialect of South Germany, with an infusion of English. 8vo. 3s. 6d.

HALLOCK, CHARLES, The Sportsman's Gazetteer and General Guide to the Game Animals, Birds, and Fishes of North America. Maps and Portrait. Cr. 8vo. 15s.

HAMILTON. Memoirs of Arthur Hamilton, B.A., of Trinity College, Cambridge. Cr. 8vo. 6s.

HARRIS, EMILY M., Narrative of the Holy Bible. Cr. 8vo. 5s.

HARRISON, CLIFFORD, In Hours of Leisure. Second Edition. Cr. 8vo. 5s.

HARRISON, Col. R., Officer's Memorandum Book for Peace and War. Fourth Edition, revised. Oblong 32mo. red basil, with pencil, 3s. 6d.

HARRISON, J. A., and **BASKERVILL, W.,** Handy Dictionary of Anglo-Saxon Poetry. Sq. 8vo. 12s.

HART, J. W. T., Autobiography of Judas Iscariot. A Character Study. Cr. 8vo. 3s. 6d.

HARTMANN, EDUARD von, Philosophy of the Unconscious. Translated by W. C. COUPLAND. 3 vols. Post 8vo. 31s. 6d. (*Philosophical Library.*)

HARTMANN, FRANZ, Magic, White and Black; or, The Science of Finite and Infinite Life. Cr. 8vo. 7s. 6d.

The Life of Paracelsus, and the Substance of his Teachings. Post 8vo. 10s. 6d.

Life and Doctrines of Jacob Boehme: an Introduction to the Study of his Works. Post 8vo. 10s. 6d.

HARTMANN, R., Anthropoid Apes. With 63 Illustrations. Second Edition. Cr. 8vo. 5s. (*I.S.S.*)

HARVEY, W. F., Simplified Grammar of the Spanish Language. Cr. 8vo. 3s. 6d.

HAUG, M., Essays on the Sacred Language, Writings, and Religion of the Parsis. Third Edition. Edited and Enlarged by E. W. WEST. Post 8vo. 16s. (*Trübner's Oriental Series.*)

HAWEIS, H. R., Current Coin. Materialism—The Devil—Crime—Drunkenness—Pauperism—Emotion—Recreation—The Sabbath. Sixth Edition. Cr. 8vo. 5s.
Arrows in the Air. Fifth Edition. Cr. 8vo. 5s.
Speech in Season. Sixth Edition. Cr. 8vo. 5s.
Thoughts for the Times. Fourteenth Edition. Cr. 8vo. 5s.
Unsectarian Family Prayers. Fourth Edition. Fcp. 8vo. 1s. 6d.
HAWTHORNE, NATHANIEL, Works. Complete in 12 vols. Large post 8vo. 7s. 6d. each.
HEAD, BARCLAY V., The Numismata Orientalia. Part III. The Coinage of Lydia and Persia, from the Earliest Times to the Fall of the Dynasty of the Achæmenidæ. With 3 Plates. Royal 4to. Paper wrapper, 10s. 6d.
HEALES, Major ALFRED, The Architecture of the Churches of Denmark. 8vo. 14s.
HEATH, FRANCIS GEORGE, Autumnal Leaves. With 12 Coloured Plates. Third and Cheaper Edition. 8vo. 6s.
Sylvan Winter. With 70 Illustrations. 14s.
HEATH, RICHARD, Edgar Quinet: His Early Life and Writings. With Portraits, Illustrations, and an Autograph Letter. Post 8vo. 12s. 6d. (*Philosophical Library.*)
HECKER, J. F. C., The Epidemics of the Middle Ages. Translated by G. B. BABINGTON. Third Edition. 8vo. 9s. 6d.
HEGEL'S Philosophy of Fine Art, The Introduction to, translated by BERNARD BOSANQUET. Cr. 8vo. 5s.
HEIDENHAIN, RUDOLPH, Hypnotism, or Animal Magnetism. With Preface by G. J. ROMANES. Second Edition. Sm. 8vo. 2s. 6d.
HEILPRIN, Prof. A., Bermuda Islands. 8vo. 18s.
Geographical and Geological Distribution of Animals. With Frontispiece. Cr. 8vo. 5s. (*I.S.S.*)
HEINE, H., Religion and Philosophy in Germany. Translated by J. SNODGRASS. Post 8vo. 6s. (*Philosophical Library.*)
HENDRIKS, DOM LAWRENCE, The London Charterhouse: its Monks and its Martyrs. Illustrated. 8vo. 15s.
HENEY, THOMAS, In Middle Harbour, and other Verse, chiefly Australian. Sm. cr. 8vo. 3s. 6d.
HENSLOW, Prof. G., Origin of Floral Structures through Insect and other Agencies. With 88 Illustrations. Cr. 8vo. 5s.
HEPBURN, J. C., Japanese and English Dictionary. Second Edition. Imp. 8vo. half-roan, 18s.
Japanese-English and English-Japanese Dictionary. Third Edition. Royal 8vo. half-morocco, cloth sides, 30s. Pocket Edition, square 16mo. 14s.
HERMES TRISMEGISTUS, Works. Translated by J. D. CHAMBERS. Post 8vo. 7s. 6d.
The Virgin of the World. Translated and Edited by the Authors of 'The Perfect Way.' Illustrations. 4to. imitation parchment, 10s. 6d.
HERSHON, P. J., Talmudic Miscellany; or, One Thousand and One Extracts from the Talmud, the Midrashim, and the Kabbalah. Post 8vo. 14s. (*Trübner's Oriental Series.*)
HILLEBRAND, KARL, France and the French in the Second Half of the 19th Century. From the third German Edition. Post 8vo. 10s. 6d.
HINTON. Life and Letters of James Hinton. With an Introduction by Sir W. W. GULL, and Portrait engraved on steel by C. H. JEENS. Sixth Edition. Cr. 8vo. 8s. 6d.
Philosophy and Religion. Selections from the Manuscripts of the late James Hinton. Edited by CAROLINE HADDON. Second Edition. Cr. 8vo. 5s.
The Law-Breaker and **The Coming of the Law.** Edited by MARGARET HINTON. Cr. 8vo. 6s.
The Mystery of Pain. New Edition. Fcp. 8vo. 1s.

HODGSON, B. H., Essays on the Languages, Literature, and Religion of Nepal and Tibet. Roy. 8vo. 14*s.*
Essays relating to Indian Subjects. 2 vols. Post 8vo. 28*s.* (*Trübner's Oriental Series.*)
HODGSON, J. E., Academy Lectures. Cr. 8vo. 7*s.* 6*d.*
HOLE, W. G., Amoris Imago. 16mo. 5*s.*
Procris, and other Poems. Fcp. 8vo. 3*s.* 6*d.*
HOLMES-FORBES, A. W., The Science of Beauty: an Analytical Inquiry into the Laws of Æsthetics. Second Edition. Post 8vo. 3*s.* 6*d.*
HOLMES, OLIVER WENDELL, John Lothrop Motley: a Memoir. Cr. 8vo. 6*s.*
Life of Ralph Waldo Emerson. With Portrait. English Copyright Edition. Cr. 8vo. 6*s.*
HOLTHAM, E. G., Eight Years in Japan, 1873-1881. With 3 Maps. Large Cr. 8vo. 9*s.*
HOMER'S Iliad. Greek Text, with Translation by J. G. CORDERY. 2 vols. 8vo. 14*s.* Translation only, cr. 8vo. 5*s.*
HOOPER, MARY, Little Dinners: How to Serve them with Elegance and Economy. Twenty-first Edition. Cr. 8vo. 2*s.* 6*d.*
Cookery for Invalids, Persons of Delicate Digestion, and Children. Fifth Edition. Cr. 8vo. 2*s.* 6*d.*
Every-day Meals: being Economical and Wholesome Recipes for Breakfast, Luncheon, and Supper. Seventh Edition. Cr. 8vo, 2*s.* 6*d.*
HOPKINS, ELLICE, Work amongst Working Men. Sixth Edition. Cr. 8vo. 3*s.* 6*d.*
HOPKINS, E. W., Ordinances of Manu. Translated from the Sanskrit. With an Introduction by the late A. C. BURNELL. Post 8vo. 12*s.* (*Trübner's Oriental Series.*)
HOPKINS, F. L., Elementary Grammar of the Turkish Language. With a few Easy Exercises. Cr. 8vo. 3*s.* 6*d.*
HORATIUS FLACCUS, Q., Opera. Edited by F. A. CORNISH. With Frontispiece. Elzevir 8vo. vellum, 7*s.* 6*d.*; parchment or cloth, 6*s.* (*Parchment Library.*)
HORNADAY, W. T., Two Years in a Jungle. With Illustrations. 8vo. 21*s.*
Taxidermy and Zoological Collecting; with Chapters on Collecting and Preserving Insects, by W. J. HOLLAND, D.D. With 24 Plates and 85 Illustrations. 8vo. 10*s.* 6*d.*
HOSPITALIER, E., The Modern Applications of Electricity. Translated and Enlarged by JULIUS MAIER. Second Edition, revised, with many Additions and Numerous Illustrations. 2 vols. 8vo. 25*s.*
HOWE, HENRY MARION, The Metallurgy of Steel. Vol. I. Second Edition, revised and enlarged. Royal 4to. £2. 12*s.* 6*d.*
HUGHES, H., Principles of Natural and Supernatural Morals. Vol. I. Natural Morals. 8vo. 12*s.* Vol. II. Supernatural Morals. 8vo. 12*s.*
HULME, F. EDWARD, Mathematical Drawing Instruments, and How to Use Them. With Illustrations. Fifth Edition, imperial 16mo, 3*s.* 6*d.*
HUMBOLDT, Baron W. von, The Sphere and Duties of Government. From the German by J. COULTHARD. Post 8vo, 5*s.*
HUNTER, HAY, and WHYTE, WALTER. My Ducats and My Daughter. With Frontispiece. Cr. 8vo. 6*s.*
HUNTER, Sir W. W., The Indian Empire: its History, People, and Products. Second Edition, revised, with Map. 8vo. £1. 1*s.* (*Trübner's Oriental Series.*)
Brief History of the Indian People. Fourth Edition, with Map. Cr. 8vo. 3*s.* 6*d.*
The Indian Musalmans. Third Edition. 8vo. 10*s.* 6*d.*
HUSMANN, G., American Grape Growing and Wine Making. Illustrated. 12mo. 7*s.* 6*d.*

HUTCHINSON, A. B., The Mind of Mencius; or, Political Economy founded upon Moral Philosophy. A Systematic Digest of the Doctrines of the Chinese Philosopher Mencius. Translated from the German of FABER, with Additional Notes. Post 8vo. 10s. 6d. (*Trübner's Oriental Series.*)

HUTCHINSON, Colonel, and MACGREGOR, Major, Military Sketching and Reconnaissance. Fifth Edition, with 16 Plates. Sm. cr. 8vo. 4s. (*Military Handbooks*.)

HUXLEY, Prof. T. H., The Crayfish: an Introduction to the Study of Zoology. With 82 Illustrations. Fifth Edition. Cr. 8vo. 5s. (*I.S.S.*)

IHNE, W., Latin Grammar for Beginners. Ahn's System. 12mo. 3s.

IM THURN, EVERARD F., Among the Indians of Guiana: Sketches, Chiefly Anthropologic, from the Interior of British Guiana. With 53 Illustrations and a Map. 8vo. 18s.

INGELOW, JEAN, Off the Skelligs: a Novel. With Frontispiece. Cr. 8vo. 6s.

INMAN, JAMES, Nautical Tables. Designed for the use of British Seamen. New Edition, revised and enlarged. 8vo. 16s.

IVANOFF'S Russian Grammar. Sixteenth Edition. Translated, Enlarged, and Arranged for use of Students by Major W. E. GOWAN. 8vo. 6s.

JACOB, G. A., Manual of Hindu Pantheism: the Vedântasâra. Third Edition, post 8vo. 6s. (*Trübner's Oriental Series.*)

JAPP, ALEXANDER H., Days with Industrials: Adventures and Experiences among Curious Industries. With Illustrations. Cr. 8vo. 6s.

JÄSCHKE, H. A., Tibetan Grammar. Prepared by Dr. H. WENZELL. Second Edition. Cr. 8vo. 5s.

JEAFFRESON, HERBERT H., The Divine Unity and Trinity. 8vo. 12s.

Magnificat: a Course of Sermons. With Frontispiece. Cr. 8vo. 2s. 6d.

JENKINS, E., A Modern Paladin: Contemporary Manners. Cr. 8vo. 5s.

JENKINS, E., and RAYMOND, J., Architect's Legal Handbook. Fourth Edition, revised. Cr. 8vo. 6s.

JENKINS, JABEZ, Vest-Pocket Lexicon. An English Dictionary of all except Familiar Words, including the principal Scientific and Technical Terms. 64mo. roan, 1s. 6d.; cloth, 1s.

JENKINS, Canon R. C., Heraldry, English and Foreign. With a Dictionary of Heraldic Terms and 156 Illustrations. Sm. 8vo. 3s. 6d.

JENNINGS, HARGRAVE, The Indian Religions; or, Results of the Mysterious Buddhism. 8vo. 10s. 6d.

JESSOP, C. MOORE, Saturn's Kingdom; or, Fable and Fact. Cr. 8vo. 6s.

Jesus, the Carpenter of Nazareth. By a LAYMAN. Second Edition, revised. Cr. 8vo. 5s. Also in Two Parts, price 2s. 6d. each.

JEVONS, W. STANLEY, Money and the Mechanism of Exchange. Ninth Edition. Cr. 8vo. 5s. (*I.S.S.*)

JOEL, L., Consul's Manual, and Shipowner's and Shipmaster's Practical Guide in their Transactions Abroad. 8vo. 12s.

JOHNSON, J. B., Theory and Practice of Surveying. Designed for use of Students in Engineering. Illustrated. Second Edition. 8vo. 15s.

JOHNSON, S. W., How Crops Feed: a Treatise on the Atmosphere and the Soil as related to Nutrition of Plants. Illustrated. Cr. 8vo. 10s.

How Crops Grow: a Treatise on the Chemical Composition, Structure, and Life of the Plant. Illustrated. Cr. 8vo. 10s.

JOHNSON, SAMUEL, Oriental Religions and their Relation to Universal Religion—Persia. 8vo. 18s.

Oriental Religions and their Relation to Universal Religion—India. 2 vols. 21s. (*Philosophical Library.*)

JOHNSTON, H. H., The Kilima-njaro Expedition: a Record of Scientific Exploration in Eastern Equatorial Africa. With 6 Maps and 80 Illustrations. 8vo. 21s.

History of a Slave. With 47 Illustrations. Square 8vo. 6s.

JOLLY, JULIUS, Naradiya Dharma-Sastra: or, The Institutes of Narada. Translated from the Sanskrit. Cr. 8vo. 10s. 6d.

Manava-Dharma-Castra: the Code of Manu. Original Sanskrit Text. With Critical Notes. Post 8vo. 10s. 6d. (*Trübner's Oriental Series.*)

JOLY, N., Man before Metals. With 148 Illustrations. Fourth Edition. Cr. 8vo. 5s. (*I.S.S.*)

JONCOURT, Madame MARIE DE, Wholesome Cookery. Fifth Edition. Cr. 8vo. cloth, 1s. 6d.; paper covers, 1s.

JORDAN, FURNEAUX, Character as seen in Body and Parentage. Cr. 8vo. boards, 2s.

Body, Parentage and Character in History: Notes on the Tudor Period. Cr. 8vo. boards, 2s.

JUDD, Prof. J. W., Volcanoes: what they are and what they teach. With 96 Illustrations on Wood. Fourth Edition. Cr. 8vo. 5s. (*I.S.S.*)

KARCHER, THÉODORE, Questionnaire Français: Questions on French Grammar, Idiomatic Difficulties, and Military Expressions. Fourth Edition. Cr. 8vo. 4s. 6d.; interleaved with writing paper, 5s. 6d.

KARMARSCH, KARL, Technological Dictionary. Fourth Edition, revised. Imp. 8vo. 3 vols.
Vol. 1.—German-English-French, 12s.
Vol. 2.—English-German-French, 12s.
Vol. 3.—French-German-English, 15s.

KAUFMANN, M., Socialism: its Nature, its Dangers, and its Remedies considered. Cr. 8vo. 7s. 6d.

Utopias; or, Schemes of Social Improvement, from Sir Thomas More to Karl Marx. Cr. 8vo. 5s.

Christian Socialism. Cr. 8vo. 4s. 6d.

KAY, JOSEPH, Free Trade in Land. Edited by his WIDOW. With Preface by Right Hon. JOHN BRIGHT. Seventh Edition. Cr. 8vo. 5s. Cheap Edition. Cloth, 1s. 6d.; paper covers, 1s.

KEATS, JOHN, Poetical Works. Edited by W. T. ARNOLD. Large Cr. 8vo. choicely printed on hand-made paper, with etched portrait, vellum, 15s.; parchment or cloth, 12s. Cheap edition, crown 8vo, cloth, 3s. 6d.

KEBLE, J., Christian Year. With Portrait. Elzevir 8vo. vellum, 7s. 6d.; parchment or cloth, 6s. (*Parchment Library.*)

KELKE, W. H. H., An Epitome of English Grammar. For the Use of Students. Adapted to London Matriculation Course. Cr. 8vo. 4s. 6d.

KEMPIS, THOMAS À, The Imitation of Christ. Revised Translation. Elzevir 8vo. (*Parchment Library*), vellum, 7s. 6d.; parchment or cloth, 6s. Red line Edition, fcp. 8vo. 2s. 6d. Cabinet Edition, sm. 8vo. 1s. 6d.; cloth limp, 1s. Miniature Edition, 32mo. with red lines, 1s. 6d.; without red lines, 1s.

A Metrical Version. By H. CARRINGTON. Cr. 8vo. 5s.

KENDALL, HENRY, The Kinship of Men: an Argument from Pedigrees; or, Genealogy viewed as a Science. With Diagrams. Cr. 8vo. 5s.

KENT, C. B. ROYLANCE, Essays in Politics. Cr. 8vo. 5s.

KETTLEWELL, S., Thomas à Kempis and the Brothers of Common Life. With Portrait. Cr. 8vo. 7s. 6d.

KHAYYÁM, OMAR, The Quatrains of. Persian Text, with an English Verse Translation. Post 8vo. 10s. 6d. Translation only, 5s. (*Trübner's Oriental Series.*)

KIDD, JOSEPH, Laws of Therapeutics. Second Edition. Cr. 8vo. 6s.
KINAHAN, G. H., Valleys and their Relation to Fissures, Fractures, and Faults. Cr. 8vo. 7s. 6d.
KING, Mrs. HAMILTON, The Disciples. Tenth Edition. Elzevir 8vo. 6s. ; sm. 8vo. 5s.
   A Book of Dreams. Third Edition. Cr. 8vo. 3s. 6d.
   Sermon in the Hospital (from 'The Disciples'). Fcp. 8vo. 1s. Cheap Edition, 3d.
   Ballads of the North, and other Poems. Cr. 8vo. 5s.
KINGSFORD, ANNA, The Perfect Way in Diet: a Treatise advocating a Return to the Natural and Ancient Food of our Race. Sixth Edition. Sm. 8vo. 2s.
   Spiritual Hermeneutics of Astrology and Holy Writ. Illustrated. 4to. parchment, 10s. 6d.
KINGSFORD, ANNA, and MAITLAND, EDWARD, The Virgin of the World of Hermes Mercurius Trismegistus, rendered into English. 4to. imit. parchment, 10s. 6d.
   The Perfect Way; or, The Finding of Christ. Third Edition, revised. Square 16mo. 7s. 6d.
KINGSFORD, W., History of Canada. 4 vols. 8vo. 15s. each.
KINGSLEY, J. S., Natural History. 'Riverside' Edition. With 2,200 Illustrations. 6 vols. 4to. £6. 6s.
KISTNA, OTTO, Buddha and His Doctrines: a Bibliographical Essay. 4to. 2s. 6d.
KITTON, FRED. G., John Leech, Artist and Humourist: a Biographical Sketch. 18mo. 1s.
KNOWLES, J. HINTON, Folk-Tales of Kashmir. Post 8vo. 16s. (*Trübner's Oriental Series.*)
KNOX, A. A., The New Playground; or, Wanderings in Algeria. New and Cheaper Edition. Large cr. 8vo. 6s.
KOLBE, F. W., A Language-Study based on Bantu: an Inquiry into the Laws of Root-formation. 8vo. 6s.
KRAMER, J., Pocket Dictionary of the Dutch Language. Fifth Edition. 16mo. 4s.
KRAPF, L., Dictionary of the Suahili Language. 8vo. 30s.
KRAUS, J., Carlsbad: its Thermal Springs and Baths, and how to use them. Fourth Edition, revised and enlarged. Cr. 8vo. 6s. 6d.
KUNZ, G. F., Gems and Precious Stones of North America. Illustrated with 8 Coloured Plates and numerous Engravings. Super-royal 8vo. £2. 12s. 6d.

LAGRANGE, F., Physiology of Bodily Exercise. Second Edition. Cr. 8vo. 5s. (*I.S.S.*)
LAIDLAW, SYDNEY, The Powers which Propel and Guide the Planets. With Comments. Cr. 8vo. 3s. 6d.
LANDON, JOSEPH, School Management; including a General View of the Work of Education, Organisation, and Discipline. Seventh Edition. Cr. 8vo. 6s. (*Education Library.*)
LANE, E. W., Selections from the Koran. New Edition, with Introduction by STANLEY LANE-POOLE. Post 8vo. 9s. (*Trübner's Oriental Series.*)
LANG, ANDREW, In the Wrong Paradise, and other Stories. Cr. 8vo. 6s.
   Ballades in Blue China. Elzevir 8vo. 5s.
   Rhymes à la Mode. With Frontispiece. Second Edition. Elzevir 8vo. 5s.
   Lost Leaders. Cr. 8vo. 5s.
LANGDON-DAVIES, C., An Explanation of the Phonophore, and more especially of the Simplex Phonophore Telegraph. 4to. 4s.

LANGE, Prof. F. A., History of Materialism, and Criticism of its present importance. Authorised Translation by ERNEST C. THOMAS. 3 vols. Post 8vo. 10s. 6d. each. (*Philosophical Library.*)

LANGE, F. K. W., German Grammar Practice. Cr. 8vo. 1s. 6d.
Colloquial German Grammar. Cr. 8vo. 4s. 6d.
Germania: a German Reading-book. Part I. Anthology of Prose and Poetry, with vocabulary. Part II. Essays on German History and Institutions. 8vo. 2 vols. 5s. 6d.; separately, 3s. 6d. each.

LANGSTROTH on the Hive and Honey Bee. Revised and Enlarged Edition. With numerous Illustrations. 8vo. 9s.

LARMOYER, M. de, Practical French Grammar. Cr. 8vo. Two Parts. 3s. 6d. each.

LARSEN, A., Dano-Norwegian Dictionary. Cr. 8vo, 10s. 6d.

LAURIE, S. S., Rise and Early Constitution of Universities. With a Survey of Mediæval Education. Cr. 8vo. 6s.

LEE, G., Manual of Politics. Sm. cr. 8vo. 2s. 6d.

LEE, MATTHEW HENRY, Diaries and Letters of Philip Henry, M.A., of Broad Oak, Flintshire. Cr. 8vo. 7s. 6d.

LEFEVRE, Right Hon. G. SHAW, Peel and O'Connell. 8vo. 10s. 6d.
Incidents of Coercion: a Journal of Visits to Ireland. Third Edition. Cr. 8vo. limp cloth, 1s. 6d.; paper covers, 1s.
Irish Members and English Gaolers. Cr. 8vo. limp cloth, 1s. 6d.; paper covers, 1s.
Combination and Coercion in Ireland: Sequel to 'Incidents of Coercion.' Cr. 8vo. cloth, 1s. 6d.; paper covers, 1s.

LEFFMANN, HENRY, and BEAM, W., Examination of Water for Sanitary and Technical Purposes. Second Edition, revised and enlarged. With Illustrations. Cr. 8vo. 5s.

LEGGE, J., Chinese Classics. Translated into English. Popular Edition. Cr. 8vo.
Vol. I. Life and Teachings of Confucius. 6th edition, 10s. 6d.
Vol. II. Works of Mencius. 12s.
Vol. III. She-King, or Book of Poetry, 12s.

LELAND, C. G., Breitmann Ballads. The only Authorised Edition. Including Nineteen Original Ballads, illustrating his Travels in Europe. Cr. 8vo. 6s. Cheap Edition, 3s. 6d. (*Lotos Series.*)
Gaudeamus: Humorous Poems from the German of JOSEPH VICTOR SCHEFFEL and others. 16mo. 3s. 6d.
English Gipsies and their Language. Second Edition. Cr. 8vo. 7s. 6d.
Fu-Sang; or, The Discovery of America by Chinese Buddhist Priests in the 5th Century. Cr. 8vo. 7s. 6d.
Pidgin-English Sing-Song; or, Songs and Stories in the China-English Dialect. Third Edition. Cr. 8vo. 5s.
The Gipsies. Cr. 8vo. 10s. 6d.

LEOPARDI, GIACOMO, Essays and Dialogues. Translated by CHARLES EDWARDES, with Biographical Sketch. Post 8vo. 7s. 6d. (*Philosophical Library.*)

LESLEY, J. P., Man's Origin and Destiny. Sketches from the Platform of the Physical Sciences. Second Edition. Cr. 8vo. 7s. 6d.

LESSING, GOTTHOLD E., Education of the Human Race. From the German by F. W. Robertson. Fcp. 8vo. 2s. 6d.

LEVI, Prof. LEONE, International Law, with Materials for a Code of International Law. Cr. 8vo. 5s. (*I.S.S.*)

LEWES, GEORGE HENRY, Problems of Life and Mind. 8vo.
Series I. Foundations of a Creed. 2 vols. 28s.
Series II. Physical Basis of Mind. With Illustrations, 16s.
Series III. The Study of Psychology. 2 vols. 22s. 6d.

Kegan Paul, Trench, Trübner, & Co.'s Publications. 29

Light on the Path. For the Personal Use of those who are Ignorant of the Eastern Wisdom. Written down by M. C. Fcp. 8vo. 1s. 6d.

LEYTON, F., Shadows of the Lake, and other Poems. Second Edition. Cr. 8vo. 5s.

LILLIE, ARTHUR, Popular Life of Buddha. Containing an Answer to the Hibbert Lectures of 1881. With Illustrations. Cr. 8vo. 6s.

Buddhism in Christendom; or, Jesus the Essene. With Illustrations. 8vo. 15s.

LILLY, W. S., Characteristics from the Writings of Cardinal Newman. Selections from his various Works. Eighth Edition. With Portrait. Cr. 8vo. 6s.

LINDSAY, Lady, Lyrics, and other Poems. Second Edition. Elzevir 8vo. 5s.

LINTON, W. J., Rare Poems of the 16th and 17th Centuries. Cr 8vo. 5s.

LINTON, W. J., and **STODDARD, R. H., English Verse.** CHAUCER TO BURNS— TRANSLATIONS—LYRICS OF THE NINETEENTH CENTURY—DRAMATIC SCENES AND CHARACTERS—BALLADS AND ROMANCES. 5 vols. Cr. 8vo. 5s. each.

LIOY, DIODATO, The Philosophy of Right, with special reference to the Principles and Development of Law. Translated from the Italian by W. HASTIE, B.D. 2 vols. Post 8vo. 21s. (*Philosophical Library.*)

LOCHER, CARL, Explanation of Organ Stops. With Hints for Effective Combinations. 8vo. 5s.

LOCKER, F., London Lyrics. Eleventh Edition. With Portrait. Elzevir 8vo. 5s.

LOCKHART, W., Life of Antonio Rosmini-Serbati. With Portraits. 2 vols. Cr. 8vo. 7s. 6d.

LOCKYER, J. NORMAN, Studies in Spectrum Analysis. With 6 Photographic Illustrations of Spectra, and numerous Engravings on Wood. Fourth Edition. Cr. 8vo. 6s. 6d. (*I.S.S.*)

LOMMEL, Dr. EUGENE, Nature of Light. With a General Account of Physical Optics. With 188 Illustrations and a Table of Spectra in Chromo-lithography. Fifth Edition. Cr. 8vo. 5s. (*I.S.S.*)

LONG, J., Eastern Proverbs and Emblems, illustrating Old Truths. Post 8vo. 6s. (*Trübner's Oriental Series.*)

LONGFELLOW. Life of H. Wadsworth Longfellow. By HIS BROTHER. With Portraits and Illustrations. 3 vols. 8vo. 42s.

LONSDALE, MARGARET, Sister Dora: a Biography. With Portrait. Thirtieth Edition. Small 8vo. 2s. 6d.

George Eliot: Thoughts upon her Life, her Books, and Herself. Second Edition. Small 8vo. 1s. 6d.

LOVAT, Lady, Seeds and Sheaves: Thoughts for Incurables. Cr. 8vo. 5s.

LOWDER. Charles Lowder: a Biography. By the Author of 'St. Teresa.' Twelfth Edition. With Portrait. Cr. 8vo. 3s. 6d.

LOWE, R. W., Thomas Betterton. Cr. 8vo. 2s. 6d. (*Eminent Actors.*)

LOWELL, JAMES RUSSELL, Biglow Papers. Edited by THOMAS HUGHES, Q.C. Fcp. 8vo. 2s. 6d.

LUBBOCK, Sir JOHN, Ants, Bees, and Wasps: a Record of Observations on the Habits of the Social Hymenoptera. With 5 Chromo-lithographic Plates. Tenth Edition. Cr. 8vo. 5s. (*I.S.S.*)

On the Senses, Instincts, and Intelligence of Animals. With Special Reference to Insects. With 118 Illustrations. Third Edition. Cr. 8vo. 5s. (*I.S.S.*)

LÜCKES, EVA C. E., Lectures on General Nursing, Delivered to the Probationers of the London Hospital Training School for Nurses. Third Edition. Cr. 8vo. 2s. 6d.

LUKIN, J., Amateur Mechanics' Workshop: Plain and Concise Directions for the Manipulation of Wood and Metals. Sixth Edition. Numerous Woodcuts. 8vo. 6*s.*

The Lathe and its Uses: or, Instruction in the Art of Turning Wood and Metal. Seventh Edition. Illustrated. 8vo. 10*s.* 6*d.*

Amongst Machines: a Description of Various Mechanical Appliances Used in the Manufacture of Wood, Metal, &c. A Book for Boys. Third Edition. With 64 Engravings. Cr. 8vo. 3*s.* 6*d.*

The Boy Engineers: What They Did, and How They Did It. A Book for Boys. With 30 Engravings. Third Edition. Imp. 16mo. 3*s.* 6*d.*

The Young Mechanic: a Book for Boys Containing Directions for the Use of all Kinds of Tools, and for the Construction of Steam-engines and Mechanical Models, including the Art of Turning in Wood and Metal. Seventh Edition. With 70 Engravings. Cr. 8vo. 3*s.* 6*d.*

LUYS, J., The Brain and its Functions. With Illustrations. Third Edition. Cr. 8vo. 5*s.* (*I.S.S.*)

LYALL, Sir ALFRED, Verses written in India. Second Edition. Elzevir 8vo. gilt top, 5*s.*

LYSCHINSKA, M. J., and MONTEFIORE, T. G., Froebel's Ethical Teaching: Two Essays. Fcp. 8vo. 2*s.* 6*d.*

LYTTON, Earl of, Life, Letters, and Literary Remains of Edward Bulwer, Lord Lytton. With Portraits, Illustrations, and Facsimiles. 8vo. 2 vols. 32*s.*

Lucile. Illustrated. 16mo. 4*s.* 6*d.*

MACAULAY'S Essays on Men and Books: Lord Clive, Milton, Earl of Chatham, Lord Byron. Edited by ALEX. II. JAPP. Pott 8vo. 3*s.* 6*d.* (*Lotos Series.*)

MacCARTHY, DENIS FLORENCE, Calderon's Dramas. Translated by. Post 8vo. 10*s.*

MACDONALD, D. C., Birthright in Land. Cr. 8vo. 7*s.* 6*d.*

MACDONALD, GEORGE, Malcolm. With Portrait of the Author engraved on Steel. Cr. 8vo. 6*s.* New and Cheaper Edition, 3*s.* 6*d.*

Castle Warlock. With Frontispiece. Cr. 8vo. 6*s.* New and Cheaper Edition, 3*s.* 6*d.*

There and Back. With Frontispiece. 6*s.*

Donal Grant. With Frontispiece. Cr. 8vo. 6*s.*

Home Again. With Frontispiece. Cr. 8vo. 6*s.*

The Marquis of Lossie. With Frontispiece. Cr. 8vo. 6*s.*

St. George and St. Michael. With Frontispiece. Cr. 8vo. 6*s.*

What's Mine's Mine. With Frontispiece. Cr. 8vo. 6*s.*

Annals of a Quiet Neighbourhood. With Frontispiece. Cr. 8vo. 6*s.*

The Seaboard Parish: a Sequel to 'Annals of a Quiet Neighbourhood.' With Frontispiece. Cr. 8vo. 6*s.*

Wilfred Cumbermede: an Autobiographical Story. With Frontispiece. Cr. 8vo. 6*s.*

Thomas Wingfold, Curate. With Frontispiece. Cr. 8vo. 6*s.*

Paul Faber, Surgeon. With Frontispiece. Cr. 8vo. 6*s.*

The Elect Lady. With Frontispiece. Cr. 8vo. 6*s.*

There and Back. With Frontispiece. Cr. 8vo. 6*s.*

Flight of the Shadow. With Frontispiece. Cr. 8vo. 6*s.*

MADDEN, F. W., The Numismata Orientalia. Vol. II. Coins of the Jews. Being a History of the Jewish Coinage and Money in the Old and New Testaments. With 279 Woodcuts and Plate. Royal 4to. £2.

McGRATH, TERENCE, Pictures from Ireland. New Edition. Cr. 8vo. 2*s.*

MACHIAVELLI, NICCOLÒ, Discourses on the First Decade of Titus Livius. From the Italian by N. HILL THOMPSON. Large cr. 8vo. 12*s.*

Kegan Paul, Trench, Trübner, & Co.'s Publications. 31

MACKAY, DONALD J.,. Bishop Forbes: a Memoir. With Portrait and Map. Cr. 8vo. 7s. 6d.

MACKAY, ERIC, A Lover's Litanies, and other Poems. With Portrait of Author. 3s. 6d. (*Lotos Series.*)

MAC KENNA, S. J., Plucky Fellows: a Book for Boys. With 6 Illustrations. Fifth Edition. Cr. 8vo. 3s. 6d.

MACKONOCHIE. Alexander Heriot Mackonochie: a Memoir. By E. A. T. Edited, with Preface, by E. F. RUSSELL. With Portrait and Views Large cr. 8vo. 7s. 6d. Cheap Edition, cr. 8vo. 3s. 6d.

MACNEILL, J. G. SWIFT, How the Union was Carried. Cr. 8vo. cloth, 1s. 6d. ; paper covers, 1s.

MACRITCHIE, DAVID, The Testimony of Tradition. With 20 Illustrations, 8vo. 7s. 6d.

MADDEN, F. W., Coins of the Jews; being a History of the Jewish Coinage and Money in the Old and New Testaments. With 279 Woodcuts and a Plate of Alphabets. Roy. 4to. £2. 2s.

MAGNUS, Lady, About the Jews since Bible times. Sm. Cr. 8vo. 6s.

MAGNUS, Sir PHILIP, Industrial Education. Cr. 8vo. 6s. (*Education Library.*)

MAGUIRE, W. R., Domestic Sanitary Drainage and Plumbing. 8vo. 12s.

MAHAFFY, Prof., Old Greek Education. Second Edition. Cr. 8vo. 3s. 6d. (*Education Library.*)

MAIMONIDES, Guide of the Perplexed. Translated and annotated by M. FRIEDLÄNDER. 3 vols. post 8vo. 31s. 6d. (*Philosophical Library.*)

MALET, LUCAS, Little Peter: a Christmas Morality for Children of any Age. With numerous Illustrations. Fourth Thousand. Imp. 16mo. 5s.

Colonel Enderby's Wife. With Frontispiece. Cr. 8vo. 6s.

A Counsel of Perfection. With Frontispiece. Cr. 8vo. 6s.

MALLET, Right Hon. Sir LOUIS, Free Exchange. Papers on Political and Economical Subjects, including Chapters on the Law of Value and Unearned Increment. Edited by BERNARD MALLET. 8vo. 12s.

MANNING. Towards Evening: Selections from the Writings of CARDINAL MANNING. Fifth Edition. 16mo. 2s.

Many Voices. Extracts from Religious Writers of Christendom from the 1st to the 16th Century. With Biographical Sketches. Cr. 8vo. 6s.

MARCHANT, W. T., In Praise of Ale: Songs, Ballads, Epigrams, and Anecdotes. Cr. 8vo. 10s. 6d.

MAREY, Prof. E. J., Animal Mechanism: a Treatise on Terrestrial and Aërial Locomotion. With 117 Illustrations. Third Edition. Cr. 8vo. 5s. (*I.S.S.*)

MARKHAM, Capt. ALBERT HASTINGS, R.N., The Great Frozen Sea: a Personal Narrative of the Voyage of the *Alert* during the Arctic Expedition of 1875-6. With Illustrations and Maps. Sixth and Cheaper Edition. Cr. 8vo. 6s.

MARSDEN, WILLIAM, Numismata Orientalia Illustrata. 57 Plates of Oriental Coins, from the Collection of the late WILLIAM MARSDEN, F.R.S., engraved from drawings made under his directions. 4to. 31s. 6d.

MARTIN, G. A., The Family Horse: its Stabling, Care, and Feeding. Cr. 8vo. 3s. 6d.

MARTINEAU, GERTRUDE, Outline Lessons on Morals. Sm. cr. 8vo. 3s. 6d.

MARTINEAU, HARRIET, The Positive Philosophy of Auguste Comte. Translated and condensed. Second Edition. 2 vols. post 8vo. 25s.

MARTINEAU, JAMES, Essays, Philosophical and Theological. 2 vols. cr. 8vo. £1. 4s.

MASON, CHARLOTTE M., Home Education: a Course of Lectures to Ladies. Cr. 8vo. 3s. 6d.

MASON, Capt. F. H., **Life and Public Service of James A. Garfield, President U.S.A.** With a Preface by BRET HARTE. Portrait. Cr. 8vo. 2s. 6d.

MASON, ERNEST, **Womanhood in the God-man.** Cr. 8vo. 6s.

MATHER, G., and BLAGG, C. J., **Bishop Rawle**: a Memoir. Large cr. 8vo. 7s. 6d.

MATHERS, S. L. M., **The Key of Solomon the King.** Translated from ancient MSS. in the British Museum. With Plates. Cr. 4to. 25s.

The Kabbalah Unveiled. Containing the Three Books of the Zohar, translated from the Chaldee and Hebrew Text. Post 8vo. 10s. 6d.

The Tarot: its Occult Signification, use in Fortune-telling, and method of Play. With pack of 78 Tarot Cards, 5s.; without the Cards, 1s. 6d.

MATUCE, H. OGRAM, **A Wanderer.** Cr. 8vo. 5s.

MAUDSLEY, H., **Body and Will**: an Essay concerning Will, in its Metaphysical, Physiological, and Pathological Aspects. 8vo. 12s.

Natural Causes and Supernatural Seemings. Second Edition. Cr. 8vo. 6s.

Responsibility in Mental Disease. Fourth Edition. Cr. 8vo. 5s. (*I.S.S.*)

MAXWELL, W. E., **Manual of the Malay Language.** Second Edition. Cr. 8vo. 7s. 6d.

MEAD, C. M., D.D., **Supernatural Revelation**: an Essay concerning the basis of the Christian Faith. Royal 8vo. 14s.

MEAKIN, J. E. BUDGETT, **Introduction to the Arabic of Morocco.** English-Arabic Vocabulary, Grammar, Notes, &c. Fcp. 8vo. 6s.

Meditations on Death and Eternity. Translated from the German by FREDERICA ROWAN. Published by Her Majesty's gracious permission. Cr. 8vo. 6s.

Meditations on Life and its Religious Duties. Translated from the German by FREDERICA ROWAN. Published by Her Majesty's gracious permission. Cr. 8vo. 6s.

MEDLICOTT, H. B., **The Evolution of Mind in Man.** 8vo. 1s.

MENDELSSOHN'S **Letters to Ignaz and Charlotte Moscheles.** Translated by FELIX MOSCHELES. Numerous Illustrations and Facsimiles. 8vo. 12s.

MERRILL, G. P., **Stones for Building and Decoration.** Royal 8vo. 21s.

MEYER, G. HERMANN von, **Organs of Speech and their Application in the Formation of Articulate Sounds.** With 47 Illustrations. Cr. 8vo. 5s. (*I.S.S.*)

MEYNELL, WILFRID, **John Henry Newman, the Founder of Modern Anglicanism, and a Cardinal of the Roman Church.** Cr. 8vo. 2s. 6d.

MILL, JOHN STUART, **Auguste Comte and Positivism.** Third Edition. Post 8vo. 3s. 6d. (*Philosophical Library.*)

MILLER, EDWARD, **The History and Doctrines of Irvingism**; or, The So-called Catholic and Apostolic Church. 2 vols. Large post 8vo. 15s.

MILLER, ELLEN E., **Alone Through Syria.** With Introduction by Prof. A. H. SAYCE. With 8 Illustrations. Second Edition. Cr. 8vo. 5s.

MILLHOUSE, JOHN, **Italian Dictionary.** 2 vols. 8vo. 12s.

Manual of Italian Conversation. 18mo. 2s.

MILLS, HERBERT, **Poverty and the State**; or, Work for the Unemployed. Cr. 8vo. 6s.; cheap edition, limp cloth, 1s. 6d.; paper covers, 1s.

MILNE, Prof. J., **Earthquakes and other Earth Movements.** With 38 Figures. Second Edition. Cr. 8vo. 5s. (*I.S.S.*)

MILTON, JOHN, **Prose Writings.** Edited by E. MYERS. Elzevir 8vo. vellum, 7s. 6d.; parchment or cloth, 6s. (*Parchment Library.*)

Poetical Works. 2 vols. elzevir 8vo. vellum, 7s. 6d.; parchment or cloth, 6s. (*Parchment Library.*)

Sonnets. Edited by MARK PATTISON. With Portrait. Elzevir 8vo. vellum, 7s. 6d.; parchment or cloth, 6s. (*Parchment Library.*)

MITCHELL, E. H., Forty Days in the Holy Land. With 6 Illustrations. Cr. 8vo. 6s.

MITCHELL, LUCY M., History of Ancient Sculpture. With Numerous Illustrations. Super-royal 8vo. 42s.

MIVART, ST. GEORGE, On Truth. 8vo. 16s.
Origin of Human Reason. 8vo. 10s. 6d.

MOLTKE, Count Von, Notes of Travel. Cr. 8vo. 2s. 6d.

MONCEL, Count DU, The Telephone, the Microphone, and the Phonograph. With 74 Illustrations. 3rd Edition. Sm. 8vo. 5s.

MONIER-WILLIAMS, Sir M., Modern India and the Indians: a Series of Impressions, Notes, and Essays. Fifth Edition. Post 8vo. 14s. (*Trübner's Oriental Series.*)

MOORE, AUBREY L., Essays, Scientific and Philosophical. With Memoir of the Author. Cr. 8vo. 6s.
Lectures and Papers on the History of the Reformation in England and on the Continent. 8vo. 16s.
Science and the Faith: Essays on Apologetic Subjects. Cr. 8vo. 6s.

MOORE, T. W., Treatise and Handbook of Orange Culture in Florida, Louisiana, and California. Fourth Edition Enlarged. 18mo. 5s.

MORFILL, W. R., Simplified Grammar of the Polish Language. Cr. 8vo. 3s. 6d.
Simplified Serbian Grammar. Crown 8vo. 4s. 6d.

MORFIT, CAMPBELL, Manufacture of Soaps. With Illustrations. 8vo. £2. 12s. 6d.
Pure Fertilizers, and the Chemical Conversion of Rock Guanos, &c., into various Valuable Products. With 28 Plates. 8vo. £4. 4s.

MORISON, J. COTTER, The Service of Man: an Essay towards the Religion of the Future. Cr. 8vo. 5s.

MORRIS. Diary and Letters of Gouverneur Morris, Minister of the U.S. to France. With Portraits. 2 vols. 8vo. 30s.

MORRIS, HENRY, Simplified Grammar of the Telugu Language. With Map of India showing Telugu Country. Cr. 8vo. 10s. 6d.

MORRIS, LEWIS, Poetical Works. New and Cheaper Edition. 5 vols. fcap. 8vo. 5s. each.
Songs of Two Worlds. Thirteenth Edition. Fcap. 8vo. 5s.
The Epic of Hades. Twenty-fifth Edition. Fcap. 8vo. 5s.
Gwen, and the Ode of Life. Ninth Edition. Fcap. 8vo. 5s.
Songs Unsung, and Gycia. Fifth Edition. Fcap. 8vo. 5s.
Songs of Britain. Fourth Edition. Fcap. 8vo. 5s.
Poetical Works. Sixth Thousand. In 1 vol. cr. 8vo. 6s. Cloth extra, gilt edges, 7s. 6d.
The Epic of Hades. With 16 Autotype Illustrations, after the Drawings of the late GEORGE R. CHAPMAN. 4to. cloth extra, gilt edges, 21s.
The Epic of Hades. Presentation Edition. 4to. cloth extra, gilt edges, 10s. 6d. Elzevir Edition, 6s.
A Vision of Saints. Fcap. 8vo. 6s.
Birthday Book. Edited by S. S. COPEMAN. With Frontispiece. 32mo. cloth extra, gilt edges, 2s.; cloth limp, 1s. 6d.

MORSE, E. S., First Book of Zoology. With numerous Illustrations. New Edition. Cr. 8vo. 2s. 6d.

MORSELLI, Prof. H., Suicide: an Essay on Comparative Moral Statistics. Second Edition, with Diagrams. Cr. 8vo. 5s. (*I.S S.*)

MOSENTHAL, J. De, and **HARTING, JAMES E., Ostriches and Ostrich Farming.** Second Edition. With 8 full-page Illustrations and 20 woodcuts, royal 8vo. 10s. 6d.

MUIR, JOHN, Original Sanskrit Texts, on the Origin and History of the People of India. 5 vols. 8vo.
Mythical and Legendary Accounts of the Origin of Caste. Third Edition. £1. 1s. Also issued as a volume of *Trübner's Oriental Series*, at the same price.
The Trans-Himalayan Origin of the Hindus. Second Edition. £1. 1s.
The Vedas. Second Edition. 16s.
Comparison of the Vedic with the Principal Indian Deities. Second Edition. £1. 1s.
Cosmogony, Mythology, &c., of the Indians in the Vedic Age. Third Edition. £1. 1s.
Metrical Translations from Sanskrit Writers. Post 8vo. 14s. (*Trübner's Oriental Series.*)

MULHOLLAND, ROSA, Marcella Grace: an Irish Novel. Cr. 8vo. 6s.
A Fair Emigrant. With Frontispiece. Cr. 8vo. 6s.

MÜLLER, E., Simplified Grammar of the Pali Language. Cr. 8vo. 7s. 6d.

MÜLLER, F. MAX, Outline Dictionary, for the Use of Missionaries, Explorers, and Students of Language. 12mo. morocco, 7s. 6d.
Sacred Hymns of the Brahmins, as preserved in the oldest Collection of Religious Poetry, the Rig-Veda-Sanhita. Vol. I. Hymns to the Maruts, or the Storm-Gods. 8vo. 12s. 6d.
Hymns of the Rig-Veda, in the Sanhita and Pada Texts. 2 vols. Second Edition. 8vo. £1. 1s.

Munchausen's Travels and Surprising Adventures. Illustrated by ALFRED CROWQUILL. 3s. 6d. (*Lotos Series.*)

My Lawyer; or, the People's Legal Adviser. A Concise Abridgement of and Popular Guide to the Laws of England. By a BARRISTER-AT-LAW. Second Edition. Cr. 8vo. 6s. 6d.

NARADIYA DHARMA-SASTRA; or, The Institutes of Narada. Translated by Dr. JULIUS JOLLY. Cr. 8vo. 10s. 6d.

Navy in the Civil War (American). 3 vols. 5s. each.

NEWHOUSE, S., Trapper's Guide; a Manual of Instructions for Capturing all Kinds of Fur-bearing Animals, and Curing their Skins, &c. Eighth, Revised Edition. 8vo. 5s.

NEWMAN. Characteristics from the Writings of Cardinal Newman. Selections from his various Works, arranged by W. S. LILLY. Eighth Edition. With Portrait. Cr. 8vo. 6s.
*** Portrait of the late Cardinal Newman, mounted for framing, 2s. 6d.

NEWMAN, F. W., Comments on the Text of Æschylus and Euripides. 8vo. 6s.
Supplement to Studies in Æschylus and Notes on Euripides. 6s.
Miscellanies. 8vo. Vol. I., Chiefly Addresses, Academical and Historical, 7s. 6d. Vol. II., Essays, Tracts or Addresses, Moral and Religious, 12s. Vol. III., Essays, Tracts or Addresses, Political and Social, 12s. Vol. IV., Political Economy, or The Science of the Market, especially as affected by Local Law, 10s. 6d. Vol. V., chiefly Academic, 12s.
Phases of Faith; or, Passages from the History of my Creed. Cr. 8vo. 3s. 6d.
The Soul: her Sorrows and her Aspirations. Tenth Edition. Post 8vo. 3s. 6d.
A Handbook of Modern Arabic. Post 8vo. 6s.
Dictionary of Modern Arabic. Anglo-Arabic and Arabo-English. 2 vols. Cr. 8vo. £1. 1s.
Contributions, chiefly to the Early History of the late Cardinal Newman. Cr. 8vo. 3s. 6d.

NICOLS, ARTHUR, Chapters from the Physical History of the Earth: an Introduction to Geology and Palæontology. With numerous Illustrations. Cr. 8vo. 5*s*.

NILSSON, L. G., WIDMARK, P. F., and COLLIN, A. Z., Swedish Dictionary. New Edition. 8vo. 16*s*.

NOEL, Hon. RODEN, Essays on Poetry and Poets. 8vo. 12*s*.

A Little Child's Monument. Third Edition. Sm. cr. 3*s*. 6*d*.

A Modern Faust, and other Poems. Sm. cr. 8vo. 5*s*.

NOIRIT, JULES, French Course in Ten Lessons. Cr. 8vo. 1*s*. 6*d*.

French Grammatical Questions, for the use of Gentlemen preparing for the Army, Civil Service, Oxford Examinations, &c. Cr. 8vo. 1*s*.; interleaved, 1*s*. 6*d*.

NOPS, M., Class Lessons on Euclid. Cr. 8vo. 2*s*. 6*d*.

Notes on Cavalry Tactics, Organisation, &c. By a CAVALRY OFFICER. With Diagrams. 8vo. 12*s*.

NUGENT'S French Pocket Dictionary. 24mo. 3*s*.

Numismata Orientalia (The), Royal 4to. in Paper Wrapper. Part I. Ancient Indian Weights, by E. THOMAS, with a Plate and Map, 9*s*. 6*d*. Part II. Coins of the Urtuki Turkumáns, by S. LANE POOLE, with 6 Plates, 9*s*. Part III. Coinage of Lydia and Persia, by BARCLAY V. HEAD, with 3 Plates, 10*s*. 6*d*. Part IV. Coins of the Tuluni Dynasty, by E. T. ROGERS, with 1 Plate, 5*s*. Part V. Parthian Coinage, by PERCY GARDNER, with 8 Plates, 18*s*. Part VI. Ancient Coins and Measures of Ceylon, by T. W. RHYS DAVIDS, with 1 Plate, 10*s*.

Vol. I. containing Six Parts, as specified above, half-bound, £3. 13*s*. 6*d*.

Vol. II. **Coins of the Jews:** being a History of the Jewish Coinage in the Old and New Testaments. By F. W. MADDEN. With 279 Woodcuts and Plate. Royal 4to. £2.

Vol. III. Part I. **The Coins of Arakan, of Pegu, and of Burma.** By Lieut.-General Sir ARTHUR PHAYRE. Also contains the Indian Balhara, and the Arabian Intercourse with India in the Ninth and following Centuries. By EDWARD THOMAS. With 5 Illustrations. Royal 4to. 8*s*. 6*d*.

Vol. III. Part II. **The Coins of Southern India.** By Sir W. ELLIOT. With Map and Plates. Royal 4to. 25*s*.

OATES, FRANK, Matabele Land and the Victoria Falls: a Naturalist's Wanderings in the Interior of South Africa. Edited by C. G. OATES. With numerous Illustrations and 4 Maps. Second Edition. 8vo. 21*s*.

O'BRIEN, R. BARRY, Irish Wrongs and English Remedies, with other Essays. Cr. 8vo. 5*s*.

Home Ruler's Manual. Cr. 8vo. cloth, 1*s*. 6*d*.; paper covers, 1*s*.

Life and Letters of Thomas Drummond, Under-Secretary in Ireland, 1835-40. 8vo. 14*s*.

O'CONNELL, Mrs. MORGAN J., The Last Colonel of the Irish Brigade, Count O'Connell, and Old Irish Life at Home and Abroad, 1745-1833. 2 vols. 8vo. 25*s*.

O'CONNOR, EVANGELINE, Index to Shakspere's Works. Cr. 8vo. 5*s*.

OLCOTT, Colonel, Posthumous Humanity: a Study of Phantoms, from the French of Adolphe D'Assier. With Appendix and Notes. Cr. 8vo. 7*s*. 6*d*.

Theosophy, Religion, and Occult Science, with Glossary of Eastern words. Cr. 8vo. 7*s*. 6*d*.

OLLENDORFF. Metodo para aprender a Leer, escribir y hablar el Inglés, segun el sistema de Ollendorff. 8vo. 7*s*. 6*d*. Key, 4*s*.

Metodo para aprender a Leer, escribir y hablar el Frances, segun el sistema de Ollendorff. Cr. 8vo. 6*s*. Key, 3*s*. 6*d*.

OMAN, F. G., Swedish Dictionary. Cr. 8vo. 8*s*.

O'MEARA, KATHLEEN, Henri Perreyve and his Counsels to the Sick. Sm. cr. 8vo. 5s.

One-and-a-Half in Norway. By EITHER and BOTH. Sm. cr. 8vo. 3s. 6d.

OTTÉ E. C., Dano-Norwegian Grammar: a Manual for Students of Danish, based on the Ollendorffian System. Third Edition. Cr. 8vo. 7s. 6d. Key, 3s.

Simplified Grammar of the Danish Language. Cr. 8vo. 2s. 6d.

Simplified Grammar of the Swedish Language. Cr. 8vo. 2s. 6d.

OWEN, ROBERT DALE, Footfalls on the Boundary of another World. With Narrative Illustrations. Post 8vo. 7s. 6d.

Debatable Land between this World and the Next. With Illustrative Narrations. Second Edition. Cr. 8vo. 7s. 6d.

Threading My Way: Twenty-seven Years of Autobiography. Cr. 8vo. 7s. 6d.

PALGRAVE, W. GIFFORD, Hermann Agha: an Eastern Narrative. Third Edition. Cr. 8vo. 6s.

PALMER, E. H., English-Persian Dictionary. With Simplified Grammar of the Persian Language. Royal 16mo. 10s. 6d.

Persian-English Dictionary. Second Edition. Royal 16mo. 10s. 6d.

Simplified Grammar of Hindustani, Persian, and Arabic. Second Edition. Cr. 8vo. 5s.

Papers relating to Indo-China. Reprinted from Dalrymple's 'Oriental Repertory,' 'Asiatic Researches,' and the 'Journal' of the Asiatic Society of Bengal. Post 8vo. 2 vols. 21s.

MISCELLANEOUS ESSAYS ON SUBJECTS CONNECTED WITH THE MALAY PENINSULA AND THE INDIAN ARCHIPELAGO. From the Journals of the Royal Asiatic, Royal Geographical Societies, &c. Edited by R. ROST. With 5 Plates and a Map. Second Series, 2 vols. 25s. (*Trübner's Oriental Series.*)

PARAVICINI, FRANCES de, Early History of Balliol College. 8vo. 12s.

PARKER, G. W., Concise Grammar of the Malagasy Language. Cr. 8vo. 5s.

PARKER, THEODORE, Discourse on Matters pertaining to Religion. People's Edition. Cr. 8vo. cloth, 2s.; paper covers, 1s. 6d.

Collected Works of Theodore Parker, Minister of the Twenty-eighth Congregational Society at Boston, U.S. 14 vols. Cr. 8vo. 6s. each.

PARRY, EDWARD ABBOTT, Charles Macklin. Cr. 8vo. 2s. 6d. (*Eminent Actors.*)

PARRY, E. GAMBIER, Biography of Reynell Taylor, C.B., C.S.I. With Portrait and Map. 8vo. 14s.

PARSLOE, JOSEPH, Our Railways: Sketches, Historical and Descriptive. With Information as to Fares and Rates, &c. Cr. 8vo. 6s.

PASCAL, BLAISE, Thoughts. Translated by C. KEGAN PAUL. Large cr. 8vo. Parchment, 12s.; vellum, 15s. Cheap edition. Cr. 8vo. 6s.

PATON, A. A., History of the Egyptian Revolution, from the Period of the Mamelukes to the Death of Mohammed Ali. Second Edition. 2 vols. 8vo. 7s. 6d.

PAUL, ALEXANDER, Short Parliaments. History of National Demand for Frequent General Elections. Sm. cr. 8vo. 3s. 6d.

PAUL, C. KEGAN, Faith and Unfaith, and other Essays. Cr. 8vo. 7s. 6d.

Biographical Sketches. Second Edition. Cr. 8vo. 7s. 6d.

Confessio Viatoris. Fcp. 8vo. 2s.

Thoughts of Blaise Pascal. Translated. Large cr. 8vo. Parchment, 12s.; vellum, 15s. Cheap Edition, cr. 8vo. 6s.

Paul of Tarsus. By the Author of 'Rabbi Jeshua.' Cr. 8vo. 4s. 6d.

PAULI, REINHOLD, Simon de Montfort, Earl of Leicester, the Creator of the House of Commons. Cr. 8vo. 6s.

PEMBERTON, T. EDGAR, Charles Dickens and the Stage: a Record of his Connection with the Drama. Cr. 8vo. 6s.

PERRY, ARTHUR LATHAM, Principles of Political Economy. Large post 8vo. 9s.

PESCHEL, OSCAR, The Races of Man and their Geographical Distribution. Second Edition. Large cr. 8vo. 9s.

PETTIGREW, J. B., Animal Locomotion; or, Walking, Swimming, and Flying. With 130 Illustrations. Third Edition. Cr. 8vo. 5s. (*I.S.S.*)

PHAYRE, Lieut.-Gen. Sir A., History of Burma. Including Burma Proper, Pegu, Taungu, Tenasserim, and Arakan, from the Earliest Time to the end of the First War with British India. Post 8vo. 14s. (*Trübner's Oriental Series.*)

PHAYRE, Lieut.-Gen. Sir A., and THOMAS, E., Coins of Arakan, of Pegu, and of Burma. With 5 Illustrations. Royal 4to. 8s. 6d. (*Numismata Orientalia.*)

PHILLIPS, W., Manual of British Discomycetes. With Descriptions of all the Species of Fungi hitherto found in Britain included in the Family, and Illustrations of the Genera. Cr. 8vo. 5s. (*I.S.S.*)

'PHYSICUS,' Candid Examination of Theism. Second Edition. Post 8vo. 7s. 6d. (*Philosophical Library.*)

PICARD, A., Pocket Dictionary of the Dutch Language. Fifth Edition. 16mo. 10s.

PICCIOTTO, JAMES, Sketches of Anglo-Jewish History. 8vo. 12s.

PICKFORD, JOHN, Maha-vira-Charita; or, the Adventures of the Great Hero Rama. From the Sanskrit of BHAVABHÚTI. Cr. 8vo. 5s.

PIESSE, C. H., Chemistry in the Brewing Room: a Course of Lessons to Practical Brewers. Fcp. 8vo. 5s.

PLIMSOLL, SAMUEL, Cattle Ships. Being the Fifth Chapter of 'An Appeal for our Seamen.' With 46 Illustrations. Cr. 8vo. 5s.; Cheap Edition, paper covers, 1s.

PLOWRIGHT, C. B., British Uredineæ and Ustilagineæ. With Illustrations. 8vo. 10s. 6d.

PLUMPTRE, C. J., Lectures on Elocution, delivered at King's College. Fourth Edition. Post 8vo. 15s.

POE, EDGAR ALLAN, Poems. Edited by ANDREW LANG. With Frontispiece. Elzevir 8vo. vellum, 7s. 6d.; parchment or cloth, 6s. (*Parchment Library.*)

The Raven. With Commentary by JOHN H. INGRAM. Cr. 8vo. parchment, 6s.

POLE, W., Philosophy of Music. Lectures delivered at the Royal Institution. Second Edition. Post 8vo. 7s. 6d. (*Philosophical Library.*)

POLLEN, JOHN, Rhymes from the Russian. Translations from the best Russian Poets. Cr. 8vo. 3s. 6d.

PONSARD, F., Charlotte Corday: a Tragedy. Edited by Professor C. CASSAL. Third Edition. 12mo. 2s. 6d.

L'Honneur et l'Argent: a Comedy. Edited by Professor C. CASSAL. Second Edition. 12mo. 3s. 6d.

PONTOPIDDAN, HENRIK, The Apothecary's Daughters. Translated from the Danish by GORDIUS NIELSEN. Cr. 8vo. 3s. 6d.

POOLE, STANLEY LANE, The Numismata Orientalia. Part II. Coins of the Urtuki Turkumáns. With 6 Plates. Royal 4to. Paper wrapper, 9s.

POOLE, W. F., Index to Periodical Literature. Revised Edition. Royal 8vo. £3. 16s. FIRST SUPPLEMENT, 1882 to 1887. Royal 8vo. £1. 16s.

POSNETT, H. M., Comparative Literature. Crown 8vo. 5s. (*I.S.S.*)

POULTON, E. B., Colours of Animals: their Meaning and Use, especially considered in the case of Insects. With Coloured Frontispiece and 66 Illustrations in Text. Cr. 8vo. 5s. (*I.S.S.*)

Practical Guides, to see all that ought to be seen in the shortest period and at the least expense. 113th Thousand, Illustrated. Sm. 8vo. paper covers. France, Belgium, Holland, and the Rhine, 1s. Italian Lakes, 1s. Wintering Places of the South, 2s. Switzerland, Savoy, and North Italy, 2s. 6d. General Continental Guide, 5s. Geneva, 1s. Paris, 1s. Bernese Oberland, 1s. Italy, 4s.

PRATT, GEORGE, Grammar and Dictionary of the Samoan Language. Second Edition. Cr. 8vo. 18s.

PRATT, Lieut.-Colonel S. C., Field Artillery: its Equipment, Organisation, and Tactics. Fourth Edition. Sm. cr. 8vo. 6s. (*Military Handbooks.*)

Military Law: its Procedure and Practice. Sixth revised Edition. Sm. cr. 8vo. 4s. 6d. (*Military Handbooks.*)

PREL, CARL DU, Philosophy of Mysticism. Translated from the German by C. C. Massey. 2 vols. 8vo. cloth, 25s.

PRICE, Prof. BONAMY, Chapters on Practical Political Economy. New Edition. Cr. 8vo. 5s.

PRIG, The Prigment: 'The Life of a Prig,' 'Prig's Bede,' 'How to Make a Saint,' 'Black is White.' Second Edition. In 1 vol. Cr. 8vo. 6s.

A Romance of the Recusants. Cr. 8vo. 5s.

Dulce Domum. Fcap. 8vo. 5s.

Black is White; or, Continuity Continued. Second Edition. Fcp. 8vo. 3s. 6d.

Prig's Bede: the Venerable Bede Expurgated, Expounded, and Exposed. Second Edition. Fcp. 8vo. 3s. 6d.

PRIOR, MATTHEW, Selected Poems. Edited by Austin Dobson. Elzevir 8vo. vellum, 7s. 6d.; parchment or cloth, 6s. (*Parchment Library.*)

Professor, The, and other Poems. By the Author of 'Moods' &c. Cr. 8vo. 5s.

PROTHERO, G. W., Henry Bradshaw: a Memoir, with Portrait and Facsimile. 8vo. 16s.

PROWER, NELSON, Reggie Abbot: an Historical Romance. 8vo. 6s.

Psalms of the West. Second Edition. Sm. 8vo. 1s. 6d.

Pulpit Commentary, The (Old Testament Series). Edited by the Very Rev. Dean H. D. M. Spence, D.D., and the Rev. J. S. Exell. Super royal 8vo.
  Genesis, by the Rev. T. Whitelaw, D.D.; Homilies by the Very Rev. J. F. Montgomery, D.D., Rev. Prof. R. A. Redford, Rev. F. Hastings, Rev. W. Roberts; Introduction to the Study of the Old Testament, by Ven. Archdeacon Farrar, D.D.; Introductions to the Pentateuch, by the Right Rev. H. Cotterill, D.D., and Rev. T. Whitelaw, D.D. Ninth Edition. 15s.
  Exodus, by the Rev. Canon Rawlinson; Homilies by the Rev. J. Orr, D.D., Rev. D. Young, Rev. C. A. Goodhart, Rev. J. Urquhart, and the Rev. H. T. Robjohns. Fifth Edition. 2 vols. 9s. each.
  Leviticus, by the Rev. Prebendary Meyrick; Introductions by the Rev. R. Collins, Rev. Professor A. Cave; Homilies by the Rev. Prof. Redford, Rev. J. A. Macdonald, Rev. W. Clarkson, Rev. S. R. Aldridge, and Rev. McCheyne Edgar. Fourth Edition. 15s.
  Numbers, by the Rev. R. Winterbotham; Homilies by the Rev. Prof. W. Binnie, D.D., Rev. E. S. Prout, Rev. D. Young, Rev. J. Waite; Introduction by the Rev. Thomas Whitelaw, D.D. Fifth Edition. 15s.
  Deuteronomy, by the Rev. W. L. Alexander, D.D.; Homilies by the Rev. C. Clemance, D.D., Rev. J. Orr, D.D., Rev. R. M. Edgar, Rev. J. D. Davies. Fourth Edition. 15s.
  Joshua, by the Rev. J. J. Lias; Homilies by the Rev. S. R. Aldridge, Rev. R. Glover, Rev. E. de Pressensé, D.D., Rev. J. Waite, Rev. W. F. Adeney; Introduction by the Rev. A. Plummer, D.D. Sixth Edition. 12s. 6d.
  Judges and Ruth, by the Bishop of Bath and Wells, and Rev. J. Morison, D.D.; Homilies by the Rev. A. F. Muir, Rev. W. F. Adeney, Rev. W. M. Statham, and Rev. Prof. J. Thomson. Fifth Edition. 10s. 6d.

Kegan Paul, Trench, Trübner, & Co.'s Publications. 39

Pulpit Commentary, The (Old Testament Series)—
1 and 2 Samuel, by the Very Rev. R. PAYNE SMITH, D.D.; Homilies by the Rev. DONALD FRASER, D.D., Rev. Prof. CHAPMAN, Rev. B. DALE, and Rev. G. WOOD. Seventh Edition. 2 vols. 15*s*. each.
1 Kings, by the Rev. JOSEPH HAMMOND; Homilies by the Rev. E. DE PRESSENSÉ, D.D., Rev. J. WAITE, Rev. A. ROWLAND, Rev. J. A. MACDONALD, and Rev. J. URQUHART. Fifth Edition. 15*s*.
2 Kings, by the Rev. Canon RAWLINSON; Homilies by the Rev. J. ORR, D.D., Rev. D. THOMAS, D.D., and Rev. C. H. IRWIN. 15*s*.
1 Chronicles, by the Rev. Prof. P. C. BARKER; Homilies by the Rev. Prof. J. R. THOMSON, Rev. R. TUCK, Rev. W. CLARKSON, Rev. F. WHITFIELD, and Rev. RICHARD GLOVER. Second Edition. 15*s*.
2 Chronicles, by the Rev. PHILIP C. BARKER; Homilies by the Rev. W. CLARKSON and Rev. T. WHITELAW, D.D. 15*s*.
Ezra, Nehemiah, and Esther, by the Rev. Canon G. RAWLINSON; Homilies, by the Rev. Prof. J. R. THOMSON, Rev. Prof. R. A. REDFORD, Rev. W. S. LEWIS, Rev. J. A. MACDONALD, Rev. A. MACKENNAL, Rev. W. CLARKSON, Rev. F. HASTINGS, Rev. W. DINWIDDIE, Rev. Prof. ROWLANDS, Rev. G. WOOD, Rev. Prof. P. C. BARKER, and the Rev. J. S. EXELL. Seventh Edition. 12*s*. 6*d*.
Job, by the Rev. Canon G. RAWLINSON. Homilies by the Rev. T. WHITELAW, D.D., the Rev. Prof. E. JOHNSON, the Rev. Prof. W. F. ADENEY, and the Rev. R. GREEN. 21*s*.
Proverbs, by the Rev. W. J. DEANE and the Rev. S. T. TAYLOR-TASWELL. Homilies by the Rev. Prof. W. F. ADENEY, the Rev. Prof. E. JOHNSON, and the Rev. W. CLARKSON. 15*s*.
Ecclesiastes and Song of Solomon, by the Rev. W. J. DEANE and Rev. Prof. R. A. REDFORD. Homilies by the Rev. T. WHITELAW, D.D., Rev. B. C. CAFFIN, Rev. Prof. J. R. THOMSON, Rev. S. CONWAY, Rev. D. DAVIES, Rev. W. CLARKSON, and Rev. J. WILLCOCK.
Isaiah, by the Rev. Canon G. RAWLINSON; Homilies by the Rev. Prof. E. JOHNSON, Rev. W. CLARKSON, Rev. W. M. STATHAM, and Rev. R. TUCK. Third Edition. 2 vols. 15*s*. each.
Jeremiah and Lamentations, by the Rev. Canon T. K. CHEYNE, D.D.; Homilies by the Rev. Prof. J. R. THOMSON, Rev. W. F. ADENEY, Rev. A. F. MUIR, Rev. S. CONWAY, Rev. D. YOUNG, Rev. J. WAITE. 2 vols. Third Edition. 15*s*. each.
Ezekiel (Vol. I.), by the Very Rev. E. H. PLUMPTRE, D.D. Homilies by the Rev. Prof. W. F. ADENEY, the Rev. Prof. J. R. THOMSON, the Rev. J. D. DAVIES, the Rev. W. JONES, and the Rev. W. CLARKSON. Introduction by the Rev. T. WHITELAW, D.D. 12*s*. 6*d*.
Hosea and **Joel,** by the Rev. Prof. J. J. GIVEN, D.D.; Homilies by the Rev. Prof. J. R. THOMSON, Rev. A. ROWLAND, Rev. C. JERDAN, Rev. J. ORR, D.D., and Rev. D. THOMAS, D.D. 15*s*.

Pulpit Commentary, The (New Testament Series). Edited by the Very Rev. H. D. M. SPENCE, D.D., and Rev. JOSEPH S. EXELL.
St. Matthew, by the Rev. A. L. WILLIAMS. Homilies by the Rev. B. C. CAFFIN, Rev. Prof. W. F. ADENEY, Rev. P. C. BARKER, Rev. M. DODS, D.D., Rev. J. A. MACDONALD, and Rev. R. TUCK.
St. Mark, by the Very Rev. Dean E. BICKERSTETH, D.D.; Homilies by the Rev. Prof. J. R. THOMSON, Rev. Prof. J. J. GIVEN, D.D., Rev. Prof. E. JOHNSON, Rev. A. ROWLAND, Rev. A. F. MUIR, and Rev. R. GREEN. Sixth Edition. 2 vols. 10*s*. 6*d*. each.
St. Luke, by the Very Rev. Dean H. D. M. SPENCE; Homilies by the Rev. J. MARSHALL LANG, D.D., Rev. W. CLARKSON, and Rev. R. M. EDGAR. Second Edition. 2 vols. 10*s*. 6*d*. each.
St. John, by the Rev. Prof. H. R. REYNOLDS, D.D.; Homilies by the Rev. Prof. T. CROSKERY, D.D., Rev. Prof. J. R. THOMSON, Rev. D. YOUNG, Rev. B. THOMAS, and Rev. G. BROWN. Third Edition. 2 vols. 15*s*. each.

Pulpit Commentary, The (New Testament Series)—
The Acts of the Apostles, by the Right Rev. Bishop of BATH and WELLS; Homilies by the Rev. Prof. P. C. BARKER, Rev. Prof. E. JOHNSON, Rev. Prof. R. A. REDFORD, Rev. R. TUCK, Rev. W. CLARKSON. Fourth Edition. 2 vols. 10s. 6d. each.
Romans, by the Rev. J. BARMBY; Homilies by Rev. Prof. J. R. THOMSON, Rev. C. H. IRWIN, Rev. T. F. LOCKYER, Rev. S. R. ALDRIDGE, and Rev. R. M. EDGAR. 15s.
Corinthians and Galatians, by the Ven. Archdeacon FARRAR, D.D., and Rev. Prebendary E. HUXTABLE; Homilies by the Rev. Ex-Chancellor LIPSCOMB, Rev. DAVID THOMAS, D.D., Rev. DONALD FRASER, D.D., Rev. R. TUCK, Rev. E. HURNDALL, Rev. Prof. J. R. THOMSON, Rev. R. FINLAYSON, Rev. W. F. ADENEY, Rev. R. M. EDGAR, and Rev. T. CROSKERY, D.D. 2 vols. Vol I., containing I. Corinthians, Fourth Edition, 15s. Vol. II, containing Corinthians and Galatians, Second Edition, 21s.
Ephesians, Philippians, and Colossians, by the Rev. Prof. W. G. BLAIKIE, D.D., Rev. B. C. CAFFIN, and Rev. G. G. FINDLAY; Homilies by the Rev. D. THOMAS, D.D., Rev. R. M. EDGAR, Rev. R. FINLAYSON, Rev. W. F. ADENEY, Rev. Prof. T. CROSKERY, D.D., Rev. E. S. PROUT, Rev. Canon VERNON HUTTON, and Rev. U. R. THOMAS, D.D. Third Edition. 21s.
Thessalonians, Timothy, Titus, and Philemon, by the Right Rev. Bishop of BATH and WELLS, Rev. Dr. GLOAG, and Rev. Dr. EALES; Homilies by the Rev. B. C. CAFFIN, Rev. R. FINLAYSON, Rev. Prof. T. CROSKERY, D.D., Rev. W. F. ADENEY, Rev. W. M. STATHAM, and Rev. D. THOMAS, D.D. Second Edition. 15s.
Hebrews and James, by the Rev. J. BARMBY, and Rev. Prebendary E. C. S. GIBSON; Homilies by the Rev. C. JERDAN and Rev. Prebendary E. C. S. GIBSON, Rev. W. JONES, Rev. C. NEW, Rev. D. YOUNG, Rev. J. S. BRIGHT, and Rev. T. F. LOCKYER. Third Edition. 15s.
Peter, John, and Jude, by the Rev. B. C. CAFFIN, Rev. A. PLUMMER, D.D., and Rev. Prof. S. D. F. SALMOND, D.D.; Homilies by the Rev. A. MACLAREN, D.D., Rev. C. CLEMANCE, D.D., Rev. Prof. J. R. THOMSON, Rev. C. NEW, Rev. U. R. THOMAS, Rev. R. FINLAYSON, Rev. W. JONES, Rev. Prof. T. CROSKERY, D.D., and Rev. J. S. BRIGHT, D.D. Second Edition. 15s.
Revelation. Introduction by the Rev. T. RANDELL, principal of Bede College, Durham. Exposition by the Rev. A. PLUMMER, D.D., assisted by Rev. T. RANDELL and A. T. BOTT. Homilies by the Rev. C. CLEMANCE, D.D., Rev. S. CONWAY, Rev. R. GREEN, and Rev. D. THOMAS, D.D. Second Edition. 15s.

PUSEY. **Sermons for the Church's Seasons from Advent to Trinity.** Selected from the published Sermons of the late EDWARD BOUVERIE PUSEY, D.D. Cr. 8vo. 5s.

PYE, W., **Surgical Handicraft:** a Manual of Surgical Manipulations, &c. With 235 Illustrations. Third Edition, Revised and Edited by T. H. R. CROWLE. Cr. 8vo. 10s. 6d.

Elementary Bandaging and Surgical Dressing, for the use of Dressers and Nurses. 18mo. 2s.

Public Schools (Our): Eton, Harrow, Winchester, Rugby, Westminster, Marlborough, and The Charterhouse. Cr. 8vo. 6s.

QUATREFAGES, Prof. A. de, **The Human Species.** Fifth Edition. Cr. 8vo. 5s. (I.S.S.)

QUINCEY, DE, **Confessions of an English Opium Eater.** Edited by RICHARD GARNETT. Elzevir 8vo. vellum, 7s. 6d.; parchment or cloth, 6s. (*Parchment Library.*)

RALSTON, W. R. S., **Tibetan Tales,** derived from Indian Sources. Done into English from the German of F. ANTON VON SCHIEFNER. Post 8vo. 14s. (*Trübner's Oriental Series.*)

Kegan Paul, Trench, Trübner, & Co.'s Publications. 41

Rare Poems of the 16th and 17th Centuries. Edited by W. J. LINTON. Cr. 8vo. 5s.
RASK, ERASMUS, Grammar of the Anglo-Saxon Tongue. From the Danish, by B. THORPE. Third Edition. Post 8vo, 5s. 6d.
READE, WINWOOD, The Martyrdom of Man. Fourteenth Edition. Cr. 8vo. 7s. 6d.
REANEY, Mrs. G. S., Waking and Working; or, From Girlhood to Womanhood. New and Cheaper Edition, with Frontispiece. Cr. 8vo. 3s. 6d.
— **Blessing and Blessed :** a Sketch of Girl Life. New and Cheaper Edition. Cr. 8vo. 3s. 6d.
— **Rose Gurney's Discovery :** a Story for Girls, dedicated to their Mothers. Cr. 8vo. 3s. 6d.
— **English Girls :** their Place and Power. With Preface by the Rev. R. W. DALE. Fifth Edition. Fcp. 8vo. 2s. 6d.
— **Just Anyone,** and other Stories. With 3 Illustrations. 16mo. 1s. 6d.
— **Sunbeam Willie,** and other Stories. With 3 Illustrations. 16mo. 1s. 6d.
— **Sunshine Jenny,** and other Stories. With 3 Illustrations. 16mo. 1s. 6d.

REDHOUSE, J. W., Simplified Grammar of the Ottoman-Turkish Language. Cr. 8vo. 10s. 6d.
— **Turkish Vade-Mecum of Ottoman Colloquial Language.** English-Turkish and Turkish-English, the whole in English Characters, the Pronunciation being fully indicated. Third Edition. 32mo. 6s.
— **The Mesnevi** (usually known as the Mesnevīyi Sherīf, or Holy Mesnevī) of Mevlānā (Our Lord) Jelālu'd-Din Muhammed Er-Rūmi. Illustrated by a selection of Characteristic Anecdotes. Post 8vo. £1. 1s. (*Trübner's Oriental Series.*)
— **History, System, and Varieties of Turkish Poetry.** Illustrated by Selections in the original English Paraphrase. 8vo. 2s. 6d.
— **Tentative Chronological Synopsis of the History of Arabia and its Neighbours,** from B.C. 500,000 (?) to A.D. 679. 8vo. 2s.

REES, J. D., H.R.H. The Duke of Clarence and Avondale in Southern India. With a Narrative of Elephant Catching in Mysore, by G. P. SANDERSON. With Map, Portraits, and Illustrations. Medium 8vo. 31s. 6d.
Remedy for Landlordism ; or, Free Land Tenure. Sm. cr. 8vo. 2s. 6d.
RENAN, ERNEST, Philosophical Dialogues and Fragments. Post 8vo. 7s. 6d.
— **Age and Antiquity of the Book of Nabathæan Agriculture.** Cr. 8vo. 3s. 6d.
— **Life of Jesus.** Cr. 8vo. 1s. 6d. ; paper covers, 1s.
— **The Apostles.** Cr. 8vo. 1s. 6d. ; paper covers, 1s.

RENDELL, J. M., Handbook of the Island of Madeira. With Plan and Map. Second Edition. Fcp. 8vo. 1s. 6d.

REYNOLDS, J. W., The Supernatural in Nature : a Verification by Free Use of Science. Third Edition, Revised and Enlarged. 8vo. 14s.
— **Mystery of the Universe our Common Faith.** 8vo. 14s.
— **Mystery of Miracles.** Third Edition, Enlarged. Cr. 8vo. 6s.
— **The World to Come :** Immortality a Physical Fact. Cr. 8vo. 6s.

REYNOLDS, Sir JOSHUA, Discourses. Edited by E. GOSSE. Elzevir 8vo. vellum, 7s. 6d. ; parchment or cloth, 6s. (*Parchment Library.*)

RHOADES, JAMES, The Georgics of Virgil. Translated into English verse. Second Edition. Cr. 8vo. 2s. 6d.

RHOIDIS, EMMANUEL, Pope Joan : an Historical Study. From the Greek by C. H. COLLÉTTE. 12mo. 2s. 6d.

RHYS, JOHN, Lectures on Welsh Philology. Second Edition. Cr. 8vo. 15s.

42 Kegan Paul, Trench, Trübner, & Co.'s Publications.

RIBOT, Prof. Th., Diseases of Memory: an Essay in the Positive Psychology. Third Edition. Cr. 8vo. 5s. (*I.S.S.*)
Heredity: a Psychological Study of its Phenomena, Laws, Causes, and Consequences. Second Edition. Large cr. 8vo. 9s.
English Psychology. Cr. 8vo. 7s. 6d.
RICHARD, Ap, Marriage and Divorce. Including the Religious, Practical, and Political Aspects of the Question. Cr. 8vo. 5s.
RICHARDSON, AUSTIN, ' What are the Catholic Claims ? ' With Introduction by Rev. LUKE RIVINGTON. Cr. 8vo. 3s. 6d.
RICHARDSON, M. T., Practical Blacksmithing. With 400 Illustrations. 4 vols. Cr. 8vo. 5s. each.
Practical Horse-shoer. With 170 Illustrations. Cr. 8vo. 5s.
RICHTER, Prof. VICTOR von, Text-book of Inorganic Chemistry. Authorised Translation. By EDGAR F. SMITH. Third American Edition, from the Fifth German Edition. Cr. 8vo. 8s. 6d.
Chemistry of the Carbon Compounds; or, Organic Chemistry. Authorised Translation. By EDGAR F. SMITH. Second American Edition, from the Sixth German Edition. Cr. 8vo. 20s.
RIOLA, HENRY, How to learn Russian: a Manual for Students. Based upon the Ollendorffian System. Fourth Edition. Cr. 8vo. 12s. Key, 5s.
Russian Reader. With Vocabulary. Cr. 8vo. 10s. 6d.
RIVINGTON, LUKE, Authority; or, A Plain Reason for Joining the Church of Rome. Fifth Edition. Cr. 8vo. 3s. 6d.
Dependence; or, The Insecurity of the Anglican Position. Cr. 8vo. 5s.
ROBERTS, H., Grammar of the Khassi Language. Cr. 8vo. 10s. 6d.
ROBERTSON, F. W., Life and Letters. Edited by STOPFORD BROOKE.
 I. Library Edition. With Portrait. 8vo. 12s.
 II. Two vols. With Portrait. Cr. 8vo. 7s. 6d.
 III. Popular Edition. Cr. 8vo. 6s.
Sermons. Five Series. Sm. 8vo. 3s. 6d. each.
Notes on Genesis. New and Cheaper Edition. Sm. 8vo. 3s. 6d.
St. Paul's Epistles to the Corinthians: Expository Lectures. New Edition. Sm. 8vo. 5s.
Lectures and Addresses. With other Literary Remains. New Edition. Sm. 8vo. 5s.
Analysis of Tennyson's ' In Memoriam.' Dedicated by Permission to the Poet-Laureate. Fcp. 8vo. 2s.
Education of the Human Race. Translated from the German of GOTTHOLD EPHRAIM LESSING. Fcp. 8vo. 2s. 6d.
*** Portrait of the late Rev. F. W. Robertson, mounted for framing, 2s. 6d.
ROBINSON, A. MARY F., The Fortunate Lovers. Twenty-seven Novels of the Queen of Navarre. Frontispiece by G. P. JACOMB HOOD. Large cr. 8vo. 10s. 6d.
The Crowned Hippolytus. Sm. cr. 8vo. 5s.
A Handful of Honeysuckle. Fcp. 8vo. 3s. 6d.
ROBINSON, Sir J. C., The Dead Sailor, and other Stories. Cr. 8vo. 5s.
ROCHE, A., French Grammar. Adopted by the Imperial Council of Public Instruction. Cr. 8vo. 3s.
Prose and Poetry, from English Authors. For Reading, Composition, and Translation. Second Edition. Fcp. 8vo. 2s. 6d.
ROCKHILL, W. W., Life of the Buddha and the Early History of his Order. Derived from Tibetan Works in the Bkah-Hgyur and the Bstan-Hgyur. Post 8vo. 9s. (*Trübner's Oriental Series.*)
 UDANAVARGA: a Collection of Verses from the Buddhist Canon. Compiled by DHARMATRÂTA and Translated from the Tibetan. Post 8vo. 9s. (*Trübner's Oriental Series.*)

RODD, E. H., Birds of Cornwall and the Scilly Islands. Edited by J. E. HARTING. With Portrait and Map. 8vo. 14s.

ROGERS, E. T., The Numismata Orientalia. Part IV. The Coins of the Tuluni Dynasty. With 1 Plate. Royal 4to. Paper wrapper, 5s.

ROGERS, WILLIAM, Reminiscences. Compiled by R. H. HADDEN. With Portrait. Cr. 8vo. 6s. ; Cheap Edition, 3s. 6d.

ROMANES, G. J., Mental Evolution in Animals. With Posthumous Essay on Instinct by CHARLES DARWIN. 8vo. 12s.
  Mental Evolution in Man: Origin of the Human Faculty. 8vo. 14s.
  Animal Intelligence. Fourth Edition. Cr. 8vo. 5s. (*I.S.S.*)
  Jelly-Fish, Star-Fish, and Sea-Urchins: being a Research on Primitive Nervous Systems. With Illustrations. Second Edition. Cr. 8vo. 5s. (*I.S.S.*)

ROOD, OGDEN N., Colour: a Text-book of Modern Chromatics. With Applications to Art and Industry. With 130 Original Illustrations. Third Edition. Cr. 8vo. 5s. (*I.S.S.*)

ROOT, A. I., A B C of Bee Culture. A Cyclopædia of everything pertaining to the care of the Honey Bee. Illustrated. Royal 8vo. 7s. 6d.

ROOSEVELT, THEODORE, Hunting Trips of a Ranchman. With 26 Illustrations. Royal 8vo. 18s.

ROSENTHAL, Prof. J., General Physiology of Muscles and Nerves. Third Edition. With 75 Illustrations. Cr. 8vo. 5s. (*I.S.S.*)

ROSING, S., Danish Dictionary. Cr. 8vo. 8s. 6d.

ROSMINI. Life of Antonio Rosmini. By W. LOCKHART. With Portraits. 2 vols. Cr. 8vo. 7s. 6d.
  Rosmini's Origin of Ideas. Translated from Fifth Italian Edition. 3 vols. 8vo. 10s. 6d. each.
  Psychology. 3 vols. 8vo. 10s. 6d. each.
  Compendium of the Philosophical System of Antonio Rosmini-Serbati. Translated by T. DAVIDSON. Second Edition. 8vo. 10s. 6d.

ROSS, JANET, Italian Sketches. With 14 full-page Illustrations. Cr. 8vo. 7s. 6d.

ROSS, PERCY, A Professor of Alchemy. Cr. 8vo. 3s. 6d.

ROSS, Lieut.-Col. W. A., Alphabetical Manual of Blowpipe Analysis. Cr. 8vo. 5s.
  Pyrology, or Fire Chemistry. Sm. 4to. 36s.

ROUTLEDGE, Canon C. F., History of St. Martin's Church, Canterbury. Cr. 8vo. 5s.

ROUTLEDGE, JAMES, English Rule and Native Opinion in India. 8vo. 10s. 6d.

ROWBOTHAM, J. F., The Human Epic. Cr. 8vo. 7s.

Rowing at Westminster, 1813-1883: Extracted from the School Water-Ledgers. Cr. 8vo. 5s.

RULE, MARTIN, Life and Times of St. Anselm, Archbishop of Canterbury and Primate of the Britains. 2 vols. 8vo. 32s.

RUTHERFORD, MARK, Autobiography of Mark Rutherford, and Mark Rutherford's Deliverance. Edited by REUBEN SHAPCOTT. Fourth Edition. Cr. 8vo. 5s.
  Revolution in Tanner's Lane. Edited by REUBEN SHAPCOTT. Cr. 8vo. 7s. 6d.
  Miriam's Schooling, and other Papers. Edited by REUBEN SHAPCOTT. Cr. 8vo. 6s.

ST. CLAIR, GEORGE, Buried Cities and Bible Countries. Large cr. 8vo. 7s. 6d.

SAINTSBURY G., Specimens of English Prose Style from Malory to Macaulay. Selected and Annotated. With Introductory Essay. Large cr. 8vo. Printed on hand-made paper. Vellum, 15s.; parchment antique or cloth, 12s.

SALAMAN, J. S., Trade Marks: their Registration and Protection. Cr. 8vo. 5s.

SALMONÉ, H. A., Arabic-English Dictionary, comprising about 120,000 Arabic Words, with English Index of about 50,000 Words. 2 vols. post 8vo. 36s.

SAMUELSON, JAMES, India, Past and Present: Historical, Social, and Political. With Map, Woodcuts, Views, Portraits, &c. 8vo. 21s.
History of Drink: Social, Scientific, and Political. 2nd Edition. 8vo. 6s.
Bulgaria, Past and Present: Historical, Political, and Descriptive. With Map and numerous Illustrations. 8vo. 10s. 6d.

SANDWITH, F. M., Egypt as a Winter Resort. Cr. 8vo. 3s. 6d.

SANTIAGOE, DANIEL, Curry Cook's Assistant. Fcp. 8vo. 1s. 6d.; paper covers, 1s.

SAYCE, A. H., Introduction to the Science of Language. New and Cheaper Edition. 2 vols. cr. 8vo. 9s.

SCANNELL, THOMAS B., and WILHELM, JOSEPH, D.D., Manual of Catholic Theology, based on SCHEEBEN'S 'Dogmatik.' Vol. I. 15s.

SCHAW, Col. H., Defence and Attack of Positions and Localities. 4th Edition. Cr. 8vo. 3s. 6d.

SCHLAGINTWEIT, EMIL, Buddhism in Tibet. Illustrated by Literary Documents and Objects of Religious Worship. With 20 Plates. 2 vols. roy. 8vo. and folio, £2. 2s.

SCHLEICHER, AUGUST, Comparative Grammar of the Indo-European, Sanskrit, Greek, and Latin Languages. From the Third German Edition by H. BENDALL. 8vo. 13s. 6d.

SCHMIDT, Prof. O., Doctrine of Descent and Darwinism. With 26 Illustrations. Seventh Edition. Cr. 8vo. 5s. (I.S.S.)
Mammalia in their Relation to Primeval Times. With 51 Woodcuts. Cr. 8vo. 5s. (I.S.S.)

SCHOPENHAUER, A., The World as Will and Idea. From the German by R. B. HALDANE and J. KEMP. 3 vols. post 8vo. £2. 12s. (*Philosophical Library.*)

SCHÜTZENBERGER, Prof., Fermentation. With 28 Illustrations. Fourth Edition. Cr. 8vo. 5s. (I.S.S.)

SCHWENDLER, LOUIS, Instructions for Testing Telegraph Lines. 2 vols. 8vo. 21s.

SCOONES, W. B., Four Centuries of English Letters: a Selection of 350 Letters by 150 Writers, from the period of the Paston Letters to the Present Time. Third Edition. Large cr. 8vo. 6s.

SCOTT, JAMES GEORGE, Burma as it Was, as it Is, and as it Will Be. Cheap Edition. Cr. 8vo. 2s. 6d.

SCOTT, ROBERT H., Elementary Meteorology. Fifth Edition. With numerous Illustrations. Cr. 8vo. 5s. (I.S.S.)

SEDDING, JOHN D., Gardencraft, Old and New. With Memorial Notice by the Rev. E. F. RUSSELL. 16 Illustrations. 8vo. 12s.

SELBY, H. M., Shakespeare Classical Dictionary; or, Mythological Allusions in the Plays of Shakespeare explained. Fcap. 8vo. 1s.

SEMPER, KARL, Natural Conditions of Existence as they affect Animal Life. With 2 Maps and 106 Woodcuts. Fourth Edition. Cr. 8vo. 5s. (*I.S.S.*)

SERJEANT, W. C. ELDON, The Astrologer's Guide (Anima Astrologiæ). 8vo. 7s. 6d.

SEVERNE, FLORENCE, The Pillar House. With Frontispiece. Cr. 8vo. 6s.

SEYMOUR, W. DIGBY, Home Rule and State Supremacy. Cr. 8vo. 3s. 6d.

SHAKSPERE. WORKS. Avon Edition. In One Volume. With Glossarial Index. Super roy. 8vo. 7s. 6d.

Works. Avon Edition. 12 vols. Elzevir 8vo. (*Parchment Library*), vellum, 7s. 6d. per vol.; parchment or cloth, 6s. per vol.; Cheap Edition, 1s. 6d. per vol.

*** The Cheap Edition may also be had complete, 12 vols. in cloth box, 21s., or bound in 6 vols. 15s.

Works. New Variorum Edition. Edited by HORACE HOWARD FURNESS. Roy. 8vo. Vol. I. Romeo and Juliet, 18s. Vol. II. Macbeth, 18s. Vols. III. and IV. Hamlet, 2 vols. 36s. Vol. V. King Lear, 18s. Vol. VI. Othello, 18s. Vol. VII. Merchant of Venice, 18s. Vol. VIII. As You Like It, 18s.

Concordance to Shakspere's Poems. By Mrs. FURNESS. Roy. 8vo. 18s.

Sonnets. Edited by EDWARD DOWDEN. With Frontispiece. Elzevir 8vo. (*Parchment Library*), vellum, 7s. 6d.; parchment or cloth, 6s.

SHAW, FLORA L., Castle Blair: a Story of Youthful Days. Cr. 8vo. 3s. 6d.

SHAW, Lieut.-Col. WILKINSON, Elements of Modern Tactics practically applied to English Formations. Seventh Edition. With 31 Plates and Maps. Small cr. 8vo. 9s. (*Military Handbooks.*)

'SHEILA,' Sketches from Nature. A Book of Verses. Sm. cr. 8vo. 2s. 6d.

SHELLEY. Life of P. B. Shelley. By EDWARD DOWDEN, LL.D. With Portraits. 2 vols. 8vo. 36s.

Poems. Edited, with Preface, by RICHARD GARNETT. Frontispiece. Elzevir 8vo. vellum, 7s. 6d.; parchment or cloth, 6s. (*Parchment Library.*)

Select Letters. Edited by RICHARD GARNETT. Elzevir 8vo. vellum, 7s. 6d.; parchment or cloth, 6s. (*Parchment Library.*)

SHORE. Journal of Emily Shore. With Portrait and Facsimile. Cr. 8vo. 6s.

SIBREE, JAMES, The Great African Island, Madagascar: its Physical Geography, &c. With Maps and Illustrations. 8vo. 10s. 6d.

SIDGWICK, A., Fallacies: a View of Logic from the Practical Side. Second Edition. Cr. 8vo. 5s. (*I.S.S.*)

SIDNEY, Sir PHILIP, Knt., The Countess of Pembroke's Arcadia. Edited by H. OSKAR SOMMER. The original 4to. Edition (1590) in Photographic Facsimile, with Bibliographical Introduction.

SIMCOX, EDITH, Episodes in the Lives of Men, Women, and Lovers. Cr. 8vo. 7s. 6d.

Natural Law: an Essay in Ethics. Second Edition, Post 8vo. 10s. 6d. (*Philosophical Library.*)

SIME, JAMES, Lessing: his Life and Writings. Second Edition, with Portraits. 2 vols. Post 8vo. 21s. (*Philosophical Library.*)

SIMONNÉ, Metoda para aprender a Leer Escribir y hablar el Frances, segun el verdadero sistema de Ollendorff. Cr. 8vo. 6s. Key, 3s. 6d.

SIMPSON, M. C. M., Letters and Recollections of Julius and Mary Mohl. With Portraits and 2 Illustrations. 8vo. 15s.

SINCLAIR, F., German Vocabulary. Cr. 8vo. 2s.

SINCLAIR, MAY, Essays in Verse. Sm. cr. 8vo. 2s. 6d.

SINCLAIR, THOMAS, Travel Sketch. Cr. 8vo. 5s.

SINGER, I., Simplified Grammar of the Hungarian Language. Cr. 8vo. 4s. 6d.

SINNETT, A. P., The Occult World. Sixth Edition. Cr. 8vo. 3s. 6d.
Incidents in the Life of Madame Blavatsky. With Portrait. 8vo. 10s. 6d.
The Rationale of Mesmerism. Cr. 8vo. 3s. 6d.

Sister Augustine, Superior of the Sisters of Charity at the St. Johannis Hospital at Bonn. Translated by HANS THARAU. Cheap Edition. Large cr. 8vo. 4s. 6d.

SKINNER. James Skinner: a Memoir. By the Author of 'Charles Lowder.' With Preface by the Rev. Canon CARTER, and Portrait. Large cr. 8vo. 7s. 6d. Cheap Edition, cr. 8vo. 3s. 6d.

SMITH, A. H., Chinese Characteristics. 8vo. 7s. 6d.

SMITH, E., Foods. With numerous Illustrations. Ninth Edition. Cr. 8vo. 5s. (I.S.S.)

SMITH, EDGAR F., Electro-Chemical Analysis. With 25 Illustrations. Square 16mo. 5s.

SMITH, H. PERCY, Glossary of Terms and Phrases. Cheap Edition. Medium 8vo. 3s. 6d.

SMITH, HAMILTON, Hydraulics: the Flow of Water through Orifices, over Weirs, and through open Conduits and Pipes. With 17 plates. Royal 4to. 30s.

SMITH, HUNTINGTON, A Century of American Literature: Benjamin Franklin to James Russell Lowell. Cr. 8vo. 6s.

SMITH, JAMES C., The Distribution of the Produce. Cr. 8vo. 2s. 6d.

SMITH, L. A., The Music of the Waters: Sailors' Chanties and Working Songs of the Sea. Words and Music. 8vo. 12s.

SMITH, M., and HORNEMAN, H., Norwegian Grammar. With a Glossary for Tourists. Post 8vo, 2s.

SMYTH, R. BROUGH, The Aborigines of Victoria. Compiled for the Government. With Maps, Plates, and Woodcuts. 2 vols, royal 8vo. £3. 3s.

SOPHOCLES. The Seven Plays in English Verse. Translated by Prof. LEWIS CAMPBELL. Cr. 8vo. 7s. 6d.

Spanish Mystics. By the Editor of 'Many Voices.' Cr. 8vo. 5s.

Specimens of English Prose Style from Malory to Macaulay. Selected and Annotated. With an Introductory Essay by GEORGE SAINTSBURY. Large cr. 8vo, printed on hand-made paper, vellum, 15s.; parchment antique or cloth, 12s.

SPEDDING, JAMES, Life and Times of Francis Bacon. 2 vols. Post 8vo. 21s.

SPENCER, HERBERT, Study of Sociology. Fifteenth Edition. Cr. 8vo. 5s. (I.S.S.)

SPINOZA, BENEDICT DE, Ethic Demonstrated in Geometrical Order and Divided into Five Parts, which treat (1) of God, (2) of the Nature and Origin of the Mind, (3) of the Origin and Nature of the Affects, (4) of Human Bondage, or of the Strength of the Affects, (5) of the Power of the Intellect, or of Human Liberty. From the Latin by W. HALE WHITE. Post 8vo. 10s. 6d. (*Philosophical Library.*)

SPINOZA. Life, Correspondence, and Ethics of Spinoza. By R. WILLIS. 8vo. 21s.

SPRAGUE, CHARLES E., Handbook of Volapuk, the International Language. Second Edition. Cr. 8vo. 5s.

STALLO, J. B., Concepts and Theories of Modern Physics. Third Edition. Cr. 8vo. 5s. (I.S.S.)

STARCKE, C. N., The Primitive Family in its Origin and Development. Cr. 8vo. 5s. (I.S.S.)

STEBBING, T. R. R., The Naturalist of Cumbrae: a True Story, being the Life of David Robertson. Cr. 8vo. 6s.

Kegan Paul, Trench, Trübner, & Co.'s Publications. 47

STEELE, TH., An Eastern Love-Story : Kusa Jâtakaya. Cr. 8vo. 6s.
STEPHEN, CAROLINE E., Quaker Strongholds. Second Edition. Cr. 8vo. 5s.
STEVENSON, W. FLEMING, Hymns for the Church and Home. 32mo. 1s.
STEWART, BALFOUR, Conservation of Energy. With 14 Illustrations. Seventh Edition. Cr. 8vo. 5s. (*I.S.S.*)
STORR, F., and **TURNER, H.,** Canterbury Chimes ; or, Chaucer Tales Re-told to Children. With 6 Illustrations from the Ellesmere Manuscript. Third Edition. Fcap. 8vo. 3s. 6d.
STRACHEY, Sir JOHN, India. With Map. 8vo. 15s.
STRAHAN, S. A. K., Marriage and Disease. A Study of Heredity and the more important Family Degenerations. Cr. 8vo. 6s.
Stray Papers on Education, and Scenes from School Life. By B. H. Second Edition. Sm. cr. 8vo. 3s. 6d.
STRECKER, ADOLPH, Text-book of Organic Chemistry. Edited by Prof. WISLICENUS. Translated and Edited, with Extensive Additions, by W. R. HODGKINSON and A. J. GREENAWAY. Second and Cheaper Edition. 8vo. 12s. 6d.
STREET, J. C., The Hidden Way across the Threshold ; or, The Mystery which hath been Hidden for Ages and from Generations. With Plates. Large 8vo. 15s.
STRETTON, HESBA, David Lloyd's Last Will. With 4 Illustrations. New Edition. Royal 16mo, 2s. 6d.
  Through a Needle's Eye ; a Story. With Frontispiece. Cr. 8vo. 6s.
SULLY, JAMES, Pessimism : a History and a Criticism. 8vo. 10s. 6d.
  Illusions : a Psychological Study. Third Edition. Cr. 8vo. 5s. (*I.S.S.*)
SUMNER, W. G., What Social Classes owe to Each Other. 18mo. 3s. 6d.
SWINBURNE, ALGERNON CHARLES, A Word for the Navy. (Only 250 copies printed.) Imperial 16mo. paper covers, 5s.
SWINBURNE. Bibliography of A. C. Swinburne, 1857-87. Cr. 8vo. vellum gilt, 6s.
SYME, DAVID, On the Modification of Organisms. Cr. 8vo. 5s.
  Representative Government. Second Edition. Cr. 8vo. 6s.
SYMONDS, JOHN ADDINGTON, Vagabunduli Libellus. Cr. 8vo. 6s.
SWIFT, JON., Letters and Journals. Edited by STANLEY LANE-POOLE. Elzevir 8vo. vellum, 7s. 6d. ; parchment or cloth, 6s. (*Parchment Library.*)
  Prose Writings. Edited by STANLEY LANE-POOLE. With Portrait. Elzevir 8vo. vellum, 7s. 6d. ; parchment or cloth, 6s. (*Parchment Library.*)

TARRING, C. J., Elementary Turkish Grammar. Cr. 8vo. 6s.
'TASMA,' A Sydney Sovereign, and other Tales. Crown 8vo. cloth, 6s.
  In her Earliest Youth. Cheap Edition. Cr. 8vo. 6s.
TAYLOR, Col. MEADOWS, Seeta : a Novel. With Frontispiece. Cr. 8vo. 6s.
  Tippoo Sultaun : a Tale of the Mysore War. With Frontispiece. Cr. 8vo. 6s.
  Ralph Darnell. With Frontispiece. Cr. 8vo. 6s.
  A Noble Queen. With Frontispiece. Cr. 8vo. 6s.
  The Confessions of a Thug. With Frontispiece. Cr. 8vo. 6s.
  Tara : a Mahratta Tale. With Frontispiece. Crown 8vo. 6s.
TAYLOR, Canon ISAAC, The Alphabet : an Account of the Origin and Development of Letters. With numerous Tables and Facsimiles. 2 vols. 8vo. 36s.
  Leaves from an Egyptian Note-Book. Cr. 8vo. 5s.
TAYLOR, R. WHATELEY COOKE, The Modern Factory System. 8vo. 14s.

TAYLOR, Sir H., Works. 5 vols. Cr. 8vo. 30s.
  Philip Van Artevelde. Fcap. 8vo. 3s. 6d.
  The Virgin Widow, &c. Fcap. 8vo. 3s. 6d.
  The Statesman. Fcap. 8vo. 3s. 6d.

  Technological Dictionary of the Terms employed in the Arts and Sciences (Architecture, Engineering, Mechanics, Shipbuilding and Navigation, Metallurgy, Mathematics, &c.), with Preface by KARL KAMARSCH. Fourth Revised Edition. 3 vols. imperial 8vo.
  Vol. I. German-English-French. 12s.
  Vol. II. English-German-French. 12s.
  Vol. III. French-German-English. 15s.

THACKERAY, S. W., The Land and the Community. Crown 8vo. 3s. 6d.

THACKERAY, W. M., Essay on the Genius of George Cruickshank. Reprinted verbatim from the *Westminster Review*. With 40 Illustrations. Royal 8vo. 7s. 6d.

  Sultan Stork, and other Stories and Sketches, 1829-44, now first collected; to which is added the Bibliography of Thackeray. Large 8vo. 10s. 6d.

Theology and Piety alike Free, from the point of view of Manchester New College, Oxford : a Contribution to its effort offered by an Old Student. 8vo. 9s.

THOM, J. HAMILTON, Laws of Life after the Mind of Christ. Two Series. Third Edition. Cr. 8vo. 7s. 6d. each.

THOMAS, E., The Numismata Orientalia. Part I. Ancient Indian Weights. With Plate and Map of the India of MANU. Royal 4to. paper wrapper, 9s. 6d.

THOMPSON, A. R., Dialogues, Russian and English. Cr. 8vo. 5s.

THOMPSON, Sir H., Diet in Relation to Age and Activity. Fcp. 8vo. 1s. 6d.; paper covers, 1s.
  Modern Cremation. Second Edition, revised and enlarged. Cr. 8vo. 2s.; paper covers, 1s.

Through North Wales with a Knapsack. By FOUR SCHOOLMISTRESSES. With a Sketch Map. Sm. 8vo. 2s. 6d.

Through To-day. A Novel. Cr. 8vo. 5s.

THURSTON, Prof. R. H., History of the Growth of the Steam Engine. With numerous Illustrations. Fourth Edition. Cr. 8vo. 5s. (*I.S.S.*)
  Manual of the Steam Engine. For Engineers and Technical Schools. Parts I. and II. Royal 8vo. 31s. 6d. each Part.

TIELE, Prof. C. P., Outlines of the History of Religion to the Spread of the Universal Religions. From the Dutch by J. ESTLIN CARPENTER. Fourth Edition. Post 8vo. 7s. 6d. (*Philosophical Library, and Trübner's Oriental Series.*)
  History of the Egyptian and Mesopotamian Religions. Translated by J. BALLINGAL. Post 8vo. 7s. 6d. (*Trübner's Oriental Series.*)

TIRARD, H. M. and N., Sketches from a Nile Steamer, for the use of Travellers in Egypt. With Map and numerous Illustrations. Cr. 8vo. 6s.

TISDALL, W. ST. CLAIR, Simplified Grammar and Reading Book of the Panjābī Language. Cr. 8vo. 7s. 6d.

TOLSTOI, Count LEO, Christ's Christianity. Translated from the Russian. Large cr. 8vo. 7s. 6d.

TORCEANU, R., Simplified Grammar of the Roumanian Language. Cr. 8vo. 5s.

TORREND, J., Comparative Grammar of the South African Bantu Languages, comprising those of Zanzibar, Mozambique, the Zambezi, Kafirland, Benguela, Angola, The Congo, The Ogowe, The Cameroons, the Lake Region, &c. Super-royal 8vo. 25s.

Kegan Paul, Trench, Trübner, & Co.'s Publications. 49

TOSCANI, G., Italian Conversational Course. Fourth Edition. 12mo. 5*s.*
Italian Reading Course. Fcp. 8vo. 4*s.* 6*d.*
TRANT, WILLIAM, Trade Unions: their Origin, Objects, and Efficacy. Sm. 8vo. 1*s.* 6*d.*; paper covers, 1*s.*
TRENCH. Letters and Memorials of Archbishop Trench. By the Author of 'Charles Lowder.' With 2 Portraits. 2 vols. 8vo. 21*s.*
TRENCH, Archbishop, English Past and Present. Fourteenth Edition, revised and improved. Fcp. 8vo. 5*s.*
On the Study of Words. Twenty-first Edition, revised. Fcp. 8vo. 5*s.*
Notes on the Parables of Our Lord. Fourteenth Edition. 8vo. 12*s.*; Cheap Edition, 59th thousand, 7*s.* 6*d.*
Notes on the Miracles of Our Lord. Twelfth Edition. 8vo. 12*s.*; Cheap Edition, 48th thousand, 7*s.* 6*d.*
Household Book of English Poetry. Fourth Edition, revised. Extra fcp. 8vo. 5*s.*
Essay on the Life and Genius of Calderon. With Translations from his 'Life's a Dream' and 'Great Theatre of the World.' Second Edition, revised and improved. Extra fcp. 8vo. 5*s.* 6*d.*
Gustavus Adolphus in Germany, and other Lectures on the Thirty Years' War. Third Edition, enlarged. Fcp. 8vo. 4*s.*
Plutarch: His Life, His Lives, and His Morals. Second Edition, enlarged. Fcp. 8vo. 3*s.* 6*d.*
Remains of the late Mrs. Richard Trench. Being Selections from her Journals, Letters, and other Papers. Edited by her Son, Archbishop TRENCH. New and Cheaper Edition. With Portraits. 8vo. 6*s.*
Lectures on Mediæval Church History. Being the substance of Lectures delivered at Queen's College, London. 2nd edition, 8vo. 12*s.*
Poems. Tenth Edition. Fcp. 8vo. 7*s.* 6*d.* Library Edition. 2 vols. sm. 8vo. 10*s.*
Proverbs and their Lessons. Eighth Edition, enlarged. Fcp. 8vo. 4*s.*
Sacred Latin Poetry, chiefly Lyrical. Third Edition, corrected and improved. Fcp. 8vo. 7*s.*
Select Glossary of English Words used formerly in Senses different from their present. Seventh Edition, revised and enlarged. Fcp. 8vo. 5*s.*
Brief Thoughts and Meditations on some Passages in Holy Scripture. Third Edition. Cr. 8vo. 3*s.* 6*d.*
Commentary on the Epistles to the Seven Churches in Asia. Fourth Edition, revised. 8vo. 8*s.* 6*d.*
On the Authorised Version of the New Testament. Second Edition. 8vo. 7*s.*
Sermons New and Old. Cr. 8vo. 6*s.*
Westminster and other Sermons. Cr. 8vo. 6*s.*
The Sermon on the Mount: an Exposition drawn from the Writings of St. Augustine. Fourth Edition, enlarged. 8vo. 10*s.* 6*d.*
Shipwrecks of Faith: three Sermons preached before the University of Cambridge. Fcap. 8vo. 2*s.* 6*d.*
Studies in the Gospels. Fifth Edition, revised. 8vo. 10*s.* 6*d.*
Synonyms of the New Testament. Eleventh Edition, enlarged. 8vo. 12*s.*
TRENCH, Major-General, Cavalry in Modern War. Sm. cr. 8vo. 6*s.* (*Military Handbooks.*)
TRIMEN, ROLAND, South African Butterflies: a Monograph of the Extra-tropical Species. With 12 Coloured Plates. 3 vols. 8vo. £2. 12*s.* 6*d.*
TROUESSART, E. L., Microbes, Ferments, and Moulds. With 107 Illustrations. Second Edition. Cr. 8vo. 5*s.* (*I.S.S.*)
TROWBRIDGE, J. M., The Cider Maker's Handbook: a Complete Guide for Making and Keeping Pure Cider. Illustrated. Cr. 8vo. 5*s.*

D

TRÜBNER'S Bibliographical Guide to American Literature. From 1817 to 1857. 8vo. half-bound, 18s.

Catalogue of Dictionaries and Grammars of the Principal Languages and Dialects of the World. Second Edition. 8vo. 5s.

TRUMBULL, H. CLAY, The Blood-Covenant : a Primitive Rite and its Bearings on Scripture. Post 8vo. 7s. 6d.

TURNER, C. E., Count Tolstoï, as Novelist and Thinker. Lectures delivered at the Royal Institution. Cr. 8vo. 3s. 6d.

Modern Novelists of Russia. Lectures delivered at the Taylor Institution, Oxford. Cr. 8vo. 3s. 6d.

TWEEDIE, Mrs. ALEC, Ober-Ammergau Passion Play, 1890. Sm. 8vo. 2s. 6d.

Tyll Owlglass' Marvellous and Rare Conceits. Translated by KENNETH MACKENZIE. Illustrated by ALFRED CROWQUILL. 3s. 6d. (*Lotos Series.*)

TYLOR, HUGH, The Morality of Nations. Cr. 8vo. 6s.

TYNAN, KATHARINE, Louise de la Vallière, and other Poems. Sm. 8vo. 3s. 6d.

Shamrocks. Sm. cr. 8vo. 5s.

Ballads and Lyrics. Sm. cr. 8vo. 5s.

A Nun: her Friends and her Order. Being a Sketch of the Life of Mother Mary Xaveria Fallon. Cr. 8vo. 5s.

TYNDALL, J., Forms of Water : in Clouds and Rivers, Ice and Glaciers. With 25 Illustrations. Tenth Edition. Cr. 8vo. 5s. (*I.S.S.*)

TYRRELL, WALTER, Nervous Exhaustion : its Causes, Outcomes, and Treatment. Cr. 8vo. 3s.

UMLAUFT, Prof. F., The Alps. Translated by LOUISA BROUGH. With 110 Illustrations. 8vo. 25s.

VAN EYS, W., Outlines of Basque Grammar. Cr. 8vo. 3s. 6d.

VAN LAUN, H., Grammar of the French Language. Cr. 8vo. Accidence and Syntax, 4s.; Exercises, 3s. 6d.

VELASQUEZ, M. de la CADENA, Dictionary of the Spanish and English Languages. For the use of Young Learners and Travellers. Cr. 8vo. 6s.

Pronouncing Dictionary of the Spanish and English Languages. Royal 8vo. £1. 4s.

New Spanish Reader. Passages from the most approved Authors, with Vocabulary. Post 8vo. 6s.

Introduction to Spanish Conversation. 12mo. 2s. 6d.

VELASQUEZ and SIMONNE, New Method of Learning the Spanish Language. Adapted to Ollendorff's system. Revised and corrected by Senor VIVAR. Post 8vo. 6s.; Key, 4s.

VERE, AUBREY DE, Poetical Works. Sm. 8vo.
   I. THE SEARCH AFTER PROSERPINE, 3s. 6d.
   II. THE LEGENDS OF ST. PATRICK, 3s. 6d.
   III. ALEXANDER THE GREAT, 3s. 6d.

The Foray of Queen Meave, and other Legends of Ireland's Heroic Age. Sm. 8vo. 3s. 6d.

Legends of the Saxon Saints. Sm. 8vo. 3s. 6d.

Legends and Records of the Church and the Empire. Sm. 8vo. 3s. 6d.

VESCELIUS-SHELDON, LOUISE, An I.D.B. in South Africa. Illustrated. Cr. 8vo. 7s. 6d.

VIEYRA'S Pocket Dictionary of the Portuguese and English Languages. 2 vols. Post 8vo. 10s.

VIGNOLI, TITO, Myth and Science : an Essay. Third Edition. With Supplementary Note. Cr. 8vo. 5s. (*I.S.S.*)

VINCENT, FRANK, Around and About South America. Twenty Months of Quest and Query. With Maps, Plans, and 54 Illustrations. Medium 8vo. 21s.

VIRGIL. The Georgics of Virgil. Translated into English Verse by J. RHOADES. Sm. cr. 8vo. 5s.

VOGEL, HERMANN, Chemistry of Light and Photography. With 100 Illustrations. Fifth Edition. Cr. 8vo. 5s. (*I.S.S*)

VOLCKXSOM, E. W. von, Catechism of Elementary Modern Chemistry. Sm. cr. 8vo. 3s.

Vox Clamantis. Cr. 8vo. 6s.

WAITE, A. E., Lives of Alchemystical Philosophers. 8vo. 10s. 6d.

Magical Writings of Thomas Vaughan. Sm. 4to. 10s. 6d.

Real History of the Rosicrucians. With Illustrations. Cr. 8vo. 7s. 6d.

Mysteries of Magic : a Digest of the Writings of Eliphas Lévi. With Illustrations. 8vo. 10s. 6d.

The Occult Sciences. Cr. 8vo. 6s.

WAKE, C. S., Serpent-Worship, and other Essays. With a chapter on Totemism. 8vo. 10s. 6d.

Development of Marriage and Kinship. 8vo. 18s.

WALLACE, ALFRED RUSSELL, Miracles and Modern Spiritualism. Second Edition. Cr. 8vo. 5s.

WALPOLE, C. G., Short History of Ireland. With 5 Maps and Appendices. Third Edition. Cr. 8vo. 6s.

WALSHE, W. H., Dramatic Singing Physiologically Estimated. Cr. 8vo. 3s. 6d.

WALTERS, J. CUMING, In Tennyson Land : a Brief Account of the Home and Early Surroundings of the Poet-Laureate. With Illustrations. 8vo. 5s.

WANKLYN, J. A., Milk Analysis : a Practical Treatise on the Examination of Milk and its Derivatives, Cream, Butter, and Cheese. Second Edition. Cr. 8vo. 5s.

Tea, Coffee, and Cocoa : a Practical Treatise on the Analysis of Tea, Coffee, Cocoa, Chocolate, and Maté (Paraguay tea). Cr. 8vo. 5s.

WANKLYN, J. A., and COOPER, W. J., Bread Analysis : a Practical Treatise on the Examination of Flour and Bread. Cr. 8vo. 5s.

Air Analysis : a Practical Treatise. With Appendix on Illuminating Gas. Cr. 8vo. 5s.

WANKLYN, J. A., and CHAPMAN, E. T., Water Analysis : a Treatise on the Examination of Potable Water. Eighth Edition. Entirely re-written. Cr. 8vo. 5s.

WARD, H. MARSHALL. The Oak : a Popular Introduction to Forest Botany. Cr. 8vo. 2s. 6d. (*Modern Science Series.*)

WARD, WILFRID, The Wish to Believe : a Discussion concerning the Temper of Mind in which a reasonable Man should undertake Religious Inquiry. Sm. 8vo. 5s.

WARD, W. G., Essays on the Philosophy of Theism. Edited, with an Introduction, by WILFRID WARD. 2 vols. 8vo. 21s.

WARNER, Prof. F., Physical Expression : its Modes and Principles. With 50 Illustrations. Second Edition. Cr. 8vo. 5s. (*I.S.S.*)

WARTER, J. W., An old Shropshire Oak. 4 vols. 8vo. 56s.

WATERHOUSE, Col. J., Preparation of Drawings for Photographic Reproduction. With Plates. Cr. 8vo. 5s.

WATSON, JOHN FORBES, Index to the Native and Scientific Names of Indian and other Eastern Economic Plants and Products. Imp. 8vo. £1. 11s. 6d.

WATSON, R. G.. Spanish and Portuguese South America during the Colonial Period. 2 vols. Post 8vo. 21s.

WEAVER, F. W., Wells Wills. Arranged in Parishes, and Annotated. 8vo. 10s. 6d.

WEBER, A., History of Indian Literature. From the German by J. MANN and T. ZACHARIAE. Second Edition. Post 8vo. 10s. 6d. (*Trübner's Oriental Series.*)

WEDDING'S Basic Bessemer Process. Translated from the German by W. B. PHILLIPS and ERNST PROCHASKA. Roy. 8vo. 18s.

WEDGWOOD, H., Dictionary of English Etymology. Fourth Edition. Revised and Enlarged. 8vo. £1. 1s.

Contested Etymology in the Dictionary of the Rev. W. W. Skeat. Cr. 8vo. 5s.

WEDGWOOD, JULIA, The Moral Ideal: an Historic Study. Second Edition. 8vo. 9s.

WEISBACH, JULIUS, Theoretical Mechanics: a Manual of the Mechanics of Engineering. Designed as a Text-book for Technical Schools and for the Use of Engineers. From the German by E. B. COXE. With 902 Woodcuts. 8vo. 31s. 6d.

WELLER, E., Improved French Dictionary. Roy. 8vo. 7s. 6d.

WESTROPP, HODDER M., Primitive Symbolism as Illustrated in Phallic Worship; or, The Reproductive Principle. With Introduction by Major-Gen. FORLONG. 8vo. 7s. 6d.

WHEELDON, J. P., Angling Resorts near London: the Thames and the Lea. Cr. 8vo. paper covers, 1s. 6d.

WHEELER, J. TALBOYS, History of India from the Earliest Ages. 8vo. (Vol. I. *out of print*.) Vol. II., 21s. Vol. III., 18s. Vol. IV., Part I., 14s. Vol. IV., Part II., 12s.

⁎ Vol. III. is also published as an independent work under the title of 'History of India: Hindu, Buddhist, and Brahmanical.'

Early Records of British India: a History of the English Settlements in India, as told in the Government Records and other Contemporary Documents. Roy. 8vo. 15s.

WHERRY, E. M., Comprehensive Commentary to the Quran. With SALE'S Preliminary Discourse, Translation and Additional Notes. Post 8vo. (Vol. I. *out of print.*) Vols. II. and III. 12s. 6d. each. Vol. IV. 10s. 6d. (*Trübner's Oriental Series.*)

WHIBLEY, CHAS., In Cap and Gown: Three Centuries of Cambridge Wit. Second Edition. Cr. 8vo. 7s. 6d.

WHINFIELD, E. H., The Quatrains of Omar Khayyám. The Persian Text, with an English Verse Translation. Post 8vo. 10s. 6d.; Translation only, 5s. (*Trübner's Oriental Series.*)

Masnavi I Ma'navi: the Spiritual Couplets of Mauláná Jalálu-'d-Din Muhammad I Rúmí. Translated and Abridged. Post 8vo. 7s. 6d. (*Trübner's Oriental Series.*)

WHITAKER, FLORENCE, Christy's Inheritance: a London Story. Illustrated. Roy. 16mo, 1s. 6d.

WHITMAN, SIDNEY, Conventional Cant: its Results and Remedy. Cr. 8vo. 6s.

WHITNEY, Prof. W. D., Life and Growth of Language. Sixth Edition. Cr. 8vo. 5s. (*I.S.S.*)

Essentials of English Grammar. Second Edition. Cr. 8vo. 3s. 6d.

Language and the Study of Language. Fourth Edition. Cr. 8vo. 10s. 6d.

Language and its Study. With especial Reference to the Indo-European Family of Languages. Edited by R. MORRIS. Second Edition. Cr. 8vo. 5s.

Sanskrit Grammar. Including both the Classical Language and the older Dialects of Veda and Brahmana. Second Edition. 8vo. 12s.

WHITWORTH, G. C., Anglo-Indian Dictionary: a Glossary of Indian Terms used in English, and of such English or other non-Indian Terms as have obtained Special Meanings in India. 8vo. cloth, 12s.

WICKSON, E. J., California Fruits, and How to Grow Them. 8vo. 18s.

WIECHMANN, FERDINAND G., Sugar Analysis. For Refineries, Sugar-Houses, Experimental Stations, &c. 8vo. 10s. 6d.

WIGSTON, W. F. C., Francis Bacon, Poet, Prophet, Philosopher, *versus* Phantom Captain Shakespeare, the Rosicrucian Mask. 8vo. 15s.

WILBERFORCE. Life of Bishop Wilberforce of Oxford and Winchester. By HIS SON. Cr. 8vo. 9s.

WILDRIDGE, T. TYNDAL, The Dance of Death, in Painting and in Print. With Woodcuts. Sm. 4to. 3s. 6d.

WILLARD, X. A., Practical Dairy Husbandry. Complete Treatise on Dairy Farms and Farming. Illustrated. 8vo. 15s.

Practical Butter Book. Complete Treatise on Butter Making, &c. 12mo. 5s.

WILLIAMS, S. WELLS, Syllabic Dictionary of the Chinese Language: arranged according to the Wu-Fang Yuen Yin, with the Pronunciation of the Characters as heard in Pekin, Canton, Amoy, and Shanghai. Third Edition. 4to. £3. 15s.

WILLIS, R., Life, Correspondence, and Ethics of Benedict de Spinoza. 8vo. 21s.

WILSON, H. H., Rig-Veda-Sanhita: a Collection of Ancient Hindu Hymns. From the Sanskrit. Edited by E. B. COWELL and W. F. WEBSTER. 6 vols. 8vo. (Vols. I. V. VI. 21s. each; Vol. IV. 14s.; Vols. II. and III. in sets only.)

The Megha-Duta (Cloud Messenger). Translated from the Sanskrit of KALIDASA. New Edition. 4to. 10s. 6d.

Essays and Lectures, chiefly on the Religion of the Hindus. Collected and Edited by Dr. REINHOLD ROST. 2 vols. 21s.

Essays, Analytical, Critical, and Philological, on Subjects connected with Sanskrit Literature. Collected and Edited by Dr. REINHOLD ROST. 3 vols. 36s.

Vishnu Puráná: a System of Hindu Mythology and Tradition. From the Original Sanskrit. Illustrated by Notes derived chiefly from other Puránás. Edited by FITZEDWARD HALL. 6 vols. (including Index), £3. 4s. 6d.

Select Specimens of the Theatre of the Hindus. From the Original Sanskrit. Third Edition. 2 vols. 21s.

WILSON, Mrs. R. F., The Christian Brothers: their Origin and Work. With Sketch of Life of their Founder. Cr. 8vo. 6s.

Within Sound of the Sea. With Frontispiece. Cr. 8vo. 6s.

WOLTMANN, ALFRED, and WOERMANN, KARL, History of Painting. With numerous Illustrations. Med. 8vo. Vol. I. Painting in Antiquity and the Middle Ages, 28s. Vol. II. The Painting of the Renascence, 42s. The two volumes may be had bound in cloth with bevelled boards and gilt leaves, price 30s. and 45s. respectively.

WOOD, M. W., Dictionary of Volapük: Volapük-English and English-Volapük. Cr. 8vo. 10s. 6d.

WOODBURY, CHAS. J., Talks with Ralph Waldo Emerson. Cr. 8vo. 5s.

WORDSWORTH Birthday Book. Edited by ADELAIDE and VIOLET WORDSWORTH. 32mo. 2s.; cloth limp, 1s. 6d.

WORDSWORTH, Selections from. By WILLIAM KNIGHT and other Members of the Wordsworth Society. Printed on hand-made paper. Large cr. 8vo. With Portrait. Vellum, 15s.; parchment, 12s. Cheap Edition, cr. 8vo. 4s. 6d.

WORSAAE, CHAMBERLAIN J. J. A., The Pre-history of the North. Based on contemporary Memorials. Translated by H. F. MORLAND SIMPSON. Cr. 8vo. 6s.

WORTHAM, B. HALE, Satakas of Bhartrihari. Translated from the Sanskrit. Post 8vo. 5s. (*Trübner's Oriental Series.*)

WORTHY, CHARLES, Practical Heraldry: an Epitome of English Armoury. With 124 Illustrations. Cr. 8vo. 7s. 6d.

WRIGHT, G. FREDERICK, The Ice Age in North America, and its Bearing upon the Antiquity of Man. With Maps and Illustrations. 8vo. 21s.

WRIGHT, THOMAS, The Homes of other Days: a History of Domestic Manners and Sentiments during the Middle Ages. With 350 Illustrations, Drawn and Engraved by F. W. FAIRHOLT. Medium 8vo. 21s.

Anglo-Saxon and Old English Vocabularies. Second Edition. Edited by R. P. WULCKER. 2 vols. 8vo. 28s.

The Celt, the Roman, and the Saxon: a History of the Early Inhabitants of Britain down to the Conversion of the Anglo-Saxons to Christianity. Corrected and Enlarged Edition. With nearly 300 Engravings. Cr. 8vo. 9s.

Feudal Manuals of English History. A Series of Popular Sketches of our National History. Now first Edited from the original Manuscripts. 8vo. 15s.

WRIGHT, W., The Book of Kalilah and Dimnah. Translated from Arabic into Syriac, with Preface and Glossary in English. 8vo. 21s.

WURTZ, Prof., The Atomic Theory. Translated by E. CLEMINSHAW. Fifth Edition. Cr. 8vo. 5s. (*I.S.S.*)

WYLDE, W. The Inspection of Meat: a Guide and Instruction Book to Officers supervising Contract Meat, and to all Sanitary Inspectors. With 32 Coloured Plates. 8vo. 10s. 6d.

WYNNE, FRANCES, Whisper! Poems. Sm. cr. 8vo. 2s. 6d.

YOUNG, Prof. C. A., The Sun. With Illustrations. Third Edition. Cr. 8vo. 5s. (*I.S.S.*)

YOUMANS, ELIZA A., First Book of Botany. Designed to Cultivate the Observing Powers of Children. With 300 Engravings. New and Cheaper Edition. Cr. 8vo. 2s. 6d.

Kegan Paul, Trench, Trübner, & Co.'s Publications. 55

SHAKSPERE'S WORKS.

THE AVON EDITION,

Printed on thin opaque paper, and forming 12 handy volumes, cloth, 18*s*., or bound in 6 volumes, 15*s*.

The set of 12 volumes may also be had in a cloth box (*see Illustration*), price 21*s*., or bound in roan, persian, crushed persian levant, calf, or morocco, and enclosed in an attractive leather box, at prices from 31*s*. 6*d*. upwards.

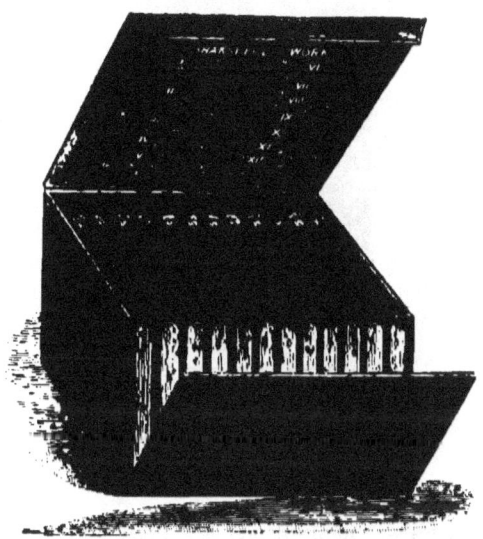

THE PARCHMENT LIBRARY EDITION,

In 12 volumes elzevir 8vo., choicely printed on hand-made paper, and bound in parchment or cloth, price £3. 12*s*., or in vellum, price £4. 10*s*.

The set of 12 volumes may also be had in a strong cloth box, price £3. 17*s*., or with an oak hanging shelf (*see Illustration*), £3. 18*s*.

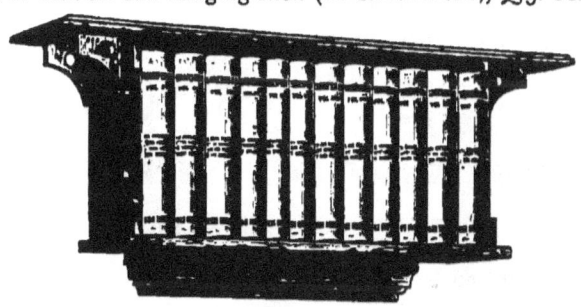

LONDON: KEGAN PAUL, TRENCH, TRÜBNER, & CO., LTD.

THE AMERICAN PATENT
REVOLVING BOOKCASE.

The Revolving Bookcase will be found a great convenience by those who wish to have from 80 to 200 volumes accessible while seated at a table or by the fireside. They occupy no more space than an ordinary whatnot, and can be wheeled from one part of a room to another. They are particularly suitable for Private Libraries, for Studies, and for the Consulting Chambers of Barristers, Physicians, &c.

Size No. 1, 36 inches high.

PRICE FROM 4 GUINEAS.

These Bookcases are made in various sizes, 24 inches square, 36 to 59 inches high, with eight, twelve, or sixteen shelves, in ash, walnut, mahogany, oak, and ebonised, and neatly finished so as to form handsome pieces of furniture. A special form of Revolving Bookcase has been designed to hold the set of 'Encyclopædia Britannica.'

Specimens of the different sizes and woods can be seen in use at

PATERNOSTER HOUSE,
CHARING CROSS ROAD, LONDON.

KEGAN PAUL, TRENCH, TRÜBNER, & CO., Ltd.,
SOLE AUTHORISED AGENTS.

Illustrated Price List on receipt of one Stamp.

www.ingramcontent.com/pod-product-compliance
Lightning Source LLC
Chambersburg PA
CBHW050844300426
44111CB00010B/1117